COLLECTIBLES
PRICE GUIDE **2009**

COLLECTIBLES
PRICE GUIDE **2009**

Judith Miller
and Mark Hill

MILLER'S

Miller's Collectables Price Guide 2009

First American edition published in 2008 by Miller's, a division of Mitchell Beazley,
imprints of Octopus Publishing Group Ltd, 2-4 Heron Quays, London E14 4JP, UK.
Miller's is a registered trademark of Octopus Publishing Group Ltd.
An Hachette Livre UK Company.
www.octopusbooks.co.uk

While every care has been exercised in the compilation of this guide,
neither the authors nor publishers accept any liability for any financial or
other loss incurred by reliance placed on the information contained in
Miller's Collectibles Price Guide 2009.

ISBN 978 1 84533 454 3

A CIP catalogue record for this book is available from the Library of Congress.

Set in Frutiger

Color reproduction by Fine Arts, Hong Kong
Printed and bound in China by C&C Offset Printing Co., Ltd

Distributed in the United States and Canada by
Sterling Publishing Co., Inc.,
387 Park Avenue South, New York, NY 10016-8810

Authors Judith Miller & Mark Hill

Publishing Manager Julie Brooke
Editors Sara Sturgess & Daniel Goode
Editorial Assistants John Parton & Katy Armstrong

Photography Graham Rae, Jeremy Martin, Robin Saker

Design Tim & Ali Scrivens, TJ Graphics;
additional design by Jeremy Tilston, The Oak Studio
& Philip Gilderdale
Indexer Hilary Bird
Production Lucy Carter
Jacket Design Tim Foster & Juliette Norsworthy

Photographs of Judith Miller and Mark Hill by Graham Rae

CONTENTS

LIST OF CONSULTANTS

ADVERTISING

Joe & Sharon Happle
Mill Antiques Center, Lafayette, NJ

CERAMICS

Greg Belhorn
Belhorn Auction Services, Columbus, OH

Holly Gnaedinger
Twice Found, Toronto, Canada

David Rago
David Rago Auctions, Lambertville, NJ

Gerald Schultz
The Antique Gallery, Philadelphia, PA

COSTUME JEWELRY

Barbara Blau
South Street Antiques Market, Philadelphia, PA

EYEWEAR

Esther Harris
Vintage Eyewear of New York City

HOLIDAY MEMORABILIA & ADVERTISING

Joe & Sharon Happle
Mill Antiques Center, Lafayette, NJ

MARBLES

Mark Block
blockglass.com

Robert Block
Private Collector

WATCHES

Mark Laino
Mark of Time, Philadelphia, PA

We are also very grateful to our friends and experts who gave us so much help and support - Conrad Biernacki and Brian Musselwhite of the Royal Ontario Museum, Toronto; Cynthia Findlay and the team at Antiques on King, Toronto; Sasha Keen of Neetorama, Somerville NJ;

Bonnie Reeder of the Antiques Emporium, Somerville NJ; everyone at the South Street Antiques Market, Philadelphia, PA; and Dick & Eileen at The Black Horse Antiques Center, Denver, PA.

HOW TO USE THIS BOOK

Subcategory Heading Indicates the sub-category of the main heading.

Caption The description of the item illustrated, including when relevant, the period, the maker or factory, medium, the year it was made, dimensions and condition. Many captions have **footnotes** which explain terminology or give identification or valuation information.

Essential reference and **expert eye** These are where we show identifying aspects of a factory or maker, point out rare colors or shapes, and explain why a particular piece is so desirable.

The price guide These price ranges give a ball-park figure for what you should pay for a similar item. The great joy of collectibles is that there is not a recommended retail price. The price ranges in this book are based on actual prices, either what a dealer will take or the full auction price. They are expressed in US$ (even for Canadian collectibles). Canadian readers should refer to the latest conversion rates at http://financeyahoo.com

Page tab This appears on every page and identifies the main category heading as identified in the Contents List on pages 5-6.

Essential reference Gives key facts about the factory, maker or style, along with stylistic identification points, value tips and advice on fakes.

The object The collectibles are shown in full color. This is a vital aid to identification and valuation. With many objects, a slight color variation can signify a large price differential.

Source code Every item has been specially photographed at an auction house, a dealer, an antiques market or a private collection. These are credited by code at the end of the caption, and can be checked against the Key to Illustrations on pages 486-489.

An Alvin the Chipmunk novelty telephone, licensed by Bagdasarian Productions and made in Hong Kong.
1984   15in (38cm) high
$25-35   AEM

INTRODUCTION

The world of collectibles has never been so vibrant and international. When I produced the first edition of Miller's Collectibles Price Guide 21 years ago, I could never have envisaged the speed at which the market would change and develop. Of course, much of this has been due to the internet which has given collectors from Chicago to London to Sydney unprecedented easy access to all manner of items in countries across the world. This has resulted in a general leveling of prices, regardless of whether the collector and object are in the same country, or thousands of miles apart.

But this doesn't mean prices have fallen, in fact many collectible areas have seen prices rise as the number of collectors and demand grow. It seems we still can't resist the lure of adding that elusive piece to our collections, the pull of nostalgic yearning for our childhoods, or the joy of finding something simply great that just 'speaks' to us in some way.

Like our desire to collect, another thing that hasn't changed is our need for accurate information. The internet may be an excellent place to buy or sell, but knowing what you're looking at, and how much it is really worth, is as important as ever. Just think of the lucky buyers who spotted a rare Worcester jug on eBay. Mis-described as being Italian, they bought it for $200 and shortly after sold it at auction for $100,000! Had the unfortunate seller known what he had, the story would have been very different.

That's where a copy of a Miller's price guide is essential. Useful as the internet is, information is not always accurate, and is often conflicting. Buying a copy of Miller's each year will enable you to build up an invaluable and reliable library that will help you make the most from buying, selling and collecting – be it at a flea market, estate sale, dealer's shop, or via eBay.

To celebrate my return this year to the company I co-founded, we've had a make-over. As you will see, the book is bigger than ever before, with larger images and more color, enabling you to see even greater detail that might make all the difference. We've also increased the number of 'Expert Eye', 'Essential Reference' and footnote features to help you understand more, and pick up tricks of the trade.

Another exciting development is our new Miller's website, www.millersantiquesguide.com, which will be launched in October 2008. This has been developed over the past year and aims to provide a site for everyone who loves the world of antiques and collectibles. It will appeal to both the committed expert and the inquiring novice. You can search our database of tens of thousands of antiques and collectibles from around the world – each with fully authenticated captions and price ranges. We also include useful and easy to understand extra information, including top tips and special features to look for. In addition, you have access to fully illustrated features by myself, Mark Hill and our team of experts including many names from the Antiques Roadshow, both in the UK and the US. The best dealers and auctioneers can be tracked down through our dealer and auctioneers locator, which is linked to Google Maps. We'll keep you up to date with antiques news, and you'll also be able to view videos that will help you get more out of antiques and collectibles as we walk you through all aspects of buying, selling, identifying and valuing. We may be involved in treasures of the past, but we also embrace the technology of the future.

This year's edition offers as much variety as ever, from advertising to ceramics, fashion, glass, toys and games, and even collectible hair! Popular markets that have remained strong, such as Roseville, are well represented with longer sections. Miller's also keeps up with the latest trends, bringing you hot, new collecting areas such as Nicodemus ceramics and postwar Czech glass. With pieces from auction houses, dealers and private collectors from across the world, Mark Hill and I have ensured that Miller's continues to reflect the market today – vibrant and international.

Judith Miller

A pair of 1950s Herbert Levine printed slingbacks. Worth $150-200

A 1950s-70s Czechoslovakian Borské Sklo 'Large Olives' pattern optical ball vase. Worth $150-250

A Roseville Futura four-sided vase. Worth $350-450

A Coca-Cola printed and embossed tinplate thermometer sign, with gold-colored bottle.

1936　　　*15.75in (40cm) high*

$280-320　　　**SOTT**

A Coca-Cola printed tinplate 'silhouette lady' thermometer sign.

1939　　　*16in (40.5cm) high*

$150-200　　　**SOTT**

A 1950s Coca-Cola enameled tin bottle sign.

12.5in (31.5cm) high

$180-220　　　**SOTT**

EXPERT EYE – A DR PEPPER TIP TRAY

These rare items used to sell for around $900, but Dr Pepper collectibles have fallen out of fashion slightly, which has affected prices.

Dr Pepper advertising memorabilia is harder to find than that for Coca-Cola. Early examples include a period after the 'Dr'.

Furthermore, as examples have become more widely and easily available via the Internet, prices have been further affected.

The artwork of the pug puppies is appealing, adding to the desirability.

A very rare Dr Pepper printed tinplate tip tray, with pug dogs and scalloped rim.

2.5in (6.5cm) diam

$500-600　　　**SOTT**

A Coca-Cola printed celluloid sign.

c1950　　　*9.25in (23cm) high*

$150-200　　　**SOTT**

A Coca-Cola printed Masonite sign.

Masonite is a type of hardboard made from wooden chips that are blasted with steam to form fibers, it is then heated and compressed into boards. No glue or other material is used. It was developed in 1924 by William H. Mason of Laurel, Mississippi, with manufacturing beginning in 1929. It is also used for roofing, desktops and even canoes.

1952　　　*14.25in (36cm) high*

$150-200　　　**SOTT**

A Dr Pepper 'Hot or Cold' printed tinplate thermometer sign.

16.25in (41cm) high

$180-220　　　**SOTT**

ADVERTISING

ESSENTIAL REFERENCE

- Vintage advertising and packaging provides a fascinating and accessible record of social trends and aspirations over the past century and more. Collectors tend to focus on one subject area, such as tobacco advertising, or on one type of object, such as tin signs. Some also focus on a particular brand, such as Kellogg's, or even a character, such as Buster Brown. As such, these categories tend to attract the most collectors, and so the highest values.
- Most pieces found by collectors will date from the early 20thC or later, with 19thC examples generally being scarcer. Much of the market is driven by nostalgia or an interest in design and brands of the past. Advertising diversified rapidly during the early years of the 20thC, and as the market expanded with more and more manufacturers. It became all-important to catch people's attention and make them buy a particular product over another.
- Tins and signs are two of the most important and sought-after areas. Both have typically eye-catching visuals, with bright colors and use of logos and characters. Always examine surfaces closely for signs of damage, such as scratches or loss of the surface, and dents. The more colors

used in a printed design, and the better it is printed, the more valuable it is likely to be. Look for cross-market interest, such as railway or automobile related themes or motifs, as this can increase value.
- Always look for items in good condition that represent the brand, subject area or period well. Items produced during the late 1920s and '30s that are in the popular Art Deco style will generally be desirable. Those from the late 19thc and early 20thC and in the Art Nouveau style will be similarly sought-after, as will those with typically 1950s artwork. The colors, style of lettering and often the logo used will help you to date a piece to a period.
- Also consider items that would have usually been thrown away. Although many may have been produced, fewer may have survived, making them sought-after today. Much packaging falls under this category, and was not made to last, making surviving examples in mint condition the most desirable. Nevertheless, the presence of the original contents does not necessarily add to value unless the package has intact seals or sealing labels, such as the tax seals on tobacco packets.

A Good Mfg Co. Inc. 'Magic' porcelain, tile and enamel cleaner tin, with paper label, unopened.

5in (12.5cm) high

$18-22   SOTT

A Palco Products 'Cleanser For The Kitchen' tin, with printed paper label, unopened.

1931   5in (12.5cm) high

$20-30   SOTT

An Oxo 'Sparkle' Cleanser tin, with printed label of a housewife going about her chores, unopened.

5in (12.5cm) high

$22-28   SOTT

A rare Amity Chemical of Chicago 'Bluebird Cleanser' tin, with paper label, unopened.

5.5in (13.5cm) high

$50-70   SOTT

A 1950s Permatex 'Airplane Wash' color-printed tin, with contents.

The artwork on this tin is particularly good, and typical of its period.

7.75in (19.5cm) high

$3-5   AEM

A 1950s tin of Oxo Cleanser powder, with printed paper label showing a housewife brandishing a sparkling clean frying pan, unopened and covered with protective cellophane.

This is a rare tin, made more desirable by the attractive period artwork and colors.

4.75in (12cm) high

$30-40   SOTT

A Canadian Imperial Tobacco Company 'Forest and Stream' pipe tobacco pocket tin, with a mallard taking flight over a lake.

4in (10cm) high

$180-220   **SOTT**

A City Club Crushed Cubes tobacco pocket tin.

4.5in (11.5cm) high

$180-220   **SOTT**

EXPERT EYE – A TOBACCO POCKET TIN

These slim, sometimes curving, tins were made to fit snugly inside the pocket of a gentleman's jacket without causing an unsightly bulge.

This is a scarce tin and also has an image of a fisherman that would appeal to collectors of fishing memorabilia.

Bold colors and strong imagery are also highly sought-after – look out especially for patriotic themes or those that cross collecting areas.

Condition is important, this tin is in good condition, scratched and dented examples will not be worth as much.

A Canadian Imperial Tobacco Company 'Forest And Stream' pipe tobacco pocket tin, with scene of a fisherman.

4.5in (11.5cm) high

$200-300   **SOTT**

A Penn Tobacco Co. 'Honey Moon' tobacco pocket tin.

The vibrant and charming artwork that shows the languid relaxation of pipe smoking makes this tin particularly desirable.

4.25in (11cm) high

$150-200   **SOTT**

A rare Ben-Hur Curry Powder tin, complete with contents.

3.25in (8.5cm) high

$12-18   **AEM**

A Golden Fluffo tin, with paper label.

6in (15cm) high

$10-15   **AEM**

A small Stag Tobacco pipe tobacco pocket tin.

This is a popular tin and was produced in various sizes. This is the smallest and also the rarest.

3.5in (9cm) high

$80-100   **SOTT**

A Dickinson's 'Big Buster' yellow pop corn tin, with color transfer-printed design of a drummer, complete with original contents.

4.75in (12cm) high

$100-150   BH

A Lady Jane Thin Butter Pretzels tin.

8.75in (22cm) high

$8-12   AEM

A Rival Dog Food miniature sample tin, converted into a money bank.

2.75in (7cm) high

$7-10   AEM

A 'Between The Acts' cigar tin, with printed design.

5.75in (14.5cm) wide

$32-38   SOTT

A Tak-A-Lax chocolate laxative printed tinplate small tin.

3.75in (9.5cm) wide

$55-65   SOTT

A Julius Schmid of New York, NY, 'Ramses' condom tin.

Early condom tins are now highly collectible, and some can be rare. Sold discreetly during a more prudish time when talk of sex was largely forbidden, they were often thrown away rather than being re-used around the home, like other tins.

1947   *2.75in (7cm) wide*

$50-70   SOTT

A 1920s-30s R.J. Reynolds Prince Albert Crimp Cut cigarette tobacco tin, with pull-off lid and transfer-printed design.

The Prince Albert this tobacco was named after was not husband to the UK's Queen Victoria, but rather their eldest son who became King Edward VII in 1901. The brand itself was mystifyingly launched with his previous title after his Coronation, in 1907. The tobacco is still produced today, but saw its heyday during the 1930s.

6.5in (16.5cm) high

$45-55   AEM

An Esso 'Sprite' 2-T liter oil can, with artwork of 'Happy' and his girlfriend on a scooter, with some scratches and denting.

Happy the oil drip and his un-named girlfriend promoted Esso's 'Happy Motoring' campaign.

9.25in (23.5cm) high

$15-25   BH

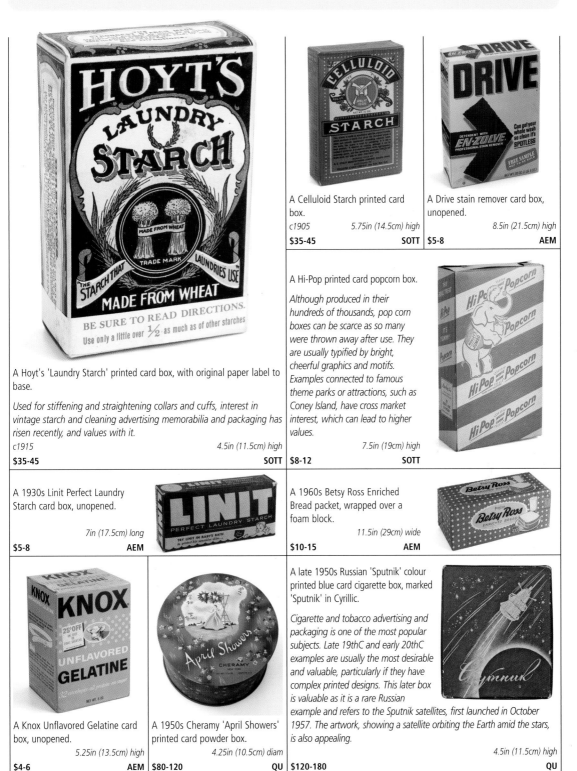

A Hoyt's 'Laundry Starch' printed card box, with original paper label to base.

Used for stiffening and straightening collars and cuffs, interest in vintage starch and cleaning advertising memorabilia and packaging has risen recently, and values with it.

c1915   4.5in (11.5cm) high

$35-45   **SOTT**

A Celluloid Starch printed card box.

c1905   5.75in (14.5cm) high

$35-45   **SOTT**

A Drive stain remover card box, unopened.

8.5in (21.5cm) high

$5-8   **AEM**

A Hi-Pop printed card popcorn box.

Although produced in their hundreds of thousands, pop corn boxes can be scarce as so many were thrown away after use. They are usually typified by bright, cheerful graphics and motifs. Examples connected to famous theme parks or attractions, such as Coney Island, have cross market interest, which can lead to higher values.

7.5in (19cm) high

$8-12   **SOTT**

A 1930s Linit Perfect Laundry Starch card box, unopened.

7in (17.5cm) long

$5-8   **AEM**

A 1960s Betsy Ross Enriched Bread packet, wrapped over a foam block.

11.5in (29cm) wide

$10-15   **AEM**

A Knox Unflavored Gelatine card box, unopened.

5.25in (13.5cm) high

$4-6   **AEM**

A 1950s Cheramy 'April Showers' printed card powder box.

4.25in (10.5cm) diam

$80-120   **QU**

A late 1950s Russian 'Sputnik' colour printed blue card cigarette box, marked 'Sputnik' in Cyrillic.

Cigarette and tobacco advertising and packaging is one of the most popular subjects. Late 19thC and early 20thC examples are usually the most desirable and valuable, particularly if they have complex printed designs. This later box is valuable as it is a rare Russian example and refers to the Sputnik satellites, first launched in October 1957. The artwork, showing a satellite orbiting the Earth amid the stars, is also appealing.

4.5in (11.5cm) high

$120-180   **QU**

ADVERTISING

A 1920s The Edwards Manufacturing Co., Cincinnati for The Diamond Match Co printed tinplate '2 Books Diamond Matches' counter-top match dispenser, marked "Patent Applied For".

The condition and color of this country store dispenser are excellent, particularly for its age and after so much use.

13.5in (34cm) high

$500-600   **SOTT**

EXPERT EYE – A COUNTRY STORE DISPLAY STAND

Often large and comparatively complex items, country store display pieces and counter-top dispensers form a collecting area of their own and are usually valuable.

This 1920s example rotates and has sliding doors revealing shelves for different hairnets.

Many were used, damaged and thrown away, being replaced by more modern models as time went by. This rare survivor is in excellent condition.

The artwork was meant to be as appealing as possible to catch customers' attention and draw them to buy the product. Here the artwork of beautiful ladies frolicking on a beach or washing their hair is delightful.

A 1920s West Electric Hair Curler Co. printed tinplate 'West Hairnets' revolving counter-top dispenser, marked "Copyright 1921 by Augustus West".

19.5in (49cm) high

$800-1,100   **SOTT**

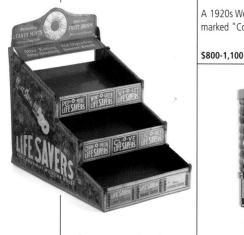

A Life Savers printed tinplate counter-top shop display dispenser.

Life Savers is a popular brand with collectors. This colorful vintage display is in excellent condition.

14.75in (37cm) high

$600-800   **SOTT**

A 1950s turquoise lacquered metal and plastic counter-top bubblegum dispenser.

18in (45.5cm) high

$180-220   **QU**

A 1940s-50s Sears Roebuck hat gift exchange hat-shaped token and box.

These clever miniature plastic hats were bought when someone wanted to buy a hat as a gift, but didn't know the size the recipient wore. It's hard to find them with their original gift boxes, as here.

Box 4.25in (11cm) high

$45-55   **BH**

A Pristalit salesman's sample of a miniature enameled metal Dutch oven.

5.5in (13.5cm) wide

$50-70   **BH**

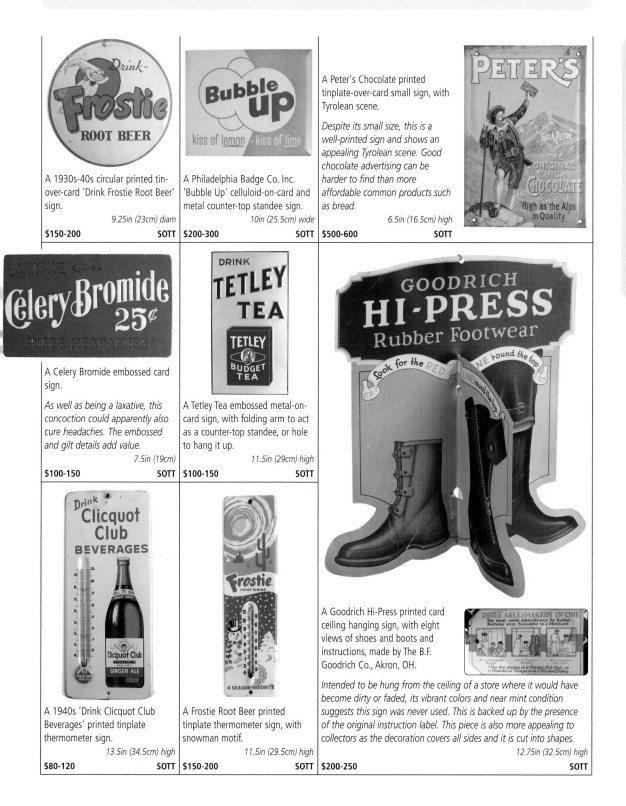

A 1930s-40s circular printed tin-over-card 'Drink Frostie Root Beer' sign.

9.25in (23cm) diam

$150-200 **SOTT**

A Philadelphia Badge Co. Inc. 'Bubble Up' celluloid-on-card and metal counter-top standee sign.

10in (25.5cm) wide

$200-300 **SOTT**

A Peter's Chocolate printed tinplate-over-card small sign, with Tyrolean scene.

Despite its small size, this is a well-printed sign and shows an appealing Tyrolean scene. Good chocolate advertising can be harder to find than more affordable common products such as bread.

6.5in (16.5cm) high

$500-600 **SOTT**

A Celery Bromide embossed card sign.

As well as being a laxative, this concoction could apparently also cure headaches. The embossed and gilt details add value.

7.5in (19cm)

$100-150 **SOTT**

A Tetley Tea embossed metal-on-card sign, with folding arm to act as a counter-top standee, or hole to hang it up.

11.5in (29cm) high

$100-150 **SOTT**

A 1940s 'Drink Clicquot Club Beverages' printed tinplate thermometer sign.

13.5in (34.5cm) high

$80-120 **SOTT**

A Frostie Root Beer printed tinplate thermometer sign, with snowman motif.

11.5in (29.5cm) high

$150-200 **SOTT**

A Goodrich Hi-Press printed card ceiling hanging sign, with eight views of shoes and boots and instructions, made by The B.F. Goodrich Co., Akron, OH.

Intended to be hung from the ceiling of a store where it would have become dirty or faded, its vibrant colors and near mint condition suggests this sign was never used. This is backed up by the presence of the original instruction label. This piece is also more appealing to collectors as the decoration covers all sides and it is cut into shapes.

12.75in (32.5cm) high

$200-250 **SOTT**

ADVERTISING

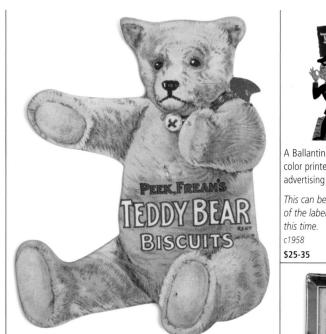

A Ballantine Brewer's Gold beer color printed and die-cut advertising standee.

This can be dated from the design of the label that changed around this time.

c1958   18.5in (47cm) high

$25-35   BH

A Riecks Ice Cream printed tinplate tray, made by the American Art Works Co, Coshocton, MASS.

1908

$300-400   SOTT

A Persil washing powder printed tinplate advertising tip tray.

4.75in (12cm) high

$20-30   SOTT

A Laxol castor oil printed tinplate tip tray, also printed "Chas W. Shonk, Litho Chicago No. 8.59".

4.25in (10.5cm) diam

$100-150   SOTT

A Peek, Frean's Teddy Bear Biscuits die-cut card advertising sign.

Advertising showing teddy bears is both hard to find and enormously appealing to teddy bear collectors. The craze began in 1902 when Theodore Roosevelt refused to shoot a bear on a hunting trip. The outstretched arms inviting a hug are a nice touch.

4.25in (11cm) high

$60-80   SOTT

EXPERT EYE – A RISING SUN BREWING CO. TRAY

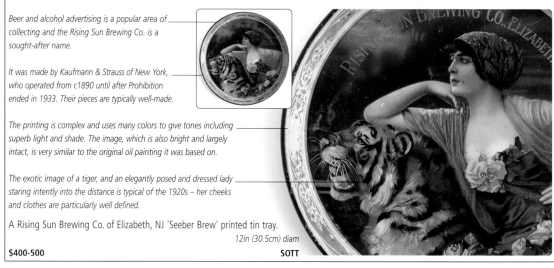

Beer and alcohol advertising is a popular area of collecting and the Rising Sun Brewing Co. is a sought-after name.

It was made by Kaufmann & Strauss of New York, who operated from c1890 until after Prohibition ended in 1933. Their pieces are typically well-made.

The printing is complex and uses many colors to give tones including superb light and shade. The image, which is also bright and largely intact, is very similar to the original oil painting it was based on.

The exotic image of a tiger, and an elegantly posed and dressed lady staring intently into the distance is typical of the 1920s – her cheeks and clothes are particularly well defined.

A Rising Sun Brewing Co. of Elizabeth, NJ 'Seeber Brew' printed tin tray.

12in (30.5cm) diam

$400-500   SOTT

ESSENTIAL REFERENCE – BUSTER BROWN

Buster Brown was created as a cartoon strip character by illustrator Richard Outcault in 1902. Appearing in the New York Herald, the strip covered the adventures and misadventures of the attractive but mischievous boy who typically ended up being spanked by his mother at the end of each strip. His sidekick Tige the dog often commented on his master's misdeeds and is said to be the first talking animal to appear in a cartoon. At the St Louis World's Fair in 1904, an executive for Brown's Shoes met Outcault and acquired the rights to use the name for a new brand of children's shoes. Acting as an early type of merchandising, Buster's popularity took off to the extent that dwarves were hired to visit towns across the US with Tige-like dogs in travelling shows from 1904 until 1930. Entire towns would turn out to meet Buster and see performances. In 1906, Outcault moved to newspapers owned by William Randolph Hearst. The Herald sued Hearst and won – although Outcault could take the characters, he couldn't take the name. Buster continued in the Herald drawn by other cartoonists until 1911, and Outcault's version continued until the early 1920s. Even though the comic strip has faded from public knowledge, the Buster Brown brand continues today as strong as ever. Vintage advertising pieces connected with his name are extremely popular and include signs, children's novelties and dolls. For a pair of Buster Brown shoes, see page 236.

A Buster Brown painted plaster advertising sign, showing a winking Buster and a grinning Tige molded in high relief.

18in (45.5cm) high

$200-250   **JDJ**

A Buster Brown Shoes printed tinplate advertising whistle.

2.5in (6.5cm) high

$50-70   **SOTT**

A Buster Brown Shoes printed tinplate advertising clicker.

1.75in (4.5cm) long

$55-65   **SOTT**

A Buster Brown Shoes printed tinplate and wood spinning top.

1.5in (4cm) diam

$35-45   **SOTT**

A Villeroy & Boch Mettlach transfer-printed 'Drink Hires Rootbeer' mug, the base impressed "3095".

4.5in (11cm) high

$250-350   **SOTT**

A Lipton Tea transfer-printed advertising mug.

3.75in (9.5cm) high

$4-6   **AEM**

A Delaval printed tinplate wall-hanging match safe, made by L.T. Savage, NY.

This is a scarce piece, particularly in blue.

c1908   6.25in (16cm) high

$250-350   **SOTT**

EXPERT EYE – AN ADVERTISING ALBUM

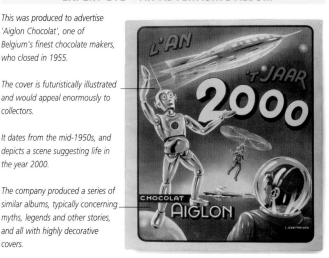

This was produced to advertise 'Aiglon Chocolat', one of Belgium's finest chocolate makers, who closed in 1955.

The cover is futuristically illustrated and would appeal enormously to collectors.

It dates from the mid-1950s, and depicts a scene suggesting life in the year 2000.

The company produced a series of similar albums, typically concerning myths, legends and other stories, and all with highly decorative covers.

A Belgian Chocolat Aiglon 'L'An 'T Jaar 2000' Dutch and French bi-lingual advertising picture card collectors album, with robot and rocket cover, in excellent condition.

c1950   12in (30.5cm) high

$300-400   **QU**

A Mr Peanut molded plastic money bank.

8.25in (21cm) high

$12-18   **AEM**

A Kellogg's Frosties 'Tony The Tiger' advertising plush stuffed toy, made in China.

1997   8in (20cm) high

$4-6   **AEM**

A 1920s chalkware hand-painted dog, unmarked.

9in (22.5cm) high

$80-120   **ANT**

A 1920s chalkware hand-painted cat, with ribbon and bow, unmarked.

Molded chalkware figurines such as this were given away as prizes at carnivals and fairs from the 1920s onwards. They are usually hand-painted, but often clumsily, and animals are typical subjects. Despite their gaudy appearance, they are becoming very popular as a form of 'folk art'. Paint losses and particularly chips devalue a piece considerably.

9in (22.5cm) high

$80-120   **ANT**

An American Cycle Trades League tiny pin-back.

0.75in (2cm) diam

$25-35   SOTT

A 1920s chalkware hand-painted bird, unmarked.

10.5in (26.5cm) high

$80-120   **ANT**

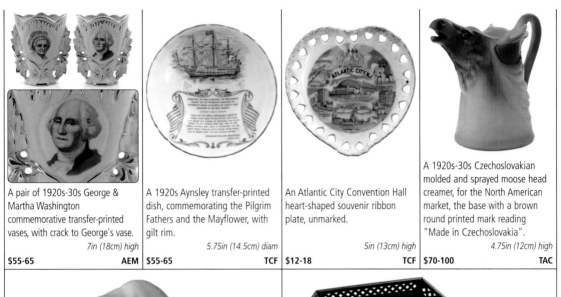

A pair of 1920s-30s George & Martha Washington commemorative transfer-printed vases, with crack to George's vase.

7in (18cm) high

$55-65   **AEM**

A 1920s Aynsley transfer-printed dish, commemorating the Pilgrim Fathers and the Mayflower, with gilt rim.

5.75in (14.5cm) diam

$55-65   **TCF**

An Atlantic City Convention Hall heart-shaped souvenir ribbon plate, unmarked.

5in (13cm) high

$12-18   **TCF**

A 1920s-30s Czechoslovakian molded and sprayed moose head creamer, for the North American market, the base with a brown round printed mark reading "Made in Czechoslovakia".

4.75in (12cm) high

$70-100   **TAC**

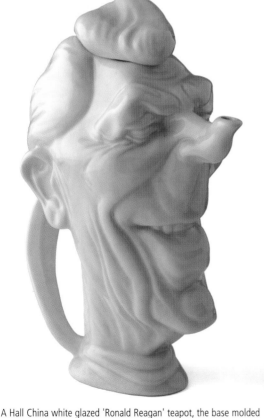

A Hall China white glazed 'Ronald Reagan' teapot, the base molded "Made in U.S.A."

10in (25.5cm) high

$350-450   **ANT**

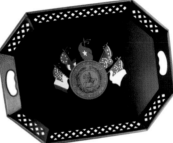

A tôle ware commemorative tin tray, the back painted "Made Expressly for Maier & Berkeley Charles Willis Atlanta", the front with hand-painted North Carolina state seal and the five proposed flags of the Confederate States of America.

This was made for the Higgs-Smith family during the 1930s.

20.25in (51cm) wide

$200-250   **AEM**

A New Orleans Mardi Gras sterling silver souvenir spoon, the bowl engraved "Mardi Gras 1899".

c1899   *5.75in (14.5cm) long*

$80-100   **BB**

A 1940s 'Rosie The Riveter' home-made fabric doll, with hand-painted features, the sash handwritten with 'Rosie The Riveter US World War II Worker'.

8.75in (22cm) high

$80-120   **BH**

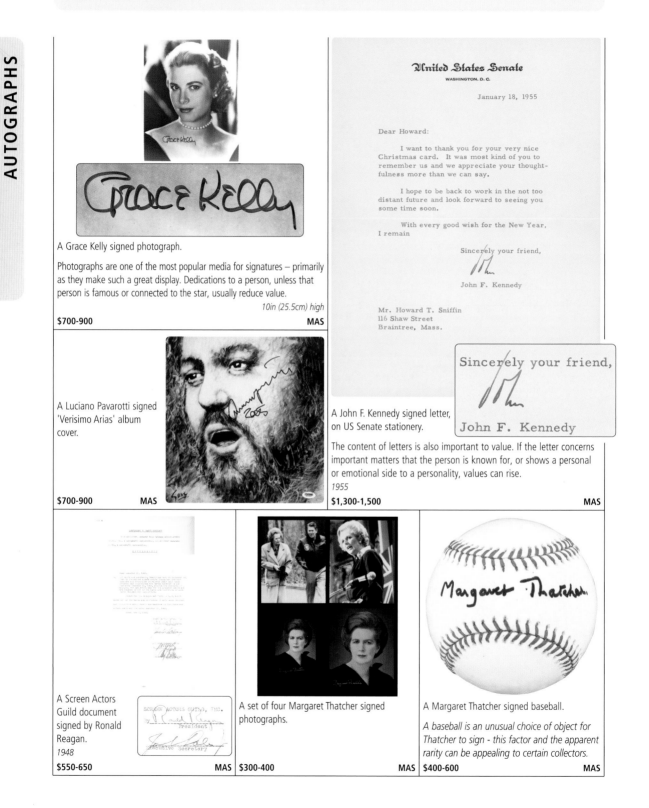

A Grace Kelly signed photograph.

Photographs are one of the most popular media for signatures – primarily as they make such a great display. Dedications to a person, unless that person is famous or connected to the star, usually reduce value.

10in (25.5cm) high

$700-900   MAS

A Luciano Pavarotti signed 'Verisimo Arias' album cover.

$700-900   MAS

A John F. Kennedy signed letter, on US Senate stationery.

The content of letters is also important to value. If the letter concerns important matters that the person is known for, or shows a personal or emotional side to a personality, values can rise.

1955

$1,300-1,500   MAS

A Screen Actors Guild document signed by Ronald Reagan.

1948

$550-650   MAS

A set of four Margaret Thatcher signed photographs.

$300-400   MAS

A Margaret Thatcher signed baseball.

A baseball is an unusual choice of object for Thatcher to sign - this factor and the apparent rarity can be appealing to certain collectors.

$400-600   MAS

ESSENTIAL REFERENCE

- Notaphily, the collecting of paper money, has grown in popularity since the 1960s. As the area is so wide, many choose to focus on one area, such as particular country or time period. Some also focus on an element or theme in the design, such as wildlife, battles or famous people. As well as being decorative, the complex designs were aimed to foil counterfeiters.
- Look out for large denominations, as generally fewer of

these were produced. Variations including errors can also affect value. Early notes are not always valuable, so consult a reference book if you are planning on building a collection. Condition has an enormous effect on value, with notes in truly mint, un-circulated condition being highly sought-after. Store banknotes flat in specially produced wallets and handle them as little as possible.

An Algerian ten dinar note.

1964   *7.5in (19cm) long*

$20-30   **CN**

A Bahamian one pound note, featuring King George VI.

c1950s   *6in (15cm) long*

$150-200   **CN**

A Biafran five shilling note.

1967   *4.5in (11.5cm) long*

$8-10   **CN**

A Jordanian one dinar note, featuring King Hussein of Jordan.

c1960s   *7in (18cm) long*

$15-20   **CN**

A Maltese five pound note.

This was the highest denomination available at the time. Apart from British notes, five pound notes from any Commonwealth country at this time showing Queen Elizabeth II are generally desirable. For example, a Jamaican five pound note may be worth anything from $1,000 to $2,000. Condition, however, is vital, with values plummeting downward if the note is not in truly mint condition.

1968   *6in (15cm) long*

$150-200   **CN**

A Libyan one dinar note, featuring Colonel Gaddaffi.

1990   *6.5in (16.5cm) long*

$2-4   **CN**

A WWII Maltese emergency issue one shilling overprint on two shilling note.

4.5in (11.5cm) long

$80-100   **CN**

BOOKS

ESSENTIAL REFERENCE

- True first editions are those from the first print run (impression) of the first published hardback edition of a book. A first edition may then have subsequent impressions, which may be changed in some way, such as errors being corrected. Paperback first editions can also be collectible, but tend to be less valuable, and are not yet as widely collected.
- Numbers of true 'firsts' are limited – value rises as desirability increases. Very famous, iconic titles will always be prized, but a classic title published at the height of an author's career will often be worth less than an early or less-well received work, mainly as fewer copies of the 'first' will have been printed.
- To check if you have a first edition, learn how to recognise the different styles of numbering. Look for a number '1' in the series of numbers on the inside copyright page. Some publishers state clearly that a book is a first edition, and some use a sequence of letters. Always check that the publishing date and copyright date match, and check the original publishing date and publisher in a reference book. In general, book club editions tend to be ignored by collectors.
- The smaller the edition is, and the more renowned the title, the higher the price. Authors' signatures add value to a first edition, particularly if it is a limited or special edition. Dedications are less desirable, unless the recipient is famous in their own right, or connected to the author in some way.
- There are many consistently popular authors such as Ian Fleming, but fashion plays a large role in value. First editions can also rise in value if the story is adapted into a successful movie or TV series. Jacket artwork can also make a difference to value.
- Always consider condition. Dust jackets should be clean, unfaded and undamaged – values can fall by over 50 percent without them. However, damage can often be restored. Check the book is complete, and has not been damaged or defaced. Books in truly perfect condition will always fetch a premium, particularly if from a smaller print run.

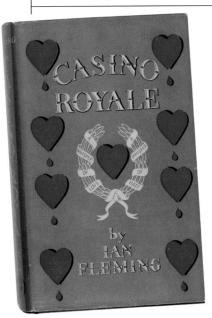

Ian Fleming, "Casino Royale", first edition, first issue, published by Cape, overall a fine copy with dust jacket, some rubbing and wear to extremities.

Being a first issue of the first edition of Fleming's first Bond book, this example is a true first edition. Under 5,000 of these were printed, many going to libraries. As it is signed in the same year it was published with a charming dedication, it is all the more desirable.
1953

$13,000-15,000   BLO

Ian Fleming, "Moonraker", first edition, published by Cape, with dust jacket, some scratches and spine slightly dulled, otherwise an unusually fine example.

Only 9,900 copies of the first edition were printed, making this example in excellent condition very rare.
1955

$6,500-7,500   BLO

Ian Fleming, "Dr. No", first edition, published by Cape, with dust jacket, some foxing and marks, and ink scribbles to front endpaper, otherwise a very good example.
1958

$900-1,100   BLO

Ian Fleming, "For Your Eyes Only", first edition, published by Cape, with dust jacket, slightly darkened to spine, otherwise a near fine copy.
1960

$650-750   BLO

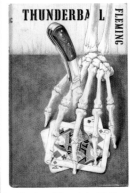

Ian Fleming, "Thunderball", first edition, published by Cape, with dust jacket, minor rubbing to corners, light spotting to top edge, otherwise an unusually fine example.
1961
$1,400-1,600 BLO

Ian Fleming, "On Her Majesty's Secret Service", first edition, published by Cape, with dust jacket, bookplate inscribed by Ian Fleming to 'Eileen' [Cond].

Eileen M. Cond was a socialite and book collector who sent bookplates to a number of authors, requesting their signatures. Fleming corresponded with her and signed a number of his books for her.
1963
$3,000-4,000 BLO

EXPERT EYE – FROM RUSSIA WITH LOVE

Fleming's fifth Bond novel is widely said to be his best book, as well as the best movie. As such it attracts a large number of fans keen to own copies.

Although it bears a personal inscription seemingly unrelated to Fleming, it is still nicely signed by the author, which adds to its value.

15,000 copies of the first edition were printed. Although the very first batch of printed pages were sent to a book club due to their poor quality, this effective second printing – marked Cape – is considered the true first edition.

The cover was the first to be designed by artist Richard Chopping, who worked closely with Fleming over the designs. His style has become a hallmark of Fleming's first editions.

Ian Fleming, "You Only Live Twice", first edition, with dust jacket, an unusually fine and bright example.

1964
$500-700 BLO

Ian Fleming, "From Russia, With Love", first edition, near full-page signed inscription from the author on front free endpaper, original boards, dust jacket, price-clipped, otherwise a fine example.

Inscribed to Geoffrey van Dantzig.
1957
$13,000-15,000 BLO

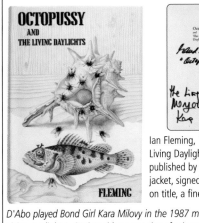

Ian Fleming, "Octopussy and The Living Daylights", first edition, published by Cape, with dust jacket, signed by Maryam D'Abo on title, a fine copy.

D'Abo played Bond Girl Kara Milovy in the 1987 movie version of 'The Living Daylights'. Copies with no remains of price stickers and unclipped jackets, like this one, are preferable.
1966
$650-750 BLO

Ian Fleming, "Thrilling Cities", first edition, published by Cape, with dust jacket, the bookplate signed and inscribed by Ian Fleming to 'Eileen' [Cond].

This is a collection of travel articles Fleming wrote for the Sunday Times following trips in 1959 and 1960. His travels appear to have influenced some of his future Bond novels and short stories.
1963
$2,000-3,000 BLO

J.G. Ballard, "The Drought", first edition, published by Jonathan Cape, with fellow author Angela Carter's bookplate on front paste-down, skillfully restored spine ends and corners, lightly rubbed.

This is an expanded version of "The Burning World", published in 1964.
1965
$400-600   BLO

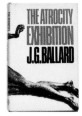

J.G. Ballard, "The Crystal World", first edition, published by Jonathan Cape, with dust jacket, rubbed at extremities, otherwise very good.
1966
$200-300   BLO

J.G. Ballard, "The Atrocity Exhibition", first edition, published by Jonathan Cape, with dust jacket, a little darkening, otherwise very good.
1970
$160-240   BLO

J.G. Ballard, "Crash", first edition, published by Jonathan Cape, with dust jacket, small inked name to upper fore-corner of front paste-down, with slight rubbing and one tear.

"Crash" is a controversial novel dealing with the sexual fetishism of car-crashes. It was made into an equally controversial movie by David Cronenberg in 1996, which was nominated for the Golden Palm at the Cannes Film Festival and won the Special Jury Prize.
1973
$700-900   BLO

J.G. Ballard, "High Rise", first edition, published by Jonathan Cape, with dust jacket, with minor creasing and a tear, but overall a very good copy.
1975
$200-300   BLO

J.G. Ballard, "The Unlimited Dream Company", first edition, published by Jonathan Cape, with dust jacket, unclipped but without price sticker.
1979
$25-35   BLO

Peter Benchley, "Jaws", first edition, published by Bantam, New York, signed by the author, very slightly chipped at spine ends, otherwise a fine copy.

Both the cover artwork and the one-sheet movie poster for the Spielberg movie version were drawn by Roger Kastel, who was also responsible for the 'Gone with the Wind' style poster for 'The Empire Strikes Back'.
1974
$500-700   BLO

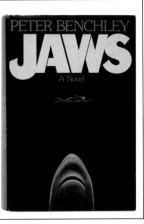

Raymond Benson, "The World is Not Enough", first edition, with dust jacket, signed by Goldie on front free endpaper, two cut signatures of the author loosely inserted.

Drum and bass legend Goldie, signed this copy both as Goldie and "The Bull", the character he played in the movie, with a bull monogram.
1999
$240-360   BLO

Raymond Chandler, "The Little Sister", first edition, published by Hamish Hamilton, with price-clipped dust jacket, worn at joints and fore-edges with slight loss to spine ends.

1949

$600-800   BLO

Tracy Chevalier, "Girl With a Pearl Earring", first edition, first issue, published by HarperCollins, with dust jacket and misspelling on lower panel, a fine copy.

1999

$300-400   BLO

Arthur C. Clarke, "2001, A Space Odyssey", first UK edition, published by Hutchinson, with dust jacket, with author's signature on loosely inserted card.

This was published by New American Library in the US, which can be worth up to $2,000 in similar fine condition.

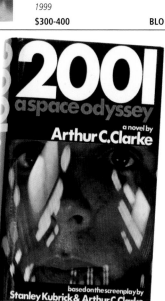

1968

$1,000-1,200   BLO

Richard Chopping, "The Fly", first edition, published by Secker & Warburg, with dust jacket.

Best known as the cover artist for most of Fleming's James Bond titles, this was Chopping's first novel – naturally he designed the cover too. The story is unrelated to the 1986 movie with Jeff Goldblum.

1965

$450-550   BLO

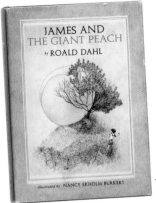

Roald Dahl, "James and the Giant Peach", first US edition, first issue, published by Alfred Knopf, with dust jacket, illustrations and plates by Nancy Ekholm Burkert, inked name on front paste-down.

1961

$1,400-1,800   BLO

Arthur Conan Doyle, "Uncle Bernac", first edition, published by Smith Elder, with 12 plates, and original cloth, slightly cocked and bumped, otherwise very good.

1897

$100-160   BLO

Arthur Conan Doyle, "The Green Flag", first US edition, published by McClure Phillips, with original pictorial cloth, spine very slightly sunned, otherwise a fine copy.

1900

$100-160   BLO

Lawrence Durrell, "Justine", first edition, published by Faber & Faber, signed and dated in 1985 by the author on title page, with price-clipped dust jacket, frayed at corners and spine ends.
1957

$1,000-1,200   **BLO**

EXPERT EYE – A JOHN GARDNER BOOK

John Gardner revived the James Bond series in 1981, finishing in 1996. Raymond Benson took over until recently, with Sebastian Faulks writing 'Devil May Care' which was published in May 2008.

This was Gardner's ninth Bond story. This example is signed by the author on the title page. Unsigned it may still be worth around $800-1,000.

As well as being the first UK edition, it was also first of the Armchair Detective Library trade editions.

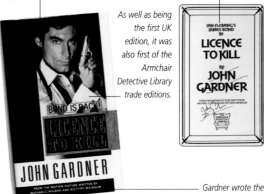

Gardner wrote the novel based on Richard Maibaum and Michael G. Wilson's movie script for the 1989 movie. Although accurate to the movie's plot, many consider the book to be much better, although both have inconsistencies related to certain characters, such as Felix Leiter.

John Gardner, "Licence to Kill", first UK edition, published by the Armchair Detective Library, with dust jacket, signed by the author on the title page, slight darkening to page edges, an excellent copy.
1990

$1,300-1,500   **BLO**

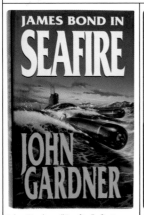

John Gardner, "Seafire", first edition with dust jacket, published by Hodder & Stoughton, signed by the author on the title page, and signed by the jacket artist with stamp on front free endpaper.
1994

$300-400   **BLO**

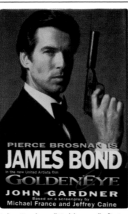

John Gardner, "Goldeneye", first edition, third impression, published by Hodder & Stoughton, with dust jacket, signed by the author on the title page.
1995

$200-400   **BLO**

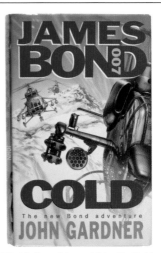

John Gardner, "COLD", first edition, published by Hodder & Stoughton, with dust jacket, signed by the author on the title page, slightly rubbed at extremities.
1996

$800-1,000   **BLO**

Nick Hornby, "Fever Pitch", first edition, published by Victor Gollancz, with price-clipped dust jacket, signed dedication by the author and inscribed on the title page.

This was the author's first novel.
1992

$400-600 BLO

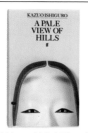

Kazuo Ishiguro, "A Pale View of Hills", first edition, published by Faber, with dust jacket, very slight sunning to spine, overall a fine copy.

This was the author's first novel.
1982

$1,100-1,300 BLO

EXPERT EYE – THE VELVETEEN RABBIT

Margery Williams Bianco (1881-1944) lived between the US and UK. She wrote 30 children's books, although this is her best known and most loved around the world.

Williams was inspired by Walter de la Mare's poetry, which focused on the imagination, and particularly a child's imagination. In the story a soft toy rabbit is loved by a boy, leading to it coming to life as a real rabbit.

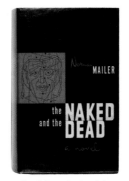

The illustrations were by William Nicholson (1872-1949), father of British abstract painter Ben Nicholson, and one of the most influential British illustrators and poster artists of the time.

Not only is this a first impression of the first edition, but it is in unusually good condition for a children's book, with bright images and only light signs of age.

Margery Williams, "The Velveteen Rabbit", first edition, first impression, published by Avon Books, with seven color plates by William Nicholson including three double-page illustrations, some marks and spotting and with skillful repair to spine, edges and corners.
1922

$8,000-10,000 BLO

Stephen King, "'Salem's Lot", first UK edition, published by New English Library, with dust jacket, a fine copy.

1976

$700-900 BLO

Alistair MacLean, "H.M.S. Ulysses", first edition, published by Collins, with dust jacket, signed by the author on the title page, with pictorial endpapers.

This was the author's first novel.
1955

$900-1,100 BLO

Norman Mailer, "The Naked and the Dead", first US edition, published by Rinehart, with dust jacket, publisher's device on the copyright page, sympathetic restoration to spine ends, corners and one edge.

1948

$400-600 BLO

Paul McCartney, Geoff Dunbar and Philip Ardagh, "High in the Clouds", first edition, published by Faber, with dust jacket, signed with doodle by McCartney on half-title, and with color illustrations throughout, in mint condition.

2005
$1,300-1,500   BLO

Arthur Miller, "Death of a Salesman", first US edition, published by Viking Press, the dust jacket with unclipped $2.50 price and pictorial endpapers, skillfully restored at spine ends and corners.

1949
$1,300-1,500   BLO

EXPERT EYE – A LARRY NIVEN BOOK

First published in 1970, Ringworld won both a Nebula award and a Locus award for Best Novel in the same year, and a Hugo award for Best Novel in 1971.

The first hardback version of this title is scarce, particularly in this excellent condition.

It is considered a classic work of science fiction and was followed by three sequels – the series is enormously popular with many fans.

The first edition of the paperback contains mistakes, the most notable being that main protagonist, Louis Wu, travels the wrong way around the Ringworld, arriving in Munich, Germany, from Greenwich, England, in an attempt to extend his birthday – later editions have him arriving in Beirut, Lebanon.

Larry Niven, "Ringworld", first UK and hardback edition, published by Gollancz, with dust jacket.
1972
$2,400-3,600   BLO

Patrick O'Brian, "Master & Commander", first edition, published by Collins, with price-clipped dust jacket, slightly frayed but otherwise very good.
1970
$1,000-1,200   BLO

Patrick O'Brian, "The Fortune of War", first edition, published by Collins, with dust jacket, spine very slightly sunned.
1979
$350-400   BLO

Patrick O'Brian, "The Surgeon's Mate", first edition, with original boards and dust jacket, a fine copy, scarce.
1980
$1,500-1,700   BLO

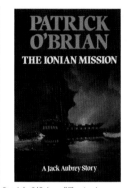

Patrick O'Brian, "The Ionian Mission", first edition, published by Collins, with dust jacket, spine slightly sunned.
1981
$500-700   **BLO**

Patrick O'Brian, "Treason's Harbour", first edition, published by Collins, with dust jacket, spine faded.
1983
$450-550   **BLO**

EXPERT EYE – BOOGIE WOOGIE

This was produced prior to the trade edition in a limited edition of only 500, each of which was signed by the author on the title page and Damien Hirst on the jacket.

The storyline parodies the New York art scene in the 1990s, and the jacket artwork alludes to the work of numerous artists involved at the time, such as Jeff Koons, Sarah Lucas and Hirst himself.

Damien Hirst designed the jacket, which is sold as an artwork by itself.

The title, the design of the title, and the game board allude to painter Piet Mondrian's 'Broadway Boogie Woogie'. The story also revolves around the sale of a Mondrian painting.

Danny Moynihan, "Boogie-Woogie", first edition, published by Duckworth Literary Entertainment, from an edition of 500 copies stamped and signed by Moynihan on the title page, jacket designed by Damien Hirst and signed by him on lower panel of jacket.
2000
$400-600   **BLO**

Philip Pullman, "Northern Lights", first edition, first issue, published by Scholastic, with dust jacket, signed inscription from the author on the half-title page, with original boards.

Philip Pullman, "His Dark Materials", three volumes of first editions, published by Scholastic, signed by the author on the title pages, comprising a first issue of "Northern Lights", the price-clipped jacket with Carnegie sticker on upper panel; "The Subtle Knife" and "The Amber Spyglass".

Prices for Pullman's first editions are beginning to rival those paid for J.K. Rowling's Harry Potter series, which previously eclipsed them. Even though it was released earlier, "Northern Lights" gained from the popularity of Rowling's books due to new interest in fantasy stories. The release of 'The Golden Compass', the movie version of "Northern Lights", in 2007 drew further attention to the series, which may continue to rise as more movies are made. Values are raised as each of these is signed, and the first bears its rare gold Carnegie Award sticker.
1995/1997/2000
$5,600-6,400   **BLO**

The book was released under the title "The Golden Compass" in the US, referring to the fictional alethiometer, a device for detecting the truth, which features on the dust jacket and prominently throughout the book.
1995
$4,400-5,600   **BLO**

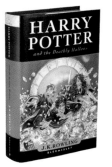

J.K. Rowling, "Harry Potter and the Deathly Hallows", first edition, published by Bloomsbury, signed with birthday greetings from the author on the title page, together with a letter of authentication from Rowling's personal assistant loosely inserted.

2007

$3,000-4,000   BLO

Robert Sabbag, "Snowblind", first edition, published by Rebel, from a limited edition of 1,000 with foreword by Howard Marx and packaging designed by Damien Hirst, signed by Sabbag, Hirst and Marx, complete with packaging including a rolled-up $100 bill, fake Amex credit card, original mirror covers, silver edges, slip-case with repeated $100-dollar bill design, in original publisher's box.

The cover artwork and accessories indicate the subject of the book – the cocaine trade. Always check the last three digits of the real $100 bill – these should match the edition number of the book.

1998

$2,400-3,600   BLO

EXPERT EYE – A HARRY POTTER DELUXE SET

Each of these books is a rare original first edition that has been rebound in very high quality gilt-tooled morocco leather by London's notable 'Chelsea Bindery' – each book also has its own matching slipcase.

The front covers have an inset leather image based on the illustrations on the original covers – each also bears J.K. Rowling's impressed signature in gilt.

The colors have been carefully chosen to match those of the original covers, which may have become damaged or dirty when they originally read.

Rebound books of this very high quality are scarce and sought-after by collectors and the army of Potter fans – it is also very rare to find a set of six Rowling first editions.

A set of six J.K. Rowling first 'deluxe' editions by the Chelsea Bindery, published by Bloomsbury, comprising "Harry Potter and the Philosopher's Stone"; "Harry Potter and the Chamber of Secrets"; "Harry Potter and the Prisoner of Azkaban" (first issue); "Harry Potter and the Goblet of Fire"; "Harry Potter and the Order of the Phoenix" and "Harry Potter and the Half-Blood Prince", the page edges stamped in silver with hologram stars.

1999-2005

$13,000-15,000   BLO

Alexander McCall Smith, "The No. 1 Ladies' Detective Agency", first edition, published by Pantheon, Edinburgh, with dust jacket, signed by the author on the title page.

This is the scarce true first edition. At the time of writing, a BBC TV series of the books is being filmed, and will be shown in the US on HBO.

1998

$1,000-1,200   BLO

Paul Stewart & Chris Riddell, "Stormchaser", first edition, published by Doubleday, with price-clipped dust jacket, illustrations and map endpapers.

1999

$400-600   BLO

Hunter S. Thompson, "Hell's Angels", first US edition stating "first printing", with dust jacket and small ownership inscription on front free endpaper, published by Random House.

1967

$1,400-1,600   BLO

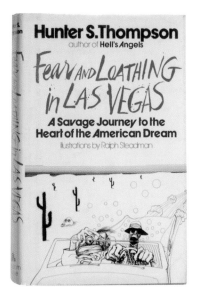

Hunter S. Thompson, "Fear and Loathing in Las Vegas", first US edition, published by Random House, with dust jacket and blind-stamp on preliminary, with illustrations by Ralph Steadman, slightly sunned at top edge.

This is Thompson's most famous novel. It was successfully filmed by Terry Gilliam in 1998, with Johnny Depp in the lead role, a character based on Thompson himself. This renewed popularity in Thompson, together with his death in 2005, has lead to an increase in prices.
1971
$1,400-1,600 **BLO**

Graham Swift, "Waterland", first edition, published by Heinemann, with dust jacket.

1983
$300-400 **BLO**

J.R.R.Tolkien, "The Lord of the Rings", published by George Allen & Unwin, comprising three first editions of "The Fellowship of the Ring", fifth impression; "The Two Towers", fourth impression; and "The Return of the King", second impression, each containing maps and with dust jackets, uniformly darkened.
1955-56
$1,000-1,400 **BLO**

William Trevor, "The Day We Got Drunk on Cake", first edition, published by Bodley Head, with dust jacket.

This is the author's first collection of short stories, and is sought-after.
1967
$1,000-1,200 **BLO**

E.B. White, "Stuart Little", first edition, first issue, published by Harper & Brothers, New York & London, with dust jacket, illustrations by Garth Williams, with "10-5 & I-U" on copyright page.
1945
$500-700 **BLO**

Douglas E. Winter (editor), "Prime Evil", produced by Donald M. Grant and published by Bantam Press, from a limited edition of 250 copies signed by the contributors, containing color plates and illustrations, and with original black rexine, black drop-back box.

Contributors include Stephen King, Clive Barker, Peter Straub, Ramsey Campbell and Whitley Strieber.
1988
$400-600 **BLO**

P.G. Wodehouse, "Summer Moonshine", first UK edition, published by Herbert Jenkins, with dust jacket, containing eight pages of advertisements, abrasions to spine, some skillful restoration to spine and edges.
1938
$800-1,200 **BLO**

John Wyndham, "The Day of the Triffids", first edition, published by Michael Joseph, with dust jacket, minor restoration to foot of spine.
1951
$1,700-1,900 **BLO**

BOOKS

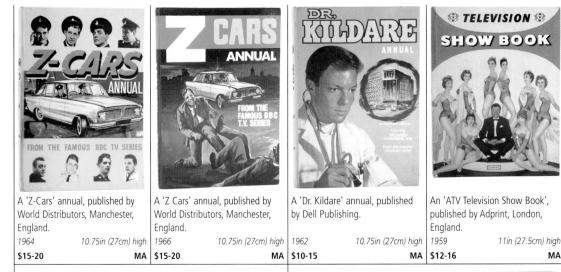

A 'Z-Cars' annual, published by World Distributors, Manchester, England.
1964   *10.75in (27cm) high*
$15-20   **MA**

A 'Z Cars' annual, published by World Distributors, Manchester, England.
1966   *10.75in (27cm) high*
$15-20   **MA**

A 'Dr. Kildare' annual, published by Dell Publishing.
1962   *10.75in (27cm) high*
$10-15   **MA**

An 'ATV Television Show Book', published by Adprint, London, England.
1959   *11in (27.5cm) high*
$12-16   **MA**

A 'Radio Fun' annual, with UFO and alien cover.

The fun and quirky cover, with the UFO and alien representing the popularity of science fiction and outer space at this time, adds to the appeal of this annual.

1957   *9.5in (24cm) high*
$15-20   **MA**

A 1950s 'This Show Business' hardback book, published by the Daily Mirror, with Jayne Mansfield 'The Girl Can't Help It' cover.

The presence of Jayne Mansfield raises the value of this book. Covers featuring popular stars who have a wide following will generally add to desirability – and often value – particularly if well photographed or showing their private lives.
1956   *10in (25.5cm) high*
$30-40   **MA**

A 'Radio Fun' annual, with Norman Wisdom cover.

1959   *9.5in (24cm) high*
$15-20   **MA**

A 1950s 'Stars Off The Record' annual, published by Eldon Press, with Johnnie Ray dust jacket and Frank Sinatra interview.
1954   *11in (28cm) high*
$12-16   **MA**

ESSENTIAL REFERENCE

- Ceramics printed with Canadian buildings or scenes were typically sold as souvenirs to tourists. Although some pieces were made by Canadian factories, such as Céramique de Beauce (see pages 37-39) and the Blue Mountain Pottery (see pages 40-45) from the 1940s onwards, large quantities were also produced in Germany, Austria and Japan, typically from the 1920s-60s. 19thC pieces, either made in Canada or showing Canadian scenes, are generally rare and valuable. Examples by makers such as F.T. Thomas of Quebec are highly sought after.

- Most examples are transfer printed, although some may have handpainted detailing. As many of these souvenirs were inexpensive, and damaged or thrown away, some can be rare today. Look out for Canadian national symbols, such as the maple leaf, and particularly the beaver.
- Items related to Canada's military history, primarily during WWII, are also sought after. An interesting story will usually increase desirability. Interest in social history and folk art is also growing. Away from scarce and valuable 19thC and earlier furniture, affordable pieces can still be found.

A 1920s-30s German souvenir ware handled vase, with coat-of-arms for Montréal and gilt highlights, the base stamped "Made in Germany".

3.5in (9cm) high

$80-120　　　　　TAC

A 1920s Austrian souvenir ware cup, transfer-printed with a scene of the University of Toronto and with hand-painted blue luster glaze and gilt highlights.

2.75in (7cm) high

$70-100　　　　　TCF

A 1920s-30s German souvenir ware teapot, with transfer-printed scene of the New Market, Bradford, and pink luster ground, marked "Made in Germany" to base.

Many of the images seen on these ceramics are also found on postcards of the time.

4.5in (11.5cm) high

$70-100　　　　　TAC

A German or Japanese souvenir ware small vase, with transfer-printed scene of the Edmonton Parliament Building, and luster glaze, unmarked.

4in (10cm) high

$50-70　　　　　TAC

A 1920s-30s German souvenir ribbon plate, with printed scene of the City Hall, Toronto, the back printed "Made in Germany".

The slots on this example could be threaded with colored ribbon, creating a decorative effect and also enabling it to be hung.

7in (17.5cm) diam

$55-65　　　　　TCF

An Aynsley bone china cup and saucer, with transfer-printed sprigs of maple leaves and the Canadian states in a ribbon, commemorating the 'centennial of the Canadian Confederation'.

c1967　　Saucer 5.75in (14.5cm) diam

$55-65　　　　　TCF

A Royal Darwood transfer-printed bone china cup and saucer, with band of gilt maple leaves, commemorating the 'centennial of the Dominion of Canada'.

c1967　　5.75in (14.5cm) diam

$25-35　　　　　TCF

CANADIANA

A Royal Doulton commemorative plate, transfer-printed with a 'Centennial Map of Canada', from the Canadian Commemorative Series 1867-1967, with printed marks to back.

c1967   10.5in (27cm) diam

$80-120   **TCF**

A Wedgwood 'H.M.S. Discovery' transfer-printed plate, from the Historical Canadian Vessels series, the back impressed "Wedgwood 3Z54" and with commemorative wording to reverse.

Captain Cook's 'Resolution' and Captain Clerke's 'Discovery' landed at Nootka Sound, Vancouver, in February 1778.

10.75in (27cm) diam

$35-45   **TCF**

A 1990s Canadian Folk Art tinplated steel gold miner's pan, hand-painted with a view of 'A Tien Atlin, British Columbia', by W. Klossner.

Gold miner's pans have been decorated and sold as popular decorative mementos since the 1920s. 'A Tien Atlin' is the Tinglit term for 'Big Water'.

16.5in (41.5cm) diam

$200-250   **THA**

A late 19thC Canadian Rose & LaFlamme Soda Fountain Supplies printed stoneware bottle.

12in (30.5cm) high

$120-180   **TAM**

A late 19thC Wentworth Mineral Water Ltd printed stoneware bottle, from Hamilton, Ontario.

7.75in (19.5cm) high

$70-90   **TAM**

A Canadian 'Canvas Back' showbird decoy, carved by Ron James.

Contemporary decoys are produced primarily as decorative items or Folk Art, rather than as functional objects. Carvers can therefore take more time to add realistic features to their birds. Note the crossed tail feathers and the delicately marked out feathers around the duck's head. Carved by a notable artist, this 'showbird' won the second prize at 1983 Sportmen's Show.

1983   15in (38cm) long

$450-550   **RAON**

A late 19thC photograph of a family, seated on the edge of Luna Island, off Goat Island, in front of the American Falls, Niagara Falls, mounted and framed.

Tourist images such as this are becoming increasingly sought-after, particularly if they are of a good age, showing a well-known landmark and are well-composed.

Image 8.75in (22cm) high

$70-100   **TCF**

A panorama photograph of cadets at the Royal Military College of Canada in Kingston, Ontario.

One of the men in the front row center, to the right of generals has been identified as Basil Collett of Kelowna B.C.

1945   33.5in (85cm) long

$100-140   **TPF**

A WWII Royal Canadian Air Force woollen uniform, complete with trousers, scarf, and tunic with belt, pilot's insignia, ribbons and bars for medals, the trousers from Winnipeg and dated 1953, the tunic from Toronto and dated 1942.

31.5in (79cm) high

$280-320   TAM

A WWII Royal Canadian Air Force service forage woollen cap, with original brass badges.

12in (30.5cm) long

$120-180   TAM

A WWI Canadian military canvas-covered water bottle, with leather shoulder strap, marked "Hugh Barson Co. Ltd Ottawa" and dated.

1915   *9in (23cm) high*

$100-150   TAM

A set of four Canadian WWII medals and ribbons, mounted on a bar.

4in (10cm) wide

$280-320   TAM

An Agfa folding pocket camera, with Agfa PB20 Readyset lens, with Royal Canadian Air Force printed logo to front flap, and used in WWII.

Without the military transfer and connection, this camera would usually be worth around $20-30 in similar condition.

6in (15cm) high

$200-300   TAM

A Royal Canadian Air Force plane propeller, cut down and converted into a mantel clock, fitted with a Westclox electric clock.

11in (28cm) high

$220-280   TAM

A Canadian cast alloy City Police badge, for Port William, Nova Scotia, with molded town crest and motto.

2.75in (6cm) high

$80-120   TAM

A Canadian Birks enameled solid gold prize medal and ribbon, awarded by the Hudson Bay Company at the British Columbian Poultry Association Ninth Annual Show to R. Eastham for Best Bird In Show, stamped "14KT".

3in (7.5cm) high

$300-500 **TAM**

An Independent Order of The Odd Fellows enameled bronze committee medal and ribbon, commemorating the 97th Annual Session in 1921, held at the Sovereign Grand Lodge.

1921 *3.25in (8cm) high*

$65-75 **TAM**

A pair of post-WWI commemorative brass and wood bookends, with cast enlargements of original WWI badges bearing the University of Toronto crest and motto.

7.75in (19.5cm) high

$200-300 **TAM**

A Roden Bros brass double-sided second prize trophy on stand, molded "1932 Canadian National Exhibition" and awarded to E. Padden for the King George V Cup Competition, the back with molded portrait of R.B. Bennett, Prime Minister of Canada.

c1931 *Medal 2.5in (6.5cm) high*

$180-220 **TAM**

An unengraved silver-plated trophy, of Canadian interest, the cup-form trophy flanked with two beavers rampant on columns, each holding sprigs of maple leaves in their mouths, the whole mounted on a light varnished wood plinth, unmarked.

17in (43cm) high

$700-1,000 **TCF**

EXPERT EYE – A VESTA CASE

Vesta cases are highly collectible in their own right. They are often found in poor condition from use – this example is in excellent condition.

Even though this example is silver-plated, rather than being sterling silver, the enameling makes it unusual.

The Canadian themes are strong and include both maple leaves and a beaver – these make it very rare.

The enamel work is well-executed, with the use of many different colors and two-tone leaves.

A silver-plated vesta case, with enameled maple leaves surrounding a crest surmounted by a beaver.

2.5in (6cm) high

$1,200-1,700 **TCF**

ESSENTIAL REFERENCE

- In 1940, the Syndicat des Céramistes Paysans de la Beauce was founded after pottery classes were held at the Beauceville High School, Quebec. Trained by Swiss ceramicist Willie Chocard, farmers and rural workers produced ceramics that could be sold during the largely unproductive winter months. Production grew rapidly, and by 1943 the potters had moved to a factory at St Joseph de Beauce.
- Output soon grew to industrial levels, with Raymond Lewis acting as head designer. The 1940s saw production dominated by tableware, most with simple, chunky forms. Until c1948, locally sourced red clay was used, but as this could not meet the factory's growing needs, a finer white clay was imported from the state of Georgia.
- The trade name Beauceware was used from 1946 to 1964, and is typically found on the base. The recognisable 'cb' mark was designed by André Roy in 1965 and was used until the factory's closure in 1989. Mold or shape numbers were used consecutively, but this will only help with identifying when a shape was introduced, as it may have been made for many years.
- Forms and glazes can help to date a piece to a period. From the late 1940s, glazes moved away from single colors, taking on sponged, dripped or graduated effects. Patterns or motifs tended to be molded. During the 1950s, curving forms were produced, some inspired by natural leaf or shell forms. Glazes included bold chartreuse, greens and burgundy/pinks, and sometimes had graduated tones.
- During the 1960s, the expanded range took on more dramatic glaze effects. Colors were splashed, dripped, swirled or trailed over the body. Tableware remained a mainstay for the factory. A key designer at this time was Quebecois ceramicist Jacques Garnier, who joined in 1963 and introduced a Scandinavian style to the company. In 1964, Raymond Bourret replaced Raymond Lewis as head of the glaze department.
- Ceramicist Jean Cartier, a further key designer, joined in 1970 and remained there until 1974, developing an idiosyncratic style. In 1974, the factory was destroyed by a fire, but reopened in 1975. Competition from foreign manufacturers led to its closure in 1989.
- The popularity of, and prices for, Beauceware have been rising for the past few years and look set to continue. Unusual and characteristic designs by Garnier or Cartier are usually more desirable. Although some pieces from between the 1940s and '50s are sought-after and expensive, many simply formed pieces can be found affordably.

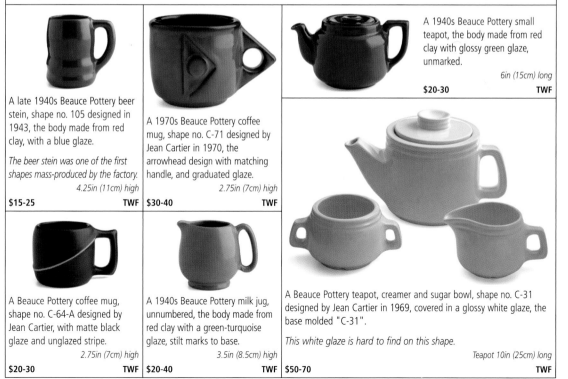

A late 1940s Beauce Pottery beer stein, shape no. 105 designed in 1943, the body made from red clay, with a blue glaze.

The beer stein was one of the first shapes mass-produced by the factory.

4.25in (11cm) high

$15-25   TWF

A 1970s Beauce Pottery coffee mug, shape no. C-71 designed by Jean Cartier in 1970, the arrowhead design with matching handle, and graduated glaze.

2.75in (7cm) high

$30-40   TWF

A 1940s Beauce Pottery small teapot, the body made from red clay with a glossy green glaze, unmarked.

6in (15cm) long

$20-30   TWF

A Beauce Pottery coffee mug, shape no. C-64-A designed by Jean Cartier, with matte black glaze and unglazed stripe.

2.75in (7cm) high

$20-30   TWF

A 1940s Beauce Pottery milk jug, unnumbered, the body made from red clay with a green-turquoise glaze, stilt marks to base.

3.5in (8.5cm) high

$20-40   TWF

A Beauce Pottery teapot, creamer and sugar bowl, shape no. C-31 designed by Jean Cartier in 1969, covered in a glossy white glaze, the base molded "C-31".

This white glaze is hard to find on this shape.

Teapot 10in (25cm) long

$50-70   TWF

EXPERT EYE – A BEAUCE TEAPOT

This teapot represented an enormous departure in design for Canadian potteries that had previously looked to Oriental examples and studio pottery for inspiration.

Beauce produced it with black, white, blue or pink lids.

Although examples were initially made in Goyer-Bonneau's studio, the company received so many orders for the teapot at 'Accent On Design' (a US trade show), that they sold the licence to Beauce who made it from 1985 to 1989.

Goyer-Bonneau's examples tend to have thinner, more delicate walls and are often signed on the base.

A 1980s Beauce Pottery teapot, designed by Denise Goyer and Alain Bonneau in 1976, with glossy black glaze, the base with blue paper "Madison Design" label.

10in (25cm) diam

$80-120   TWF

A Beauce Pottery wine carafe, shape no. 2184 designed in 1968, and four beakers, shape no. 1186 designed in 1954, the base of the carafe marked "Canada 2184 cb".

According to records, this carafe and six beakers cost $15.95 Canadian dollars in 1975.

Carafe 9.5in (24cm) high

$80-120   TWF

A 1970s Beauce Pottery 'Ptarmigan' teapot, creamer and sugar bowl, designed by Doug Funk in c1972, glazed in white with black printed geometric motifs, marked with a maple leaf between two arrows to base.

The radical forms were inspired both by a sense of speed and also by the Canadian white grouse. Plates and bowls were not designed, as these pieces were intended to be matched to plain white examples.

Teapot 11.5in (29cm) long

$100-150   TWF

A 1970s Beauce Pottery 'Ptarmigan' lidded casserole dish, shape no. CCD-54 designed by Doug Funk in c1972, glazed in white with black printed geometric motifs, the base molded "CCD-54".

10.25in (26cm) long

$60-70   TWF

A 1970s Beauce Pottery clay baker, shape C-50 designed by Jean Cartier in 1970, the top half decorated with hand-painted stylised wheat and barley designs.

17in (43cm) long

$70-100   TWF

A Beauce Pottery 'Bluestone' pattern gravy boat, shape no. cb C-87 designed by Jean Cartier in 1970, the base molded "cb C-87".

8.25in (21cm) long

$30-40   TWF

A Beauce Pottery candle-holder, shape no. G-209 designed by Jacques Garnier c1965, with glossy burgundy glazed exterior and black glazed interior.

A Beauce Pottery organic form candle-holder, shape no. C.4 designed by Jean Cartier in 1969, pierced with holes and covered with a matte green glaze, the base molded "C.4".

6.75in (17cm) high

$30-50   TWF

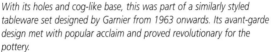

With its holes and cog-like base, this was part of a similarly styled tableware set designed by Garnier from 1963 onwards. Its avant-garde design met with popular acclaim and proved revolutionary for the pottery.

4.25in (10.5cm) high

$30-40   TWF

A 1950s-60s Beauce Pottery ribbed vase, shape no. 416, with green-gray glazed exterior and green glazed interior, the base impressed "Beauceware 416 Canada".

9.25in (23.5cm) high

$80-120   TWF

A Beauce Pottery baluster vase, shape no. 1978 designed in 1967, decorated with a turquoise glaze and black chevrons, the base molded "Beauce cb 1978 Canada".

9in (23cm) high

$100-150   TWF

A Beauce Pottery large bottle vase, the yellow glaze dripped over with green and white, the base with "cb 1916 Canada" molded mark.

18in (45.5cm) high

$80-120   TWF

A 1970s Beauce Pottery shaped vase, shape C-3018 designed by Jean Cartier in 1972, with two openings.

As well as innovative shapes, Cartier's designs for Beauce are characterised by mottled glazes, as here.

7.5in (19cm) high

$80-120   TWF

A Beauce Pottery maple leaf dish, decorated with a dripped and mottled greeny-cream glaze on a green background, the base molded "Beauce 1700 Canada".

9.5in (24cm) high

$20-25   TWF

A 1940s Beauce Pottery lotus-shaped candle-holder, the body made from red clay with a yellow mottled and dripped celadon green glaze.

Candle-holders like this, and ashtrays, were among the earliest shapes produced by the pottery.

2.75in (7cm) high

$20-40   TWF

FIND OUT MORE...

'Beauce Pottery: The Story of Beauceware and Céramique de Beauce', by Daniel Cogné, Richard Dubé and Paul Trépannier, published by Les Editions CID, Canada, 2004.

ESSENTIAL REFERENCE

- The Blue Mountain Pottery was founded by Czech immigrant Josef Weider (1909-71) in Collingwood, Ontario, just after WWII. The name was taken from the neighbouring Blue Mountains, which are a haven for skiers. Founded to provide a steady income and work throughout the year, the pottery took on fellow Czechs Dennis (Zdenek) Tupy to develop the molds and Mirek Hambálek, the glazes.

- Vases, ashtrays and bowls were sold to skiers and tourists. By 1955 production increased to cope with rising sales. Expansion continued into the 1960s, and Weider sold the successful company in 1968. After a further sale and financial problems, it was bought by Robert Blair in 1968. While the 1980s and early '90s proved strong for the company, it was forced to close in 2004 due to falling orders, the factory lease ending and competition from Far Eastern makers.

- The vast majority of pieces were made using the local red clay and a slip-molding process. The most characteristic, popular and prolifically used glaze was a streaky, flowing green, said to be inspired by the mountains' spruce and pine trees. Blue and brown were also popular. Due to the two-step, brushed and dipped production process, the glaze on each piece is unique. The glaze formulae were complex and specially developed by the company.

- Other glazes are rarer. Among the most desirable today are Harvest Gold, Autumn Mist and Cobalt Blue, and rarer glazes include Slate and Mocha. Glaze is one of the most important considerations for value. A superbly varied green glaze on a good form may be worth as much as a poor example of the rarer Slate glaze. Look at the green vases shown below for an example. In general, the stronger and more tonally varied, the better.

- Look for early pieces from the 1950s or ranges produced for short time periods, as these tend to be more desirable and valuable. Some early pieces can be identified from the presence of three pin marks on the base, left by kiln stilts. Rarer or more sought-after ranges include a series of Noah's Ark animals, Apollo, the Native Artists' Collection, and Canadian Decorator.

- Unusual or rare forms are also sought-after. Long-necked swans, stylized fish that represent the period and clean-lined modern forms all find fans. Although shapes had their own numbers, many have been given names by collectors, such as the Angel Fish. As well as the glaze, consider how sharp and detailed the molded forms are, as this counts too.

- As well as being successful within Canada, over 60 per cent of the company's production was exported abroad, 40 per cent of that to the US, with much of the remaining 20 per cent going to the UK and the rest of Europe. Prices have been growing rapidly over the past five years, but much is still affordable. As the pottery was so successful, more treasures may be waiting to be discovered.

A Blue Mountain Pottery asymmetric organic form 'Duckbill' vase, shape no. 55 designed by Dennis Tupy, with dripped green glaze.	A Blue Mountain Pottery 'Bowling Pin' jug vase or pitcher, shape no. 25a designed by Dennis Tupy, with mottled and dripped green glaze.	A Blue Mountain Pottery cylinder vase, with scooped rim, the base with molded 'three tree' mark. *The glaze on this example is not as good or desirable as on the vases on the left.*	A Blue Mountain Pottery vase, in the form of two stylized curving leaves, with green dripped glaze, the base with 'three tree' and "Canada" marks.	A 1950s Blue Mountain vase, shape no. 36 designed by Dennis Tupy, with long, flared neck, the early avocado green glaze with dripped light green and blue-tinged cream glaze.
12in (31cm) high	*19in (48cm) high*	*11.5in (29cm) high*	*11.25in (28.5cm) high*	*5.75in (14.5cm) high*
$30-50 TWF	$40-60 TWF	$30-40 TWF	$40-60 TWF	$20-40 TWF

A Blue Mountain Pottery 'Spitoon' vase, shape no. 32A, with mottled, dripped green glaze.

This is one of the most commonly seen shapes in one of the most commonly seen colorways. It is the variety of green tones on this example that makes it this valuable.

5.25in (13cm) high

$30-40 **TWF**

A Blue Mountain Pottery cornucopia vase, with a good green dripped glaze, the base with molded "BMP Canada" mark with curling "M".

This form is similar to, and may have been inspired by, the success of Royal Haeger's cornucopia vases.

10.75in (27.5cm) wide

$40-50 **TWF**

A Blue Mountain Pottery dolphin sculpture, with green dripped glaze.

16.5in (42cm) long

$30-40 **TWF**

This is one of the largest and most dramatic forms produced by Blue Mountain and was made from the early 1950s until c1986. Despite its success it was never copied by other makers.

It is usually found in this green glaze, which is well displayed by the large flat sides. Examples in Harvest Gold are rare, and it has not yet been found in any other colorway.

The production process was time-consuming as they were so large and fragile. Tupy is said to have joked that the glaze held the sides together.

Although prices have been rising in recent years, this is only for undamaged fish - always check carefully for signs of damage, particularly on the fin tips.

A Blue Mountain Pottery 'Angel Fish' vase, shape no. 58 designed by Dennis Tupy, with a graduated green dripped glaze, the base molded "BMP Canada".

17.5in (44cm) high

$150-250 **TWF**

A Blue Mountain Pottery 'Swan' tall bird sculpture, shape no. 48 designed by Dennis Tupy, with green dripped glaze, the base with Blue Mountain Pottery paper label.

Birds with elongated necks were typical forms used by glassmakers on Murano during the same period. Examine the necks carefully as they were frequently broken and reglued.

18.25in (46cm) high

$40-60 **TWF**

A Blue Mountain Pottery Fish sculpture, with long, curving tail, in a dripped and mottled green glaze.

18.5in (47cm) high

$40-60 **TWF**

A Blue Mountain Pottery 'Ginger Jar', with the 'Celadon' glaze, the base molded "750".

The form and glaze appear to be inspired by ancient Oriental ceramics. This shape was not popular at the time, making it harder to find today.

9in (22.5cm) high

$80-120   **TWF**

A pair of Blue Mountain Pottery 'Peacock' bookends, with green dripped glaze.

Peacock bookends are harder to find and more desirable than the more common horse head bookends.

8.5in (21.5cm) high

$70-90   **TWF**

A Blue Mountain Pottery camel figurine, with green dripped glaze.

8.75in (22cm) high

$50-70   **TWF**

A Blue Mountain Pottery bottle vase, with shaped bulb, tall neck and flared rim, decorated with a streaked and dripped glaze, the base with molded 'three tree' mark.

It is the highly appealing complex glaze, which contains different tones of light blue, green, cream and pink, that makes this vase so valuable.

6in (15cm) high

$150-200   **TWF**

A 1960s-70s Blue Mountain Pottery jug, with a dripped and mottled cobalt and light blue glaze, the base with molded 'three tree mark'.

10.25in (26.5cm) high

$50-70   **TWF**

A 1950s Blue Mountain vase, shape no. 36 designed by Dennis Tupy, with long, flared neck, and Aurora Borealis glaze.

5.75in (14.5cm) high

$40-60   **TWF**

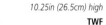

A Blue Mountain Pottery dolphin sculpture, with dripped cobalt blue glaze.

7.75in (19.5cm) high

$35-45   **TWF**

A Blue Mountain Pottery 'Spitoon' vase, shape no. 32A, with Harvest Gold glaze.

5.25in (13cm) high

$35-45   **TWF**

A Blue Mountain Pottery jug vase, shape no. 19 designed by Dennis Tupy, with handle and Harvest Gold glaze, the base with 'three tree' mark.

This glaze remains as popular with collectors today as it was with buyers during the 1970s.

13.75in (35cm) high

$50-70   **TWF**

EXPERT EYE – A BLUE MOUNTAIN VASE

The style of glaze and form are very similar to contemporary West German pottery that was being imported into Canada and sold inexpensively, competing for market share with Blue Mountain pottery.

The pitted surface and Apollo glaze name were inspired by the 1969 moon landing, and are unique to each piece as they were applied by hand.

Examples are hard to find as it was produced for only three years, from 1977 until 1980.

The thick and randomly bubbled glaze can be found on a number of different shapes including pitcher forms.

A Blue Mountain Pottery baluster shaped vase, shape no. 856, with the Apollo dripped and bubbled glaze, the base with circular factory mark and molded "856".

13.5in (34cm) high

$180-220   **TWF**

A 1970s Blue Mountain Pottery wine carafe and two goblets, each with the Mocha glaze, the base with molded "BMP" mark.

1965-84   Carafe 10.25in (26cm) high

$80-100   **TWF**

A 1970s Blue Mountain Pottery jug vase, with Mocha glaze, the base molded "BMP Canada".

Produced from 1965 until 1984, Mocha was a popular glaze during this time, undoubtedly due to its (then) fashionable color. It can be found on a large number of shapes, however, examples with the widest and most dramatic variety of tones, including the almost reflective dark brown shown here, are more desirable and valuable.

10.5in (27cm) high

$70-100   **TWF**

A late 1950-early 60s Blue Mountain Pottery tapering vase, with Plum glaze, the base impressed "B.M.P. Canada" mark.

10.5in (26.5cm) high

$80-120   **TWF**

CERAMICS

ESSENTIAL REFERENCE

- The Briglin Pottery was founded in Baker Street, central London, UK in June 1948, and took its name from the combined forenames of its founders Brigitte Appleby and Eileen Lewenstein. In 1959, the company moved south to Mayfair, London, and Lewenstein left. The company became known for its simple and functional tablewares and decorative vases and bowls that were entirely hand-potted and hand-decorated.

- The Briglin style was inspired by Scandinavian Modernism, with themes taken from the natural world, such as leaves and country flowers, placed on very simple, clean-lined forms. The natural motifs were accentuated by earthy browns and beiges, as well as creams, green and light blues. Although stocked by fashionable London department stores

such as Heal's and Peter Jones, prices were largely affordable. Briglin was, in effect, mass-produced handmade studio pottery that could be used around the home.

- The pottery was enormously successful during the 1960s and '70s, but by the 1980s fashions had changed and their handmade, naturally inspired earthy pottery was no longer fashionable. With a drop in sales and rising competition from other makers, the pottery closed in 1990. Briglin languished in charity and junk shops for around 10-to-15 years, but prices have begun to rise recently. Vases and bowls tend to be more desirable than kitchenware and novelty forms such as money boxes, but always consider the level of decoration, the rarity of the pattern and the form when assessing value.

A Briglin tapering cylinder vase, with glossy cream glaze, and copper oxide, wax-resist and sgraffito decoration of a thistle, the base impressed "Briglin".

7.75in (19.5cm) high

$120-150   GC

A Briglin vase, with wax-resist and sgraffito sycamore leaf design, the base impressed "Briglin".

9.5in (24cm) high

$80-100   GC

A Briglin cylindrical vase, with a wax-resist closed thistle on one side and an open thistle on the other, painted with a glossy cream and green oxide glaze, the base stamped "Briglin".

7.5in (19cm) high

$70-90   GC

A Briglin small vase or pen pot, with blue Japanese-style floral decoration on a glossy white ground.

4.25in (11cm) high

$40-60   GROB

A Briglin cylinder vase, with hand-painted wax-resist bamboo decoration and brushed bands, and all-over glossy glaze, the base stamped "Briglin".

Here a wax-resist has been applied over the light beige glaze to mark out the leaves, before the final brown glaze was brushed on.

9.5in (24cm) high

$60-100   GC

ESSENTIAL REFERENCE – BRIGLIN DECORATION

Briglin's decorators used three primary techniques to decorate their pottery, all executed by hand. The first, and most obvious was wax-resist, where wax would be applied to the areas where the glaze was not to appear, marking out a design. When the glaze was brushed on, it would not adhere to the wax, and when fired, the wax would burnt off, leaving the natural clay underneath. Sometimes this raw clay was colored with darker matte tones by applying manganese oxide. The second is sgraffito, where a sharp point would be used to incise lines into the leather-hard dried clay prior to firing. Sometimes lines would be scratched through a wax layer, allowing glaze to be applied in fine lines. Thirdly, a piece could be painted with a design in glaze. A combination of these techniques could be used on the same piece, as here. This is also a very rare geometric pattern, and a very large size, hence its higher value.

A 1970s Briglin large cylinder vase, with sgraffito and green mottled cream gloss glazed circle design, the base stamped "Briglin".

10.75in (27cm) high

$300-400 **GC**

A Briglin 'Scroll' pattern tall mug, with swirling wax-resist decoration.

This was Briglin's longest running pattern, and is commonly found today.

5.25in (13.5cm) high

$30-40 **GROB**

A Briglin tall mug, with wax-resist decoration of leaves against a blue-green glossy glaze, the base impressed "Briglin".

4.5in (11.5cm) high

$40-60 **GROB**

A Briglin large tankard/mug, with wax-resist flower decoration.

This is another commonly found pattern, particularly on tableware.

4.75in (12cm) high

$40-50 **GROB**

A Briglin Japanese-style teapot, with wax-resist and manganese oxide flower decoration, and bent bamboo handle.

7.5in (19cm) high

$80-120 **GROB**

A Briglin small dog money bank, with sgraffito 'fur' and cream glaze, the base stamped "Briglin".

3.5in (9cm) long

$20-30 **GC**

A Briglin small bunny money bank, with sgraffito 'fur' and cream glaze, the base stamped "Briglin".

4.5in (11.5cm) high

$20-30 **GC**

FIND OUT MORE...

'Briglin Pottery 1948-1990', by Anthea Arnold, published by Briglin Books, 2002.

CERAMICS

ESSENTIAL REFERENCE

- Wiltshaw & Robinson established the Carlton Works in Stoke-on-Trent, in 1890. Wares were produced under the trade name Carlton Ware from 1894, and it became the company's name from 1958. The company produced molded, hand-decorated ceramics in a variety of styles.
- The Art Deco styled luster range was introduced in the mid-1920s in answer to the success of Wedgwood's Fairyland Luster range designed by Daisy Makeig-Jones. Patterns were inspired by Eastern themes, Egypt, the Art Deco movement, and nature. Birds and stylized leaves and flowers were popular motifs. Colors were typically bold and strong.
- The 1930s saw the introduction of cottageware, which comprized tableware shaped like country buildings, as well as molded floral table wares. Produced into the 1950s, these

remain more affordable than the earlier luster wares, which were costly to produce and expensive at the time.
- The 1950s was one of the most productive times for the company. The 1930s luster ranges were refreshed with the Royale range, which came in Rouge, Verte, Bleu and Noire (red, green, blue and black). As before, Chinese-inspired patterns were key, and designs included Chinese landscapes, plants, birds and spider webs.
- From the 1960s onwards, the company changed with the fashion of the day, producing shapes and patterns that would have been popular at the time. These include the space age inspired Orbit and the 1970s range of Walking Ware. In 1989, the company went bankrupt, although the name and some molds were bought by Francis Joseph in 1997.

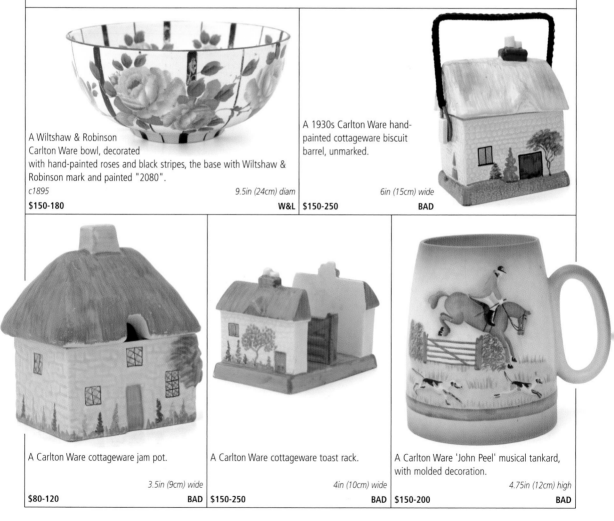

A Wiltshaw & Robinson Carlton Ware bowl, decorated with hand-painted roses and black stripes, the base with Wiltshaw & Robinson mark and painted "2080".

c1895   9.5in (24cm) diam

$150-180   **W&L**

A 1930s Carlton Ware hand-painted cottageware biscuit barrel, unmarked.

6in (15cm) wide

$150-250   **BAD**

A Carlton Ware cottageware jam pot.

3.5in (9cm) wide

$80-120   **BAD**

A Carlton Ware cottageware toast rack.

4in (10cm) wide

$150-250   **BAD**

A Carlton Ware 'John Peel' musical tankard, with molded decoration.

4.75in (12cm) high

$150-200   **BAD**

A 1930s Carlton Ware
hand-painted Handcraft charger, pattern 3801, with stylized flowers.

12in (30.5cm) diam

$400-500   **BAD**

An Art Deco Carlton Ware 'Gum Flower' pattern tapering vase, on a mottled green ground, the base painted "0/10080 3790 17".

6in (15.5cm) high

$300-400   **BEV**

A 1930s Carlton Ware 'Carnival' pattern matte Handcraft vase, the base impressed "463" and painted "6/6246 3305".

The last numbers, 3305, relate to the pattern number, which is also known as 'Carnival'. The overall design bears some similarities to Truda Carter's popular designs for Poole Pottery, produced during the same period.

4.25in (11cm) high

$500-700   **BEV**

EXPERT EYE – A CARLTON WARE VASE

Vases are more popular and desirable than jugs or shallow dishes. The form is attractive and shows the pattern off well.

There is also a hint of Oriental exoticism in the pattern. This is a theme that runs through many of Carlton Wares patterns and also the Art Deco movement.

The pattern is typical of the Art Deco era in terms of its colors and stylization.

It is a large size with no damage. The pattern is less common.

A 1930s Carlton Ware 'River Fish' pattern stepped ovoid vase, with collar neck and gilt highlights, the base with printed marks.

9.5in (24cm) high

$3,000-4,000   **FLD**

A rare 1930s Carlton Ware 'River Fish' pattern conical bowl, with gilt highlights, the base with printed marks.

9in (23cm) diam

$1,400-1,600   **FLD**

A 1930s Carlton Ware 'Rainbow Fan' pattern inkwell, with cylindrical integral well and stylized floral pattern, the base with printed marks.

8in (20.5cm) long

$1,400-1,600   **FLD**

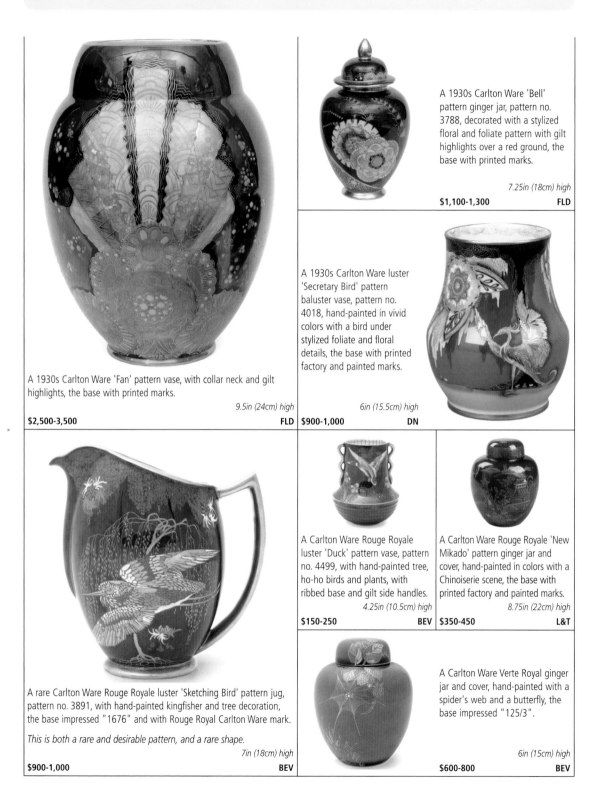

A 1930s Carlton Ware 'Bell' pattern ginger jar, pattern no. 3788, decorated with a stylized floral and foliate pattern with gilt highlights over a red ground, the base with printed marks.

7.25in (18cm) high

$1,100-1,300   **FLD**

A 1930s Carlton Ware luster 'Secretary Bird' pattern baluster vase, pattern no. 4018, hand-painted in vivid colors with a bird under stylized foliate and floral details, the base with printed factory and painted marks.

6in (15.5cm) high

$900-1,000   **DN**

A 1930s Carlton Ware 'Fan' pattern vase, with collar neck and gilt highlights, the base with printed marks.

9.5in (24cm) high

$2,500-3,500   **FLD**

A Carlton Ware Rouge Royale luster 'Duck' pattern vase, pattern no. 4499, with hand-painted tree, ho-ho birds and plants, with ribbed base and gilt side handles.

4.25in (10.5cm) high

$150-250   **BEV**

A Carlton Ware Rouge Royale 'New Mikado' pattern ginger jar and cover, hand-painted in colors with a Chinoiserie scene, the base with printed factory and painted marks.

8.75in (22cm) high

$350-450   **L&T**

A rare Carlton Ware Rouge Royale luster 'Sketching Bird' pattern jug, pattern no. 3891, with hand-painted kingfisher and tree decoration, the base impressed "1676" and with Rouge Royal Carlton Ware mark.

This is both a rare and desirable pattern, and a rare shape.

7in (18cm) high

$900-1,000   **BEV**

A Carlton Ware Verte Royal ginger jar and cover, hand-painted with a spider's web and a butterfly, the base impressed "125/3".

6in (15cm) high

$600-800   **BEV**

ESSENTIAL REFERENCE

- Carn Pottery was founded by John Beusmans in 1971, in Nancledra, near St Ives and Penzance in Cornwall, England. Beusmans' parents had produced lamp shades for Troika Pottery, Cornwall and he had studied throwing at the Redruth Art College. For each piece, Beusmans potted a master and then created a mold. This mold would be used with slip (liquid clay) to create the final range of pieces.
- Forms are linear and sculptural, ranging from simple cylindrical bottles to geometric fan vases. Patterns are abstract, yet inspired by the natural world around him. They include stylized leaves, sun rays and even pebbles on a beach. A number of molds would be made from a master

shape, each having a different pattern on the front and back. Colors are brushed on by hand with a mop, making every piece unique. Light greens, blues, beiges and creams are typical.

- Most pieces are signed with a black printed mark, but some are signed by Beusmans, typically in pencil. Examine corners, bases and rims carefully as the ceramic tends to chip easily. As with Troika, interest in, and values for, Carn have risen in recent years, but seem to have reached a plateau. Fan vases, larger sizes and cats tend to be the more collectible forms. Look for those combining two different shapes, one seen from the front and the other from the back.

A Carn Pottery rectangular vase, with low relief molded triangular pattern to one side, and a circular design of curving lines to the other, the base with factory black printed mark to base.

5.75in (14.5cm) high

$40-60   **UCT**

A Carn Pottery cylinder vase, with low relief molded circular design of curving lines and brushed brown glaze, the base with factory black printed mark.

4.75in (12cm) high

$30-50   **UCT**

A Carn Pottery hand-painted cylinder vase, with creamy green glazed circular motif, the base with factory black stamped mark.

5.25in (13cm) high

$30-50   **UCT**

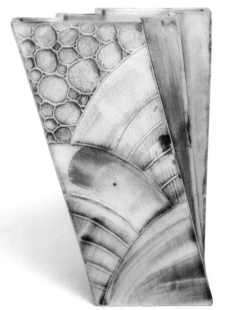

A Carn Pottery rectangular vase, one corner cut with various angles, covered with a brushed light and dark green glaze, the base with factory black printed mark.

7in (18cm) high

$60-80   **UCT**

A Carn Pottery asymmetric vase, with molded low relief stylized flower design to one side and curving, beam-like pattern to the other, with cream and brushed green and blue glazes, the base with factory black printed mark.

30-50

$30-50   **UCT**

A Carn Pottery fan vase, with low relief molded curving design to one side and stylized flower design to the other, with cream and greeny blue glazes, the base with factory black printed mark.

6in (15cm) high

$40-60   **UCT**

CERAMICS

ESSENTIAL REFERENCE

- Chinese ceramics have hit the headlines over the past few years with millions of pounds being paid for rare, early and important examples. As well as existing collectors all over the world, buyers now include collectors from mainland China. A new class of wealthy businessmen lead a burgeoning middle class, wishing to buy back their country's considerable heritage in ceramics.

- Away from these rarities, much late 19thC and 20thC export ware is comparatively affordable, with prices rarely rising above $2000 for finer examples. Some pleasing and representative pieces can even be found for under $100. Pieces such as these are attracting the attention of interior decorators and those looking for a unique or striking piece to add individuality, or a fashionable touch of the Orient, to a room.

- White ceramic pieces, hand-decorated in underglaze blue, were exported to the West in their millions, and are perhaps the most commonly found type today. Pieces include vases, bowls, dishes and larger chargers, and motifs are typically natural, including flowers, landscapes, trees, pagodas, figures, leafy vines and fish. Cargoes from shipwrecked vessels salvaged over past decades, comprised chiefly of blue and white export wares, and examples of these from the 16thC can be had for as little as $100.

- Also popular are polychrome (multicolored) wares, including famille rose (pink), famille jaune (yellow) and famille vert (green), all named after the dominant color in the palette used. View museum collections and examples being sold at auction or in dealers' shops to enable you to spot finer quality pieces. The decoration should be well applied in sympathetic colors with a good level of detail. Marks can help with identification, so consult a specialist guide. However, it is worth bearing in mind that many early marks were applied to later pieces out of respect for, and in veneration of, ancestors.

A Chinese famille rose pear-shaped vase, probably 20thC, with flared rim, decorated with figures and an attendant beneath a pine tree, the base with Qianlong seal mark.

9in (23cm) high

$640-760   **DN**

One of a pair of large 19thC-20thC Chinese famille rose vases, of shouldered form, the flared rim enameled with floral scrolls leading to a slender neck, the body finely painted in orange, red, green and blue to show a fishing hamlet.

22in (56cm) high

$600-1,000 (pair)   **FRE**

A large Chinese Republic period famille rose vase, of tapering ovoid form with a short slender neck, the body painted with a continuous landscape of green rock work, mountains and seascape, with small black inscription to shoulder.

15in (38cm) high

$440-560   **FRE**

A 20thC Chinese famille rose large vase, decorated with panels on a leaf scroll ground, some damage.

c1900   *22.5in (57cm) high*

$900-1,100   **WW**

A small 19thC Chinese famille rose vase, painted with two panels of birds on a turquoise ground decorated with birds, flowers and foliage.

6in (15cm) high

$300-400   **WW**

A 19thC Chinese famille rose moon flask, painted with a central cartouche depicting a battle scene, the reverse with a phoenix perched on a branch, the neck restored.

8.75in (22.5cm) high

$300-400   **WW**

A large 19thC Chinese famille rose dish, painted with six figures at play.

14.5in (37cm) high

$200-300   **WW**

A 20thC Chinese famille rose dish, decorated with nine peaches issuing from leafy branches, with six character Qianlong mark.

13.75in (35cm) high

$1,000-1,400 WW

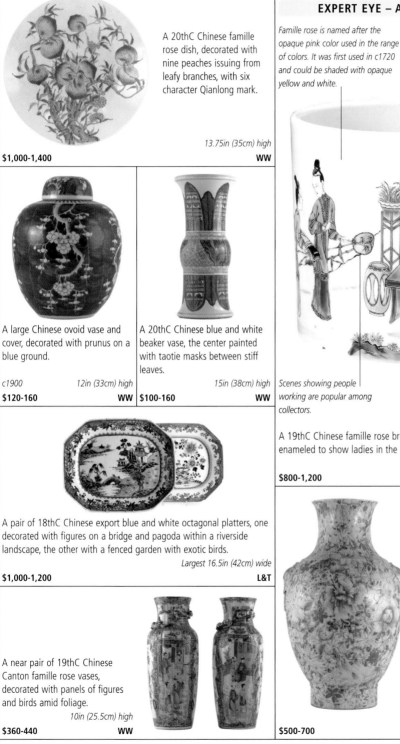

A large Chinese ovoid vase and cover, decorated with prunus on a blue ground.

c1900 *12in (33cm) high*

$120-160 WW

A 20thC Chinese blue and white beaker vase, the center painted with taotie masks between stiff leaves.

15in (38cm) high

$100-160 WW

A pair of 18thC Chinese export blue and white octagonal platters, one decorated with figures on a bridge and pagoda within a riverside landscape, the other with a fenced garden with exotic birds.

Largest 16.5in (42cm) wide

$1,000-1,200 L&T

A near pair of 19thC Chinese Canton famille rose vases, decorated with panels of figures and birds amid foliage.

10in (25.5cm) high

$360-440 WW

EXPERT EYE – A CHINESE BRUSH POT

Famille rose is named after the opaque pink color used in the range of colors. It was first used in c1720 and could be shaded with opaque yellow and white.

The decoration intentionally does not cover the entire surface, allowing the fine quality, bright flawless white porcelain to be shown off.

Scenes showing people working are popular among collectors.

Particularly good examples have faces with individual expressions, unfortunately this example does not.

A 19thC Chinese famille rose brush pot, of deep circular form, well enameled to show ladies in the pursuit of leisure, recessed base.

6.5in (16.5cm) high

$800-1,200 FRE

An early 20thC Chinese mille-fleurs large baluster vase, the base with a four character Qianlong mark, two small rim chips.

Used primarily in the 19thC, 'mille-fleurs' probably inspired the transfer-printed chintzware patterns produced by Royal Winton, Shelley and others from the 1920s to '50s.

18in (45.5cm) high

$500-700 WW

CERAMICS

ESSENTIAL REFERENCE

- Clarice Cliff was born in Tunstall, Stoke-on-Trent in 1899. Hailing from the heart of the Staffordshire Potteries, she joined the local company of Linguard Webster & Co. as an apprentice enameler in 1912. In 1916, she moved to the larger firm of A.J. Wilkinson.

- Cliff showed great promise at A.J. Wilkinson and in 1925 the company's owner, Colley Shorter, gave Cliff her own studio in the recently acquired Newport Pottery. Cliff decorated the large number of defective blank wares with vivid colors in thickly applied, striking patterns, which hid any faults in the wares. Floral designs and angled, geometric patterns are typical. A new range was developed around Cliff's designs, which was given the name Bizarre, and launched in 1928. The range proved extremely popular and was produced until 1935.

- The Bizarre name does not belong to a particular pattern or shape, but was used as a general title, as was the name Fantasque, also first used in 1928, but phased out in 1934.

- To ensure that demand for her designs was met, Cliff trained a dedicated team of female decorators at the pottery and developed a series of new modern shapes and patterns. The dates included in captions refer to the period the pattern was produced for.

- Many patterns were produced in a range of colorways, some of which are now rarer than others. Orange is a common color while blue and purple are often rarer and more valuable. Pieces in muted colors are less sought-after. Rare variations in color or pattern will tend to attract collectors' interest.

- Earlier Art Deco shapes or patterns are popular with collectors, as are pieces which display a pattern well, such as chargers, plates and Lotus shape jugs and vases. Pieces displaying a combination of an Art Deco pattern applied to an Art Deco shape will generally attract the greatest interest. Condition is very important, any damage or wear will reduce the desirability on all but the rarest pieces.

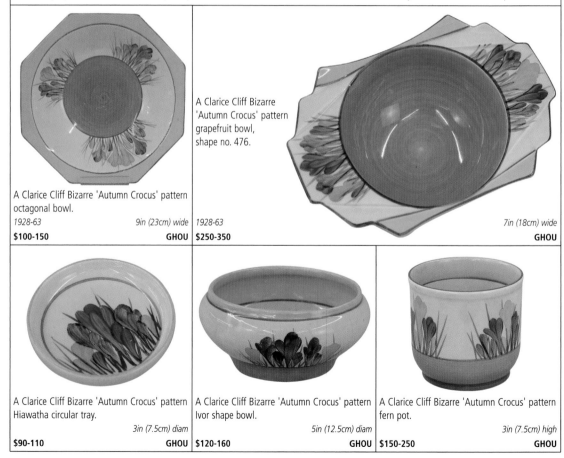

A Clarice Cliff Bizarre 'Autumn Crocus' pattern octagonal bowl.

1928-63 *9in (23cm) wide*

$100-150 GHOU

A Clarice Cliff Bizarre 'Autumn Crocus' pattern grapefruit bowl, shape no. 476.

1928-63 *7in (18cm) wide*

$250-350 GHOU

A Clarice Cliff Bizarre 'Autumn Crocus' pattern Hiawatha circular tray.

3in (7.5cm) diam

$90-110 GHOU

A Clarice Cliff Bizarre 'Autumn Crocus' pattern Ivor shape bowl.

5in (12.5cm) diam

$120-160 GHOU

A Clarice Cliff Bizarre 'Autumn Crocus' pattern fern pot.

3in (7.5cm) high

$150-250 GHOU

A Clarice Cliff Bizarre 'Cafe Au Lait Autumn' stepped jardinière, with printed marks to base.

Café au Lait is the term used to described the mottled brown glaze effect. The technique was used on a number of patterns between 1931 and 1933, with a special 'Café au Lait' mark being used on bases.

1931-33   3.5in (9cm) high

$600-800   **WW**

EXPERT EYE – A BRIDGEWATER CONICAL VASE

Bridgewater was only produced in 1934 in two color variations – on the other, the tree has green foliage.

This was part of the Conical range, introduced in May 1929, which was inspired by a metal bowl produced by French company Desny.

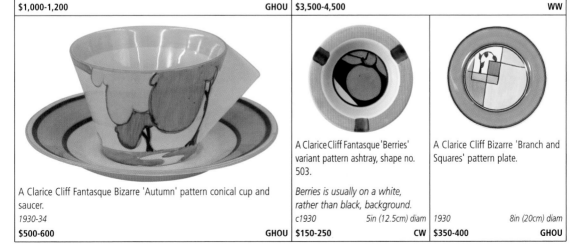

Modern, geometric forms such as this, with its conical body supported on triangular feet, are very popular with collectors and typify the Art Deco style.

A much rarer lidded biscuit jar can also be found in this shape. The lid is a smaller version of the bottom half of the body.

A Clarice Cliff Fantasque Bizarre 'Blue Autumn' pattern vase, shape 360.

1930-34   8in (20.5cm) high

$1,000-1,200   **GHOU**

A Clarice Cliff Bizarre 'Orange Bridgewater' pattern Conical vase, shape no. 400, painted in colors, with printed factory mark.

1934   6in (15cm) high

$3,500-4,500   **WW**

A Clarice Cliff Fantasque Bizarre 'Autumn' pattern conical cup and saucer.

1930-34

$500-600   **GHOU**

A Clarice Cliff Fantasque 'Berries' variant pattern ashtray, shape no. 503.

Berries is usually on a white, rather than black, background.

c1930   5in (12.5cm) diam

$150-250   **CW**

A Clarice Cliff Bizarre 'Branch and Squares' pattern plate.

1930   8in (20cm) diam

$350-400   **GHOU**

A Clarice Cliff Fantasque 'Melon' pattern Conical bowl candlestick, shape no. 384.

1930   4.5in (11.5cm) diam

$450-550   **GHOU**

A Clarice Cliff Bizarre 'Moonlight' pattern Conical sugar sifter.

A similar pattern but with stronger colors and orange, red and black bands, is known as 'Devon'.

1932   5.5in (14cm) high

$2,000-3,000   **GHOU**

EXPERT EYE – A STAMFORD TEA SET

The 'Mountain' pattern was produced only briefly from 1931 until 1932 and is very rare.

Any single piece would be a challenge to find, particularly the teapot, but to find a complete teaset in such excellent condition is very unusual.

The geometric, Art Deco Stamford shape with its shaped teapot and milk jug, and Conical cups with triangular handles, are popular.

Note the unpainted mountain top on the sugar bowl. This is typical of Cliff's hand-painted wares, where colors used on different elements could be changed by the Bizarre Girls, or accidentally be left unpainted.

A Clarice Cliff Bizarre range 'Mountain' pattern Stamford shape tea for two part service, comprizing teapot, milk jug, sugar bowl, two teacups and saucer and a side plate, with date mark for 1932.

1932   Teapot 4.75in (12cm) high

$25,000-30,000   **WW**

A Clarice Cliff Bizarre 'Orange Patina Tree' pattern spherical vase, with spatter effect ground, the base with printed marks.

Patina has a lightly textured surface as it was splashed with liquid clay prior to being decorated. Difficult to paint over, a small number of patterns were produced including 'Tree' shown above, and the landscape 'Coastal' and 'Country'.

1932   6in (15cm) high

$1,000-1,200   **FLD**

A Clarice Cliff Bizarre 'Blue Patina Tree' pattern stepped cylindrical vase, with tapered neck, the base with printed marks.

1932   7in (18cm) high

$1,000-1,200   **FLD**

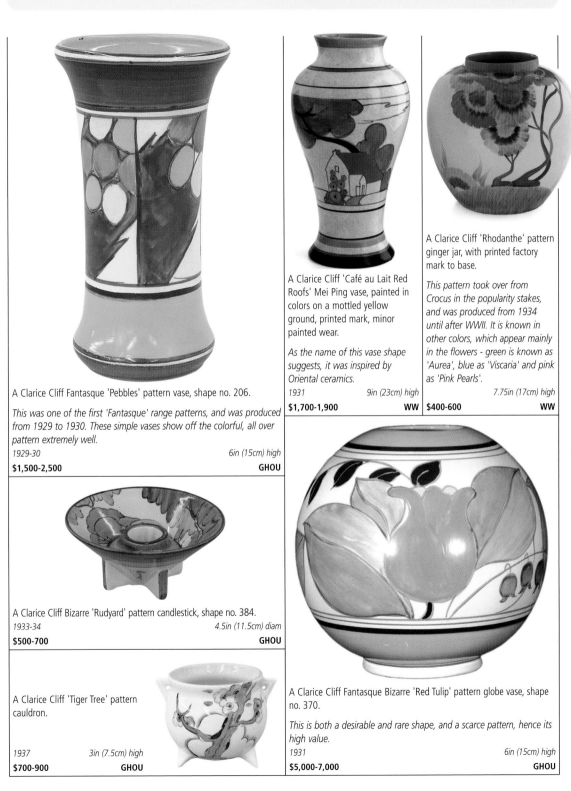

A Clarice Cliff Fantasque 'Pebbles' pattern vase, shape no. 206.

This was one of the first 'Fantasque' range patterns, and was produced from 1929 to 1930. These simple vases show off the colorful, all over pattern extremely well.

1929-30   *6in (15cm) high*
$1,500-2,500   **GHOU**

A Clarice Cliff Bizarre 'Rudyard' pattern candlestick, shape no. 384.
1933-34   *4.5in (11.5cm) diam*
$500-700   **GHOU**

A Clarice Cliff 'Tiger Tree' pattern cauldron.

1937   *3in (7.5cm) high*
$700-900   **GHOU**

A Clarice Cliff 'Café au Lait Red Roofs' Mei Ping vase, painted in colors on a mottled yellow ground, printed mark, minor painted wear.

As the name of this vase shape suggests, it was inspired by Oriental ceramics.

1931   *9in (23cm) high*
$1,700-1,900   **WW**

A Clarice Cliff 'Rhodanthe' pattern ginger jar, with printed factory mark to base.

This pattern took over from Crocus in the popularity stakes, and was produced from 1934 until after WWII. It is known in other colors, which appear mainly in the flowers - green is known as 'Aurea', blue as 'Viscaria' and pink as 'Pink Pearls'.

7.75in (17cm) high
$400-600   **WW**

A Clarice Cliff Fantasque Bizarre 'Red Tulip' pattern globe vase, shape no. 370.

This is both a desirable and rare shape, and a scarce pattern, hence its high value.

1931   *6in (15cm) high*
$5,000-7,000   **GHOU**

A Clarice Cliff Fantasque 'Trees & House' pattern ashtray.

Although the house is missing, the pattern can be recognized from the style and color of the tree and clouds.

1929   5in (12.5cm) diam
$200-300   **CW**

A Clarice Cliff Bizarre ashtray, shape no. 503.

The gate and trees, seen above, appear in a pattern from 1934 called 'Tulips'.

c1934   5in (12.5cm) diam
$300-500   **CW**

A Clarice Cliff Fantasque 'Umbrellas and Rain' pattern hexagonal vase, the base with printed marks.

1929   7.5in (19cm) high
$900-1,100   **FLD**

ESSENTIAL REFERENCE – FAKE LOTUS JUGS

Lotus jugs are one of the most popular and collectable shapes produced and are generally valuable. As a result, they are often faked, and early geometric patterns like this are the most common targets. The simplest way to identify a fake is to look at the inside edge of the handle. If a small hole is found towards the top, it is a modern reproduction or a fake. The interiors of reproductions and fakes also tend to be glazed 'too well'. Originals often have glaze runs or an uneven application of glaze. The color tones of glazes also tend to be different. Always examine marks closely as many are not right, despite appearing so. Always compare marks to examples in a reference book. Lastly, look at the base and exterior for signs of wear over time, as these are often not present.

An authentic Clarice Cliff Bizarre 'Whisper' pattern Lotus jug.
1929   11.5in (29cm) high
$3,000-4,000   **GHOU**

A Clarice Cliff Fantasque 'Umbrellas and Rain' pattern angular vase with flared rim, the base with printed marks.
1929   7.75in (19.5cm) high
$1,000-1,200   **FLD**

A Clarice Cliff Fantasque Bizarre 'Windbells' pattern conical sugar sifter.

1933   5.5in (14cm) high
$1,000-1,200   **GHOU**

A limited edition Wedgwood Clarice Cliff Age of Jazz 'Latona Red Roses' figure, printed and painted marks, boxed.

A series of company mergers and acquisitions led to Wedgwood owning the right to the Clarice Cliff name, brand and designs. During the 1990s, at the height of the market, the company released limited numbers of reproductions to allow collectors to own designs they may not be able to afford in vintage form. Produced until 2002, they are clearly marked on the base and should not be deemed 'fakes'. Always aim to buy examples that are complete with their boxes and paperwork, as these have already begun to rise in value.

8.25in (21cm) high

$150-250 WW

A Newport Pottery Clarice Cliff Fantasque Bizarre 'Windbells' pattern octagonal side plate.

1933   5.75in (14.5cm) wide

$550-650 GHOU

A Newport Pottery Clarice Cliff Fantasque Bizarre 'Windbells' pattern George shape jug, the base with printed factory mark.

1933   6.75in (17cm) high

$600-800 WW

A limited edition Wedgwood Clarice Cliff Age of Jazz 'Twin Dancers', shape no. 434, from an edition of 1,000, with box and certificate.

5in (12.5cm) high

$200-300 GHOU

A limited edition Wedgwood Clarice Cliff Bizarre 'Farmhouse' pattern Mei Ping vase, from an edition of 250, boxed.

12in (30.5cm) high

$150-250 GHOU

A limited edition Wedgwood Clarice Cliff Bizarre 'May Avenue' pattern Isis vase, from a limited edition of 250, with box and certificate.

8in (20.5cm) high

$150-250 GHOU

A Wedgwood Clarice Cliff Bizarre 'Red Roofs' pattern vase, shape no. 461, with box and certificate.

7.5in (19cm) high

$80-150 GHOU

CERAMICS

A Royal Doulton cup and saucer, in dark red with gilt panels, marked "10" in gilt.

Saucer 4.25in (11cm) wide

$80-120   **BAD**

A Royal Worcester cup and saucer, decorated with a pale blue band and hand-painted floral sprays, with gilt trim.

Saucer 5.5in (14cm) diam

$100-120   **W&L**

A 1980s Sarah Grosse cup and saucer, with printed and painted pattern of boxers, the base with printed marks.

c1986   Saucer 6.5in (16cm) diam

$15-20   **MTS**

A Royal Albert Crown China trio set, decorated with a transfer-printed and hand-painted with roses in dark blue and iron red, and with gilt highlights, the base painted "2946".

Plate 6in (15cm) diam

$35-45   **W&L**

A 1930s Old Royal China trio set, decorated in blue mottled 'malachite' effect and transfer-printed gilt trim.

Saucer 6.25in (16cm) wide

$40-50   **W&L**

A Royal Doulton cup and saucer, marked "702 852".

Saucer 4.25in (11cm) wide

$70-90   **BAD**

A Royal Crown Derby trio set, with cobalt blue and transfer-printed gilt decoration, the base painted "8309S".

Plate 7.25in (18cm) diam

$110-130   **W&L**

A 1930s Melba bone china trio set, with hand-painted yellow flowers.

Note the angled handle, which is typically 1930s, as well as echoing popular, and now desirable, designs by Shelley.

6.25in (15.5cm) diam

$35-45   **W&L**

ESSENTIAL REFERENCE

- Danish-born Kjeld and Erica Deichmann founded their pottery in Moss Glen, New Brunswick, Canada in 1935, two years after leaving Denmark. They brought with them experience of Scandinavian pottery, and are considered pioneers of studio pottery and the craft tradition in Canada.
- Kjeld was responsible for the shapes and potting, while Erica made and applied the glazes. Their wares were highly popular during the 1940s and '50s, and they experimented with over 5,000 glaze types. When Kjeld died in 1963, Erica closed the pottery and production ceased. Values have risen dramatically over the past few years. Always look on the base for their inscribed marks and monogram.

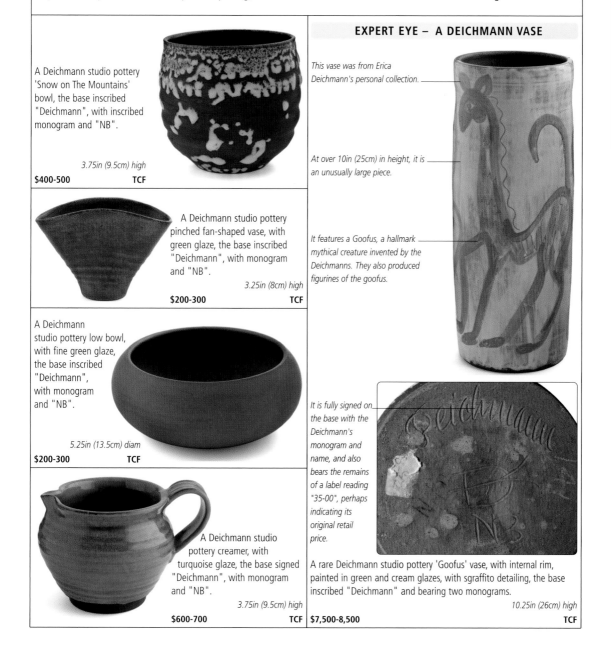

A Deichmann studio pottery 'Snow on The Mountains' bowl, the base inscribed "Deichmann", with inscribed monogram and "NB".

3.75in (9.5cm) high

$400-500   **TCF**

A Deichmann studio pottery pinched fan-shaped vase, with green glaze, the base inscribed "Deichmann", with monogram and "NB".

3.25in (8cm) high

$200-300   **TCF**

A Deichmann studio pottery low bowl, with fine green glaze, the base inscribed "Deichmann", with monogram and "NB".

5.25in (13.5cm) diam

$200-300   **TCF**

A Deichmann studio pottery creamer, with turquoise glaze, the base signed "Deichmann", with monogram and "NB".

3.75in (9.5cm) high

$600-700   **TCF**

EXPERT EYE – A DEICHMANN VASE

This vase was from Erica Deichmann's personal collection.

At over 10in (25cm) in height, it is an unusually large piece.

It features a Goofus, a hallmark mythical creature invented by the Deichmanns. They also produced figurines of the goofus.

It is fully signed on the base with the Deichmann's monogram and name, and also bears the remains of a label reading "35-00", perhaps indicating its original retail price.

A rare Deichmann studio pottery 'Goofus' vase, with internal rim, painted in green and cream glazes, with sgraffito detailing, the base inscribed "Deichmann" and bearing two monograms.

10.25in (26cm) high

$7,500-8,500   **TCF**

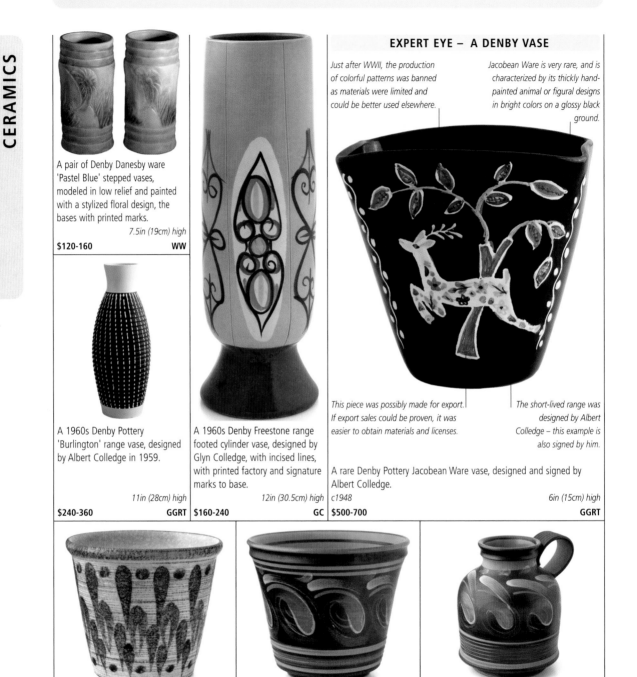

A pair of Denby Danesby ware 'Pastel Blue' stepped vases, modeled in low relief and painted with a stylized floral design, the bases with printed marks.

7.5in (19cm) high

$120-160 WW

A 1960s Denby Pottery 'Burlington' range vase, designed by Albert Colledge in 1959.

11in (28cm) high

$240-360 GGRT

A 1960s Denby Freestone range footed cylinder vase, designed by Glyn Colledge, with incised lines, with printed factory and signature marks to base.

12in (30.5cm) high

$160-240 GC

EXPERT EYE – A DENBY VASE

Just after WWII, the production of colorful patterns was banned as materials were limited and could be better used elsewhere.

Jacobean Ware is very rare, and is characterized by its thickly hand-painted animal or figural designs in bright colors on a glossy black ground.

This piece was possibly made for export. If export sales could be proven, it was easier to obtain materials and licenses.

The short-lived range was designed by Albert Colledge – this example is also signed by him.

A rare Denby Pottery Jacobean Ware vase, designed and signed by Albert Colledge.

c1948

6in (15cm) high

$500-700 GGRT

A Denby flower pot, with factory marks and "WTL 1970" printed to base.

1970

5.5in (14cm) high

$50-70 GC

A 1980s Denby Savannah range footed plant pot, designed by Glyn Colledge in 1978, with hand-painted swirled pattern and fluted bands.

5.25in (13.5cm) high

$40-60 GC

A 1980s Denby Savannah range jug vase, designed by Glyn Colledge in 1978, with hand-painted swirled pattern and fluted bands.

7in (17.5cm) high

$40-60 GC

A Doulton Lambeth cylindrical biscuit barrel, decorated by Hannah Barlow with a central band of sgraffito ponies in a landscape, with a silver-plated rim, handle and cover, the base with impressed and incized marks.

Barlow is well-known for her designs incorporating horses and other animals.

6.75in (17cm) high

$1,500-2,500 **FLD**

EXPERT EYE – A DOULTON LAMBETH ISOBATH

The Isobath is a rare inkwell. It was made for Thomas De La Rue Ltd, who later made fountain pens, many under the 'Onoto' brand introduced in 1905.

The lid and hemisphere are often missing, which reduces the value by over 50 per cent. This example retains both.

They were made in a wide variety of forms with different styles of decoration, some with trays with crimped edges that act as pen rests.

The interior contains a swinging black hard rubber hemisphere, the weight of which forces ink into the side well, meaning a consistent level of ink is maintained.

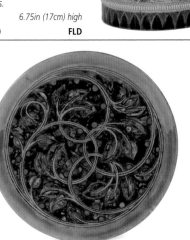

A Doulton Lambeth large circular wall plaque, by Harry Simeon, decorated with an incized and glazed stylized interwoven floral pattern, the base with impressed and painted marks.

13.5in (34cm) diam

$500-600 **FLD**

A rare Doulton Lambeth 'Isobath' stoneware inkwell, designed by Thomas De La Rue Ltd, with lid, stylized floral and foliate decoration and impressed and inscribed factory and decorators' marks to base.

4.75in (12cm) high

$400-600 **L&T**

A Royal Doulton Slater's Patent baluster form vase, painted in colors with bands of flowers and foliage, impressed mark and "X2031 A.M." to base.

Slater's Patent involved the use of real lace impressed onto the body to act as a guide for the colored pattern, which was hand-enameled over the glaze.

17.25in (44cm) high

$200-300 **ROS**

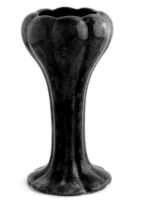

A Royal Doulton flambé vase, designed by Charles Noke, modeled as a lotus flower and covered in a rich flambé glaze, printed marks and Noke facsimile signature.

7.5in (19cm) high

$600-800 **WW**

A Royal Doulton Brangwyn ware ovoid vase, designed by Frank Brangwyn, painted with stylized flowers and foliage on a graduated creamy ground, with green border to base, the base with printed marks and painted "D5081".

7.25in (18.5cm) high

$200-300 **WW**

CERAMICS

ESSENTIAL REFERENCE

- The Fulper Pottery Co. was founded in 1814, in Flemington, New Jersey and operated until 1935, when it was acquired by another company. It began by producing simple utilitarian wares, releasing its Vasekraft art pottery ranges in 1909, at the height of the art pottery boom. Shapes were slip-molded and typically simple, with some being inspired by ancient Oriental ceramics.

- The company's production is sought-after today for its varied, rich glazes. These were often streaked or dripped in different colors The company also experimented with flambé, metallic, matte and gloss glazes. Crystalline glazes became a speciality. Higher prices are usually paid for pieces produced before WWI, which have finer quality glazes that have had more attention to their application.

A Fulper vase, with olive green over a micro-crystalline glaze, waisted body and square, curving rim, marked with the vertical Fulper oval ink stamp, with few burst glaze bubbles.

6.75in (17cm) high

$150-200   **BEL**

A Fulper octagonal baluster vase, with typical graduated green glaze and greek key molded design to rim, the base inscribed "Fulper".

8in (20.5cm) high

$300-500   **WW**

A Fulper faceted vase, covered in khaki green, cobalt, and 'cat's eye' flambé glaze, with vertical Fulper oval ink stamp, glaze flake to base.

9.75in (24.5cm) high

$500-600   **DRA**

A Fulper baluster vase, with black over tan dripped glazes, the base marked with the Fulper vertical oval ink stamp.

7.5in (19cm) high

$280-320   **BEL**

A Fulper canoe-shaped vase, with dripped Crystalline green glaze with brown highlights, with the Fulper vertical oval ink stamp.

5.5in (14cm) high

$150-200   **BEL**

A Fulper canoe-shaped vase, with frothy Electric Blue matte glaze, the base marked with the Fulper vertical oval ink stamp.

5.5in (14cm) high

$150-200   **BEL**

A Fulper rope-twist handled basket, with Electric Blue glaze, the base marked twice with the vertical Fulper oval ink stamp.

12in (30.5cm) wide

$180-220   **BEL**

ESSENTIAL REFERENCE

- German ceramics maker Goebel first produced Hummel figurines in 1935 using drawings of children by a nun, Sister Berta Hummel (1909-46), as inspiration. The first was 'Puppy Love' and was part of a range of 46 modeled by Arthur Moeller. Many of these original designs are still available today, although the range has grown to over 500 figurines, offering great scope to collectors.
- Three key points to consider are the date of the figurine, its size, and variations in modelling or color. Earlier examples from the 1930s-40s are generally the most valuable. Familiarise yourself with the marks on the base as they changed over time and this is the easiest way to attribute a figurine to a period. Impressed 'Crown' marks are usually the earliest and were used from 1936 until 1950, but if printed together with the words 'Goebel' and 'Germany', the figurine will date from between 1991 and 2000.
- Hummel's most famous mark is the 'bee in a V' mark. Used from 1940 until c1980, the style changed over time. The larger the bee is, the earlier a piece will be. By 1958, the bee had shrunk in size, become very stylized and moved inside the 'V'. Dates shown here relate to the period the mark on the base was in use, combined with the dates that the model was produced.

- Impressed numbers relate to the mold number (often called the 'Hum number' by collectors) and the size. Numbers or Roman numerals after a '/' indicate the size. Roman numerals indicate a larger than standard size – the higher the number, the larger the piece. Arabic numbers indicate a smaller than standard size – the higher the number, the smaller the piece. Larger figurines can be worth many times more than standard sizes pieces.
- Also look out for variations in color or molded form, as these can affect value. Some forms were remodeled over time, and earlier examples are usually more desirable and valuable. All authentic Hummel figurines are properly marked. Beware of unmarked pieces and those of poorer quality as reproductions and fakes produced in the Far East are common.
- Always examine pieces closely before buying as the bisque used is fragile and easily chipped or cracked. Also be careful when moving them around on display shelves. Crazing of the glaze can also affect desirability. Many figurines are still being produced today, so consult a reference book to check production dates. Prices for figurines that are still available will usually be much lower than for those which are no longer produced.

A Goebel Hummel 'Hello' figurine, no. 124, the base impressed "124/0" and painted "G80" with 'three line mark'.

Designed by Arthur Moeller and introduced in 1939, alternative names have included 'The Boss'. Look out for variations wearing green trousers and a pink waistcoat with the brown coat, as these are the rarest and most valuable. The earliest models have gray trousers and coats.

1964-72   5.75in (14.5cm) high
$80-120   BH

A Goebel Hummel 'Valentine Joy' figurine, no. 399, the base impressed "399" and printed "Exclusive Limited Edition for Members of the Goebel Collectors Club Goebel W. Germany 1979".

Designed by Gerhard Skrobek in 1979, this figurine was released in 1980 and was the fourth special edition available only to Collectors' Club members.
1979   5.5in (14cm) high
$70-100   BH

A Goebel Hummel 'Merry Wanderer' figurine, no. 11, with stylized bee "W. Germany" mark.

1958-72   4.25in (11cm) high
$30-40   BH

A Goebel Hummel 'Little Tooter' figurine, no. 214H, the base with printed 'three line' mark.

1964-72   4in (10cm) high
$60-80   BH

A Goebel Hummel 'March Winds' figurine, no. 43, the base with printed stylized bee mark.

1958-72   5in (12.5cm) high
$60-80   BH

CERAMICS

A Goebel Hummel 'Begging His Share' figurine, no. 9, with candle-holder hole in cake, the base with stylized bee mark.

A Goebel Hummel 'Good Hunting' figurine, no. 307, with brown rabbit, the base with 'two line' Goebel bee mark.

1972-79   5.25in (13.5cm) high

$150-200   **BH**

Designed by Arthur Moeller in 1935, this was originally intended to be a candle-holder – hence the hole in the cake. In 1964, the figurine was redesigned and the hole was removed, making this particular figurine easy to date. Very early examples have brightly colored socks.

1958-64   *5.5in (14cm) high*

$80-120   **BH**

A Goebel Hummel 'Band Leader', no. 129, the base impressed "129", and with 'full bee' mark.

1940-59   6in (15cm) high

$70-100   **BH**

A Goebel Hummel 'Apple Tree Boy' figurine, no. 142, the base with 'three line' mark.

1964-72   4in (10cm) high

$50-70   **BH**

A Goebel Hummel 'Umbrella Boy' large figurine, no. 152, the base impressed "152/0A", with 'three line' mark.

Designed by Arthur Moeller in the early 1940s, this figurine has a companion piece, 'Umbrella Girl'. It has the same model number but was introduced a few years later, in the late 1940s.

1964-72   *4.75in (12cm) high*

$250-350   **BH**

EXPERT EYE – A HUMMEL FIGURINE

Designed in 1996 by Helmut Fischer, this figurine was released in the US in 1999 costing $185. It has now been discontinued.

Her companion piece is 'Pretzel Boy', no. 2093, which is still available new.

A number of Special Event collectors' versions have been issued, including one with two US flags, but values are roughly the same.

A Goebel Hummel 'Girl with Doll' figurine, no. 239B, the base with printed "Goebel Germany" crown mark.

1991-99   3.5in (9cm) high

$20-30   **BH**

Pieces produced in the inaugural year bear the 'First Issue 1999' stamp, as on this example.

A Goebel Hummel 'Pretzel Girl' figurine, no. 2004, the base impressed "2004 16" and "1996", and printed "First Issue 1999" in blue.

1999   *4in (11cm) high*

$70-100   **BH**

A Goebel Hummel 'Knitting Lesson' figurine, no. 256, the base with 'three line mark' and impressed "256 33 1963".

Although impressed "1963", which probably indicates the year of design and copyright, the figurine was introduced a year later in 1964.

1964-72   7.25in (18.5cm) high

$180-220   BH

A Goebel Hummel 'Little Thrifty' figurine, no. 118, the base impressed "118" and with "Goebel W. Germany" 'two line' bee mark.

This can also be found as a money bank. Examples made before 1963 have a thicker base than later examples.

1972-79   5in (13cm) high

$70-100   BH

A Goebel Hummel 'Auf Wiedersehen' figurine, no. 153, the base impressed "153/0" and with stylized bee mark.

1958-72   5.75in (14.5cm) high

$80-120   BH

A Goebel Hummel 'Wash Day' figurine, no. 321, the base impressed "321" and with 'three line mark'.

Look out for examples with 'longer' washing that looks like a pair of bloomers. These are much earlier in date and are much rarer and more valuable, often being worth over four times the value of this version.

1964-72   5.75in (14.5cm) high

$55-75   BH

A Goebel Hummel 'Blessed Event' figurine, no. 333, the base impressed "333", and with 'three line mark'.

Although this was designed in 1955, it was not released until 1964. However, a small quantity of trade samples were made in the late 1950s, bearing the 'full bee' mark. These are extremely rare and can be worth up to ten times the amount as this more common example.

5.25in (13.5cm) high

$150-200   BH

A Goebel Hummel 'Little Gardener' figurine, no. 74, the base with printed large stylized bee and "W. Germany" mark.

Examples from before the 1960s have an oval shaped base.

c1963-72   4.25in (11cm) high

$40-60   BH

A Goebel Hummel 'Happiness' figurine, no. 86, the base with 'three line' mark.

1964-72   4.75in (12cm) high

$30-50   BH

A Goebel Hummel 'Friends' figurine, no. 136, the base with printed 'three line' mark.

1964-72   5in (12.5cm) high

$25-35   BH

FIND OUT MORE...

'The No.1 Price Guide to M.I. Hummel Figurines, Plates & More', by Robert L. Miller, published by Reverie Publishing Company, 2006.

ESSENTIAL REFERENCE

- Italian ceramics of the 1950s to '70s have grown in popularity over the past few years, alongside West German ceramics of the same period. At the time of production, the influx of money and the renewed confidence of postwar Italy saw many potteries producing and exporting large numbers of brightly colored, affordable ceramics.
- Shapes were typically simple and traditional with hand-painted patterns, which were sometimes highlighted with sgraffito, where a design is inscribed into the surface of the clay with a point. Patterns tended to be abstract, inspired by modern art of the day, and often based on natural or figural motifs. Most pieces were slip-molded, meaning bodies could be turned out on a factory production line.
- Examples were sold in design shops, department stores and lower market discount shops. They were imported by numerous companies including Raymor in the US and Hutcheson & Son Ltd in the UK. The primary indicators to value are the style, colors and quality of the application of the design – abstract and modern patterns on unusual

forms are highly desirable. The size is also important, and whimsical pieces can similarly be desirable.
- The most valuable pieces are by notable designers such as Guido Gambone (1909-69) and Marcello Fantoni (b.1915). Their work also influenced many other potteries stylistically. Another popular name is Bitossi, who produced a range known as 'Rimini Blu', designed by Aldo Londi in 1953. The range is typified by rows of impressed geometrical motifs, and can be found in red, yellow and a scarce speckled orange.
- Most pieces are marked simply on the base with a number and the word 'Italy'. Currently, very little is known about the factories or designers that produced these designs. The name of a town or resort is also often found on the base – this indicates that a piece may have been sold as a souvenir to tourists, although some towns, such as Deruta, had a long established reputation for ceramics. Always examine pieces closely as the ceramic is generally fragile and easy to chip.

A 1950s-60s Italian Ronzan table centerpiece, modeled as a mermaid and child riding the back of a large fish, with circular dish below decorated in a turquoise glaze, with painted and printed marks.

15.75in (40cm) high

$3,000-4,000 **FLD**

An Italian Lenci figurine of a child playing with a ball, with transfer-printed floral pattern, and painted marks to base.

7in (18cm) wide

$700-900 **WW**

A 1950s Italian Lenci pottery jug, of angular form, covered in a green and brown glaze, with painted marks "11-7-57".

11.75in (30cm) high

$600-800 **WW**

A 1950s Italian Guido Gambone vase, of asymmetric form, decorated with white panels with green lines over a textured black oxide ground, the base with hand-painted signature.

13.25in (32.5cm) high

$3,000-4,000 **FLD**

A 1950s Italian Guido Gambone faience vase, painted with horses, signed "Gambone Italy" with donkey motif.

12in (30.5cm) high

$900-1,400 **SDR**

A 1950s Italian ovoid vase, with flared rim, decorated with a pattern of turquoise, red and white leaping horses with sgraffito outlines on a black ground, restored rim.

11.5in (29cm) high

$200-300 QU

EXPERT EYE – AN ITALIAN VASE

The flower form with its petal-like rim echoes the floral pattern.

It is made from a fragile white ceramic, but has remained undamaged. It is also a large size. Smaller sizes have been found and can be worth around $60.

Like most Italian ceramics of the period, the abstract design was inspired by both modern art and nature. It is signed by the artist and dated "64".

The irregular form and the presence of ribs inside shows it was coil-built on a wheel by hand, rather than being slip-cast as many others were.

A 1960s Italian hand-built vase, the exterior painted with a multi-colored abstract design, illegibly signed, and dated.

1964 *15.5in (34.5cm) high*

$400-600 BEV

An Italian pottery vase, painted with a figure on horseback in the style of Marino Marini, in rough textured glazes, indistinct painted factory marks to base.

8.75in (22.5cm) high

$200-400 WW

A 1950s Italian vase, with a curving rim, decorated with a stylized lady's head in sgraffito and gloss glaze, unmarked.

8.75in (22cm) high

$60-80 GC

A 1950s-60s Italian blue textured jug, with hand-painted black lines and multicolored ovals, the base painted "6320 Italy".

7in (17.25in) high

$40-60 GC

A 1950s-60s Italian vase, the crazed, thick white glaze with hand-painted multicolored stripes, and yellow interior, unmarked.

7.25in (18.5cm) high

$60-80 GC

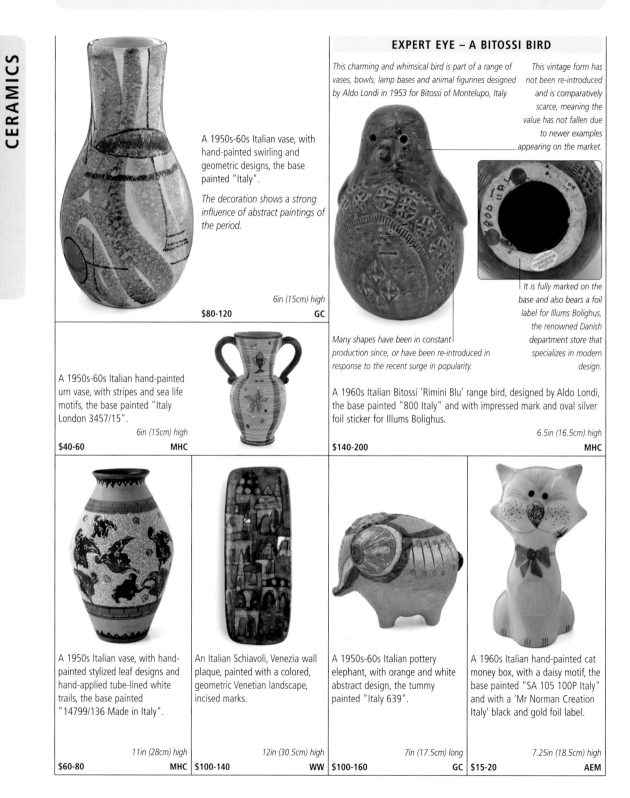

A 1950s-60s Italian vase, with hand-painted swirling and geometric designs, the base painted "Italy".

The decoration shows a strong influence of abstract paintings of the period.

6in (15cm) high

$80-120   GC

A 1950s-60s Italian hand-painted urn vase, with stripes and sea life motifs, the base painted "Italy London 3457/15".

6in (15cm) high

$40-60   MHC

EXPERT EYE – A BITOSSI BIRD

This charming and whimsical bird is part of a range of vases, bowls, lamp bases and animal figurines designed by Aldo Londi in 1953 for Bitossi of Montelupo, Italy.

This vintage form has not been re-introduced and is comparatively scarce, meaning the value has not fallen due to newer examples appearing on the market.

It is fully marked on the base and also bears a foil label for Illums Bolighus, the renowned Danish department store that specializes in modern design.

Many shapes have been in constant production since, or have been re-introduced in response to the recent surge in popularity.

A 1960s Italian Bitossi 'Rimini Blu' range bird, designed by Aldo Londi, the base painted "800 Italy" and with impressed mark and oval silver foil sticker for Illums Bolighus.

6.5in (16.5cm) high

$140-200   MHC

A 1950s Italian vase, with hand-painted stylized leaf designs and hand-applied tube-lined white trails, the base painted "14799/136 Made in Italy".

11in (28cm) high

$60-80   MHC

An Italian Schiavoli, Venezia wall plaque, painted with a colored, geometric Venetian landscape, incised marks.

12in (30.5cm) high

$100-140   WW

A 1950s-60s Italian pottery elephant, with orange and white abstract design, the tummy painted "Italy 639".

7in (17.5cm) long

$100-160   GC

A 1960s Italian hand-painted cat money box, with a daisy motif, the base painted "SA 105 100P Italy" and with a 'Mr Norman Creation Italy' black and gold foil label.

7.25in (18.5cm) high

$15-20   AEM

ESSENTIAL REFERENCE

- While the market for Chinese ceramics has boomed in recent years, a weak domestic stock market and lack of wider interest has meant the Japanese market has not enjoyed such popularity. Many pieces, therefore, are more affordable at present, particularly items dating from the late 19thC and first half of the 20thC. As with Chinese ceramics of these periods, many are collected for their decorative nature.
- Popular styles include the detailed Nabeshima, which is typically found in underglaze blue, but can also have red, green and yellow enamel highlights; the gilt and colored Satsuma; and the vibrant and bold blue, red and white Imari. Look at examples in museums and compare pieces to learn how to spot the more finely painted examples. As well as a greater level of detail, faces may have individual expressions on better quality pieces.
- Along with more traditional, historic styles, Japan exported vast numbers of hand-decorated Western style ceramics from the 1910s onwards. A company founded in 1904 by Ichizaemon Morimura, became a major force. Later in the century this company became known as Noritake. Brightly painted roses and other flowers are typical, usually combined with lavish gilding. In general, the more gilding present, the earlier the piece.
- The first mass-produced designs were exported in 1910, and the company produced its first dinnerware for the US market in 1914. The US was its largest market, but pieces were also exported to Europe. Marks on bases can help with dating, and look for well-painted pieces with realistic and detailed imagery. Examine gilding for signs of wear as this reduces value, as does any damage.
- After WWII, production continued, and pieces were marked 'Made in Occupied Japan' between 1947 and 1952. The production of novelty figurines and other small objects which grew during the 1930s, also continued. As with tableware and decorative objects, the subject, motifs and how well they are executed will indicate value.

An early 19thC Japanese Nabeshima footed dish, of blue floral underglaze, decorated with floral sprigs and a tightly painted 'comb' pattern to the well-potted foot.

8in (20.5cm) diam

$240-360   FRE

A Japanese Nabeshima footed dish, probably Edo period or later, with underglazed, blue floral motif to white ground, floral underglaze to underside and 'comb' design foot.

$200-300   FRE

A 19thC Japanese Nabeshima footed dish, with blue underglaze decoration and enameled with yellow, iron-red and green to show a junk transporting auspicious items over a ground of red scrolling sea, well underglazed coin and ribbon to underside and 'comb' design foot, some wear to base, minor wear generally.

8.25in (21cm) diam

$360-440   FRE

A 19thC Japanese Nabeshima footed dish, slightly rounded over a short foot, painted with red and yellow seeded fruit and green and blue leaves, ribbon coins to underside, 'comb' design foot, some wear to base of foot.

7in (18cm) diam

$600-800   FRE

An 18thC/19thC Japanese Kakiemon octagonal bowl, with brown rim, interior of rim painted with blue, green and yellow enamel to show blossoms issuing from scrolling leaves, the central medallion a floral spray flanked by eight floral garlands painted in reverse.

8.5in (21.5cm) diam

$800-1,000   FRE

A 19thC Japanese studio earthenware baluster vase, painted to show hagi (Japanese clover) and other autumn flowers and sprays, moon applied in light relief, signed and impressed "Itozan".

9in (23cm) high

$900-1,100   FRE

CERAMICS

A 20thC Japanese porcelain bowl, decorated with two frogs and an octopus on a brown ground.

5in (12.5cm) high

$100-160   **DN**

A Japanese porcelain vase, decorated with two panels containing figures, the remaining body decorated with a profusion of flowers and birds, restored rim.

c1880   18.5in (47cm) high

$400-600   **SWO**

A pair of Japanese celadon ground ovoid vases, Meiji period, each decorated with a bird standing beneath flowers and foliage, each with a six character mark.

14in (35.5cm) high

$300-500   **WW**

A Japanese blue and white rectangular vase and cover, each side painted with scenes of lakes before mountains, and with elaborate dragon and ring handles to the shoulders, the base with four character mark, some restoration and staining.

c1900   7in (17.5cm) high

$200-400   **WW**

EXPERT EYE – A PAIR OF KAKIEMON VASES

The double gourd form is made from a single piece and requires great skill to create – however, the example on the left leans slightly, a fault which probably occurred in the kiln.

Despite appearing to be a pair, there are differences in the sizes and proportions. This indicates they were not produced as a pair, which reduces the value.

The gourd form is considered auspicious, and is the Taoist symbol of longevity and good health. In Feng Shui it is a receptacle of good fortune.

Decorated over the glaze in the Kakiemon palette, if they had stronger and richer colors, they would be more valuable.

A matched pair of late 19thC/early 20thC Japanese Kakiemon vases, of double gourd form, with long slender necks, and molded bodies decorated in iron-red, blue and green to show mythical ho-o birds.

8in (20.5cm) high

$800-1,200   **FRE**

A Japanese blue and white model of a well bucket, painted with sparrows in flight above breaking waves, with six character mark.

c1900   7in (17.5cm) high

$200-300   **WW**

A small Japanese blue and white teapot and cover, probably 19thC, painted with small huts in a rocky landscape.

5in (13cm) high

$50-70   **WW**

ESSENTIAL REFERENCE – NORITAKE MARKS

The Morimura brothers' company, that became Noritake, has used a large number of different marks in its history. Three of the most common are shown here. The 'M' stands for the family name and the laurel wreath is derived from their family crest.

Marks with the 'M' in a wreath and 'Nippon' (the native name for Japan) were used from 1911–21. In 1921, the second McKinley Tariff Act declared that pieces imported into the US should have the country of origin marked in English. Hence, the wording 'Japan', and 'Made in Japan', replaced 'Nippon' from that date.

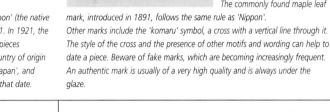

During the 1920s, the word 'Noritake' also replaced 'Hand Painted' on some marks. In 1953, the 'M' was replaced with an 'N' for the company name. The commonly found maple leaf mark, introduced in 1891, follows the same rule as 'Nippon'.

Other marks include the 'komaru' symbol, a cross with a vertical line through it. The style of the cross and the presence of other motifs and wording can help to date a piece. Beware of fake marks, which are becoming increasingly frequent. An authentic mark is usually of a very high quality and is always under the glaze.

A Japanese Nippon chocolate set, comprising chocolate pot and six cups and saucers, hand-painted with roses over black lines in bands, the base with printed blue "Hand Painted Elite Nippon" with 'B' in wreath motif mark.

Pot 8.25in (21cm) high

$200-300 (set)   **BH**

A Japanese Noritake coffee set, comprising teapot, four cups and saucers and matching tray, each with hand-painted and transfer-printed gilt stylized floral and scrolling design, the bases with printed "Made in Japan Handpainted No. 37532" mark, together with "M" in a laurel wreath motif.

Pot 6.75in (17cm) high

$200-300   **BH**

A Japanese Nippon melon or gourd form teaset, comprising teapot, creamer and sugar, ornately decorated with roses in medallions on a blue and white ground, with gilt highlights.

Teapot 8in (20.5cm) wide

$150-200

     BH

A Japanese Noritake creamer and sugar bowl, hand-painted with pink magnolia blooms and autumnal leaves over a transfer-printed gilt band, with gilded feet and printed marks to bases.

Bowl 7.5in (19cm) wide

$100-150   **BH**

CERAMICS

A Japanese Noritake China chocolate pot, painted in gilt with a stylized leaf design, the base with "Handpainted Japan" mark with an "M" in laurel wreath motif.

10in (25.5cm) high

$50-70   **BH**

A Japanese Nippon low pitcher, with shaped lip and scroll handle, hand-painted with pink and red roses, the base marked with printed leaf mark, also marked "Nippon Handpainted".

5.5in (14cm) high

$150-200   **BH**

A Japanese Nippon sugar shaker, hand-painted with a pink floral and foliate garland and with gilt highlights, the base with blue "M" mark in a laurel wreath.

5in (12.5cm) high

$70-100   **BH**

A Nippon three-piece condensed milk container, hand-painted with green bands and panels with gilt highlights, and frames containing pink flowers, the base with "Japan Handpainted" mark with leaf motif.

6.25in (16cm) high

$200-300   **BH**

A Japanese Nippon coffee pot, with hand-painted pink roses on a blue and white ground, with gilt highlights, and scroll handle, unmarked.

10in (25.5cm) high

$220-280   **BH**

A Japanese Nippon covered bowl, with hand-painted red and gold borders and pink and red roses, unmarked.

10in (20.5cm) wide

$200-250   **BH**

A Japanese Nippon baluster vase, hand-painted with roses, other flowers and leaves on a graduated cream ground, the rim and foot with gilt bands, the base with printed green "M" in laurel wreath mark.

8.5in (21.5cm) high

$70-100   **BH**

A Japanese Nippon baluster vase, with hand-painted stems and traditional roses on graduated brown, green and yellow ground, the base with printed blue "Nippon Handpainted" leaf motif mark.

6.25in (16cm) high

$100-150   **BH**

A Japanese purple and gold flower slightly waisted gourd-type vase, with blue leaf and 'hand painted' script to right logo.

6.25in (16cm) high

$150-200   **BH**

A Japanese Imperial Nippon three-handled vase, with hand-painted scene of native Americans under a palm tree at a riverside watching a boat, the base with printed circular light blue "Nippon Hand Painted" mark.

8.5in (21.5cm) high

$220-280   **BH**

EXPERT EYE – A NIPPON VASE

It is marked with a patent date identifying the earliest year it can be dated to – dated patent markings are more common in the 1930s-40s.

This is a pleasant and well-proportioned form, with restrained use of gilding.

Coralene is the term given to tiny glass beads that are sprinkled on to the surface. They are a very unusual feature and typically wore off over time.

The form of the vase and the floral motif recalls US art pottery by companies such as Rookwood – albeit in much more vibrant colors.

A Nippon vase, decorated with yellow and orange lilies on a shaded ground, with gilt and Coralene highlights, some wear to gilding, the base stamped "US Patent 917, Feb 9.1909".

8.75in (22cm) high

$1,000-1,500   **DRA**

A Japanese tapered cylindrical vase, with small neck and flared rim, painted with foliage and trees in a stylized lakeside setting, the base with indistinct printed red "Handpainted Japan" mark.

A Japanese spherical tripod vase, with double handles modeled as branches, with hand-painted pink and white flowers on a blue and white ground with gilt highlights, the base with printed "Japan Handpainted" mark.

A Japanese Nippon plate, with three gilt-framed panels containing small hand-painted landscape vignettes, with printed marks to base.

10.25in (26cm) high

$150-200   **BH**

5.5in (14cm) high

$100-150   **BH**

7.75in (19.5cm) diam

$70-100   **BH**

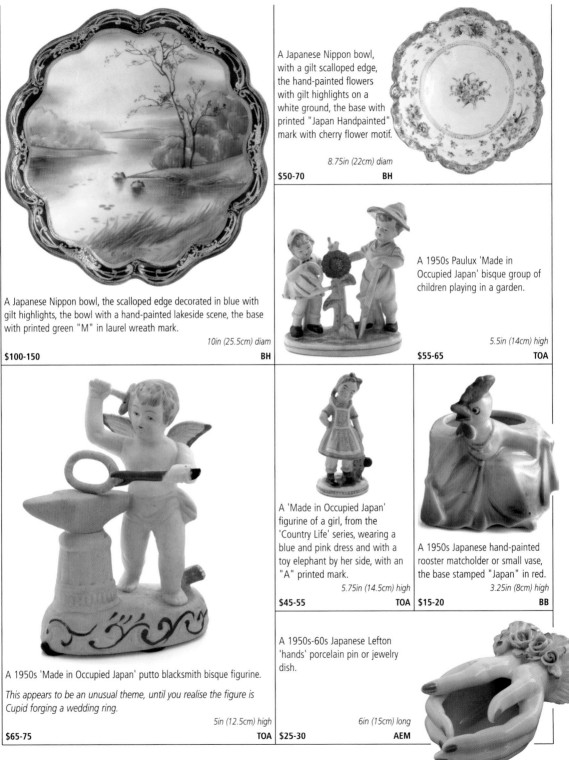

A Japanese Nippon bowl, with a gilt scalloped edge, the hand-painted flowers with gilt highlights on a white ground, the base with printed "Japan Handpainted" mark with cherry flower motif.

8.75in (22cm) diam

$50-70   **BH**

A Japanese Nippon bowl, the scalloped edge decorated in blue with gilt highlights, the bowl with a hand-painted lakeside scene, the base with printed green "M" in laurel wreath mark.

10in (25.5cm) diam

$100-150   **BH**

A 1950s Paulux 'Made in Occupied Japan' bisque group of children playing in a garden.

5.5in (14cm) high

$55-65   **TOA**

A 'Made in Occupied Japan' figurine of a girl, from the 'Country Life' series, wearing a blue and pink dress and with a toy elephant by her side, with an "A" printed mark.

5.75in (14.5cm) high

$45-55   **TOA**

A 1950s Japanese hand-painted rooster matcholder or small vase, the base stamped "Japan" in red.

3.25in (8cm) high

$15-20   **BB**

A 1950s 'Made in Occupied Japan' putto blacksmith bisque figurine.

This appears to be an unusual theme, until you realise the figure is Cupid forging a wedding ring.

5in (12.5cm) high

$65-75   **TOA**

A 1950s-60s Japanese Lefton 'hands' porcelain pin or jewelry dish.

6in (15cm) long

$25-30   **AEM**

ESSENTIAL REFERENCE

- Lorenzen pottery was first produced in 1945, in Dieppe, New Brunswick, Canada, by husband and wife team Alma and Ernst Lorenzen. Started as a hobby, Ernst threw pots while Alma modeled and sculpted in clay. Demand grew rapidly, and by 1946, they had set up a shop. In 1949, they were offered, and accepted, land in Lantz, Nova Scotia, enabling them to expand.

- Although Ernst continued to throw pots, it is perhaps Alma's mushroom sculptures that have become the most popular. With its damp and moderate climate, Nova Scotia is a haven for fungi. The many species that grow there captivated Alma on her regular country walks. Using detailed watercolors to record forms and color tones, Alma would carefully sculpt groups of mushrooms, with Ernst providing the delicately toned, yet vibrant glazes that were colored with local minerals.

- The pair carefully adhered to form, and ensured that the genus was correctly recorded on the base. Since Alma's death in 1998, her daughter Dinamarca has continued to make sculptures, and grow the business. Over 230 different varieties have been made and values depend on the color and the complexity of the form. Complex and finely modeled example are generally more desirable.

- Lorenzen's mushroom sculptures are collected by both public institutions and private collectors, and are highly sought-after. Some can take over 10 days to create. Other forms are also popular, but tend not to be as valuable. Pieces with surface designs tend to be more desirable. Always examine the edges of mushrooms caps for signs of damage or repair as this reduces value.

A Lorenzen studio pottery yellow 'Cantharellus Cibarius' mushroom sculpture, the base inscribed "Cantharelluscibarius" and with inscribed signature.

3in (7.5cm) high

$300-400   **TAC**

A Lorenzen studio pottery 'Cantharellus Nitidus' mushroom sculpture, with painted signature on base.

2.75in (7cm) high

$250-350   **TWF**

A Lorenzen studio pottery pink and yellow 'Russula Mariae' mushroom sculpture, with one unopened mushroom to rear, the base painted "Russulamariae" and with painted signature.

2.5in (6cm) high

$300-400   **TAC**

A Lorenzen studio pottery 'Russula Olivaceae' mushroom sculpture, with painted "Lantz Nova Scotia" signature to base.

2.5in (6.5cm) high

$250-350   **TWF**

A Lorenzen studio pottery 'Mycena Pura' mushroom sculpture, inscribed on the base, one stem restored.

2.5in (6cm) high

$180-220   **TWF**

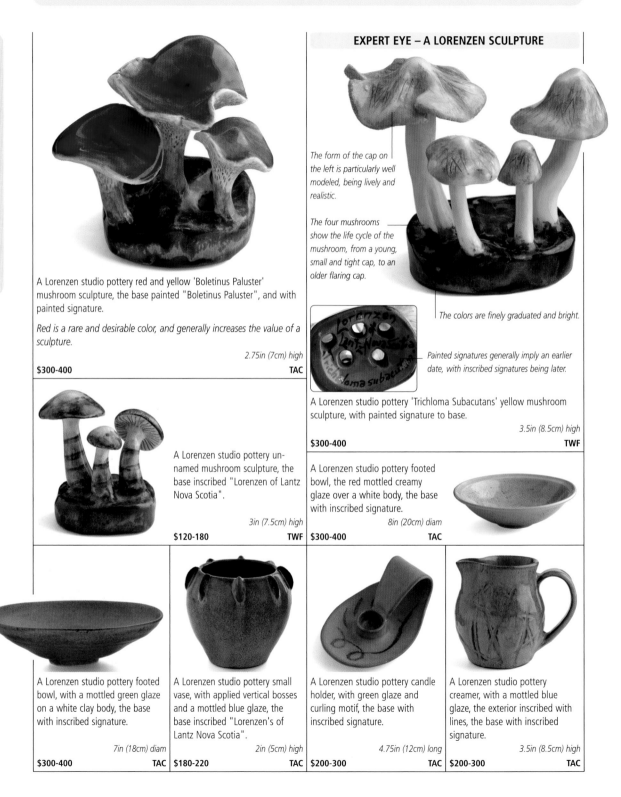

A Lorenzen studio pottery red and yellow 'Boletinus Paluster' mushroom sculpture, the base painted "Boletinus Paluster", and with painted signature.

Red is a rare and desirable color, and generally increases the value of a sculpture.

2.75in (7cm) high

$300-400   **TAC**

A Lorenzen studio pottery un-named mushroom sculpture, the base inscribed "Lorenzen of Lantz Nova Scotia".

3in (7.5cm) high

$120-180   **TWF**

EXPERT EYE – A LORENZEN SCULPTURE

The form of the cap on the left is particularly well modeled, being lively and realistic.

The four mushrooms show the life cycle of the mushroom, from a young, small and tight cap, to an older flaring cap.

The colors are finely graduated and bright.

Painted signatures generally imply an earlier date, with inscribed signatures being later.

A Lorenzen studio pottery 'Trichloma Subacutans' yellow mushroom sculpture, with painted signature to base.

3.5in (8.5cm) high

$300-400   **TWF**

A Lorenzen studio pottery footed bowl, the red mottled creamy glaze over a white body, the base with inscribed signature.

8in (20cm) diam

$300-400   **TAC**

A Lorenzen studio pottery footed bowl, with a mottled green glaze on a white clay body, the base with inscribed signature.

7in (18cm) diam

$300-400   **TAC**

A Lorenzen studio pottery small vase, with applied vertical bosses and a mottled blue glaze, the base inscribed "Lorenzen's of Lantz Nova Scotia".

2in (5cm) high

$180-220   **TAC**

A Lorenzen studio pottery candle holder, with green glaze and curling motif, the base with inscribed signature.

4.75in (12cm) long

$200-300   **TAC**

A Lorenzen studio pottery creamer, with a mottled blue glaze, the exterior inscribed with lines, the base with inscribed signature.

3.5in (8.5cm) high

$200-300   **TAC**

ESSENTIAL REFERENCE

- William Moorcroft (1872-1945) began working as a designer at James Macintyre & Co. in 1897, being promoted to manager of Ornamental Ware in 1898. His first designs were the Florian and Aurelian ranges, which are typified by their complex Moorish-inspired symmetrical patterns of natural themes including leaves and flowers. Highly stylized, they are typical of the Art Nouveau style prevalent at the time.
- Moorcroft's hand-thrown shapes were decorated with a tube-lining process, where liquid clay was piped onto the surface, outlining the desired pattern. The 'cells' within the pattern were then filled with liquid glaze. Moorcroft left Macintyre in 1912 in order to found his own company with backing from important London retailer Liberty. By 1929, Moorcroft had been awarded the Royal Warrant.
- Colors are typically rich and deep, and patterns continued to be inspired by the natural world, although the Art Nouveau stylization was abandoned and new ranges were introduced. After William's death, his son Walter took over and continued many of his father's designs as well as introducing some of his own.
- The most desirable and valuable ranges tend to be early, from the 1900s to '20s, and include Florian, Claremont and any of the landscape patterns. Many of William's patterns were so popular, they were produced throughout the 20thC. However, more modern ranges produced by recent designers including Sally Tuffin and Rachel Bishop are also growing in value on the secondary market, particularly if they are from a limited edition or an unusual variation in terms of color, form or pattern.
- Patterns produced for long periods tend to be the most affordable, particularly if the piece is small. The pattern, shape, size and type of marks on the base can help to date a piece. Always examine the entire body for signs of damage.

A James Macintyre & Co. 'Honesty' pattern Florian ware footed double gourd vase, designed by William Moorcroft, with two-tone blue glaze over a stippled ground, the base with impressed monogram and green painted signature.

11in (28cm) high

$2,500-3,000   **FLD**

A James Macintyre & Co. 'Blue Poppy' pattern Florian ware jardiniére, designed by William Moorcroft, with white ground and frilled rim, the base with printed and painted signatures.

6.75in (17cm) high

$2,500-3,500   **FLD**

A James Macintyre & Co. large 'Dianthus' pattern Florian ware vase, designed by William Moorcroft, of slender high-shouldered form with a slightly everted rim, the base with printed marks and full green flash signature, with small restoration to rim.

12in (30.5cm) high

$1,400-1,600   **FLD**

A Moorcroft 'Anemone' pattern vase, designed by William Moorcroft, the base with impressed factory marks, signed "W.M." in green and dated "11-20-80".

1980 12.5in (31.5cm) high

$350-450   **BEL**

A Moorcroft 'Anemone' pattern vase.

c1940   3.25in (8.5cm) high

$450-550   **PGO**

CERAMICS

A 1940s-50s Moorcroft
'Anemone' pattern vase, designed
by Walter Moorcroft, with a green
background, the base with
impressed and painted marks.

5.5in (14cm) high

$400-600   **PGO**

A Moorcroft
'Revived Cornflower'
or 'Brown Chrysanthemum'
pattern circular footed fruit
bowl, designed by
William Moorcroft, with an ochre ground and applied loop handles, the
base with green painted flash signature and dated "November 1913".
1913   *8.5in (21.5cm) wide*

$1,500-2,000   **FLD**

A Moorcroft 'Dahlia' pattern ovoid vase, designed by Walter Moorcroft
in 1960, the base with impressed and painted marks.

*This is reputed to be one of only 50 produced in this pattern, which
was used experimentally.*

8.5in (21.5cm) high

$1,200-1,400   **FLD**

EXPERT EYE – A MOORCROFT VASE

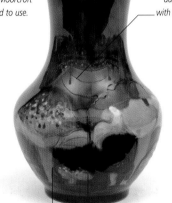

*Claremont is an early design that
was produced and sold under the
Liberty name – in fact, Liberty
devised the name for the
range, which Moorcroft
then continued to use.*

*Early examples have dark green and
blue mottled backgrounds similar to
the Hazeldene design. They became
darker and stronger
during the 1920s,
with bolder designs.*

*The pattern was registered in
October 1903 and was
produced for nearly 40 years.*

*The design is comparatively scarce, and
highly desirable. This form is also appealing
and the pattern is designed to fit the form.*

A Moorcroft 'Claremont' pattern ovoid shouldered vase, designed by
William Moorcroft, the base with impressed marks and full blue
painted signature.

7in (17.5cm) high

$4,000-5,000   **FLD**

A Moorcroft 'Finches
Blue' pattern wall
charger, designed by
Sally Tuffin in 1988,
the reverse with green
WM monogram.

14in (35.5cm) diam

$550-650   **WW**

A 1960s-70s Moorcroft 'Hibiscus'
pattern bowl, designed by Walter
Moorcroft in 1949, the base with
printed and painted marks.

3.75in (9.5cm) diam

$200-300   **PGO**

A Moorcroft 'Moonlit Blue' pattern inkwell, designed by William Moorcroft, with integral cube-form well and pen rest to front, the base with impressed marks and painted signature.

Launched in 1922, 'Moonlit Blue' was the first of three landscape designs that also included 'Eventide' (1923) and 'Dawn' (1926). This is a scarce form.

9in (23.5cm) wide

$1,400-1,600   **FLD**

A Moorcroft 'Frilled Orchid' pattern baluster vase, designed by William Moorcroft, with a deep blue ground, the base with paper label.

3.75in (9.5cm) high

$300-400   **WW**

EXPERT EYE – A MOORCROFT VASE

The Pansy pattern was introduced in 1911, a year after the popular 'Pomegranate' pattern.

Early backgrounds on 'Pansy' are lighter, comprizing white, cream or celadon. After c1916, they became dark blue.

While the Florian wares that preceded them were patterned all over the body, 'Pansy' and 'Pomegranate' had single bands of decoration.

Pansy was available on tablewares and decorative wares and was produced until the late 1930s.

A James Macintyre & Co. 'Pansy' pattern baluster vase, designed by William Moorcroft, with a white glazed ground, the base with printed marks and painted signature.

3.75in (9.5cm) high

$2,500-3,500   **FLD**

A 1920s Moorcroft 'Pansy' pattern bowl, designed by William Moorcroft, the base with printed and painted marks.

6in (15cm) diam

$600-800   **PGO**

A limited edition Moorcroft 'Polar Bear' vase, designed by Sally Tuffin, from an edition of 250, with a tube-lined design on a light flambé ground, the base with impressed and painted marks, with firing crack to rim.

This design was produced for the Canadian market. The pink background is extremely unusual, as the standard colorway was white with a gently graduated pink outline accentuating the tube-lined designs. Suggesting warmth and comfort, pink is not a color usually associated with the Arctic.

1988   7in (17.5cm) high

$1,100-1,300   **WW**

A Moorcroft 'Pomegranate' pattern plate, designed by William Moorcroft, the base with impressed marks and signed in green.

8.25in (22cm) diam

$300-400   **L&T**

A Moorcroft 'Pomegranate' pattern flared cylindrical footed vase, designed by William Moorcroft, the base with impressed marks and green painted flash monogram.

The quality on this example is extremely high. A number of imitations produced in China have flooded the market recently. Often in large sizes, they are usually unmarked and the quality of decoration is very poor.

12.5in (31cm) high

$2,500-3,500   **FLD**

A Moorcroft 'Pomegranate' pattern vase, designed by William Moorcroft, the base with impressed and painted marks.

This is an unusual form.
c1928   4.5in (11.5cm) high
$600-800   **PGO**

A Moorcroft 'Pomegranate' pattern bowl, designed by William Moorcroft, the base with impressed and painted marks.

c1913-25   4.5in (11.5cm) high
$400-600   **PGO**

A Moorcroft 'Big Poppy' pattern double-handled pedestal bowl, designed by William Moorcroft, with a blue glazed ground, the base with impressed marks and painted monogram.

9in (23cm) wide
$1,500-1,700   **FLD**

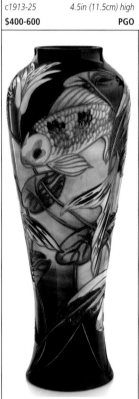

A Moorcroft 'Quiet Waters' pattern vase, designed by Philip Gibson, the base with painted and impressed marks.
2002   14.25in (36cm) high
$900-1,100   **WW**

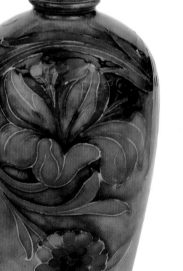

A Moorcroft 'Spanish' pattern ovoid vase, with narrow collar neck, the base with full green painted signature and date for 1914.

The richly colored Spanish pattern was introduced in 1910 and was produced into the 1930s.
1914   5.25in (13cm) high
$3,000-4,500   **FLD**

A 1920s-30s Moorcroft 'Big Poppy' bowl, designed by William Moorcroft, the base with impressed and painted marks.
6.75in (17cm) high
$800-1,000   **PGO**

A Moorcroft 'Violet' pattern vase, designed by Sally Tuffin, the base with impressed and painted marks.
1987   7in (18cm) high
$1,000-1,200   **WW**

ESSENTIAL REFERENCE – MOORCROFT MINIATURES

- Despite their diminutive size, there is nothing small about the prices of these scarce objects. Moorcroft's miniatures were most probably produced from the late 1910s to '20s as salesmen's samples, enabling traveling sales representatives to show prospective retailers the patterns available. Patterns are extremely well-applied and painted, and forms precise, despite their size. Some may also have been sold as novelties.

- The idea was revived in the 1970s, but the backstamps differ, so consult a reference work to ensure that you are buying a period piece. A further series of miniatures was offered later still, but the patterns are much later and include those by Emma Bossons and Sally Tuffin. All later examples can fetch anything from $150 to $400 depending on the date, pattern and location and type of seller. Later examples are often sold boxed in sets.

A 1970s Moorcroft 'Anemone' pattern miniature vase, designed by Walter Moorcroft, the base with printed marks.

2.5in (5.5cm) high

$250-350 WW

A 1970s Moorcroft 'Anemone' pattern miniature vase, designed by Walter Moorcroft, the base with printed marks.

2.5in (5.5cm) high

$250-350 WW

A James Macintyre & Co. 'Forget Me Nots' pattern miniature vase, designed by William Moorcroft, the base with printed marks and painted signature.

Exhibited at the 'William Moorcroft & Walter Moorcroft 1897-1973' exhibition at The Fine Art Society, London, in 1973, this vase also features in the accompanying catalogue.

3.25in (8cm) high

$3,000-4,000 WW

A rare Moorcroft 'Hazeldene' pattern miniature vase, designed by William Moorcroft, the base with painted signature, the rim restored.

Exhibited at the 'William Moorcroft & Walter Moorcroft 1897-1973' exhibition at The Fine Art Society, London, in 1973, this vase also features in the accompanying catalogue.

c1911 3.25in (8cm) high

$4,000-5,000 WW

A Moorcroft 'Pomegranate' pattern miniature vase, designed by William Moorcroft, the base painted "WM".

Exhibited at The Fine Art Society, London in 1973, and included in the catalogue.

2.5in (6cm) high

$2,500-3,500 WW

A James Macintyre & Co. 'Pomegranate' pattern miniature vase, designed by William Moorcroft, with green flash painted monogram.

2.5in (6cm) high

$1,500-1,700 FLD

A James Macintyre & Co. 'Tulip' pattern Florian ware miniature vase, designed by William Moorcroft, the base with painted signature and printed mark, with restored rim.

Exhibited at The Fine Art Society, London in 1973, and included in the catalogue.

c1902 2.5in (6.5cm) high

$2,000-3,000 WW

FIND OUT MORE...

'Moorcroft', by Paul Atterbury, published by Richard Dennis, 1996.

CERAMICS

ESSENTIAL REFERENCE

- Chester Nicodemus (1901-90) graduated from the Cleveland School of Art in 1925. For the next five years he taught at the Dayton Art Institute, before moving to the Columbus Art School. During the early 1930s, he studied with notable early ceramics designer and studio potter, Arthur Baggs (1886-1947), who had worked at Marblehead.
- In 1943 he left his full-time teaching position to focus on pottery, previously done in his spare time. Working from his garage, he used locally sourced iron-rich red clay, giving rise to one of his tradenames, 'Ferro-Stone'. He also produced some of his designs in plastic.
- The most common forms included teapots, vases, bowls, and similar homewares, but he also produced animal figurines, nativity sets and Christmas ornaments. Glazes were applied so the deep red of the clay showed through, adding warm tones. Colors include mottled greens, turquoise, ivory and golden yellows.
- Most pieces are signed on the base with either an "N", the word "Nicodemvs" or, from 1971, a paper label. Reproductions, notably of a robin figurine are known, so always compare a suspicious piece against an authentic one and consider glaze colors.
- Although Nicodemus employed a small, part-time team of assistants to help with retail commissions, he executed most of the work himself, and is best described as a studio potter. His often delicate and extremely well executed work has become highly collectible in recent years and price rises look set to continue.

A Nicodemus Pottery large spiral molded vase, covered with a speckled, light green glaze, the base impressed "Nicodemvs".

6.25in (15.5cm) high

$150-200   ANT

A Nicodemus Pottery baluster vase, with a graduated, speckled green over brown glaze.

5.5in (13.5cm) high

$350-450   ANT

A Nicodemus Pottery small double-handled urn vase, with dripped yellow over brown glaze, the base impressed "Nicodemvs".

4in (10cm) high

$70-100   ANT

A Nicodemus Pottery pot, with molded everted rim and with speckled green over brown glaze, the base signed "N".

4in (10cm) high

$250-350   ANT

A Nicodemus Pottery shaped pot, with speckled and graduated pink and greeny-cream over brown glaze.

This color of glaze is known as Pussy Willow.

2.5in (6cm) high

$180-220   ANT

A Nicodemus Pottery jar, with molded fluted columns of three lines and graduated speckled green and brown glaze, the base impressed "Nicodemvs".

3.75in (9.5cm) high

$350-450   ANT

A Nicodemus Pottery large yellow glazed creamer, the base signed "N".

4.5in (11.5cm) high

$550-650   ANT

A Nicodemus Pottery bear-shaped planter, the base stamped "Nicodemvs" and "EJ".

The "EJ" mark is for Ellen Jennings, who designed many of the smaller animal figurines.

3in (7.5cm) high

$220-280   ANT

FIND OUT MORE...

'Sanford's Guide to Nicodemus: His Potter & His Art', by Jim Riebel, published by Adelmore Press, 1998.

ESSENTIAL REFERENCE

- If George Ohr was not America's best art potter, he was certainly its most eccentric. Poor and largely uneducated, Ohr (1857-1918) studied pottery in New Orleans and founded his pottery in Biloxi, Mississippi, in 1883. He built the pottery himself and mined his own clay from a river. His early work is largely traditional and comprised pitchers and similar forms decorated with simple glazes. These are usually of the least interest to collectors.
- The 1890s saw a complete change in his style, which became more unconventional and eccentric after a fire destroyed the pottery in 1893. Vases, dishes and bowl dominated production, but were usually modified by collapsing the typically paper thin walls and rims, or twisting them. Sizes were small, generally at under 6in (15cm), and fitted into the palm of Ohr's hand allowing him to control the form.

- Glazes also exploded in a riot of color at this time and comprised of reds, greens, blues, purples and oranges – often used in combination. Red is one of the most desirable and valuable colors. In around 1903, Ohr decided to abandon all glazes as "God put no color in souls, and I'll put no color on my pottery". Pieces dating from after this period are known as 'bisque ware', and display the colors of the raw clay. He stopped potting in 1907 and gave his pottery to his sons.
- The 'Mad Potter of Biloxi's' work was forgotten after his death until around 5,000 pots were re-discovered in 1968 by an antique dealer. Pieces, such as his glazed teapots and double-handled vases from the 1890s, can be worth tens of thousands of dollars today. Ohr's work is generally signed on the base, or bears his pottery stamp.

A George Ohr demitasse cup and saucer, the cup with a rare brushed decoration of yellow leaves on gunmetal glaze, with Ohr price tag, restoration to rim.

Brushed decoration by Ohr is very unusual. Snipped-off stilt marks on the saucer indicate that he stacked other pieces, probably more saucers, in the kiln.

Cup 3.25in (8cm) high

$1,000-1,500   **DRA**

A George Ohr puzzle mug, with floral handle, covered in green and gun-metal mottled glaze, with script signature.

3.5in (9cm) high

$1,000-1,500   **DRA**

A George Ohr puzzle mug, with rabbit handle, covered in glossy amber glaze, and stamped "G.E. Ohr Biloxi".

4.25in (11cm) high

$1,800-2,200   **DRA**

A George Ohr tapered vase, covered in green and amber mottled glaze, marked "G.E. Ohr, Biloxi Miss", rim ground down and re-glazed.

6.25in (16cm) high

$1,200-1,800   **DRA**

A George Ohr vessel, with cupped neck and pronounced shoulder, covered in a rare mottled gold and gunmetal glaze, and stamped "G.E. Ohr, Biloxi, Miss."

This mottled glaze is extremely rare. The shape is also complex and challenging to make. As this vessel is by George Ohr, the fact that it leans to the right is forgivable, even desirable.

3.25in (8cm) high

$1,800-2,200   **DRA**

A Poole Pottery 'DR' pattern vase, designed by Marian Heath, painted with Art Deco flowers and foliage on a mint green ground, impressed and painted marks.

8.25in (21cm) high

$240-360   **WW**

A 1930s Poole Pottery 'Persian Deer' pattern vase, shape no. 966, designed by Truda Adams and decorated by Ruth Pavely, the base impressed "966", with painted "SK" pattern code and with decorator's mark for Ruth Pavely.

This vase was owned by Roy Holland, Poole Pottery's works manager and then managing director of Poole Pottery from 1962 to 1975. Animals, particularly gazelles, are a desirable and scarce motif in 1930s Poole designs. It could have been worth around twice this value if it wasn't cracked.

10in (25cm) high

$500-700   **WW**

EXPERT EYE – A POOLE POTTERY WALL CHARGER

The design was produced from a 1940 drawing by artist Arthur Bradbury, who also produced designs for similar ship plates.

Approximately six examples are known, of which this is one.

The town of Poole became an important commercial and military destination for flying boats. The Empire flying boats ran scheduled flights from Poole from 1939 to 1948.

Another plate was presented to US President Roosevelt's envoy, Harry Hopkins, when he passed through Poole in 1941, after finalizing the historic Lend-Lease Agreement.

A Poole Pottery 'Port of Poole Empire Airways' wall charger, designed by Arthur Bradbury and decorated by Margaret Holder, the back with printed mark.

1940   *14.5in (37cm) diam*

$7,000-8,000   **WW**

A Carter, Stabler & Adams Poole Pottery 'EC' pattern vase, designed by Truda Carter and painted by Anne Hatchard, in shades of mint, silver, brown and black, impressed and painted marks, minor hairlines to top rim.

16.5in (42cm) high

$1,600-2,000   **WW**

An early 1930s Carter, Stabler & Adams Poole Pottery 'EP' pattern large jug, shape 897, designed by Ruth Pavely, and decorated by Ann Hatchard.

The marks on the base are extremely useful. The inscribed number is the shape number, the painted letters the pattern number. The painted monogram was used by the decorator from the late 1920s onwards, and this impressed factory mark was used from 1925 to 1934.

11.5in (29cm) high

$2,000-3,000   **BEV**

A 1950s Poole Pottery 'Leipzig Girl' pattern plate, designed by Olive Bourne, the reverse with painted "HD" pattern code, printed factory marks and decorator's monogram, possibly for Gladys Hallett.

Although the design was produced in 1927 and exhibited at the Exhibition of Industrial Art in Leipzig, hence the pattern's name, this piece was made in the 1950s.
12in (30.5cm) diam

$360-440   **WW**

A Poole Pottery 'X/PT' pattern jardinière, shape no. 653, pattern designed by Ruth Pavely, from the Contemporary range, the base with printed and painted marks.
7.5in (19cm) high

$200-300   **WW**

EXPERT EYE – A POOLE POTTERY TRIAL PLATE

Ann Read was Alfred Read's daughter, and studied at the Chelsea School of Art, London, England, before joining her father at Poole Pottery.

In 1956, she produced the stylized 'Bamboo' design that was used on tableware. It comprised of similar lines on a black background.

This is from a small range of limited edition or unique examples designed and produced by Read around 1955-56.

The design is highly modern, showing the influence of art of the period, particularly Cubism, but also the early 1950s obsession with science and crystalline structures.

A trial Poole Pottery 'Rock Crystal' pattern oval plate, designed by Ann Read, painted in shades of white, purple and brown on a Black Panther ground, the back with printed and painted marks.
c1956
12.25in (31cm) wide

$480-560   **WW**

A Poole Pottery 'YFC' pattern carafe vase, shape no. 690 designed by Claude Smale and Guy Sydenham, pattern designed by Alfred Read, from the Contemporary range, the base with printed and painted marks.
12.25in (31m) high

$480-560   **WW**

A late 1950s Poole Pottery vase, shape no. 704, designed by Alfred Read and Guy Sydenham, from the Contemporary range, covered in a chocolate brown glaze, the base impressed "704", and with blue Poole Pottery printed mark.
7.5in (19cm) high

$80-120   **GC**

A trial Poole Pottery 'Philodendron' pattern oval plate, by Ann Read, painted in shades of white, black and brown on a black ground, the back with printed and painted marks.

Here, Read turns her attention to another 1950s fad – houseplants.
12.25in (31cm) wide

$480-560   **WW**

CERAMICS

A Poole Studio charger, covered in a geometric design in textured colored glazes, the reverse with printed "Studio" mark.

17in (43cm) diam

$1,000-1,200   **WW**

A Poole Studio charger, painted with a geometric abstract design in shades of green and blue, the reverse with printed blue Studio mark.

This pattern is very similar to designs by Robert Jefferson from c1962 to 1963.

13.5in (34.5cm) diam

$1,600-2,400   **WW**

EXPERT EYE – A POOLE STUDIO CHARGER

Tony Morris joined Poole in 1963 after studying at the Newport School of Art, Wales, UK.

He worked closely with Robert Jefferson to produce new colorways using bought-in glazes. The blue palette is early, dating from before 1970.

Abstract designs were typical, and also formed the basis of what was to become the immensely popular Delphis range.

This is a one-off, unique piece decorated by Morris himself and bears his monogram on the reverse. Look out for his desirable abstract face patterns.

A Poole Studio charger, designed and decorated by Tony Morris, painted in colors with an abstract landscape design, the base with painted "TM" mark.

14in (35.5cm) diam

$3,600-4,400   **WW**

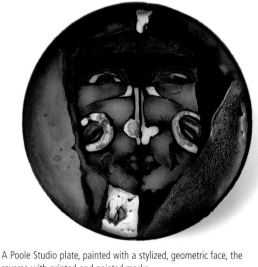

A Poole Studio plate, painted with a stylized, geometric face, the reverse with printed and painted marks.

8in (20cm) diam

$1,300-1,500   **WW**

A Poole Studio plate, painted with a geometric face pattern in shades of green and brown, the reverse with printed Studio mark.

8in (20cm) diam

$760-840   **WW**

A Poole Pottery Studio small dish, with small mark to reverse.

5.25in (13.5cm) diam

$35-45   **GAZE**

A Poole Pottery Delphis bowl, with printed and painted marks.

5in (13cm) diam

$120-160 WW

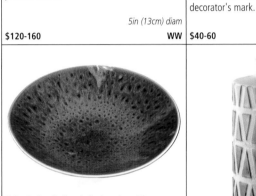

A Poole Pottery Delphis small dish, shape no. 86, the back stamped "86" and with decorator's mark.

5in (12.5cm) diam

$40-60 GAZE

A Poole Pottery Delphis tapering cylindrical footed vase, shape no. 85, covered with graduated and mottled yellow to brown to green glazes, with printed and painted marks, hairline crack to rim.

7in (18cm) high

$480-560 WW

A Poole Studio bowl, the interior with a mottled blue-green glaze, the base with printed blue Studio mark.

10.75in (27cm) diam

$200-300 WW

A Poole Studio vase, designed by Robert Jefferson and thrown by Guy Sydenham, carved with triangles in shades of blue on a creamy white ground, the base with printed mark.

Jefferson left Poole in 1966, but his influence remained strong during the following years.

15.75in (40cm) high

$1,500-1,700 WW

A Poole Studio vase, probably designed by Robert Jefferson, modeled in low relief with a grid design and glazed in green and brown, the base impressed with a triangle mark and with printed factory mark.

3.5in (9cm) high

$440-560 WW

A Poole Studio bowl, probably designed by Robert Jefferson, incised with a hatched design, with printed "Poole Studio" mark, and small glaze chip to top rim.

7.75in (19.5cm) diam

$400-600 WW

A Poole Pottery Delphis bowl, shape no. 85, carved with a geometric design and glazed in black, vivid red and orange, the reverse with printed and painted marks.

This bowl was owned by Roy Holland, managing director of Poole Pottery. It is decorated with colors typical of the Delphis range.

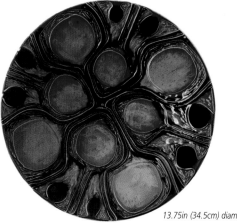

13.75in (34.5cm) diam

$1,000-1,200 WW

A Poole Pottery Delphis dish, boldly painted with a stylized design on a red ground, printed mark in black.

$240-360 LFA

A Poole Pottery Delphis charger, shape no. 54, decorated with an organic cell-like design in blues, greens, reds and oranges, with printed and painted marks to reverse.

16.25in (41cm) diam

$240-360 WW

A Poole Pottery Delphis plate, decorated with a geometric design, printed and painted marks.

10.5in (26.5cm) diam

$400-500 WW

A Poole Pottery Delphis charger, shape no. 54, painted with a geometric design in shades of yellow, orange, blue and green textured glazes, printed and painted marks.

16.25in (41cm) diam

$800-1,200 WW

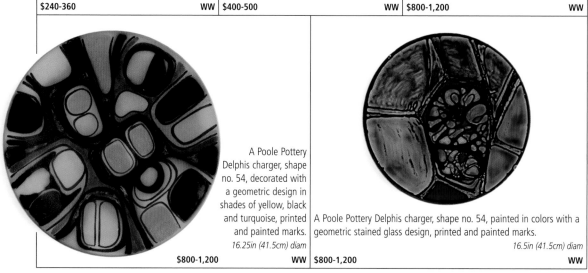

A Poole Pottery Delphis charger, shape no. 54, decorated with a geometric design in shades of yellow, black and turquoise, printed and painted marks.

16.25in (41.5cm) diam

$800-1,200 WW

A Poole Pottery Delphis charger, shape no. 54, painted in colors with a geometric stained glass design, printed and painted marks.

16.5in (41.5cm) diam

$800-1,200 WW

ESSENTIAL REFERENCE – ATLANTIS

The Atlantis range was the brainchild of talented potter Guy Sydenham (1916-2005). Sydenham joined Carter, Stabler & Adams in 1931 and worked his way up to become senior designer in 1966. He worked closely with both Alfred Read and Robert Jefferson, particularly in relation to the in-house Studio range, that grew to prominence under Jefferson and was relaunched in 1961. The range was designed between 1965 and 1966 and was produced into the 1970s. Each piece was carved, as well as glazed, by hand. Sydenham was responsible for much of the work although others also produced it. Pieces he produced are marked with his 'GS' seal, shown on the base of this vase. Pieces typically have a strong texture, with geometric patterns, and made as much use of the color of the clay as any glaze applied. Each piece is unique, with the range being as close to studio pottery as possible.

A Poole Pottery Atlantis vase, by Guy Sydenham, with carved geometric columns in shades of white and blue on a brown ground, the base with impressed and incised marks.

5.5in (14cm) high

$360-440 **WW**

A Poole Pottery Atlantis stoneware vase, carved with vertical columns and geometric design, and glazed in a creamy gloss glaze, the base with painted and incised marks.

8.25in (21cm) high

$440-560 **WW**

A Poole Pottery Atlantis stoneware vase, the carved vertical columns with a chevron design, glazed in brown and creamy gloss glazes, the base with painted and incised marks.

5.75in (14.5cm) high

$360-440 **WW**

A Poole Pottery Atlantis stoneware vase, by Guy Sydenham, carved with abstract sliced columns, the base with impressed marks and "GS" and "BB" monograms, with hairline cracks to rim.

8.25in (21cm) high

$80-120 **WW**

A Poole Pottery Atlantis vase, by Guy Sydenham, of ovoid form with impressed design, covered in an oatmeal glaze.

4in (10cm) high

$300-400 **WW**

A Poole Pottery Atlantis vase, by Jennie Haigh, with incised and applied wavy band, the base with impressed factory mark and incised "JH" monogram.

4.75in (12cm) high

$360-440 **WW**

EXPERT EYE – A POOLE POTTERY LAMP BASE

These lamp bases with internal motifs are among Sydenham's most iconic and unusual designs – they are also among the rarest.

This example has separately made, applied features, rather than being simply inscribed, impressed or painted – it would have taken longer to create.

The features inside relate closely to an important water feature made by Guy Sydenham in 1970 and installed in the old quayside Poole factory.

It is glazed in typical Poole colors. The objects inside are small bowls and vases, which relate to Poole Pottery.

A very rare Poole Pottery Atlantis 'Knight's Helmet' lamp base, by Guy Sydenham, of ovoid form internally modeled with a grimacing knight's face, the exterior modeled as chainmail, impressed "A12" and with the artist's cipher.

11.75in (30cm) high

$3,200-4,400   WW

A rare Poole Pottery Atlantis 'Mermaid' lamp base, by Guy Sydenham, of ovoid form internally modeled with a mermaid resting in a cave of 'Poole' vases, vivid orange glaze to the interior, the exterior mottled green, impressed "Poole England", with artists's cipher.

16.25in (41cm) high

$12,000-16,000   WW

A Poole Pottery Atlantis 'Pebble', shape A6, by Guy Sydenham, decorated with a spiralling pattern in slip, the base with impressed and incised marks.

4.75in (12cm) diam

$360-440   WW

A limited edition Poole Pottery 'Cathedral' wall plate, design no. 479 designed by Tony Morris, painted by C. Willis, from an edition of 1,000, with impressed, printed and painted marks.

The design was based on the 12thC stained glass window at the cathedral of Notre Dame, Chartres, France.

1973   *12.5in (32cm) diam*

$120-180   WW

A Poole Pottery 'peanut' vase, painted by Sue Pottinger, with stylized flowers in pastel colors on a banded cream and beige ground, the base with printed and painted marks.

14.25in (36cm) high

$240-360   WW

A Poole Studio Collection 'Bird' vase, designed by Sally Tuffin.

This vase was only made for approximately one year.

1996   *9in (20cm) high*

$300-360   KCS

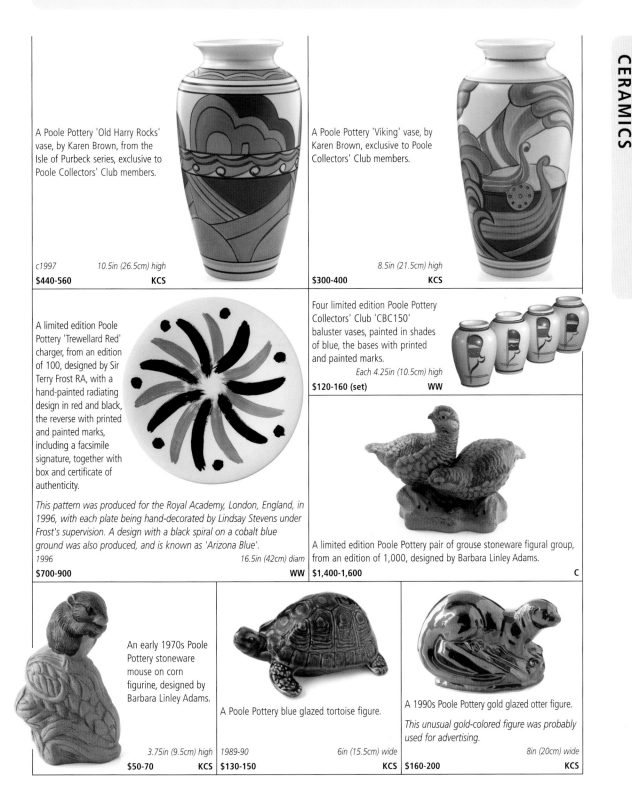

A Poole Pottery 'Old Harry Rocks' vase, by Karen Brown, from the Isle of Purbeck series, exclusive to Poole Collectors' Club members.

c1997   10.5in (26.5cm) high
$440-560   **KCS**

A Poole Pottery 'Viking' vase, by Karen Brown, exclusive to Poole Collectors' Club members.

8.5in (21.5cm) high
$300-400   **KCS**

A limited edition Poole Pottery 'Trewellard Red' charger, from an edition of 100, designed by Sir Terry Frost RA, with a hand-painted radiating design in red and black, the reverse with printed and painted marks, including a facsimile signature, together with box and certificate of authenticity.

This pattern was produced for the Royal Academy, London, England, in 1996, with each plate being hand-decorated by Lindsay Stevens under Frost's supervision. A design with a black spiral on a cobalt blue ground was also produced, and is known as 'Arizona Blue'.
1996   16.5in (42cm) diam
$700-900   **WW**

Four limited edition Poole Pottery Collectors' Club 'CBC150' baluster vases, painted in shades of blue, the bases with printed and painted marks.
Each 4.25in (10.5cm) high
$120-160 (set)   **WW**

A limited edition Poole Pottery pair of grouse stoneware figural group, from an edition of 1,000, designed by Barbara Linley Adams.
$1,400-1,600   **C**

An early 1970s Poole Pottery stoneware mouse on corn figurine, designed by Barbara Linley Adams.

3.75in (9.5cm) high
$50-70   **KCS**

A Poole Pottery blue glazed tortoise figure.

1989-90   6in (15.5cm) wide
$130-150   **KCS**

A 1990s Poole Pottery gold glazed otter figure.

This unusual gold-colored figure was probably used for advertising.

8in (20cm) wide
$160-200   **KCS**

ESSENTIAL REFERENCE

- Prattware is the generic name given to a particular type of underglaze transfer-printed ware. The patterns and manufacturers are related to pot lids of the same period. Although it is named after the prolific producer F. & R. Pratt, other companies, such as T.J. & J. Mayer, also produced it. Wares printed with color transfers first appeared during the mid-19thC and reached the peak of production and popularity in the very late 19thC.
- Shapes vary from the functional to the highly decorative. Mugs, jugs and plates are among the more common shapes, as are jars that typically held meat paste. Shape is one of the main factors in value – a scarcer or more decorative shape, such as a vase or a rare eggcup, will be worth more than a dinner plate, which tended to be sold in multiples.
- The pattern is the other major factor to consider. Many were taken from pot lid designs. Look for strong colors and good quality images that have been printed well. Some subjects,

such as Wellington's funeral, are rarer than others. Numbers given here relate to the pattern reference numbers in K.V. Mortimer's book listed at the end of this section.
- Also consider the surround, as the color and the level of eye-appeal can add to desirability. White, red, dark green, burgundy and pink are the most common colors. Yellow, pale blue and black are rarer. Some have designs such as reclining ladies or arabesques, which are often more desirable when highlighted in gold.
- The level and style of the outer border decoration can also affect value. The most common border is Classical in style and known as the '1-2-3' pattern. A pattern with curving stylized wheat sheaves between small brooch-like turquoise spotted ovals is rarer. Pieces bearing advertising are generally rare. Always examine pieces for signs of wear or damage, looking closely at edges and the surfaces of dinner service plates.

A Prattware 'Haddon Hall' plate, no. 621, with classical reclining female border in deep crimson.

This is from a series of four historic houses, and was produced for many years. Early examples have borders like this example.

9.5in (24cm) diam

$450-550   **SAS**

A Prattware 'Tremadoc' plate, no. 620, with classical reclining female border in purple, lined in pink and gilt.

9.5in (24cm) diam

$120-160   **SAS**

A Prattware 'The Poultry Yard Trentham' plate, by Elliot & Son, no. 616, with gilded border, with title and with maker's mark.

Look out for the rare flask decorated with this pattern.

9.5in (24cm) diam

$350-450   **SAS**

A Prattware 'State House in Philadelphia 1776' dessert plate, no. 672, the maroon surround with a star and panel border and gold line decoration, the reverse with "R.J. Allen, Son & Co." retailer's mark.

This was produced in 1876 to celebrate the centenary of the Declaration of Independence in 1776.

9.5in (24cm) diam

$300-400   **SAS**

A Prattware 'The Hop Queen' plate, no. 676, with malachite border and gold line decoration.

This pattern can be found on large pot lids and circular comports.

9.5in (24cm) diam

$150-200   **SAS**

A Prattware 'The Irishman' side plate, no. 126, with an orange ground and '1-2-3' border with gold line decoration.

5.5in (14cm) diam

$100-150   **SAS**

A Prattware 'The Truant' plate, no. 675, with maroon ground and '1-2-3' and scroll border with gold line decoration.

9.5in (24cm) diam

$150-250   **SAS**

A Prattware 'Pelargoniums & Moss Rose' plate, no. 459, the green border lined in yellow.

9.5in (24cm) diam

$80-120   **SAS**

A Prattware 'Shells' small side plate, no. 711, the pink border lined in green.

6.75in (17cm) diam

$200-300   **SAS**

A Prattware 'Orchids' plate, no. 454, with wavy outline, blue printed border, the reverse printed "No.94" in blue.

This is a dramatic and scarce combination with superb coloring reminiscent of 19thC botanical prints.

9.5in (24cm) diam

$600-700   **SAS**

A Prattware 'Uncle Tom and Eva' meat paste jar, no. 527, the neck with 'seaweed' ground.

The companion piece to this shows an African slave being beaten and is known as 'Uncle Tom' (no. 526). A desirable set of three can be made by finding the version of this jar showing both scenes (no. 528). That double version has no seaweed decoration on the neck.

3.5in (8.75cm) high

$800-1,000   **SAS**

A Prattware 'The Dragoon Charge, Balaklava' meat paste jar, no. 510, with minor hairline crack.

3.5in (8.75cm) high

$500-700   **SAS**

A Prattware 'Venice' meat paste jar, no. 517, by Mayer.

$140-180   **SAS**

A Prattware 'The Fall of Sebastopol, 8th Sept. 1855' meat paste jar, no. 511, by Mayer.

3.5in (8.75cm) high

$700-900   **SAS**

CERAMICS

A Prattware 'The Deer Stalker and Wild Deer' meat paste jar, no. 530, with 'Potted Meat' lid.

$450-550   **SAS**

MILLER'S COMPARES – TWO 'PASSING THE PIPE' JARS

The 'seaweed' pattern decorated neck on this example is not as fine.

As well as having a taller neck, it has a concave base. Some have internal collars.

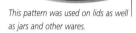

This pattern was used on lids as well as jars and other wares.

The colors are stronger on this example.

A Prattware 'Passing the Pipe' meat paste jar, no. 525, the neck with mottled ground.

3.5in (9cm) high

$500-700   **SAS**

A Prattware 'Passing the Pipe' meat paste jar, no. 525, the neck with mottled ground.

4.5in (11.5cm) high

$900-1,100   **SAS**

A Prattware 'Exhibition Buildings 1851' Princess Christian sauce bottle or vase, no. 134, with a black mottled ground.

$400-600   **SAS**

A Prattware 'Convulvulus' jug, no. 458, with hinged pewter cover, gilt lining and minor hairline crack.

11in (28cm) high

$150-200   **SAS**

A Prattware tobacco jar, plunger and cover, with 'Cows in Stream near Ruins' and 'Halt near Ruins' scenes on a blue ground, with '1-2-3'-border and gold line decoration.

4.75in (12cm) high

$500-700   **SAS**

A Prattware cylindrical loving cup, decorated with 'Passing the Pipe' no. 525 and 'The Smokers', no. 524, on a malachite ground with gold line decoration.

4.25in (11cm) high

$400-600   **SAS**

FIND OUT MORE...

'Pot-Lids And Other Colored Printed Staffordshire Wares', by K.V. Mortimer, published by Antique Collectors' Club, 2003.

ESSENTIAL REFERENCE

- The Red Wing Stoneware Co. was founded in 1868 in Red Wing, Minnesota, and produced domestic and industrial stoneware. By 1906 it had merged with its two major competitors. Around this time, they also introduced matte green-brown stained decorative pottery including urns, large vases and umbrella stands known as 'Brushedware'. This was available until around 1929, when glazed wares production began.
- In the early 1930s, pottery distributor George Rumwill entered into a partnership with Red Wing and was responsible for widening and organising their line of art pottery. Until the partnership was dissolved around 1938, these were marketed under the Rumwill Pottery name.
- New York-based designer Belle Kogan was employed in 1938 and produced 100 designs. He returned during the 1950s and '60s to design further ranges. His designs can be identified by the 'B' prefix at the start of the model number. Perhaps his most famous range was the geometric 'Prismatique', introduced in 1962.
- In 1940, Charles Murphy was hired as a staff designer and went on to produce a series of popular lines, as well as designing the majority of Red Wing's hand-painted dinnerwares. Murphy had previously worked with Guy Cowan, Viktor Schreckengost and Frederick Rhead.
- Murphy's designs, which characterised the look of much postwar Red Wing pottery, can be identified from the 'M' prefix before each model number. He left in 1947, but returned again in 1953, working there until the pottery's closure in 1967. Key themes were simple lines and bright, vibrant colours.
- Values vary depending on the size, age, complexity and appeal of each piece. Early pieces from the 1920s-30s are usually desirable, and are generally harder to find than later examples. Always examine pieces for signs of damage, particularly hairline cracks.
- Complex patterns are sought-after, particularly on dinnerware, which was originally priced depending on how many levels of hand-painting were required to complete the design. The factory closed in 1967 due to competition from less expensive imports, but the company remained as a retailer. Production under the Red Wing name recommenced in 1987 and continues today.

A Red Wing Bronze Line urn, the base marked "Red Wing USA 850".

7.25in (18.5cm) high

$18-22   **BEL**

A Red Wing urn vase, with pink interior and blue exterior and molded detailing to the foot, handles and base, the base impressed "Red-Wing U.S.A. 1173".

7.25in (18.5cm) high

$120-180   **ANT**

A Red Wing pink mottled glazed urn vase, the base molded "Redwing USA 1584".

7.5in (19cm) high

$80-120   **ANT**

A Red Wing tapered fluted vase, with flared rim and crystalline brown glaze, the base impressed "Red Wing U.S.A. 662".

11in (28cm) high

$150-200   **ANT**

A Red Wing yellow glazed vase, designed by Belle Kogan, the base impressed "Red Wing B1426".

8.25in (20.5cm) high

$150-200   **ANT**

A Red Wing baluster vase, with turquoise crackle glazed exterior and silver lustre glazed interior, the base marked "Red Wing U.S.A. 1300".

10in (25.5cm) high

$150-200   **ANT**

CERAMICS

A Red Wing vase, with horizontal molded banding leading to six 'handles', the exterior glazed in burgundy, the interior glazed in light blue, the base impressed "1359 Red Wing U.S.A."

The teacup-shaped handles on this vase have led it to be known as the 'teacup vase'.

7.75in (19.5cm) high

$150-200   **ANT**

A 1950s Red Wing waisted vase, designed by Charles Murphy, with molded swirling decoration forming a handle on each side, the exterior glazed in a brown speckled light blue glaze, the interior glazed in yellow, the base impressed "Red Wing U.S.A. M-1460".

9.25in (23.5cm) high

$200-300   **ANT**

EXPERT EYE – A RED WING VASE

The body is molded in low relief with lions. The colors of the glaze allude to the natural environment.

It was produced for a limited period from 1926 to 1929, so is comparatively scarce.

A late 1950s Red Wing footed bowl, designed by Charles Murphy, with a mottled turquoise glaze, the base impressed "M-1504".

8in (20cm) high

$80-120   **ANT**

This mottled and graduated glaze is complex and visually appealing, being comprised of a matte green dripped over a bronzed red.

It was also produced in other glazes. Those with simpler glazes are generally less desirable and can be worth at least 25 per cent less.

A Red Wing vase, covered with a mottled, dripped green glaze over a bronzey-red glaze, the base impressed "164".

7in (18cm) high

$700-1,300   **ANT**

A late 1950s Red Wing 'Bob White' pitcher.

Designed by Charles Murphy, 'Bob White' was produced from 1956-67 and became the company's best selling product at the time. It mushroomed in popularity after a coffee cup from the range featured as a prop in Playboy's February 1956 centerfold.

12.25in (31cm) high

$30-35   **AEM**

A 1950s-60s Red Wing yellow pear-shaped covered dish.

6in (15cm) long

$12-18   **AEM**

A Red Wing 'Smart Set' dinner plate, designed by Charles Murphy in 1955, with hand-painted yellow and black rectangular and square design, the base impressed "Red Wing USA".

10.75in (2.5cm) diam

$15-25   **HLM**

ESSENTIAL REFERENCE

- The Rookwood Pottery was founded in Cincinnati, Ohio, in 1880 by wealthy heiress Maria Longworth Nichols as decorating ceramics was seen as a virtuous hobby for women. Although the pottery initially lost money, the arrival of manager William Watts Tyler in 1883 turned the company's fortunes around. In 1890, Tyler took the then profitable pottery over, with Nichols remarrying and leaving.
- The pieces were thrown and decorated by hand. Taking into account the well-proportioned and balanced shapes used, the real interest in Rookwood lies in its many different glazes and patterns that were developed from the mid-1880s onwards. The first glaze is known as Standard and is typified by a graduated brown background usually painted with flower designs – portraits are rare.
- Glaze technicians were employed to reproduce ancient techniques and glaze effects, or develop new ones. Japanese ceramics were a major inspiration. The clear, glossy Iris glazes were introduced in 1894, but experimentation dated back to 1889. The green-tinted Sea Green glaze was introduced at the same time, with Vellum being launched in 1900 and Matte glazes following in 1901.
- The company also employed a number of highly skilled decorators and it is their work that has become the most collectible today, particularly early examples or large pieces with finely executed designs. As glazes are so important, crazing (a fine network of lines) tends to reduce value considerably, as does any damage that detracts from the glaze or design.
- The company's more mass produced Production wares, introduced in 1905, were not artist-signed and tend to be worth less, often under $200. Look for shapes and colors that represent the company's design ethics. The stock market crash of 1929 and the resultant Great Depression saw the pottery begin to decline, as demand for art pottery fell. Although it changed hands and revivals were attempted, the company closed in 1960.

A Rookwood Standard Glaze vase, decorated by L.A. Fry with a curving branch with yellow flowers, the base inscribed with an LF monogram, and impressed "216 Rookwood 1885".

This impressed Rookwood mark was used from 1882 to 1886, when the more commonly seen 'RP' monogram began to be used. A single 'flame' motif was added around the monogram for each year from 1887 to 1900, after that a Roman numeral was used to indicate the year. In 1884, Laura Fry introduced the use of an atomiser to the pottery, which meant that colors could be sprayed on, giving a subtle graduated effect.

12in (30.5cm) high

$2,200-2,600   **ANT**

A Rookwood Standard Glaze bottle-shaped vase, by an unidentified artist, painted with yellow roses, minimal crazing, with inscribed flame mark and "463C W".

1891   *12in (30.5cm) high*

$650-750   **DRA**

A Rookwood Standard Glaze swirling bulbous vase, painted by A.R. Valentien with violets and encased in a Sterling silver basket weave, with inscribed flame mark and "653 W A.R.V. Sterling", break to one silver strand at rim.

1893   *11.75in (30cm) high*

$1,500-2,000   **DRA**

A Rookwood Iris Glaze vase, painted by Laura Lindeman with mistletoe, with inscribed flame mark and "IV 741C LEL", restoration to rim.

1903-04   *5.75in (14.5cm) high*

$800-1,000   **DRA**

A Rookwood Scenic Vellum ovoid vase, painted by Lenore Asbury, drill hole to base obscures date, with inscribed flame mark and "L.A."

Most Vellum glazed wares have landscapes, although floral patterns and other motifs were used. Banded Scenic Vellum vases are typically less desirable – most obviously as they have a smaller amount of decoration.

c1915   9.25in (23.5cm) high

$1,000-1,500   **DRA**

A Rookwood Scenic Vellum vase, painted by Fred Rothenbusch with a mountainous landscape, with inscribed flame mark and "XXIV 1664D FR", uncrazed and undamaged.

1924   11in (28cm) high

$1,000-1,500   **DRA**

A Rookwood Vellum vase, painted by Kate Curry with a band of blue birds in flight on a pink and sand ground, with an inscribed flame mark and "XVIII 1044", artist's cipher and "X" seconded mark for glaze scaling at base.

1918   8.5in (21.5cm) high

$750-850   **DRA**

A Rookwood Jewel Porcelain vase, painted by Kataro Shirayamadani with crocuses, with inscribed flame mark "XXV 2831" and a Japanese cipher.

Japanese-born Kataro Shirayamadani (1865-1948) was perhaps Rookwood's most notable decorator, and worked for the company from 1887 until 1948. In 1991, a Sea Green vase decorated by him in 1900 sold for $198,000. This was followed in 2004 by a black Iris glaze vase with electroplated mounts that sold for a staggering $350,750.

1925   5.5in (14cm) high

$1,800-2,200   **DRA**

A Rookwood Jewel Porcelain two-handled vase, painted by Lorinda Epply with sprays of flowers, with inscribed flame mark and "XXVII 2077 LE".

1927   6in (15cm) high

$1,000-1,500   **DRA**

A Rookwood small cameo ewer, painted by an unidentified artist with a white rose, with inscribed flame mark and "40W S R", overfired around foot.

1888   6.25in (16cm) high

$350-450   **DRA**

FIND OUT MORE...

'Miller's How To Compare & Value American Art Pottery', by David Rago & Suzanne Perrault, published by Miller's, 2001.

ESSENTIAL REFERENCE

- The Roseville Pottery Company began producing stoneware in 1890, in Roseville in the 'pottery state' of Ohio. It initially produced utilitarian wares such as flowerpots, cuspidors (spittoons) and umbrella stands. As business grew, more factories were acquired and, by 1910, production was focused in the 'clay city' of Zanesville.
- Rozane, the company's first art pottery range, was designed by Ross C. Purdy in 1900 and mimicked Rookwood's successful Standard Glaze, as well as those Rookwood inspired like Weller's Louwelsa. Further successful hand-decorated art pottery ranges followed. However, by 1908, the demand for such expensive wares had declined and Roseville abandoned all but one hand-decorated range. The pottery adapted quickly, fitting a tunnel kiln to allow for less expensive mass-produced molded wares.
- Frederick Rhead designed for the company from 1904 to 1908, introducing some of its most sought-after ranges, such as Della Robbia, and the squeeze-bag technique. Many later wares were designed by Frank Ferrell, who produced designs and shapes from 1917 to 1954, and

George Krause, who worked on glazes from 1915 to 1954.
- Molded designs were typically based around flowers and natural motifs. The quality of the molding counts considerably towards value – it should be clear and crisp. Similarly, the glazes should be well and correctly applied. Dull or unintentionally pale, sloppily applied glazes are less desirable. The color of the glaze in a range can also affect value – blue is often more desirable than brown.
- Values also depend on the range itself. Common, later ranges from the 1940s, such as Bittersweet, tend to be less desirable. Although also easily found, the earlier Pinecone and Dahlrose are widely collected and desirable. Ranges that follow popular period styles, such as L'Art Nouveau and the Art Deco style Futura, are also consistently popular.
- Condition is also of paramount importance. Chips and cracks can devalue a piece by at least 50 per cent. Also beware of fakes and reproductions. Compare unusual glazes against color photographs in a book and always carefully examine marks on the base.
- The plant closed in 1954.

A Roseville pink 'Apple Blossom' pattern vase, the base marked "Roseville USA 382-7".

7.25in (18.5cm) high

$120-180   **BEL**

A Roseville pink 'Apple Blossom' pattern ewer, the base marked "Roseville USA 316-8".

8.25in (21cm) high

$120-180   **BEL**

A Roseville pink 'Apple Blossom' pattern bowl, the bowl marked "Roseville USA 326-6".

8in (20cm) wide

$60-80   **BEL**

A Roseville pink 'Apple Blossom' pattern basket, the base marked "Roseville USA 309-8".

Examine handles carefully, as they are frequently broken. Apple Blossom was introduced in 1949 in blue, pink or green and is relatively common.

8.5in (20.5cm) high

$200-250   **BEL**

A Roseville green 'Apple Blossom' pattern jardinière, the base marked "Roseville USA 300-4".

4in (10cm) high

$100-150   **BEL**

A Roseville blue 'Apple Blossom' pattern jardinière and pedestal set, both marked, very minor nick to each piece.

$450-550   **DRA**

A Roseville 'Blackberry' pattern vase, shape no. 570-5", unmarked.

Blackberry was introduced in 1933, and is highly sought-after, particularly in large, well-executed forms. Pieces tend to be labeled or unmarked.

5in (12.5cm) high

$300-400   BEL

A Roseville 'Blackberry' pattern double-handled vase, shape no. 577-10", well-glazed and molded, the base with light remnants of red crayon markings and a paper label.

10.25in (26cm) high

$850-950   BEL

A Roseville 'Blackberry' pattern double-handled vase, shape no. 578-12", with good color and mold, marked with a partial black paper label and "578" in red crayon covered by part of an old retail label.

This was the largest vase made in the Blackberry series. This is a particularly bold example.

12.25in (31cm) high

$1,200-1,800   BEL

MILLER'S COMPARES – TWO 'BLACKBERRY' PATTERN JARDINIÈRES

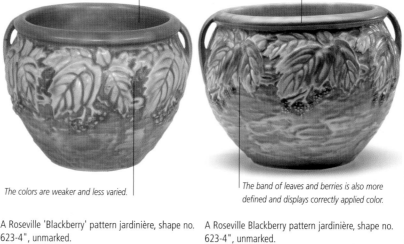

These are both the same shape, but this example is smaller in size than the other.

This example is more crisply and finely molded. This can be particularly seen by comparing the level of detail on the base.

The colors are weaker and less varied.

The band of leaves and berries is also more defined and displays correctly applied color.

A Roseville 'Blackberry' pattern jardinière, shape no. 623-4", unmarked.

8in (20.5cm) high

$280-320   BEL

A Roseville Blackberry pattern jardinière, shape no. 623-4", unmarked.

9.5in (24cm) high

$600-700   DRA

A Roseville 'Blackberry' pattern jardinière and pedestal set, with excellent mold and color, unmarked, nick to one berry, faint spiderlines to base of jardinière.

29in (73.5cm) high

$2,000-3,000   DRA

A Roseville 'Blackberry' pattern low bowl, shape no. 226-6", the base marked "226" in red crayon.

8in (20cm) high

$220-280   BEL

CERAMICS

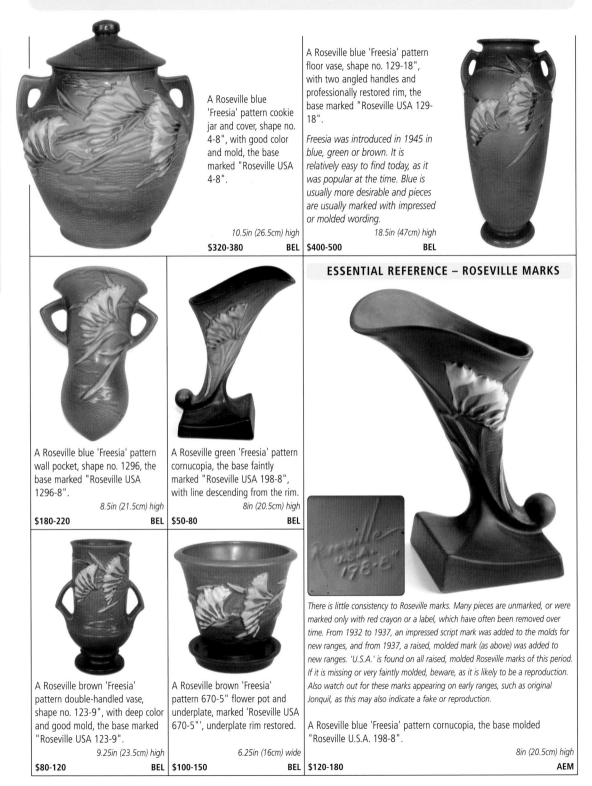

A Roseville blue 'Freesia' pattern cookie jar and cover, shape no. 4-8", with good color and mold, the base marked "Roseville USA 4-8".

10.5in (26.5cm) high

$320-380   **BEL**

A Roseville blue 'Freesia' pattern floor vase, shape no. 129-18", with two angled handles and professionally restored rim, the base marked "Roseville USA 129-18".

Freesia was introduced in 1945 in blue, green or brown. It is relatively easy to find today, as it was popular at the time. Blue is usually more desirable and pieces are usually marked with impressed or molded wording.

18.5in (47cm) high

$400-500   **BEL**

A Roseville blue 'Freesia' pattern wall pocket, shape no. 1296, the base marked "Roseville USA 1296-8".

8.5in (21.5cm) high

$180-220   **BEL**

A Roseville green 'Freesia' pattern cornucopia, the base faintly marked "Roseville USA 198-8", with line descending from the rim.

8in (20.5cm) high

$50-80   **BEL**

ESSENTIAL REFERENCE – ROSEVILLE MARKS

There is little consistency to Roseville marks. Many pieces are unmarked, or were marked only with red crayon or a label, which have often been removed over time. From 1932 to 1937, an impressed script mark was added to the molds for new ranges, and from 1937, a raised, molded mark (as above) was added to new ranges. 'U.S.A.' is found on all raised, molded Roseville marks of this period. If it is missing or very faintly molded, beware, as it is likely to be a reproduction. Also watch out for these marks appearing on early ranges, such as original Jonquil, as this may also indicate a fake or reproduction.

A Roseville blue 'Freesia' pattern cornucopia, the base molded "Roseville U.S.A. 198-8".

8in (20.5cm) high

$120-180   **AEM**

A Roseville brown 'Freesia' pattern double-handled vase, shape no. 123-9", with deep color and good mold, the base marked "Roseville USA 123-9".

9.25in (23.5cm) high

$80-120   **BEL**

A Roseville brown 'Freesia' pattern 670-5" flower pot and underplate, marked 'Roseville USA 670-5"', underplate rim restored.

6.25in (16cm) wide

$100-150   **BEL**

A Roseville 'Futura' pattern flared footed vase, with green stepped base and buttresses, unmarked, with three tight lines from rim, and a small nick to base.

12.25in (21cm) high

$1,000-1,500   **DRA**

A Roseville 'Futura' pattern cylinder vase, shape no. 381, with orange and green glazes, unmarked.

6.25in (16cm) high

$300-400   **BEL**

EXPERT EYE – A 'FUTURA' PATTERN VASE

This is a rare shape, and is also large in size. However, it is cracked, which reduces the value.

The green leaf design near the rim recalls Roseville's traditional patterning, but here they are highly stylized in line with the Art Deco style.

The form is typical of the Art Deco period, with its clean lines based on geometric shapes.

The stepped base is another typical feature of the Art Deco style.

A Roseville 'Futura' bulbous vase, with stepped neck, covered in a turquoise glaze with charcoaling near base and paper label.

12.5in (32cm) high

$800-1,200   **DRA**

A Roseville 'Futura' vase, with stepped neck, decorated with a leaf-like design, unmarked, touch-ups to rim and base.

6in (16cm) high

$350-450   **DRA**

A Roseville pink 'Futura' pattern range four-sided vase, shape no. 399-7", with chevron design in green, unmarked.

Futura was introduced in 1928 and is usually labeled or marked with a red crayon only.

6in (16cm) high

$550-650   **DRA**

A Roseville 'Futura' pattern tall vase, with flaring neck, on stepped base, unmarked, tight opposing lines to rim.

12.25in (31cm) high

$1,200-1,800   **DRA**

A Roseville 'Futura' pattern jardinière, shape no. 616, with a tiny glaze flake and some glaze pops to the rim, unmarked.

9in (23cm) diam

$150-200   **BEL**

CERAMICS

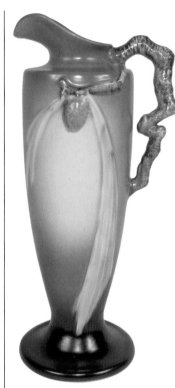

A Roseville blue 'Pine Cone' pattern ewer, shape no. 851, with branch handle and deep cobalt blue tones, two small glaze flakes to rim, the base marked "Roseville 851-15".

Designed by Frank Ferrell and rejected by other potteries, 'Pine Cone' was introduced by Roseville in 1935 and went on to become a best seller. It can be found in blue, brown or green, but blue tends to be the most desirable. Pink is extremely rare. Pieces with molded, raised marks date from after 1939.

15.5in (39.5cm) high

$700-800   BEL

A Roseville blue 'Pine Cone' pattern double-handled vase, shape no. 747-10", the base marked "Roseville 747-10", with one restored handle.

10.5in (26.5cm) high

$180-220   BEL

A Roseville blue 'Pine Cone' pattern bowl, shape no. 278, with professionally restored rim and chip to twig.

The deep and varied blue tones are particularly appealing, as is the dramatically curving pattern on this form.

7in (18cm) diam

$150-200   BEL

A Roseville blue 'Pine Cone' pattern fan vase, shape no. 472, the base marked "Roseville USA 472-6".

This is a well-molded example of an unusual and dramatic form.

6.5in (16.5cm) high

$300-400   BEL

A Roseville blue 'Pine Cone' pattern bowl, shape no. 322, the base marked "Roseville 322-12", with restored handle.

14in (35.5cm) wide

$100-150   BEL

A Roseville brown 'Pine Cone' pattern bowl, shape no. 279, the base marked "Roseville 279-9", in near mint condition with scratches to interior.

10.5in (26.5cm) long

$150-200   BEL

A Roseville brown 'Pine Cone' pattern vase, shape no. 704, with restored rim interior, the base marked "Roseville 704-7".

7.25in (18.5cm) high

$100-150   BEL

A Roseville brown 'Pine Cone' pattern cornucopia vase, shape no. 126, the base marked "Roseville USA 126-6".

6in (15cm) high

$120-180   BEL

A Roseville 'Sunflower' pattern vase, shape no. 566-4", with double loop handles, unmarked.

Sunflower was introduced in 1930 and pieces sometimes bear a paper label, but is otherwise unmarked. It can be hard to find, particularly in large sizes, and is one of the company's most popular ranges among collectors.

4in (10cm) high

$400-500   **BEL**

A Roseville 'Sunflower' pattern vase, shape no. 566-4", with two loop handles, unmarked.

4in (10cm) high

$450-550   **BEL**

A Roseville 'Sunflower' pattern rose bowl, shape no. 213-4", unmarked.

4in (10cm) high

$350-450   **BEL**

A Roseville 'Sunflower' pattern vase, shape no. 514, with two tiny side handles, with two tiny chips to the rim, unmarked.

6in (15cm) high

$350-450   **BEL**

A Roseville 'Sunflower' pattern double-handled vase, shape no. 512, with well-molded details and good color, unmarked.

5in (13cm) high

$400-500   **BEL**

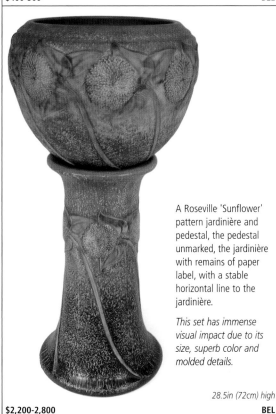

A Roseville 'Sunflower' pattern jardinière and pedestal, the pedestal unmarked, the jardinière with remains of paper label, with a stable horizontal line to the jardinière.

This set has immense visual impact due to its size, superb color and molded details.

28.5in (72cm) high

$2,200-2,800   **BEL**

A Roseville 'Sunflower' pattern wall pocket, unmarked.

7.25in (18cm) high

$850-950   **DRA**

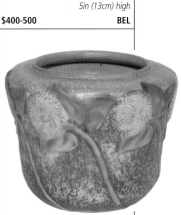

A Roseville 'Sunflower' pattern vase, shape no. 486-5", with very good mold and color, unmarked.

5in (12.5cm) high

$550-650   **BEL**

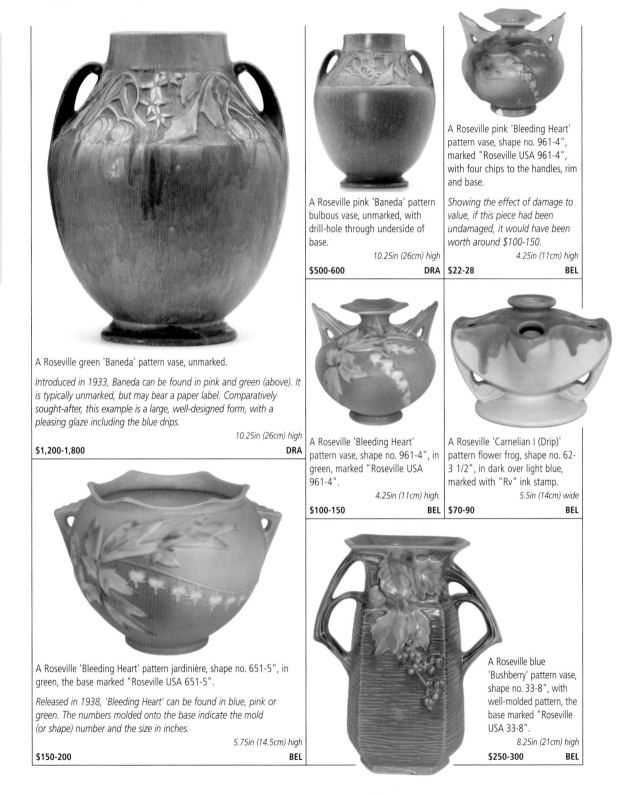

A Roseville green 'Baneda' pattern vase, unmarked.

Introduced in 1933, Baneda can be found in pink and green (above). It is typically unmarked, but may bear a paper label. Comparatively sought-after, this example is a large, well-designed form, with a pleasing glaze including the blue drips.

10.25in (26cm) high

$1,200-1,800   DRA

A Roseville 'Bleeding Heart' pattern jardinière, shape no. 651-5", in green, the base marked "Roseville USA 651-5".

Released in 1938, 'Bleeding Heart' can be found in blue, pink or green. The numbers molded onto the base indicate the mold (or shape) number and the size in inches.

5.75in (14.5cm) high

$150-200   BEL

A Roseville pink 'Baneda' pattern bulbous vase, unmarked, with drill-hole through underside of base.

10.25in (26cm) high

$500-600   DRA

A Roseville 'Bleeding Heart' pattern vase, shape no. 961-4", in green, marked "Roseville USA 961-4".

4.25in (11cm) high.

$100-150   BEL

A Roseville pink 'Bleeding Heart' pattern vase, shape no. 961-4", marked "Roseville USA 961-4", with four chips to the handles, rim and base.

Showing the effect of damage to value, if this piece had been undamaged, it would have been worth around $100-150.

4.25in (11cm) high

$22-28   BEL

A Roseville 'Carnelian I (Drip)' pattern flower frog, shape no. 62-3 1/2", in dark over light blue, marked with "Rv" ink stamp.

5.5in (14cm) wide

$70-90   BEL

A Roseville blue 'Bushberry' pattern vase, shape no. 33-8", with well-molded pattern, the base marked "Roseville USA 33-8".

8.25in (21cm) high

$250-300   BEL

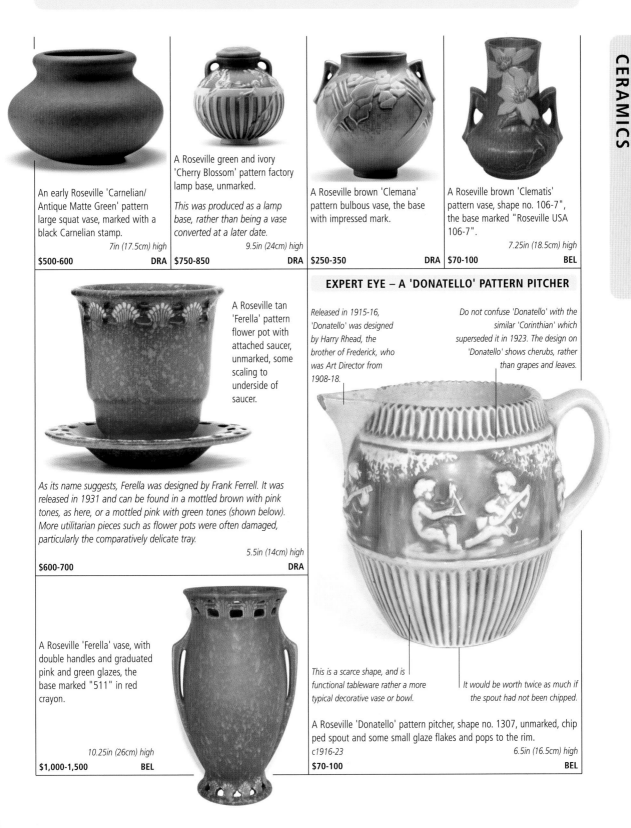

An early Roseville 'Carnelian/ Antique Matte Green' pattern large squat vase, marked with a black Carnelian stamp.

7in (17.5cm) high

$500-600 DRA

A Roseville green and ivory 'Cherry Blossom' pattern factory lamp base, unmarked.

This was produced as a lamp base, rather than being a vase converted at a later date.

9.5in (24cm) high

$750-850 DRA

A Roseville brown 'Clemana' pattern bulbous vase, the base with impressed mark.

$250-350 DRA

A Roseville brown 'Clematis' pattern vase, shape no. 106-7", the base marked "Roseville USA 106-7".

7.25in (18.5cm) high

$70-100 BEL

A Roseville tan 'Ferella' pattern flower pot with attached saucer, unmarked, some scaling to underside of saucer.

As its name suggests, Ferella was designed by Frank Ferrell. It was released in 1931 and can be found in a mottled brown with pink tones, as here, or a mottled pink with green tones (shown below). More utilitarian pieces such as flower pots were often damaged, particularly the comparatively delicate tray.

5.5in (14cm) high

$600-700 DRA

EXPERT EYE – A 'DONATELLO' PATTERN PITCHER

Released in 1915-16, 'Donatello' was designed by Harry Rhead, the brother of Frederick, who was Art Director from 1908-18.

Do not confuse 'Donatello' with the similar 'Corinthian' which superseded it in 1923. The design on 'Donatello' shows cherubs, rather than grapes and leaves.

This is a scarce shape, and is functional tableware rather a more typical decorative vase or bowl.

It would be worth twice as much if the spout had not been chipped.

A Roseville 'Donatello' pattern pitcher, shape no. 1307, unmarked, chipped spout and some small glaze flakes and pops to the rim.

c1916-23

6.5in (16.5cm) high

$70-100 BEL

A Roseville 'Ferella' vase, with double handles and graduated pink and green glazes, the base marked "511" in red crayon.

10.25in (26cm) high

$1,000-1,500 BEL

CERAMICS

A Roseville pink 'Foxglove' pattern handled vase, shape no. 162-8", the base marked "Roseville USA 162-8".

8.25in (21cm) high

$120-180　　　　　BEL

A Roseville pink 'Foxglove' pattern jardinière, shape no. 659-3", the base marked "Roseville USA 659-3".

4.75in (12cm) wide

$50-70　　　　　BEL

A Roseville blue 'Foxglove' pattern rose bowl, shape no. 418-6", the base marked "Roseville USA 418-6".

Foxglove was released in 1942 and can be found in pink, blue and green. Bases bear the raised molded Roseville mark. It is one of the least stylized of Roseville's floral patterns.

6.5in (16.5cm) high

$120-180　　　　　BEL

A Roseville pink and green 'Foxglove' pattern handled bowl, the base marked "Roseville USA 425-14".

As well as being large, this example has sharp molding and superb colors.

17in (43cm) long

$100-150　　　　　BEL

A Roseville pink 'Foxglove' pattern console bowl, shape no. 425-14", with a very good molded features, the base marked "Roseville USA 425-14".

16.75in (42.5cm) wide

$100-150　　　　　BEL

A Roseville green 'Fuchsia' pattern low handled bowl, shape no. 348-5", the base marked "Roseville 348-5".

8.5in (20.5cm) wide

$100-150　　　　　BEL

ESSENTIAL REFERENCE – FUSCHIA PATTERN

Fuchsia was introduced in 1938 in a wide variety of tones based around three colors typical for Roseville; brown, blue and green. As well as being found in different tones, these colors may also be combined with a variety of other colors. Usually bearing impressed marks on the base, it is a comparatively popular range due to its wide appeal. Beware of examples with white, pink or beige leaves on brown or green as these are fakes. This particular vase ticks a number of boxes; it is unusually large, the form is balanced, the handles are not damaged, the molding is excellent, and the vibrant color is striking. A similar example sold at the same location the previous year for over $3,000.

A Roseville blue 'Fuchsia' pattern floor vase, shape no. 905-18", with two handles, the base marked "Roseville 905-18".

18.75in (47.5cm) high

$1,200-1,800　　BEL

A Roseville green 'Fuchsia' pattern double-handled vase, shape no. 892-6", the base marked "Roseville 892-6".

6.25in (16cm) high

$180-220　　　　　BEL

A Roseville blue 'Iris' pattern handled vase, shape no. 927-10", the base faintly marked "Roseville 927-10", with restored rim and handle.

10.5in (26.5cm) high

$150-200   BEL

A Roseville red 'Laurel' pattern vase, shape no. 671-7 1/4", unmarked.

'Laurel' was introduced in 1934, and its unusual combination of Art Deco forms and lines with the curving mistletoe sprigs make it popular. It was produced in red (shown here), green and yellow and pieces are unmarked, although may bear paper labels. Shapes typical of the Art Deco style are desirable.

7.25in (18.5cm) high

$350-450   BEL

A Roseville red 'Laurel' pattern vase, shape no. 667-6", with partial foil label.

6.25in (16cm) high

$250-350   BEL

A Roseville red 'Laurel' pattern vase, shape no. 669-7 1/2", unmarked, shallow chip at the base with a bruise.

6.75in (17cm) high

$220-280   BEL

A Roseville red 'Laurel' pattern vase, shape no. 670-7 1/4", unmarked.

7.25in (18.5cm) high

$400-500   BEL

A Roseville blue 'Magnolia' pattern handled vase, shape no. 98, the base marked "Roseville USA 98-15".

Magnolia was introduced in 1940 in blue, green or brown, and bears molded marks including the shape number and size on the base. Typical of Roseville, and much loved in its day, it is comparatively easy to find today.

15.25in (39cm) high

$450-550   BEL

A Roseville blue 'Magnolia' pattern lidded cookie jar, shape no. 2-8", the base marked "Roseville USA 2-8", the base and lid repaired.

10.5in (26.5cm) high

$280-320   BEL

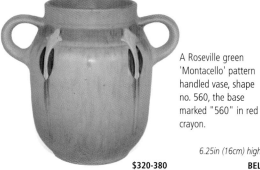

A Roseville green 'Montacello' pattern handled vase, shape no. 560, the base marked "560" in red crayon.

6.25in (16cm) high

$320-380   BEL

CERAMICS

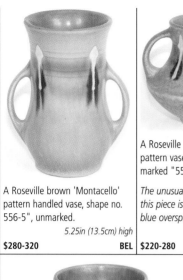

A Roseville brown 'Montacello' pattern handled vase, shape no. 556-5", unmarked.

5.25in (13.5cm) high

$280-320   **BEL**

A Roseville brown 'Montacello' pattern vase, shape no. 555-4", marked "555" in red crayon.

The unusually strong mottling on this piece is the result of a light blue overspray.

4.25in (11cm) high

$220-280   **BEL**

A Roseville green 'Morning Glory' pattern double-wall pocket, unmarked, with small nick to outer edge of rim, and chip to inner rim.

Introduced in 1935, this organic design is found with white or green backgrounds. The tones of the flowers can vary in strength.

8.5in (22cm) long

$500-600   **DRA**

A Roseville brown 'Montacello' pattern vase, shape no. 560-6", with two loop handles, unmarked.

Introduced in 1931, Montacello can be found in mottled and graduated blue, green or brown. The white motif on the band can vary from a stylized fleur-de-lys to an arrowhead form, painted over a black oval. Pieces are unmarked, but may have labels.

6.25in (16cm) high

$350-450   **BEL**

A Roseville blue 'Moss' pattern vase, shape no. 777-7", the base faintly marked "Roseville 777-7", with restored chip at base.

Moss was introduced in 1936, with its design reflecting the hanging moss draped trees of the Bayou and Southern states. Background colors vary and include a graduated green and pink, a graduated blue and cream, and a graduated green and yellow. Marks are typically impressed.

7.5in (19cm) high

$150-200   **BEL**

A Roseville green 'Panel' pattern vase, with purple flowers, the base marked with "Rv" ink stamp.

6.25in (16cm) high

$250-350   **BEL**

One of a pair of Roseville pink and sea green 'Moss' pattern candle-holders, shape no. 1109-2", the bases marked "Roseville 1109", one with restored base.

2in (5cm) high

$100-150 (pair)   **BEL**

A Roseville pink and green 'Moss' pattern vase, shape no. 773-5", with good mold, original Roseville Pottery foil label, the base marked "Roseville 773-5".

5.25in (13.5cm) high

$150-200   **BEL**

A Roseville green 'Panel' pattern flaring two-handled vase, the base with "Rv "ink mark, restoration to lines through body.

11.5in (29cm) high

$500-600   **DRA**

A Roseville pink 'Snowberry' pattern floor vase, shape no. 1V-18", the base marked "Roseville USA 1V-18", with small glaze nick.

The color on this example is particularly strong.

18.5in (47cm) high

$350-450   **BEL**

A Roseville pink 'Snowberry' pattern wall pocket, shape no. 1WP-8", the base marked "Roseville USA 1WP-8".

5.25in (13.5cm) high

$200-250   **BEL**

A Roseville blue 'Thornapple' pattern vase, marked "811-6".

6.25in (16cm) high

$120-180   **BEL**

An early Roseville 'Velmoss' pattern spherical vase, with flared rim, unmarked.

10in (25.5cm) high

$1,000-1,500   **CRA**

An early Roseville 'Velmoss' pattern bulbous vase, embossed with leaves, unmarked.

8in (20cm) high

$600-700   **DRA**

A Roseville 'Vista' pattern tall vase, unmarked, tight bruise to rim.

17.5in (44.5cm) high

$700-900   **DRA**

An early Roseville 'Velmoss' pattern jardinière, unmarked and with chip to inner rim.

13.25in (33.5cm) wide

$800-1,000   **DRA**

CERAMICS

A Roseville blue 'White Rose' pattern handled vase, shape no. 982-7", marked "Roseville USA 982-7".

7.25in (18.5cm) high

$100-150   BEL

A Roseville 'Windsor' pattern double-handled vase, shape no. 546-6", in brown with green geometric decoration around the rim, unmarked.

6.25in (16cm) high

$280-320   BEL

A Roseville blue 'Windsor' pattern bulbous vase, with yellow and green geometric rectangular design around rim, paper label, minor scaling to base edge.

6.25in (16cm) high

$500-600   DRA

A Roseville brown 'Wisteria' pattern vase, shape no. 630-6", most of the original foil label intact on the base.

6.25in (16cm) high

$350-450   BEL

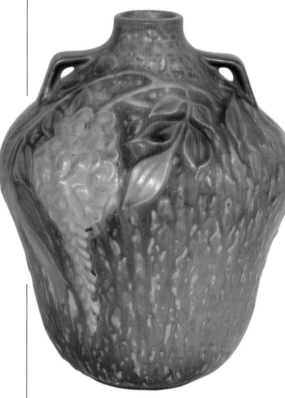

A Roseville brown 'Wisteria' pattern bowl, shape no. 243-5", unmarked.

12in (30.5cm) wide

$220-280   BEL

A Roseville blue 'Zephyr Lily' pattern hanging basket, shape no. 472, marked "USA" on the rim, and with firing flaw to rim.

7.5in (18cm) wide

$100-150   BEL

An unusual Roseville factory lamp base, with branches of yellow blossoms on a brown ground, unmarked.

8in (20cm) high

$700-800   DRA

A Roseville blue 'Wisteria' pattern vase, shape no. 636-8", with good mold and color, marked with original Roseville Pottery foil label, a few minor skips to the color and glaze.

8.25in (21cm) high

$800-1,200   BEL

FIND OUT MORE...

'Collectors' Encyclopaedia of Roseville Pottery', *by Sharon & Bob Huxford and Mike Nickel, published by Collector Books, 2001.*

'Warman's Roseville Pottery & Price Guide', *by Mark Moran, published by Krause Publications, 2004.*

ESSENTIAL REFERENCE

- Royal Copenhagen was founded in 1775 by Heinrich Frank Müller, under the royal patronage of Queen Julianne Marie of Denmark. Müller had devoted years of research into unlocking the secrets of hard paste porcelain, which was known only to a small number of European ceramics factories.
- Its first range, Blue Fluted, is still among its most popular today, but many collectors tend to focus on its 1920s to '30s, and post-WWII decorative porcelain and stoneware. Nils Thorsson was one its longest serving and most prolific designers, and other important names include Arnold Krog, Knud Kyhn, Axel Salto, and Johanne Gerber.
- Forms tend to be functional and Modernist, contrasting against the hand-painted patterns that were typically inspired by the natural environment. Colors, such as beiges, browns, and greens predominate, and patterns take the form of stylized leaves, sheaves and flowers. Abstract and surreal figural motifs were also used, often in less natural colors such as purple and blue.
- Marks on the bases can help you to find out more, including the range, the name of the designer and the decorator, whose monogram is hand-painted alongside the factory marks. Dates can often be identified by looking for a short line underneath a letter in the name 'Royal Copenhagen' and then consulting a reference table that allots a different year for each letter. Alumina marks often appear as the company acquired Royal Copenhagen in 1882.

A Royal Copenhagen Baca Fajance bottle vase, no. 704/3259, designed by Nils Thorsson, with blue on brown wax-resist design, and printed and painted marks to base.

9in (23cm) high

$140-180   **UCT**

A Royal Copenhagen Baca Fajance bottle base, no. 712/3259, designed by Nils Thorsson, with printed and painted marks to base.

9in (23cm) high

$140-180   **UCT**

A Royal Copenhagen Baca Fajance bottle vase, no. 711/3455, designed by Nils Thorsson, with printed and painted marks to base.

The monogram in the larger circular mark is that of Nils Thorsson (1898-1975), who worked at Royal Copenhagen from 1912 to 1975, becoming their chief designer in the 1950s. Collectors often call it the 'chop mark'.

7.75in (19.5cm) high

$100-150   **UCT**

A Royal Copenhagen Baca Fajance oval-section tall vase, no. 1780/3101, designed by Johanne Gerber, the base with printed and painted marks.

The mark on the base is very lightly scored through three times by a sharp knife, indicating this is a second. The more strikes through the mark, the more faults the piece contains. Despite being a second, the value is in the large size.

14.25in (36cm) high

$300-450   **UCT**

A Royal Worcester bottle vase, shape no. 2491, painted and signed by Harry Stinton, with Highland cattle, gilt rim, the base with printed crown and circle mark in puce, date code for 1915.

1915

$600-800   **NEA**

A Royal Worcester blush ground twin-handled vase, shape no. 2337, decorated by William Hale, with floral spray decoration, signed "W. Hale", factory printed and impressed marks, dated 1908.

1908   *12.25in (31cm) high*

$550-650   **SWO**

EXPERT EYE – A SCOTTIE WILSON PLATTER

Scottish born Scottie Wilson (1891-1972) turned to drawing late in life, at the age of 44, while running a second-hand shop in Toronto, Canada.

He is considered an 'outsider' artist, in other words an artist with no education or official training in art and who is not part of the 'art world'. The term is often applied to vagrants and the poor who survive by earning money from art.

After some success and his return to England in 1945, his art was admired and bought by famous artists including Pablo Picasso and Jean Dubuffet.

In in the 1960s, he was commissioned by Royal Worcester to produce a pattern for them to reproduce, which is shown below.

A Scottie Wilson hand-painted platter, decorated over the glaze in shades of yellow, rust and black with a panels of birds, flowers and fish within a stylized foliate frame, signed "Scottie" on the bottom right.

Despite claiming poverty throughout his life, and living very modestly, upon Wilson's death in 1972 bank accounts containing large sums of money were discovered – as was a suitcase full of money hidden under his bed.

15.5in (38.5cm) high

$600-800   **WW**

A Royal Worcester Art Nouveau twin-handled vase, with printed and impressed marks, restored.

16in (41cm) high

$250-350   **SWO**

A 1950s Royal Worcester transfer-printed 'Fiesta' pattern bone china plate.

8in (20cm) diam

$20-30   **BAD**

A Royal Worcester Crown Ware Tree of Life' pattern plate, designed by Scottie Wilson, with black transfer-printed decoration, the reverse with printed marks and facsimile signature.

8.25in (21cm) high

$150-250   **WW**

A Royal Worcester Crown Ware 'Tree of Life' pattern teapot, designed by Scottie Wilson, with black transfer-printed decoration, the reverse with printed marks and facsimile signature.

8.25in (21cm) high

$200-400   **WW**

ESSENTIAL REFERENCE

- Developments in Scandinavian ceramic design from the 1940s to '70s were influential and enduring, not only in Scandinavia, but across the rest of the world. Value mainly depends on the factory, the range and the designer. Also consider the form, size, glaze and production process. Learn how to recognise styles, key ranges and marks on the base. Currently few fakes are known but styles were often copied by other makers, often closely.
- Leading factories whose work is sought-after include Rorstrand (founded 1726), Gustavsberg (founded 1640), and Arabia (founded 1873). However, there are also a number of smaller factories that are growing in prominence as ranges by these main factories continue to rise in value. These include Stavangerflint (1949-79), Palshus (1949-72), and Upsala Ekeby (founded 1886).
- Designers to look out for include Stig Lindberg (1916-82), whose hand-decorated, brightly colored faience works produced at Gustavsberg between the 1940s and '60s were particularly influential. Marks on the base help with identification and dating. Look out for a large 'G' with a hand motif, some also bear the wording 'Stig L'. The works of Wilhelm Kåge for Gustavsberg, Gunnar Nylund for Rorstrand, and Bjørn Wiinblad are also popular.
- Designs often combined stark modernism with a feel for traditional crafts and the natural environment. Colors range from bright and strong primary colors to more subtle, earthy tones, the former often used for tableware. Tableware also tends to be more affordable than decorative wares, but was often just as influential. Also consider studio ceramics, as interest and values are rising, and each piece is unique. These can be harder to spot, so always look on the base for marks that often include the country of manufacture.

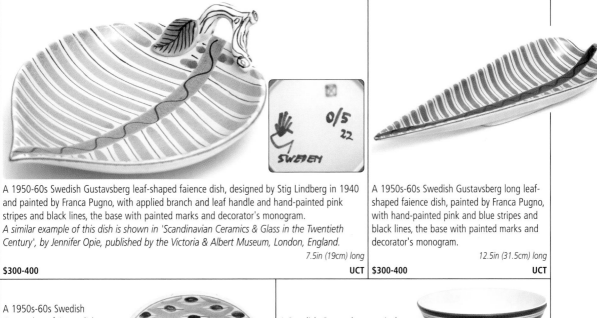

A 1950-60s Swedish Gustavsberg leaf-shaped faience dish, designed by Stig Lindberg in 1940 and painted by Franca Pugno, with applied branch and leaf handle and hand-painted pink stripes and black lines, the base with painted marks and decorator's monogram.
A similar example of this dish is shown in 'Scandinavian Ceramics & Glass in the Twentieth Century', by Jennifer Opie, published by the Victoria & Albert Museum, London, England.
7.5in (19cm) long

$300-400   **UCT**

A 1950s-60s Swedish Gustavsberg long leaf-shaped faience dish, painted by Franca Pugno, with hand-painted pink and blue stripes and black lines, the base with painted marks and decorator's monogram.
12.5in (31.5cm) long

$300-400   **UCT**

A 1950s-60s Swedish Gustavsberg faience dish, designed by Stig Lindberg and painted by Kurt Addin, with hand-painted yellow lattice design with brown dots, the base with painted marks and decorator's monogram.
5in (12.25cm) diam

$300-400   **UCT**

A Swedish Gustavsberg conical jug vase, designed by Stig Lindberg and painted by Sigrid Richter, with hand-painted blue stripes and orange lines, and applied handle, the base painted "G Sweden 159.AM.3" and with decorator's monogram.
8in (20cm) high

$350-450   **UCT**

A Swedish Gustavsberg melon-shaped vase, designed by Stig Lindberg, with pink stripes and scalloped rim.

c1940-50   8.5in (21.5cm) wide

$700-800   **GGRT**

EXPERT EYE – A GUSTAVSBERG REPTIL VASE

The molded Reptil range is sought-after by collectors and was produced from the mid-1950s to the mid-1960s.

The surface is decorated with molded scales, which gives it its name. It can be found in other colors including cobalt blue, white, yellow and a scarce olive green.

It is fully marked on the base with the Gustavsberg name and anchor mark. The label is a rare survivor.

This organic, asymmetric form is typical of the range and of Scandinavian Modernism of the time. Many shapes also have elongated necks on curving bodies.

A 1950s Swedish Gustavsberg light blue Reptil range vase, designed by Stig Lindberg, the base with impressed factory marks and foil label.

Some pieces in this range were designed by Berndt Friberg.

9in (23cm) high

$300-400   **UCT**

A Swedish Gustavsberg Domino range cylindrical vase, designed by Stig Lindberg, with brown glaze and spiralling ridges.

5.25in (13cm) high

$200-250   **UCT**

A Swedish Gustavsberg Domino range vase, designed by Stig Lindberg, with brown glaze and spiralling and chevron ridges.

5.25in (13cm) high

$240-280   **UCT**

A Swedish Gustavsberg little girl figurine, designed by Lisa Larson, with hand-painted clothes, the back with gilt foil label.

5in (12.5cm) high

$80-120   **UCT**

A Swedish Gustavsberg lion figurine, designed by Lisa Larson, with impressed and sgraffito details, the base impressed "LL".

This lion was also produced in larger sizes. Larson is better known for her popular 'Kennel' series of dog figurines.

2in (5cm) high

$80-120   **UCT**

ESSENTIAL REFERENCE – THE ARGENTA RANGE

The Argenta range of mottled jade-green glazed decorative wares embellished with silver patterns was designed by Wilhelm Kåge (1889-1960), one of the company's most notable designers. It was introduced in 1930 at the 'Stockholdsutstallingen', Stockholm's major exhibition of art and industry. Expensive to produce and buy, it was always deemed a luxury line and was sold in high-end design and department stores. Motifs are typically inspired by the natural world and are strongly stylized. Figures were also used. Small dishes and bowls are the most common shapes seen, with larger sizes and vases being more valuable. Red is a very rare variation, with blue being even rarer.

A Swedish Gustavsberg Argenta range vase, designed by Wilhelm Kåge, with silver stylized floral and foliate design, the base numbered "9780".

5.25in (13cm) high

$280-320   ANT

A Swedish Gustavsberg Argenta range tapering vase, with silver decoration of a mermaid reserved on a mottled green ground, painted and printed marks "Gustavsberg/Argenta/ 978 II".

8.25in (21cm) high

$900-1,100   L&T

A Swedish Gustavsberg Argenta range small bowl, designed by Wilhelm Kåge, with turned linear design, and silver top rim and foot rim, the base with impressed and printed mark.

The impressed name "Kåge" and the style of the other marks indicate that this is an early piece.

2.5in (6.5cm) high

$80-100   UCT

A Swedish Gustavsberg Argenta range posy vase, no. 960, designed by Wilhelm Kåge, with scalloped rim and stylized flower motifs, the base with printed marks.

2.5in (6.5cm) high

$70-90   UCT

A Swedish Gustavsberg Argenta range pin tray, no. 924, designed by Wilhelm Kåge, with floral motif and scalloped design rim, the base with gilt printed mark.

3.5in (9cm) high

$70-90   UCT

A Swedish Gustavsberg Argenta range circular dish, no. 1003I, designed by Wilhelm Kåge, with floral motif, the base with gilt printed mark.

5.25in (13cm) high

$100-150   UCT

A rare Swedish Gustavsberg red Argenta range small footed bowl, no. 1094, designed by Wilhelm Kåge, with foliate motif and scalloped design rim, the base with gilt printed mark.

3.5in (9cm) high

$100-150   UCT

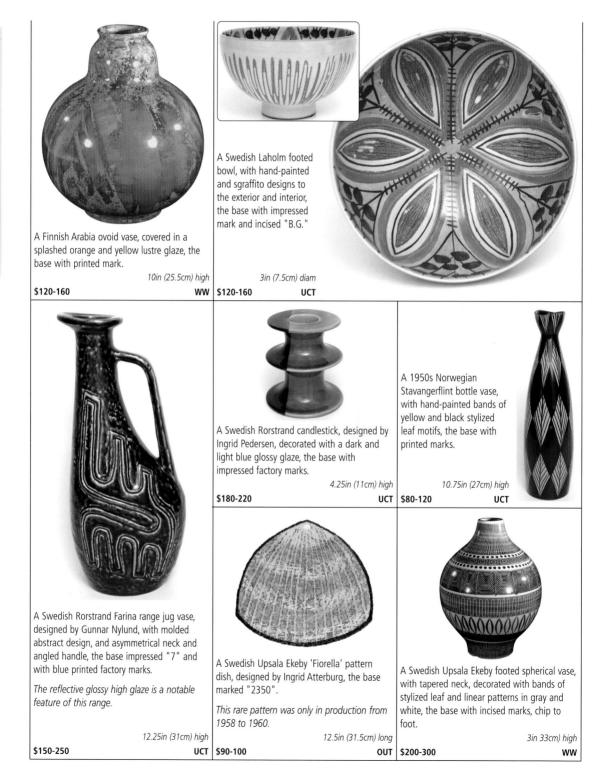

A Finnish Arabia ovoid vase, covered in a splashed orange and yellow lustre glaze, the base with printed mark.

10in (25.5cm) high

$120-160 WW

A Swedish Laholm footed bowl, with hand-painted and sgraffito designs to the exterior and interior, the base with impressed mark and incised "B.G."

3in (7.5cm) diam

$120-160 UCT

A Swedish Rorstrand candlestick, designed by Ingrid Pedersen, decorated with a dark and light blue glossy glaze, the base with impressed factory marks.

4.25in (11cm) high

$180-220 UCT

A 1950s Norwegian Stavangerflint bottle vase, with hand-painted bands of yellow and black stylized leaf motifs, the base with printed marks.

10.75in (27cm) high

$80-120 UCT

A Swedish Rorstrand Farina range jug vase, designed by Gunnar Nylund, with molded abstract design, and asymmetrical neck and angled handle, the base impressed "7" and with blue printed factory marks.

The reflective glossy high glaze is a notable feature of this range.

12.25in (31cm) high

$150-250 UCT

A Swedish Upsala Ekeby 'Fiorella' pattern dish, designed by Ingrid Atterburg, the base marked "2350".

This rare pattern was only in production from 1958 to 1960.

12.5in (31.5cm) long

$90-100 OUT

A Swedish Upsala Ekeby footed spherical vase, with tapered neck, decorated with bands of stylized leaf and linear patterns in gray and white, the base with incised marks, chip to foot.

3in 33cm) high

$200-300 WW

ESSENTIAL REFERENCE – BJØRN WIINBLAD

Bjørn Wiinblad (1918-2006) was one of the most versatile Danish artists of the 20thC, working across poster, textile, ceramic, glass and metalware design. After studying at the Royal Academy of Arts in Copenhagen he started working in ceramics with Lars Syberg, before founding his own studio in 1952. Handmade limited production studio works were made throughout his career, however, his name is more commonly associated with Nymølle and Rosenthal. He began producing transfer-printed designs for Nymølle in 1946 and bought the company in 1976 – his designs were produced until the 1990s and were exported all over the world. Wiinblad worked with Rosenthal of Germany from 1956 until he bought Nymølle, producing similar transfer-printed patterns. His instantly recognizable and characteristic designs focus on fairy tale, myth and nature, with a unique style all of his own. Mass-produced pieces such as the seasonal plaques and these plates are commonly seen. His unique hand-decorated studio works are considerably rarer and more valuable. These plates were produced in four different sizes, of which this the largest. 11in (28cm) plates may be worth around half as much. Wiinblad's recent death has increased interest from collectors.

A Danish Nymølle 'Spring' transfer-printed large charger, designed by Bjørn Wiinblad, from The Seasons series.

14.25in (36cm) diam

$150-250   GROB

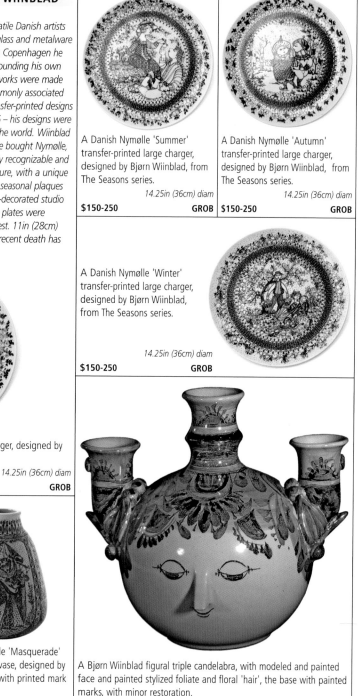

A Danish Nymølle 'Summer' transfer-printed large charger, designed by Bjørn Wiinblad, from The Seasons series.

14.25in (36cm) diam

$150-250   GROB

A Danish Nymølle 'Autumn' transfer-printed large charger, designed by Bjørn Wiinblad, from The Seasons series.

14.25in (36cm) diam

$150-250   GROB

A Danish Nymølle 'Winter' transfer-printed large charger, designed by Bjørn Wiinblad, from The Seasons series.

14.25in (36cm) diam

$150-250   GROB

A Danish Nymølle transfer-printed planter, designed by Bjørn Wiinblad.

6in (15cm) diam

$150-200   GROB

A Danish Nymølle 'Masquerade' transfer-printed vase, designed by Bjørn Wiinblad, with printed mark to base.

6.5in (16.5cm) high

$120-160   MHT

A Bjørn Wiinblad figural triple candelabra, with modeled and painted face and painted stylized foliate and floral 'hair', the base with painted marks, with minor restoration.

8.75in (22cm) high

$350-400   WW

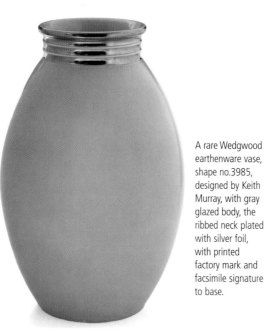

A rare Wedgwood earthenware vase, shape no.3985, designed by Keith Murray, with gray glazed body, the ribbed neck plated with silver foil, with printed factory mark and facsimile signature to base.

A Wedgwood 'Dolphin' plate, designed by Laurence Whistler, with printed and painted design including a Classical dolphin, the reverse with printed marks.

11in (27.5cm) diam

$150-200 **WW**

A Wedgwood 'Garden' pattern teapot, designed by Eric Ravilious, with transfer-printed pattern in yellow and black, the base with printed factory marks.

4in (10cm) high

$250-350 **WW**

New Zealand-born architect Murray (1892-1981) produced Modernist designs for Wedgwood during the 1930s, which were produced until the late 1960s. Even though the simple form is typical, this glossy glaze is highly unusual, as is the color. However, perhaps the most unusual feature is the silver neck, as all other designs were undecorated apart from the simple glaze and molded pattern.

12.75in (32cm) high

$3,000-4,000 **WW**

A Wedgwood Fairyland Lustre 'Leapfrogging Elves' York Cup, designed by Daisy Makeig-Jones, printed and painted in colors and gilt on a black luster ground, printed and painted marks.

4.75in (12cm) diam

$1,500-1,700 **WW**

A Wedgwood quatre-lobed teapot, cover and stand, molded with bamboo branches, impressed marks including date mark for 1870, some damages.

8in (20.5cm) high

$200-400 **WW**

EXPERT EYE – A WEDGWOOD FAIRYLAND LUSTRE BOWL

Makeig Jones (1881-1945) was heavily influenced by the illustrated fairy books she read as a child, as well as the work of illustrators such as Arthur Rackham and Edmund Dulac.

Showing elves leaping over toadstools, this was one of her more notable and popular patterns, and was designed in 1916.

Bowls are a popular form as they can be decorated inside and out, unlike vases. This interior is not decorated – this would have added considerably to the value.

Wedgwood's Fairyland Lustre inspired the later Carlton Ware luster ranges, and has grown enormously in desirability and value in recent years.

A Wedgwood Fairyland Lustre 'Leapfrogging Elves' small Empire bowl, designed by Daisy Makeig Jones, decorated in colors on a black luster ground, the base with printed factory marks.

5.25in (13cm) diam

$2,000-3,000 **WW**

ESSENTIAL REFERENCE

- Samuel Weller (1851-1925) founded his pottery in Fultonham, in the 'pottery state' of Ohio in 1872, moving to Zanesville in 1888. Initially producing utilitarian wares and crocks, his attention soon turned to the rapidly developing art pottery market. To learn how to produce complex glazed designs, he bought W.A. Long's Lonhuda Pottery in 1894.

- Within a year, Weller had learnt Long's special glazing techniques, developed by ex-Rookwood decorator Laura Fry, and the partnership was dissolved. The Lonhuda range, which featured hand-painted natural motifs on a brown glossy background, was re-launched as Louwelsa. As art pottery boomed in popularity, Weller's business grew.

- To keep the market satisfied, new, high quality hand-decorated ranges were designed and released. These included Aurelian (c1897), Eocean (1898), Dickensware (1900) and Sicardo (1902). Designers included Charles Upjohn (working 1895-1904), Jacques Sicard (1902-07), and the notable Frederick Rhead (1903-04). By 1905, Weller was the largest art pottery in the world.

- Competition became stiff, with factories copying designs and competing over price, which often meant a drop in quality. This, and a decrease in public demand for expensive art pottery during the mid-1910s, meant that most factories soon ended their hand-decorated ranges. During the 1920s, molded wares began to take over, being faster and less expensive to produce.

- Weller reacted against this by releasing the hand-painted Hudson range in 1917. However, the financial strain of the Great Depression saw even Weller move entirely to molded wares, which were still of good quality. Most were designed by Rudolph Lorber and his assistant Dorothy England Laughead. After WWII, cheap imports, a lack of innovation and a final drop in demand led to the closure of Weller in 1948.

- Today, the highest prices are reserved for the early hand-decorated lines such as Louwelsa, Eocean and Hudson. Look for large examples that are well decorated, particularly all over the surface of the body. Look for artists' signatures as these can add value. More complex molded ranges, and those by notable designers, are generally more sought-after. Damage reduces value on any example, but more so on the later molded wares. Fashion also plays a part, with the Coppertone and Art Deco styled Cretone ranges currently in vogue.

A Weller jardinière, probably Louwelsa, with a hand-painted floral design on a typical brown background, small glaze flakes at the rim and one at the base, unmarked.

8.75in (22cm) high

$120-180 BEL

A Weller Eocean jardinière, with hand-painted floral decoration, the base impressed "Weller Eocean".

11in (28cm) wide

$200-300 BEL

A Weller Sicard four-sided vase, with ruffled rim, embossed curving panel 'frames' and iridescent glazes, each panel decorated with daisies, impressed "6X".

A Weller Sicard waisted vase, with an iridescent stylized fleur-de-lys or foliate design, the base impressed "58".

6in (15cm) high

$750-950 ANT

The hand-painted Sicard line was developed in 1902 by Jacques Sicard and was produced until 1907, when Sicard left. Sicard had previously been a decorator at the French factory Clement Massier, that had developed iridescent glazes by 1889. Today, it is one of Weller's most desirable ranges. Look out for complex patterns and shapes, particularly with strong iridescence and embossing.

5in (12.5cm) high

$750-850 DRA

A Weller Golden Glow candle-holder, with three geometric arms supporting a central holder, the base marked "Weller Pottery" in script.

3.5in (9cm) high

$40-50   BEL

A Weller green Marvo fan vase, with five-sectioned opening, the base marked with Weller Pottery full kiln stamp.

8in (20cm) high

$200-300   BEL

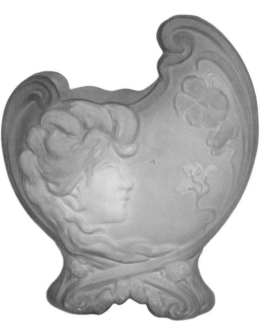

A Weller L'Art Nouveau pillow vase, molded with a long-haired beauty on the front and nautilus-style floral decoration on the reverse, decorated with pastel matte glazes, the base marked "Weller".

The original range was designed by the notable Frederick Rhead, and had glossy glazes and high-relief molded designs. Rhead worked at Weller from 1903-04.

9.75in (25cm) high

$500-600   BEL

A Weller brown Marvo jardinière, unmarked but with the remnants of a Weller label.

6.5in (16.5cm) high

$150-200   BEL

A Weller blue Panella covered ginger jar, the base marked "Weller" in script.

6.75in (17cm) high

$60-100   BEL

A Weller blue Panella basket, unmarked.

7.25in (18.5cm) high

$40-60   BEL

A Weller Silvertone fan vase, decorated by Hester Pillsbury in pink, green, lavender and yellow pastel glazes, the base "Weller Ware" ink stamp and painted "HP".

7.5in (19cm) high

$250-350   BEL

A Weller Silvertone double-handled vase, decorated by Hester Pillsbury with yellow blossoms on a background of lavender, green and yellow, the base with Weller Pottery full kiln stamp and painted "HP".

This vase has a complex form and very crisp molding. The colors also vary from strong to the typically pale tones associated with the range, making the pattern more appealing.

8in (20cm) high

$350-450   BEL

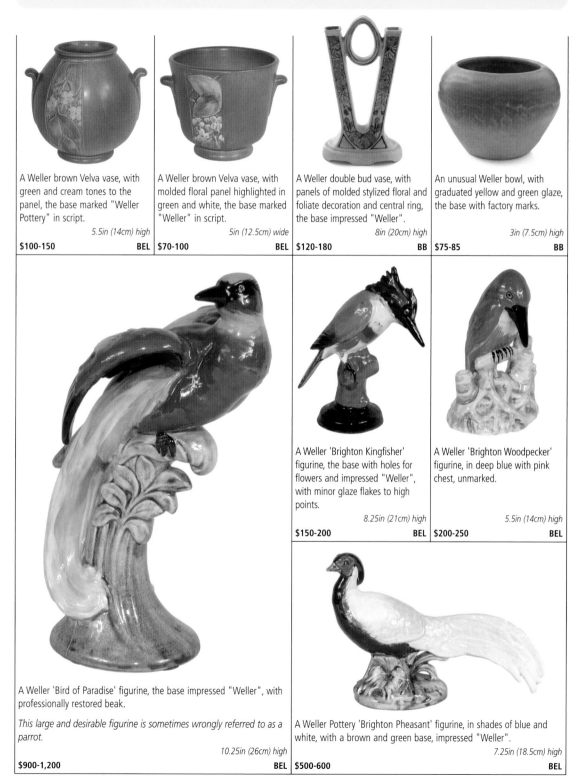

A Weller brown Velva vase, with green and cream tones to the panel, the base marked "Weller Pottery" in script.

5.5in (14cm) high

$100-150   BEL

A Weller brown Velva vase, with molded floral panel highlighted in green and white, the base marked "Weller" in script.

5in (12.5cm) wide

$70-100   BEL

A Weller double bud vase, with panels of molded stylized floral and foliate decoration and central ring, the base impressed "Weller".

8in (20cm) high

$120-180   BB

An unusual Weller bowl, with graduated yellow and green glaze, the base with factory marks.

3in (7.5cm) high

$75-85   BB

A Weller 'Brighton Kingfisher' figurine, the base with holes for flowers and impressed "Weller", with minor glaze flakes to high points.

8.25in (21cm) high

$150-200   BEL

A Weller 'Brighton Woodpecker' figurine, in deep blue with pink chest, unmarked.

5.5in (14cm) high

$200-250   BEL

A Weller 'Bird of Paradise' figurine, the base impressed "Weller", with professionally restored beak.

This large and desirable figurine is sometimes wrongly referred to as a parrot.

10.25in (26cm) high

$900-1,200   BEL

A Weller Pottery 'Brighton Pheasant' figurine, in shades of blue and white, with a brown and green base, impressed "Weller".

7.25in (18.5cm) high

$500-600   BEL

CERAMICS

ESSENTIAL REFERENCE

- Wemyss was produced at the Fife Pottery in Scotland, under the guidance of its owner Robert Methven Heron. He was assisted by his sister Hessie, works manager Robert McLaughlin and a young Austrian painter called Karel Nekola. Production boomed in popularity from the 1880s until the outbreak of WWI.
- It is typified by cheerful, brightly rendered hand-painted patterns of flowers, plants, fruit, birds and other animals. Shapes are usually simple to show the pattern off to its best advantage, and comprise bowls, vases, candlesticks, jugs and basin washing sets, and tablewares. They also produced a range of unusual pig and cat figurines – look out for small sleeping pigs as these can be worth over $20,000.

- Patterns were primarily designed by Nekola, who trained a small team to reproduce them, as well as decorating examples himself. Apart from Nekola, the most talented decorators were James Sharp and, from 1916, Edwin Sandland. Pieces decorated by them, particularly Nekola, will be worth a premium. Consider the shape as well as the pattern – even a small matchbox cover may be valued at a over a hundred dollars due to its scarcity.
- In 1930, the rights were sold to the Bovey Tracey Pottery in Devon. Karel Nekola's son Joseph moved with them, where he continued to paint until his death in 1942. Eccentric, colorful and charming, Wemyss has remained popular for many years and looks set to continue.

A Wemyss 'Gordon' pattern small plate, decorated with irises, impressed mark "Wemyss Ware/R.H. & S."

c1900   5.5in (14cm) diam

$300-400   L&T

A Wemyss 'Gordon' pattern dessert plate, decorated with purple irises, with impressed mark "Wemyss/R.H. & S.", and printed "T. Goode & Co." retailer's marks, restored.

c1900   8in (20.5cm) diam

$350-450   L&T

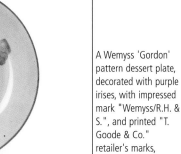

A Wemyss side plate, decorated with red clover, impressed mark "Wemyss/R.H. & S."

c1900   8.25in (21cm) diam

$350-400   L&T

A Wemyss small plate, decorated with blackcurrants on a branch, with impressed "Wemyss Ware/R.H. & S." mark, and painted "T Goode & Co." retailer's mark.

c1900   5.5in (14cm) diam

$350-450   L&T

An early 20thC Wemyss side plate, decorated with strawberries, impressed "Wemyss" mark and painted "T. Goode & Co." retailer's mark, one small chip to rim.

7.5in (19cm) diam

$300-400   L&T

CERAMICS

An early 20thC Wemyss sponge dish and liner, decorated by James Sharp with pink, purple and brown chrysanthemums, impressed and painted "Wemyss" mark and painted "T. Goode & Co." retailers mark, restoration to one handle.

7.75in (20cm) diam

$700-900   **L&T**

An early 20thC Wemyss 'Lady Eva' vase, decorated by Edwin Sandland with daffodils, impressed and painted "Wemyss" marks.

8in (20.5cm) high

$800-1,000   **L&T**

An early 20thC Wemyss frilled vase, decorated by Edwin Sandland with dragonflies, impressed and painted "Wemyss" marks, restored.

5.75in (14.5cm) high

$700-900   **L&T**

A Wemyss small beaker vase, decorated with a black cock and hen, indistinct impressed "Wemyss Ware/R.H. & S." mark.

c1900   *4.25in (11cm) high*

$300-400   **L&T**

An early 20thC Wemyss 'Bon Jour' pattern cream jug, decorated with a brown cock, inscribed "BonJour", impressed and printed marks, glaze frits to spout, stained rim.

2.75in (7cm) high

$500-700   **L&T**

A Wemyss pink glazed pig, impressed marks.

6.25in (16cm) wide

$800-1,000   **WW**

A Wemyss pig, painted in shades of black and pink on a white ground, impressed marks, re-glued ear and hairline crack.

Had this pig not been damaged, it may have been worth more than twice as much.

6in (15cm) wide

$1,000-1,500   **WW**

CERAMICS

A set of three West German ceramic vases, the bases molded "West Germany", with indistinct numbers.

7.75in (19.5cm), 9.75in (25cm) and 11.75in (30cm) high

$60-80   GAZE

A West German Bay Keramik vase, with gray speckled finish and blue band with orange circular motifs, the base molded '"West-Germany 660-20".

8in (20cm) high

$40-60   GC

A West German Scheurich vase, with red band printed with green squares, with matte textured white glazed upper and lower parts, the base molded "203-32".

12.75in (32.5cm) high

$80-120   GC

A West German baluster vase, with gun-metal matte gray and gloss red bands and white vertical scored lines, the base with hand-painted marks "KK 6196 Made in Germany Handpainted".

7.75in (19.5cm) high

$50-70   GC

A West German Bay Keramik vase, possibly designed by Bodo Mans, with glossy white and multicolored linear and splodged design on a brick red ground, the base molded "West Germany 1065-30".

12in (30.5cm) high

$80-100   GC

An Austrian Keramos waisted vase, with hand-decorated banded and dripped design, the base molded "664-18 Austria".

The survival of the original label here is useful. It shows that this piece of Austrian pottery was produced by the German company Carstens. In 1953 they had signed a deal with the Goldscheider factory to produce a number of their products.

7.25in (18.5cm) high

$50-60   GC

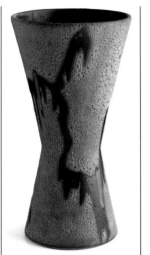

An early 1960s West German Scheurich vase, with light green pumice glaze and dripped streaks of brown and orange glaze, the base molded "Foreign 244 22".

8.75in (22cm) high

$30-40   **AEM**

A West German waisted vase, with dripped silvery gun metal gray glazed bands over a thin black lined ground, the base impressed "3769/22".

9in (23cm) high

$80-120   **GC**

A West German Carstens tapering vase, with black cross-hatched pattern over a dark green ground, the base molded "1227-21 W.Germany".

8in (20.5cm) high

$60-100   **GC**

A West German Ceramano 'Agina' pattern floor vase, with soldier and geometric pattern picked out with a creamy lava glaze, the base inscribed "106/3 'Agina' Ceramano W-Germany Handarbeit".

c1961   *18.5in (47cm) high*

$200-300   **QU**

A West German Ceramano 'Tourmalin' pattern large floor vase, shape no. 27, decorated with bands, incised marks.

Ceramano's wide range of designs have become highly sought-after recently. Each was hand decorated, so the designs vary from piece to piece. Ceramano pieces can be recognized by the marks which were inscribed by hand into the base. Typically these include the pattern name, the decorator's monogram, and the word 'Handarbeit' (handworked).

21.25in (54cm) high

$400-600   **WW**

A West German Bay Keramik 'Kongo' pattern ovoid vase, with incised lines and multicolored gloss oval patterns, the base impressed "543/30 Germany".

c1960   *13.75in (35cm) high*

$400-600   **GC**

A very rare 1970s West German Carstens double gourd vase, with purple glaze and handle, unmarked.

6in (15cm) high

$45-55   **OUT**

CERAMICS

A pair Gouda 'Juliana' pattern Ivora vases, with tapered tall necks and decorated with stylized floral motifs and scrolls, hand-painted marks to bases.

12in (30.5cm) high

$600-800 FLD

A Dutch Pieter Groeneveldt hand-built small cube vase, with a lightly textured mottled blue glaze over a brown underglaze, on four feet, unsigned.

Pieter Groeneveldt (1889-1982) studied as a painter and draughtsman at the Academy of Arts in Amsterdam. He then turned to pottery, opening his first pottery near The Hague in 1923. Much of his production, which varied between unique studio works and serial studio works, was sold through his nearby flower shop Schéhérazade. His experimental glazes were inspired by Oriental glazes and typically covered simple, modern forms such as this.

5in (12.5cm) high

$60-100 PC

A Dutch Pieter Groeneveldt cylinder vase, with deep purple grainy glaze, the base impressed "11 10".

4.75in (12cm) high

$35-45 OUT

A Grueby squat vessel, with a row of stacked rounded leaves, covered in matte green glaze, circular Pottery stamp, marked "SM 11/5/06", short, tight line to rim.

1906 *2.25in (5.5cm) high*

$1,200-1,800 DRA

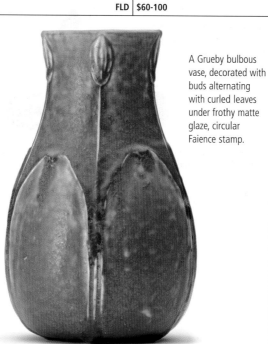

A Grueby bulbous vase, decorated with buds alternating with curled leaves under frothy matte glaze, circular Faience stamp.

The organic, bud-like form, molded stylized leaf design and thick mossy green glaze is typical of Grueby. The company was founded in 1894 by William Henry Grueby, and produced art pottery from 1897 until c1909. His green glaze became so popular in its day that it was copied by many other Arts & Crafts pottery manufacturers including Teco and Pewabic.

7.5in (19cm) high

$2,800-3,200 DRA

A scarce Grueby pig vase, with dripped three color glaze, unmarked.

4.25in (10.5cm) high

$200-300 BB

A 1930s Belgian Roger Guerin small squat vase, with mottled brown, blue, red and green glazes, the base with impressed "R. Guerin" signature, and hand inscribed "007".

2in (5cm) high

$200-300 TOJ

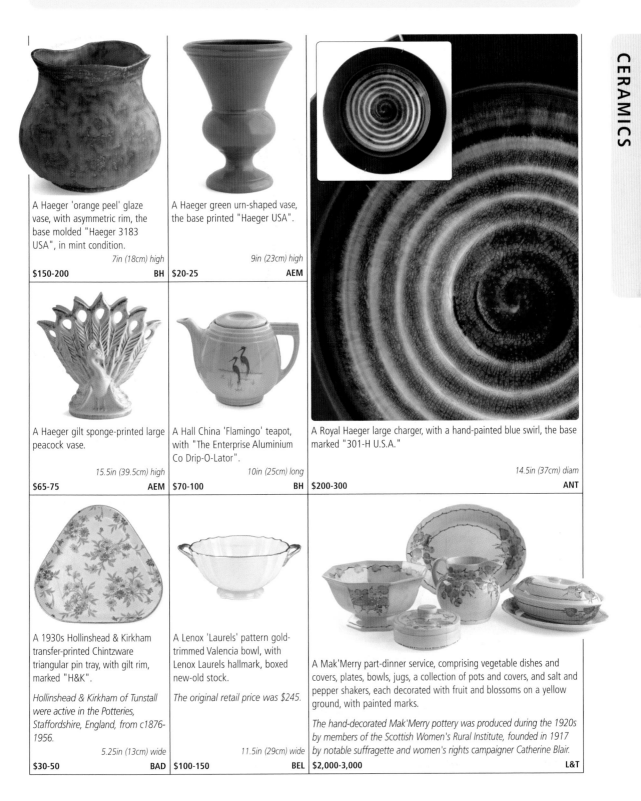

A Haeger 'orange peel' glaze vase, with asymmetric rim, the base molded "Haeger 3183 USA", in mint condition.

7in (18cm) high

$150-200   BH

A Haeger green urn-shaped vase, the base printed "Haeger USA".

9in (23cm) high

$20-25   AEM

A Haeger gilt sponge-printed large peacock vase.

15.5in (39.5cm) high

$65-75   AEM

A Hall China 'Flamingo' teapot, with "The Enterprise Aluminium Co Drip-O-Lator".

10in (25cm) long

$70-100   BH

A Royal Haeger large charger, with a hand-painted blue swirl, the base marked "301-H U.S.A."

14.5in (37cm) diam

$200-300   ANT

A 1930s Hollinshead & Kirkham transfer-printed Chintzware triangular pin tray, with gilt rim, marked "H&K".

Hollinshead & Kirkham of Tunstall were active in the Potteries, Staffordshire, England, from c1876-1956.

5.25in (13cm) wide

$30-50   BAD

A Lenox 'Laurels' pattern gold-trimmed Valencia bowl, with Lenox Laurels hallmark, boxed new-old stock.

The original retail price was $245.

11.5in (29cm) wide

$100-150   BEL

A Mak'Merry part-dinner service, comprising vegetable dishes and covers, plates, bowls, jugs, a collection of pots and covers, and salt and pepper shakers, each decorated with fruit and blossoms on a yellow ground, with painted marks.

The hand-decorated Mak'Merry pottery was produced during the 1920s by members of the Scottish Women's Rural Institute, founded in 1917 by notable suffragette and women's rights campaigner Catherine Blair.

$2,000-3,000   L&T

ESSENTIAL REFERENCE

- Trained modeler, Andrew Clark, started the Sugarlump Studio in 1995 and, inspired by his love of children's TV, created a range of figures and scenes based on numerous TV shows, including The Clangers, The Magic Roundabout, The Herbs and Sooty. The studio closed in September 2002.
- As each piece was hand-painted by a small team, production numbers are limited, even for standard pieces. The rarest piece is the Magic Roundabout 'Potting Shed', identified by its green roof, as only 90 examples were produced between April 1995 and August 1996.

- Other pieces likely to be desirable are those produced in small limited editions, or those retired early. Examples should retain their original packaging and paperwork to be worth the values given here.
- Given the short life of the studio, the limited production numbers, and the continuing popularity of the subject matter, it is likely that Sugarlump figurines will remain sought-after.
- See the company's website, which is still maintained, for a full list of figurines produced: www.sugarlumpstudio.com.

A Sugarlump Studio 'Gabriel' figurine, from the Bagpuss collection, mint and boxed.

2000-02   *3in (7.5cm) high*
$50-60   **MTB**

A Sugarlump Studio 'The Mouse Organ' figurine, from the Bagpuss collection, mint and boxed.

1999-2002   *4.5in (12cm) high*
$50-70   **MTB**

A Sugarlump Studio 'Bagpuss' figurine, from the Bagpuss collection, mint and boxed.
1999-2002   *3in (7.5cm) high*
$60-80   **MTB**

A Sugarlump Studio 'Professor Yaffle' figurine, from the Bagpuss collection, mint and boxed.

1999-2002   *3in (7.5cm) high*
$50-60   **MTB**

A Sugarlump Studio 'Major Clanger' figurine, from the Clangers collection, mint and boxed.

1996-2002   *3.3in (8.5cm) high*
$40-50   **MTB**

A Sugarlump Studio 'Tiny Clanger' figurine, from The Clangers collection, mint and boxed.

1996-2202   *3in (8cm) high*
$40-50   **MTB**

A Sugarlump Studio 'Uncle Clanger' figurine, from The Clangers collection, mint and boxed.

1997-2002   *3in (8cm) high*
$40-50   **MTB**

A set of Sugarlump Studio 'Chive' figurines, nos. 1, 2, 3 and 4, from The Herbs collection, mint and boxed.

1999-2002   *2in (5cm) high*
$40-50 (each)   **MTB**

A Sugarlump Studio 'Sage The Owl' figurine, from The Herbs collection, mint and boxed.

1999-2002
2.5in (6cm) high
$40-60   **MTB**

A Sugarlump Studio 'Parsley The Lion' figurine, from The Herbs collection, mint and boxed.

1999-2002   *3in (7.5cm) high*
$50-60   **MTB**

A Sugarlump Studio 'Sir Basil' figurine, from The Herbs collection, mint and boxed.

1999-2002   *3in (8cm) high*
$40-60   **MTB**

A Sugarlump Studio 'Tarragon The Dragon', from The Herbs collection, mint and boxed.

2000-02   *3in (7cm) high*
$40-60   **MTB**

A Sugarlump Studio 'Basil' figurine, from The Magic Roundabout collection, mint and boxed.

1998-2002   *2.5in (6.5cm) high*
$50-60   **MTB**

A limited edition Sugarlump Studio 'Buxton The Blue Cat' figurine, from an edition of 2,000, from The Magic Roundabout collection, mint and boxed.

1999   *3in (8cm) high*
$60-80   **MTB**

EXPERT EYE – A CHRISTOPHER ROBIN NURSERY BOWL AND COVER

The Ashtead Pottery was in production from 1923 to 1935, a mere 12 years. Given the factory's short life, Ashtead pieces are scarce, and are sought-after when they come to the market.

Although the pottery was praised at the time for its fresh designs, particularly its Art Deco pieces, the factory closed in part due to the death of its founder Sir Lawrence Weaver.

A Christopher Robin nursery set was presented to the future Queen Elizabeth II in 1928.

The combination of a sought-after pottery and beloved childhood characters makes this a valuable piece. Pieces were easily damaged by children, making items in excellent condition rare.

An Ashtead Pottery Christopher Robin nursery set bowl and cover, printed in colors with characters from Winnie the Pooh, based on the designs of E.H. Sheppard, printed marks.

6in (15cm) diam

$800-1,000   **WW**

A Pizza Hut The Flintstones Kids 'Wilma' glass.

1986   *6in (15cm) high*

$4-6   **AEM**

A 1950s Noddy painted wooden eggcup, by Fairy Lite Products and licensed by Noddy Subsidiary Rights Co. Ltd, mint and boxed.

During the 1960s, these were made in plastic and are less desirable. They have a value of around $10-15 in this condition.

4in (10cm) high

$24-28   **MTB**

A Howdy Doody printed cotton handkerchief.

8in (20cm) wide

$55-75   **SOTT**

A Howdy Doody painted celluloid pin.

1.5in (4cm) long

$10-15   **TSIS**

A Howdy Doody color transfer-printed tin cookie jar, by Kagran Corp.

8.5in (21.5cm) high

$100-150   **BH**

A pair of Dutch Laurel & Hardy molded plastic money banks, modeled as policemen, with scales to each side showing the level of savings.

1968   *10.5in (26.5cm) high*

$30-40   **MTB**

A 1970s Magic Roundabout squirting 'Dougal', by Bendy Toy, mint and sealed in original packaging.

Loose without its packaging, this toy is worth around $20. Always examine Bendy Toys carefully, as the foam plastic is prone to 'dissolve' into a powder.

$65-75   **MTB**

A late 1960s Welsh The Magic Roundabout 'Ermintrude' hand-made shell sculpture, licensed by Serge Danot, with conch shell body.

4.25in (10.5cm) high

$20-25   **MTB**

A late 1960s Welsh The Magic Roundabout 'Florence' hand-made shell sculpture, licensed by Serge Danot, with sea anemone shell head.

Given the delicacy of these shells, it is surprising that Florence has survived intact for over 40 years.

7.25in (18.5cm) high

$40-50   **MTB**

EXPERT EYE – A SIGMA 'MISS PIGGY' MUG

Sigma Ceramics made a number of good quality Muppet Show collectibles, many of which are highly sought-after.

As Miss Piggy and Kermit are the most popular Muppets, they are easier to find than characters such as Dr. Teeth and Animal, with Gonzo being the rarest.

As the company only made Muppet merchandise from 1978 until the early 1980s, they are hard to find today. The attention to detail, note Miss Piggy's eyes for example, also make them desirable to collectors.

As well as 14 ceramic pieces, the company also produced papier-mâché Christmas ornaments,

A Muppet Show 'Miss Piggy' hand-painted mug, by Sigma Ceramics.
1979-81   *4.25in (10.5cm) high*

$5-10   **AEM**

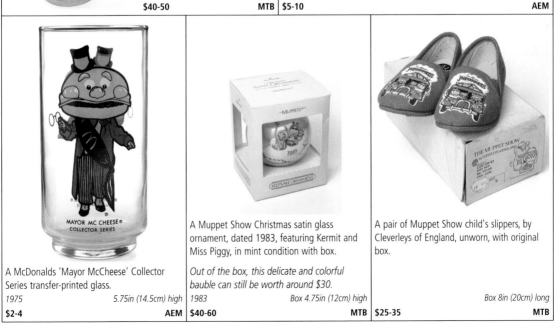

A McDonalds 'Mayor McCheese' Collector Series transfer-printed glass.
1975   *5.75in (14.5cm) high*

$2-4   **AEM**

A Muppet Show Christmas satin glass ornament, dated 1983, featuring Kermit and Miss Piggy, in mint condition with box.

Out of the box, this delicate and colorful bauble can still be worth around $30.

1983   *Box 4.75in (12cm) high*

$40-60   **MTB**

A pair of Muppet Show child's slippers, by Cleverleys of England, unworn, with original box.

Box 8in (20cm) long

$25-35   **MTB**

A Shoe People 'PC Boot' money bank, by Action Games & Toys, mint and carded.

Although comparatively popular at the time, the Shoe People cartoon ran for one season only. Merchandise is hard to find today, but values are often low as there are so few collectors.

1986   9.25in (23cm) high

$35-40   **MTB**

A Planet of The Apes 'Galen' money bank, by PlayPal Plastics Inc. and licensed by 20th Century Fox.

The character of Galen was played by Roddy McDowall in the 1974 Planet of the Apes TV series. He previously played 'Cornelius' in two films and 'Caesar' in two further prequals. PlayPal also made a 'Dr. Zauis' money bank that is worth a similar amount.

1974   10.25in (26cm) high

$15-25   **BH**

A Popeye Speed Boat, by Harmony C&D Ind. Ltd, Hong Kong, licensed by King Features Syndicate Inc.

$45-55   **MEM**

A 1980s Rainbow Brite 'Starlite' plush horse stuffed toy, with fabric tag, in good condition.

1983   12.5in (32cm) high

$8-12   **AEM**

A Marx Toys Rupert the Bear plastic friction-driven tricycle toy, licensed by Beaverbrook Newspapers, mint and boxed.

1973   Box 4.25in (11cm) high

$60-80   **MTB**

A Superman game, by Hasbro Games, nearly complete, missing one flying card.

1978   Box 19.75in (50cm) wide

$20-25   **BH**

A 1940s-50s Superman large plaster shop display figure, unmarked.

The missing 'S' logo from his chest, shows it is an unauthorized figure.

15.25in (38.5cm) high

$300-500   **BH**

A 'Superman Time Capsule!' promotional comic, for Kellogg's Sugar Smacks, with artwork by Win Mortimer and Curt Swan.

There were two other titles given away with this promotion: "Duel in Space" and "The Super Show of Metropolis". All three titles are sought-after. This title was reprinted in 'Superman' issue 250, released in April 1972.

1955   7in (17cm) long

$100-150   **TSIS**

A Tarzan badge, with artwork by Ross Manning licensed by Edgar Rice Burroughs Enterprises.

1975   3.25in (8.5cm) diam

$8-12   **BH**

A limited edition Beswick 'Dr Mopp' figurine, no. TR5, from the Trumpton Series, from an edition of 2,500, mint and boxed with matching numbered certificate.

2001   5.75in (14.5cm) high

$80-100   MTB

A limited edition Beswick 'Windy Miller' figurine, from the Trumpton Series, from an edition of 2,500, mint and boxed with matching numbered certificate.

Beware of examples that come without their matching numbered certificates and without a limited edition number inscribed into the ceramic on the base. These are seconds and are generally worth under 50 per cent of this value.

2001   5.75in (14.5cm) high

$80-100   MTB

A Wizard of Oz 'Mayor' hand-painted figurine bell, by Presents, mint with original box.

1989   6in (15cm) high

$30-50   MTB

An Annie Oakley plastic mug, with photographic insert of Gail Davis playing the character in the 1954-57 TV series.

This plastic mug came from Gail Davis' personal estate, as she used to sign them for fans.

4in (10cm) high

$12-18   BH

A Davy Crockett mug, by Norton Ceramics, with impressed factory marks to base.

4in (10cm) high

$25-35   BH

A Hopalong Cassidy Med-O-Pure Cottage Cheese printed tinplate tip tray.

4.75in (12cm) diam

$15-25   BH

A 1950s Hopalong Cassidy paper-over-card pencil case, by Hasbro.

9in (23cm) long

$40-60   BH

A Lone Ranger hair brush, with worn transfer on the wooden handle.

1939   4.25in (11cm) high

$7-10   BH

A very rare 1950s Lone Ranger carnival hand-painted chalkware figure, marked with impressed name to the base.

These cheaply made figures were given away as prizes at carnivals and fairs. Due to their fragile nature, intact examples are scarce. Collectible in their own right, the subject matter makes this even more desirable.

10.25in (26cm) high

$100-150   BH

A Metlox teddy bear cookie jar, with impressed marks to base and some damage to lip.

Without damage to the inside lid, this could be worth around $60-80.

11.75in (29.5cm) high

$18-22   **AEM**

A very rare Regal China Co. 'Goldilocks' cookie jar.

Regal's Goldilocks usually features on the top ten list of most wanted cookie jars. However, examples have been reproduced by Brush McCoy and are marked as such. Modern reproductions are also available over the Internet. Reproductions are typically smaller, and may have different over-glaze colors. Look on the base for authentic Regal marks including '405' and 'Pat-Pending'.

12.5in (31.5cm) high

$420-480   **AEM**

A McCoy 'honey bear' cookie jar.

8.25in (21cm) high

$50-80   **AEM**

An American Bisque pig cookie jar, with hairline crack to neck and some chips to the internal rim.

Had it not been damaged, it could have been worth over twice as much.

12.25in (31cm) high

$50-80   **AEM**

A Treasure Craft 'graduate' owl cookie jar.

11in (28cm) high

$18-22   **AEM**

A Treasure Craft Victorian house cookie jar, with damage to the inside rim and a few chips.

11.5in (29cm) high

$20-30   **AEM**

A Metlox apple cookie jar, the base impressed "Made in U.S.A."

7.5in (19cm) high

$35-45   **AEM**

ESSENTIAL REFERENCE

- Vibrantly colored Bakelite and plastic jewelry exploded onto the fashion scene during the 1920s. Great leaps in the development of plastics saw a wider variety of colors being introduced. They could also be molded economically, or cast, and then carved with patterns by hand or machine.
- The Great Depression caused by the Wall Street Crash of 1929 meant less money was available to spend on luxuries. While jewel-encrusted, platinum cocktail jewelry remained popular with the very wealthy, Bakelite and plastic jewelry provided an affordable, yet fashionable, alternative for others. The bright colors, novelty shapes and themes also added cheer at difficult times.
- Generally, it is the better carved, brighter colored, chunkier pieces that obtain the best prices today. Cherry red, bright green and orange are most desirable. The creamy butterscotch, also known as 'creamed corn', is similarly desirable. Duller colors such as black or brown are less so. Novelty or quirky shapes such as human faces or animals are also popular. Later plastics from the 1950s are often of poorer quality, but are still collectible.
- Also consider the work that went in to making a piece. Assembled items, made up of different parts, or chunky pieces deeply cut by hand will be worth more than a thin piece cut by machine or with molded decoration. Geometric patterns, typical of the Art Deco style, are also sought-after. Always examine a piece closely for signs of damage such as holes, cracks or chips, which are very difficult to repair.

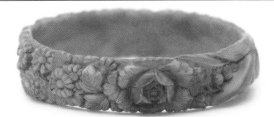

A red stained cream plastic bangle, carved with rose and leaf motifs.

2.75in (7cm) diam

$90-110   P&I

A salmon pink stained cream plastic bangle, carved with rose, daisy and leaf motifs.

2.75in (7cm) diam

$50-70   P&I

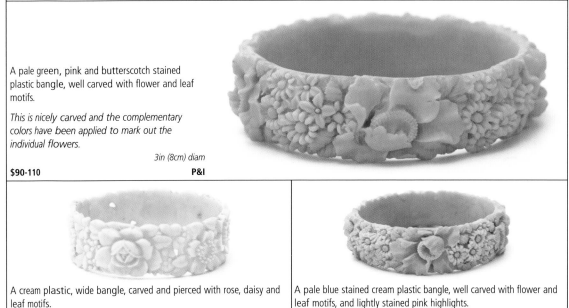

A pale green, pink and butterscotch stained plastic bangle, well carved with flower and leaf motifs.

This is nicely carved and the complementary colors have been applied to mark out the individual flowers.

3in (8cm) diam

$90-110   P&I

A cream plastic, wide bangle, carved and pierced with rose, daisy and leaf motifs.

2.75in (7cm) diam

$60-100   P&I

A pale blue stained cream plastic bangle, well carved with flower and leaf motifs, and lightly stained pink highlights.

3in (8cm) diam

$60-100   P&I

COSTUME JEWELRY

A pair of Renoir embossed copper earrings, in the form of stylized sheaves of corn.

1.25in (3cm) high

$25-35   BB

A pair of Renoir embossed copper teardrop-shaped earrings.

1.5in (3.5cm) high

$20-25   BB

EXPERT EYE – A REBAJES PIN

In 1934 Spanish jeweler and sculptor Francisco Rebajes (1906-90) opened his first shop in New York City, which he ran until he returned to Spain in 1967.

His designs are Modern in style, and were usually inspired by foreign culture or ethnic designs. Here he has been inspired by a Chinese dragon's head.

All his designs are made from die-cut and embossed copper. They have a distinctively soft patina that should not be polished.

Other makers also imitated his successful designs. All Rebajes pieces are marked on the back with his name.

A Rebajes Chinese dragon's head copper pin, stamped "Rebajes" on the reverse.

1.75in (4.5cm) high

$45-55   BB

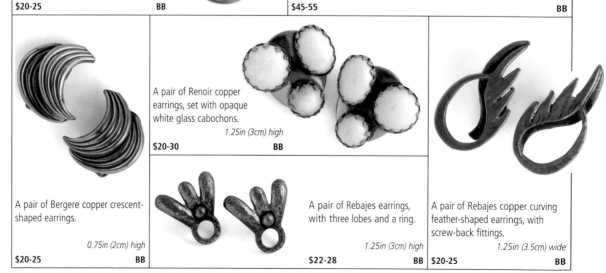

A pair of Bergere copper crescent-shaped earrings.

0.75in (2cm) high

$20-25   BB

A pair of Renoir copper earrings, set with opaque white glass cabochons.

1.25in (3cm) high

$20-30   BB

A pair of Rebajes earrings, with three lobes and a ring.

1.25in (3cm) high

$22-28   BB

A pair of Rebajes copper curving feather-shaped earrings, with screw-back fittings.

1.25in (3.5cm) wide

$20-25   BB

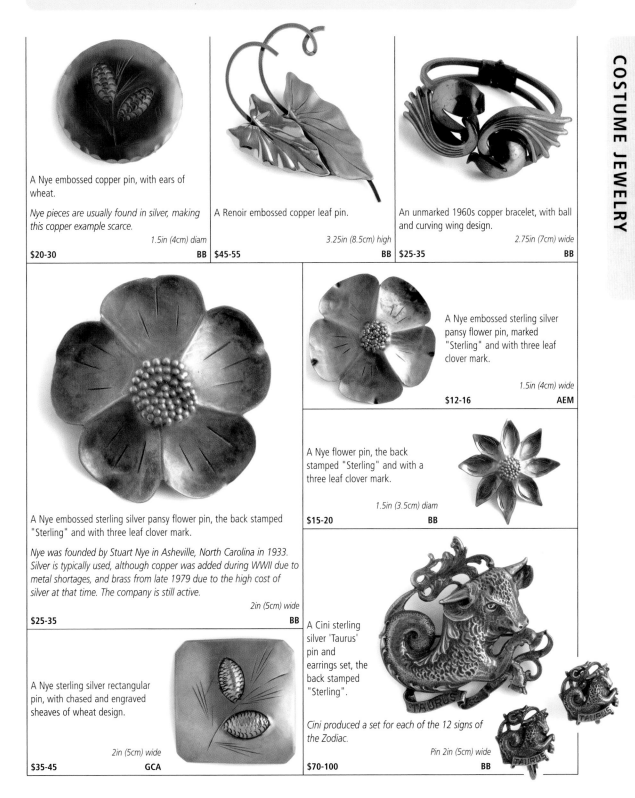

A Nye embossed copper pin, with ears of wheat.

Nye pieces are usually found in silver, making this copper example scarce.

1.5in (4cm) diam

$20-30   **BB**

A Renoir embossed copper leaf pin.

3.25in (8.5cm) high

$45-55   **BB**

An unmarked 1960s copper bracelet, with ball and curving wing design.

2.75in (7cm) wide

$25-35   **BB**

A Nye embossed sterling silver pansy flower pin, marked "Sterling" and with three leaf clover mark.

1.5in (4cm) wide

$12-16   **AEM**

A Nye flower pin, the back stamped "Sterling" and with a three leaf clover mark.

1.5in (3.5cm) diam

$15-20   **BB**

A Nye embossed sterling silver pansy flower pin, the back stamped "Sterling" and with three leaf clover mark.

Nye was founded by Stuart Nye in Asheville, North Carolina in 1933. Silver is typically used, although copper was added during WWII due to metal shortages, and brass from late 1979 due to the high cost of silver at that time. The company is still active.

2in (5cm) wide

$25-35   **BB**

A Nye sterling silver rectangular pin, with chased and engraved sheaves of wheat design.

2in (5cm) wide

$35-45   **GCA**

A Cini sterling silver 'Taurus' pin and earrings set, the back stamped "Sterling".

Cini produced a set for each of the 12 signs of the Zodiac.

Pin 2in (5cm) wide

$70-100   **BB**

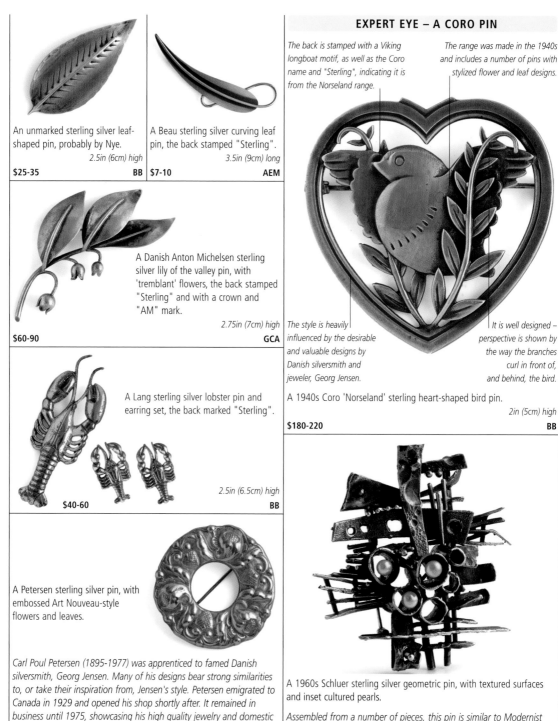

An unmarked sterling silver leaf-shaped pin, probably by Nye.

2.5in (6cm) high

$25-35   BB

A Beau sterling silver curving leaf pin, the back stamped "Sterling".

3.5in (9cm) long

$7-10   AEM

A Danish Anton Michelsen sterling silver lily of the valley pin, with 'tremblant' flowers, the back stamped "Sterling" and with a crown and "AM" mark.

2.75in (7cm) high

$60-90   GCA

A Lang sterling silver lobster pin and earring set, the back marked "Sterling".

2.5in (6.5cm) high

$40-60   BB

A Petersen sterling silver pin, with embossed Art Nouveau-style flowers and leaves.

Carl Poul Petersen (1895-1977) was apprenticed to famed Danish silversmith, Georg Jensen. Many of his designs bear strong similarities to, or take their inspiration from, Jensen's style. Petersen emigrated to Canada in 1929 and opened his shop shortly after. It remained in business until 1975, showcasing his high quality jewelry and domestic silverware designs.

$450-550   TCF

EXPERT EYE – A CORO PIN

The back is stamped with a Viking longboat motif, as well as the Coro name and "Sterling", indicating it is from the Norseland range.

The range was made in the 1940s and includes a number of pins with stylized flower and leaf designs.

The style is heavily influenced by the desirable and valuable designs by Danish silversmith and jeweler, Georg Jensen.

It is well designed – perspective is shown by the way the branches curl in front of, and behind, the bird.

A 1940s Coro 'Norseland' sterling heart-shaped bird pin.

2in (5cm) high

$180-220   BB

A 1960s Schluer sterling silver geometric pin, with textured surfaces and inset cultured pearls.

Assembled from a number of pieces, this pin is similar to Modernist wooden and metal sculptures produced at the same time.

$1,500-2,000   TCF

An unmarked strawberry fruit pin, set with faux pearl and colored rhinestone studs.

1.75in (4.5cm) high

$20-25   BB

An unmarked strawberry fruit pin, set with red rhinestones.

Note the good quality molding of the strawberry's leaves.

1.75in (4.5cm) high

$10-15   AEM

An unmarked leaf-shaped pin, set with faceted blue crystal rhinestones.

2.75in (7cm) high

$40-60   BB

A green faceted rhinestone leaf pin, with gold-plated leaf mount.

2.75in (7cm) high

$25-35   AEM

An unmarked gold-tone foliate sprig pin, with curling leaves and prong-set multicolored stones.

2.25in (6cm) high

$40-60   BB

A pair of unmarked purple faceted rhinestone earrings.

1.5in (4cm) high

$10-15   AEM

An unmarked red and clear faceted rhinestone floral spray pin.

2.75in (5.5cm) high

$25-35   AEM

COSTUME JEWELRY

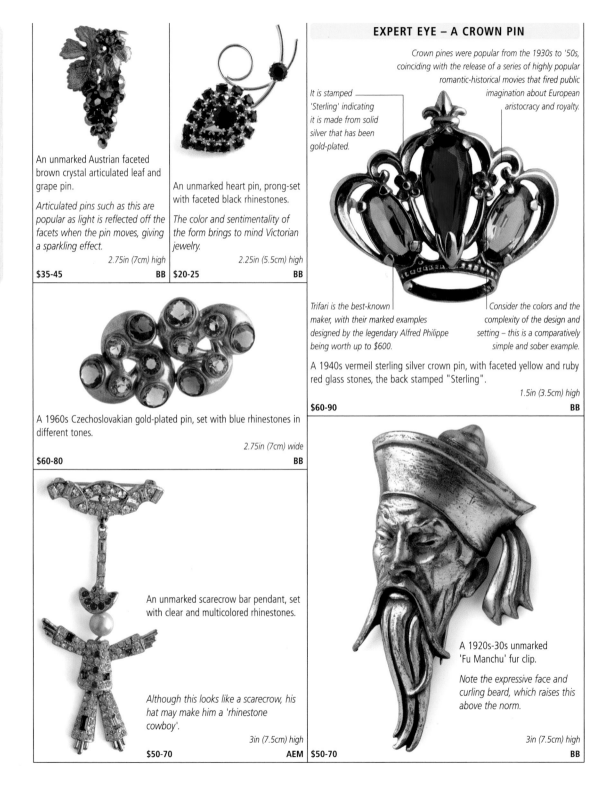

An unmarked Austrian faceted brown crystal articulated leaf and grape pin.

Articulated pins such as this are popular as light is reflected off the facets when the pin moves, giving a sparkling effect.

2.75in (7cm) high

$35-45   BB

An unmarked heart pin, prong-set with faceted black rhinestones.

The color and sentimentality of the form brings to mind Victorian jewelry.

2.25in (5.5cm) high

$20-25   BB

A 1960s Czechoslovakian gold-plated pin, set with blue rhinestones in different tones.

2.75in (7cm) wide

$60-80   BB

An unmarked scarecrow bar pendant, set with clear and multicolored rhinestones.

Although this looks like a scarecrow, his hat may make him a 'rhinestone cowboy'.

3in (7.5cm) high

$50-70   AEM

EXPERT EYE – A CROWN PIN

Crown pines were popular from the 1930s to '50s, coinciding with the release of a series of highly popular romantic-historical movies that fired public imagination about European aristocracy and royalty.

It is stamped 'Sterling' indicating it is made from solid silver that has been gold-plated.

Trifari is the best-known maker, with their marked examples designed by the legendary Alfred Philippe being worth up to $600.

Consider the colors and the complexity of the design and setting – this is a comparatively simple and sober example.

A 1940s vermeil sterling silver crown pin, with faceted yellow and ruby red glass stones, the back stamped "Sterling".

1.5in (3.5cm) high

$60-90   BB

A 1920s-30s unmarked 'Fu Manchu' fur clip.

Note the expressive face and curling beard, which raises this above the norm.

3in (7.5cm) high

$50-70   BB

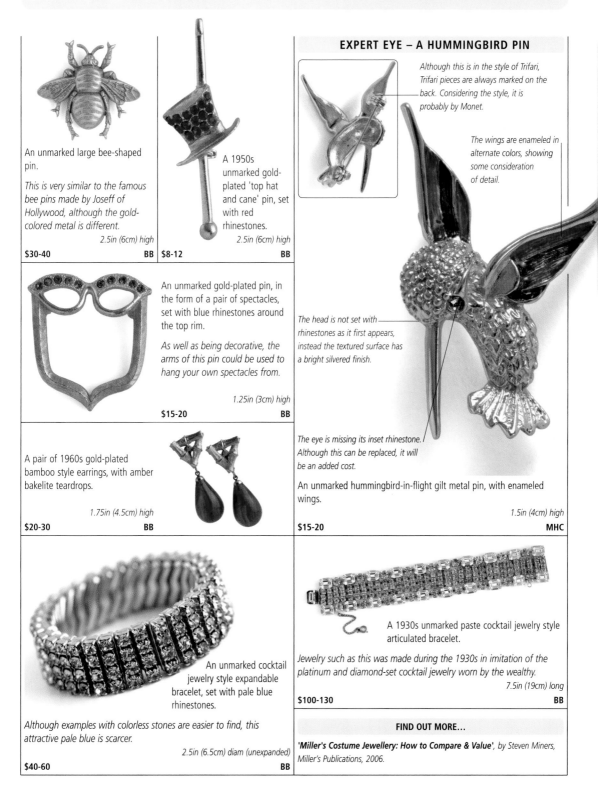

An unmarked large bee-shaped pin.

This is very similar to the famous bee pins made by Joseff of Hollywood, although the gold-colored metal is different.

2.5in (6cm) high

$30-40   BB

A 1950s unmarked gold-plated 'top hat and cane' pin, set with red rhinestones.

2.5in (6cm) high

$8-12   BB

EXPERT EYE – A HUMMINGBIRD PIN

Although this is in the style of Trifari, Trifari pieces are always marked on the back. Considering the style, it is probably by Monet.

The wings are enameled in alternate colors, showing some consideration of detail.

An unmarked gold-plated pin, in the form of a pair of spectacles, set with blue rhinestones around the top rim.

As well as being decorative, the arms of this pin could be used to hang your own spectacles from.

1.25in (3cm) high

$15-20   BB

The head is not set with rhinestones as it first appears, instead the textured surface has a bright silvered finish.

A pair of 1960s gold-plated bamboo style earrings, with amber bakelite teardrops.

1.75in (4.5cm) high

$20-30   BB

The eye is missing its inset rhinestone. Although this can be replaced, it will be an added cost.

An unmarked hummingbird-in-flight gilt metal pin, with enameled wings.

1.5in (4cm) high

$15-20   MHC

An unmarked cocktail jewelry style expandable bracelet, set with pale blue rhinestones.

Although examples with colorless stones are easier to find, this attractive pale blue is scarcer.

2.5in (6.5cm) diam (unexpanded)

$40-60   BB

A 1930s unmarked paste cocktail jewelry style articulated bracelet.

Jewelry such as this was made during the 1930s in imitation of the platinum and diamond-set cocktail jewelry worn by the wealthy.

7.5in (19cm) long

$100-130   BB

FIND OUT MORE...

'Miller's Costume Jewellery: How to Compare & Value', by Steven Miners, Miller's Publications, 2006.

DISNEYANA

ESSENTIAL REFERENCE

- The Disney animation studios were founded in 1923 by Walter Elias Disney (1901-66) and his brother Roy (b.1930). Their most famous character, Mickey Mouse, was developed in 1928. Shortly after, merchandise was also produced, and it is this pre-war memorabilia that tends to be most sought-after and valuable today.

- Look for marks, as these can help with dating. Before 1939, the wording 'Walt Disney Enterprises' or, more rarely, 'Walter E. Disney' was used. From 1939 to 1984, the mark changed to 'Walt Disney Productions', with later marks including '© Disney' and '© Disney Enterprises'. Licensed items bearing one of these marks is generally more sought-after than unlicensed items, unless very early or rare.

- The style of a character, or the characters themselves, can also help with dating. For example, Mickey Mouse lost his toothy grin in the early 1930s and became more rounded and less rodent-like over time. Mickey and some characters

have broader appeal than others, but do not ignore characters that are less well-known as they may be rarer.

- In 1961, Marx released its Disneykins ranges, which were produced until the company closed in 1973. These were tiny injection molded, hand-painted figures that were sometimes included in detailed scenes. They were affordable and fun – in the US, in 1961, the small figurines retailed at 15 cents each, while larger TV Scenes retailed at 29 cents each. With over 160 figurines to find, there are a number of ranges, with 101 Dalmations being the largest with over 47 figurines.

- Condition is important to value as most memorabilia was played with or worn, and has become damaged. Disneykins should retain their colorful and appealing boxes, which should also be in good condition, to be worth higher values. Earlier examples produced in 'British Hong Kong' tend to have better quality molding and painting.

A 1960s Louis Marx Disneykin 'Pinocchio' TV Scenes set, marked "Walt Disney Productions", mint and boxed.

3in (7.5cm) high

$40-50　　　　　　　　　　　　　　　**MTB**

A 1960s Louis Marx Disneykin 'Bambi' TV Scenes set, marked "Walt Disney Productions", mint and boxed.

3in (7.5cm) high

$40-50　　　　　　　　　**MTB**

A 1960s Louis Marx Disneykins 'Dewey' hand-painted miniature figurine, made in Hong Kong, mint and boxed.

Box 1.5in (4cm) high

$5-10　　　　　　　　　**MTB**

A 1960s Marx Disneykins 'Thumper' hand-painted miniature figurine, made in Hong Kong, mint and boxed.

Box 1.5in (4cm) high

$5-10　　　　**MTB**

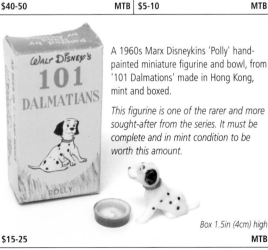

A 1960s Marx Disneykins 'Polly' hand-painted miniature figurine and bowl, from '101 Dalmations' made in Hong Kong, mint and boxed.

This figurine is one of the rarer and more sought-after from the series. It must be complete and in mint condition to be worth this amount.

Box 1.5in (4cm) high

$15-25　　　　　　　　　　　**MTB**

DISNEYANA

A 1960s Louis Marx Disneykin 'Soldier' hand-painted miniature figurine, from the Babes in Toyland series, made in Hong Kong, mint and boxed.

This series was released in 1962.

4.25in (10.5cm) high

$20-30   **MTB**

A 1960s Louis Marx Disneykin play set, including Mickey Mouse, Minnie Mouse and Pluto, made in Hong Kong, marked "Walt Disney Productions".

6.5in (16.5cm) wide

$80-120   **MTB**

A 1970s-80s Play Pal Plastic Inc. Mickey Mouse plastic money bank, impressed "Walt Disney Productions".

11.25in (28.5cm) high

$10-15   **AEM**

A Hoan Ltd Mickey Mouse cookie jar, impressed "©The Walt Disney Co."

10.75in (27cm) high

$20-30   **AEM**

A 1940s Ideal Novelty Co. Pinocchio painted composition and wood figurine, with flex-jointed arms and legs.

This Pinocchio is lacking his name, which is usually transfer-printed in white across his chest.

7.5in (19cm) high

$60-100   **AAC**

A 1970s-80s Play Pal Plastic Inc. Pinocchio plastic money bank, impressed "Walt Disney Productions".

11.25in (28.5cm) high

$15-20   **AEM**

A Snow White hand-painted carnival chalkware figure, with recently touched-up face.

These painted plaster figurines were usually sold or given away at fairs as prizes. Condition is usually very poor.

c1938   *14.5in (37cm) high*

$45-65   **BH**

A 1960s Louis Marx Mary Poppins clockwork plastic 'Whirling Toy', marked "Walt Disney Productions", mint with original printed card box.

Wind her up and she jiggles and jumps around.

10.75in (27.5cm) high

$80-120   **MTB**

DISNEYANA

A Mattel Pushmi-Pullyu double-headed llama soft toy.

This was produced in conjunction with the 1967 film 'Dr Dolittle' starring Rex Harrison as the Doctor. In the book it appeared as an antelope, but was portrayed as a llama in the film.

c1968   6.25in (16cm) high

$80-100   **MTB**

A Kohner plastic Pluto 'Peppy Puppet', marked "Walt Disney Productions", mint and carded.

1970   11in (28cm) high

$25-35   **MTB**

A unopened pack of 1950s Walt Disney Productions printed card 'Disneyland Party Decorations', including Bambi and Thumper.

13.5in (34.5cm) high

$7-10   **BH**

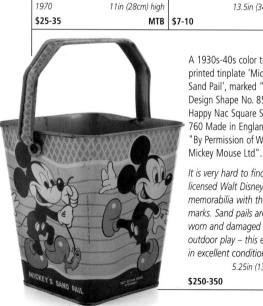

A 1930s-40s color transfer-printed tinplate 'Mickey's Sand Pail', marked "Reg'd Design Shape No. 858445 Happy Nac Square Sand Pail 760 Made in England" and "By Permission of Walt Disney Mickey Mouse Ltd".

It is very hard to find UK licensed Walt Disney memorabilia with these marks. Sand pails are usually worn and damaged through outdoor play – this example is in excellent condition.

5.25in (13.5cm) high

$250-350   **BH**

EXPERT EYE – A PAIR OF SALT & PEPPER SHAKERS

Retailer Faye Bennison acquired the Poxon China Company of Vernon, California in 1931, renaming it Vernon Kilns.

He won a contract to produce characters from Walt Disney's 'Fantasia', 'Dumbo' and 'The Reluctant Dragon' films in 1940, which lasted until late 1941.

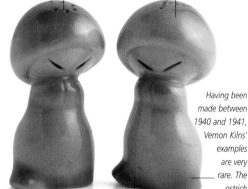

Having been made between 1940 and 1941, Vernon Kilns' examples are very rare. The ostrich ballerina figurines can be worth as much as $2,000 each.

Now being deemed a classic, Fantasia was not a commercial success when released, and sales of related memorabilia at the time were comparatively low.

A very rare pair of Vernon Kilns dancing mushroom salt and pepper shakers, from Walt Disney's 'Fantasia', impressed "Disney Copyright 1941".

The American Pottery Company continued producing some of Vernon Kiln's items, but these are not marked and are less sought-after.

1941   3.5in (9cm) high

$300-400   **BB**

A 1950s Walt Disney Productions transfer-printed metal bubblegum dispenser, with maker's mark to base.

23.5in (59.5cm) high

$500-700   **QU**

FIND OUT MORE...

www.disneykins.com
www.disney.com

ESSENTIAL REFERENCE

- The earliest dolls were generally home-made, carved from wood or sewn from scraps of fabric. The bisque-head doll industry grew in France and Germany from the 1860s onwards, and saw its golden age from the 1900s until the 1930s, when other materials such as composition (which had been traditionally been used for dolls' bodies rather than their heads), began to take over.
- The incised marks on the back of a bisque doll's head can help identify its maker, as can facial characteristics. Look for dolls by well-known makers such as Jumeau, Heubach and Armand Marseille. Collectors value clean, undamaged heads with expressive faces. Replaced bodies devalue a doll, while original clothes add considerably to value.

- Bisque and composition were used for dolls' heads from the 1900s to the 1950s when they were superseded by the more economical, and versatile, plastic.
- In recent years, hard and soft plastic dolls have seen a rise in interest and value, as those who loved them as children become collectors. Look for major names such as Madam Alexander, Terri Lee, Vogue, Ideal and Pedigree. Condition is one of the most important considerations for value. Hairstyles should also be original with restyled, and particularly cut, hair reducing value considerably. Look for detailed, original clothing and original boxes. Character dolls can also be sought-after, whether based on celebrities or story book characters.

A German Kammer & Reinhardt/Simon & Halbig bisque child doll, with weighted blue eyes, open mouth, pierced ears, brunette wig and pate, wood and composition jointed body, wearing woollen one-piece long-johns and vest, socks, leatherette shoes, green velvet pantaloons and matching jacket and cap, the head impressed "Simon & Halbig k * R 39".

Simon & Halbig made heads for Kammer & Reinhardt, who purchased the company in 1920.

16in (40cm) high

$500-700   **VEC**

A German J.D. Kestner Jr. bisque doll, with weighted brown eyes, open mouth, blonde mohair wig, five-piece composition body, painted dark blue ribbed stockings and tan and brown shoes, cotton and woollen undergarments, white muslin dress, crochet bonnet, the head impressed "192".

1900   9in (23cm) high

$300-400   **VEC**

A German Armand Marseille for Edmund Edelman Melitta bisque doll, with open mouth with missing teeth, original brown mohair wig and pate, five-piece curved limb composition body, impressed "Melitta 11", blue weighted eyes detached but present, right thumb missing, toes detached.

c1910   20in (51cm) high

$70-110   **VEC**

A German Hermann Steiner bisque doll, with weighted brown eyes, open mouth with chipped teeth, blonde wig and pate, wood and composition ball-jointed body, cotton and woollen undergarments, silk, cotton and lace dress and lace bonnet, the head impressed "H St 9".

c1910   17.5in (45cm) high

$200-300   **VEC**

A German Walther and Söhn character bisque doll, with weighted brown eyes, open mouth, original blond wig and pate, five-piece composition body, dressed in original golden thread woven dress and matching head-band, impressed "200-14/0 W&S 14/0".

This character doll may have been used as a Christmas fairy judging by its clothing.

c1922   9.25in (24cm) high

$160-240   **VEC**

A 1930s American Effanbee Patsyette composition doll, with painted brown side-glancing eyes, painted closed mouth, molded brown hair, five-piece body, impressed "Effanbee Patsyette Doll", slight crazing overall, reclothed.

9in (23cm) high

$100-150   **VEC**

A 1920s-30s molded and painted felt and fabric 'Empress of Australia' souvenir sailor doll.

10in (25.5cm) high

$40-60   **PC**

A 1930s Chad Valley felt boy doll, with painted eyes, mohair hair, wearing socks, leather shoes, cotton shirt, brown spotty tie, green velvet shorts and felt jacket, with red embroidered label to left foot "Hygienic Toys Made in England by Chad Valley Co. Ltd", minor moth damage and fading.

16in (41cm) high

$200-300   **VEC**

EXPERT EYE – A STEINER CLOCKWORK BISQUE DOLL

The tinplate boots are characteristic of Steiner.

Her face finely molded with a charming expression, and she is beautifully dressed in well-made clothes, adding to her appeal.

Mechanical walking dolls are rare. The body of this doll has been opened to repair the mechanism, which reduces the value marginally.

The head is incised 'FS & Co' indicating it was made by German maker Franz Schmidt (founded 1890). This style of marking was used on their later dolls.

A Steiner clockwork walking doll, with Franz Schmidt bisque head, original period clothes and tinplate boots

12.75in (32cm) high

$6,000-8,000   **MTB**

A 1950s Betsy McCall cloth doll, together with her McCall's pattern and instructions.

17in (43cm) high

$70-100   **BH**

An Annalee 'Kid with Kite' poseable fabric doll, with fabric and card tags, the base stamped "2335".

1992   *7in (18cm) high*

$12-18   **AEM**

A Coleco Cabbage Patch Kid, with vinyl face and wool hair, dressed in a sailor suit.

Cabbage Patch Kids were devised by Xavier Roberts in 1978 and were made from cloth. They were initially sold at craft shows and later via the Babyland General Hospital in Cleveland, Georgia. Toy maker Colec mass-produced them with vinyl faces from 1982 until they went bankrupt in 1989. Since then, they have been made by a number of companies including Mattel, Hasbro and, most recently, Play Along.

1982-89   *17.25in (44cm) high*

$7-10   **AEM**

A Chad Valley Strawberry Shortcake vinyl doll, complete with comb, and mint and boxed.

1980   7.75in (19.5cm) high

$30-40   **MTB**

An Ideal Shirley Temple vinyl doll, with original sailor suit, shoes, bow and hat, and original red coat and hat, in mint condition.

1957   12in (30.5cm) high

$140-200   **SOTT**

EXPERT EYE – A PEDIGREE MARY POPPINS

Notable UK doll company Pedigree was commissioned by the film's New Zealand distributors to produce a Mary Poppins doll to promote the film.

The clothing is very close to that worn by the character in the film, including a working dress and apron.

Pedigree used a Sindy doll with chestnut hair that was in production at the time, dressing her in Mary Poppins' clothing.

Examples are rare. Those in mint condition, complete with their boxes, are rarer still.

A Pedigree Walt Disney's 'Mary Poppins' vinyl character doll, complete with original clothes, hat and bag, and in card box.

c1965   12in (30.5cm) high

$1,100-1,300   **MTB**

A rare 1963 Alexander-kins Queen Elizabeth II doll, no. 499, in mint, complete condition, with printed card box.

Do not confuse this earlier example with the later edition from 1992, that wears a crown and is dressed differently.

1963   7.75in (19.5cm) high

$800-1,200   **BH**

A 1950s Madame Alexander Maggie hard plastic walker doll, her black skirt printed with pink roses, with shoes and laces, and label on blouse.

14.25in (36cm) high

$240-360   **BH**

A 1950s English Rosebud hard plastic doll, with original suit, duster coat and ponytail.

13.75in (35cm) high

$70-90   **MA**

A Tiny Terri Lee hard plastic doll, with original clothes, socks and shoes, with curly hairstyle and fabric tag.

10.25in (26cm) high

$160-240   **BH**

A 1960s Uneeda 'Bendable Babs' poseable fashion doll, from the Dollikin range, made in "The British Crown Colony of Hong Kong", mint in original box.

7.5in (19cm) wide

$50-70   **MTB**

A 1960s Uneeda Dollikin poseable fashion doll, with 14 different poseable body joints, mint and boxed.

11.25in (28.5cm) high

$120-160   **MTB**

A Vogue Lil' Imp soft vinyl walker doll, complete with original clothing and shoes, in excellent condition.

1959-60   *11in (28cm) high*

$120-180   **BH**

A 1950s Vogue Dolls Ginny hard plastic walker doll, with painted lashes and straight legs, mint and boxed with original leaflet.

7.5in (19cm) high

$450-550   **BH**

A Vogue Dolls Inc. 'Ginny' doll, with wrist tag and remnant of original label, in mint condition with box and instruction leaflet.

The high value of this doll and the one shown above far right can be attributed to the fact they are in complete, boxed and mint condition.

1953   *7.5in (19cm) high*

$550-650   **BH**

A Vogue Dolls Inc. 'Ginny' outfit, with dress and hat, in mint condition with original card and cellophane window box.

6.25in (16cm) wide

$60-80   **BH**

ESSENTIAL REFERENCE

- Just like salt and pepper shakers, eggcups have become a collecting field of their own. Over the past 300 years, many companies and makers have produced eggcups in different materials, with a great many being found in ceramic. Small in size, and usually affordable, they are easy to describe, ship and display. This makes them popular with shop-based dealers as well as internet-based sellers.
- There are a number of features to consider. Firstly, look for a maker's mark. Notable makers such as Spode or Wedgwood will add desirability. Secondly, look at the quality of the piece in terms of the molding and the pattern. If it is hand-painted, look for good details and careful application of paint. Although small, transfer-printed designs should be carefully applied.
- Novelty forms are also popular, particularly if they relate to popular characters, cars or aeroplanes. Most novelty eggcups found will date from the 1920s and 1960s and were often made in Japan. Examples with designs by popular children's book illustrators such as Mabel Lucie Attwell will usually be worth more. Always look carefully for signs of damage as these were made to be used and typically saw great use.

A Washington 'Old Willow' pattern transfer-printed eggcup.

1.75in (4.5cm) high

$25-35   BEV

A Copeland Spode 'Italian' pattern transfer-printed eggcup.

Spode is collected in its own right, and 'Italian' is one of the more common patterns.

1.75in (4.5cm) high

$40-50   BEV

An English urn-shaped 'Imari' eggcup, with hand-painted and transfer-printed detailing and gilt highlights, the base painted "No 824 X".

2.5in (6cm) high

$70-90   BEV

A Japanese combined whistle and 'man in a car' eggcup, the base stamped in red "Foreign".

This is valuable and desirable for a number of reasons. Combination eggcups and whistles such as this are scarce, particularly in good condition. The car shape is also highly desirable, and the level of molded detail is very good.

4.5in (11cm) long

$150-250   BEV

A Japanese lustre painted combination whistle and train eggcup, the base stamped "Foreign" in red.

4.75in (12cm) long

$50-70   BEV

A Japanese lustre painted train eggcup, unmarked.

2.5in (6.5cm) high

$40-50   BEV

A Japanese lustre painted Noah's ark eggcup, unmarked.

2.5in (6.5cm) high

$40-60   BEV

EYEWEAR

ESSENTIAL REFERENCE

- Although there are still many who collect primarily to record optical developments and changing styles, today's market for vintage eyewear is dominated by those who buy to wear, and include prolific collectors such as Elton John. A decade ago, the focus was on 19thC and earlier examples, but today this has shifted to examples from the 20thC that are visibly more wearable, colorful and fun.
- The key factors governing value are: the style or look, the condition, the name of the maker or designer, and the materials used. Examples that sum up a particular period or style tend to be most popular, with those from the 1950s and '60s currently being seen as the most stylish. These include the 'cat's eye' styles of the 1950s and the over-sized rounded forms of the 1960s.
- Those in wilder styles, or in crazy colors or shapes, tend to be the most valuable. Sought-after today to give a truly individual look, they can be hard to find as their extreme styling made them either unpopular or too expensive at the time. More standard frames that sum up the period can make affordable and useable retro alternatives to today's frames.

- Consider the materials used and the work that went into making a pair. Hand-crafted elements such as enameling, painting or complex laminating or cutting will generally add value. Look for a famous designer's name or monogram, as this will usually add value, particularly if the name is combined with great period styling. Some designers' monograms changed over time, which will help with dating.
- Always examine a set of frames closely before buying. Look for burn marks, and particularly for cracks or splits, as these cannot be repaired suitably, especially if the frames are intended to be worn. Some plastic can warp over time and bend out of shape. Providing this is not too serious, it can usually be corrected by a professional.
- The value is not usually affected if lenses are scratched, cracked or even missing entirely. Most buyers will prefer to choose whether frames are used as glasses or sunglasses, and may want to fit prescription lenses. However, if lenses were unusual, such as having a graduated tint in a matching or contrasting color, the original examples will add value. Keep hold of them even if they are replaced with prescription examples.

A pair of 1950s American dark blue 'cat's eye' frames, with inset star-shaped screws, marked "Swan U.S.A. 51/2".

4.75in (12cm) wide

$30-50   **BB**

A pair of 1950s French gray pearlescent 'cat's eye' frames, inset with rhinestones and flashes, marked "France".

5in (13cm) wide

$40-50   **BB**

A pair of 1950s French gold pearlized, blue and red laminated plastic 'cats eye' frames, marked "Made in France".

5in (13cm) wide

$140-180   **VE**

A pair of 1950s French black frames, with inset metal lines and stars, marked "Frame France".

5in (12.5cm) wide

$40-50   **BB**

A pair of 1950s Christian Dior laminated pearlescent gray and clear plastic 'cat's eye' frames, set with rhinestones in gilt metal at the corners, and with a bow-shaped bridge, marked "Frame Austria".

5in (13cm) wide

$250-350   **VE**

A pair of laminated pearlized gray and black plastic 'snake' textured frames, with extended side wings over the hinges.

5.25in (13.5cm) wide

$140-180   **VE**

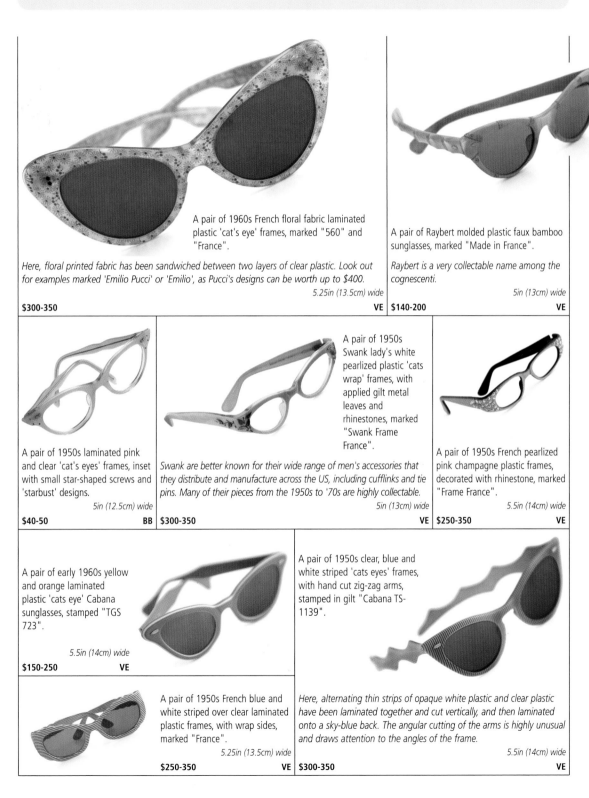

A pair of 1960s French floral fabric laminated plastic 'cat's eye' frames, marked "560" and "France".

Here, floral printed fabric has been sandwiched between two layers of clear plastic. Look out for examples marked 'Emilio Pucci' or 'Emilio', as Pucci's designs can be worth up to $400.

5.25in (13.5cm) wide

$300-350   VE

A pair of Raybert molded plastic faux bamboo sunglasses, marked "Made in France".

Raybert is a very collectable name among the cognescenti.

5in (13cm) wide

$140-200   VE

A pair of 1950s laminated pink and clear 'cat's eyes' frames, inset with small star-shaped screws and 'starbust' designs.

5in (12.5cm) wide

$40-50   BB

A pair of 1950s Swank lady's white pearlized plastic 'cats wrap' frames, with applied gilt metal leaves and rhinestones, marked "Swank Frame France".

Swank are better known for their wide range of men's accessories that they distribute and manufacture across the US, including cufflinks and tie pins. Many of their pieces from the 1950s to '70s are highly collectable.

5in (13cm) wide

$300-350   VE

A pair of 1950s French pearlized pink champagne plastic frames, decorated with rhinestone, marked "Frame France".

5.5in (14cm) wide

$250-350   VE

A pair of early 1960s yellow and orange laminated plastic 'cats eye' Cabana sunglasses, stamped "TGS 723".

5.5in (14cm) wide

$150-250   VE

A pair of 1950s clear, blue and white striped 'cats eyes' frames, with hand cut zig-zag arms, stamped in gilt "Cabana TS-1139".

Here, alternating thin strips of opaque white plastic and clear plastic have been laminated together and cut vertically, and then laminated onto a sky-blue back. The angular cutting of the arms is highly unusual and draws attention to the angles of the frame.

5.5in (14cm) wide

A pair of 1950s French blue and white striped over clear laminated plastic frames, with wrap sides, marked "France".

5.25in (13.5cm) wide

$250-350   VE

$300-350   VE

EYEWEAR

A pair of 1960s French handmade gold-colored and black laminated carved plastic sunglasses, with flower petal type decoration, the original lenses with "Fait Main Verres Filtrant" label.

The label indicates that the petal-like shapes were cut into the side of the frames by hand.

5.5in (14cm) wide

$300-350   VE

A pair of 1960s French orange and white laminated plastic frames, with hand-cut 'cookie cutter' edges, marked "Hand Made in France", with 'Fait Main' sticker.

6in (15.5cm) wide

$250-350   VE

A pair of 1960s convex 'bug eye' laminated white and black plastic frames, marked "Frame France".

A pair of 1960s black and white laminated plastic frames, unmarked.

5.5in (14cm) wide

$250-350   VE

A pair of laminated purple and white plastic 'Op Art' chequerboard frames.

5.25in (13.5cm) wide

$300-350   VE

The streaked wood effect is created by laminating thin strips or panels of black and white plastic together in different combinations and layers and then cutting it vertically to reveal the 'sandwich' of layers.

5.75in (14.5cm) wide

$300-350   VE

A pair of 1960s French translucent 'Jackie O' brown 'bug eye' sunglasses, the original lenses with sticker reading "Filtrant Vergo France", unmarked.

6in (15cm) wide

$250-350   VE

A pair of 1960s thick copper and black laminated plastic 'bug eye' frames, unmarked.

5.25in (13.5cm) wide

$250-350   VE

A pair of 1960s French laminated black and gray leopard skin effect on black plastic Lucite 'Eskimo' frames.

6.25in (16cm) wide

$50-80   BB

A pair of 1960s French transparent sky-blue plastic sunglasses, inset with metal dots and rhinestones, marked "Made in France".

5.25in (13.5cm) wide

$250-350 **VE**

A pair of 1960s French scalloped bone sunglasses, with original lenses, marked "Made in France".

5in (13cm) wide

$250-350 **VE**

EXPERT EYE – A PAIR OF DIOR SUNGLASSES

Christian Dior is a prestigious name. The frames are fully signed and retain their original case.

The large perfectly round frames and thick arms are typical of the most fashionable 1960s styles.

A pair of 1960s French 'Op Art' black plastic hexagonal oversize sunglasses, with blue circular insets, marked "Made in France".

These bring to mind the boldly colored 1960s geometric artworks of Victor Vasarely.

6in (15cm) wide

$300-350 **VE**

The brightly colored stylized floral design has been hand-painted onto the molded front, and is typical of the 1960s.

Dior also produced scarcer enameeled gold metal frames with similar decoration, inset rhinestones and glass jewels during the late 1960s. They can be worth up to $1,500.

A pair of 1960s French Christian Dior multicolored handmade plastic sunglasses, the arms with impressed 'CD' monograms, together with original gray faux leather case with Dior logo.

6in (15.5cm) wide

$800-1,000 **VE**

A pair of 1960s Op Art style white and black laminated sunglasses, stamped "Sun Sentry U.S.A."

Op Art is the name applied to an abstract style of painting comprizing geometric monochrome or repeated colors, and making use of optical effects to blur the boundaries between the picture plane and illusion. Its champion was the British painter Bridget Riley, and its effects were seen in the fashions of Andre Courreges and Pierre Cardin.

5.5in (14cm) wide

$300-350 **VE**

A pair of 1960s 'Patriotic' cream plastic square sunglasses, cut with a square of lines and then block-printed with red or blue squares.

5.5in (14cm) wide

$250-350 **VE**

A pair of late 1960s Pierre Cardin light gray transparent plastic frames, in the shape of a pair of open lips, marked "Frame France".

5.75in (14.5cm) wide

$250-350 **VE**

EYEWEAR

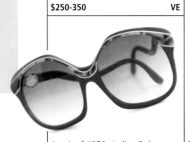

A pair of 1960s French pink-striated transparent plastic large sunglasses, stamped "Made in France".

6.25in (16cm) wide

$250-350   **VE**

A pair of 1970s Italian Delotto laminated terracotta, white and faux tortoiseshell plastic sunglasses, with wavy arms and original graduated lenses, one arm marked marked "Made in Italy, Oris 112 Brown".

6in (15.5cm) wide

$250-350   **VE**

A pair of 1970s over-sized brown and amber graduated plastic frames, with cut-out bridge, unmarked but with Paco Rabanne inset metal decal.

5.75in (14.5cm) wide

$250-350   **VE**

A pair of 1970s German Christian Dior yellow-to-amber graduated plastic Optyl frames, with triangular pierced arms, marked "Made in Germany".

$250-350   **VE**

A pair of 1960s-70s transparent graduated green, pink and clear plastic frames.

5.5in (14cm) wide

$30-40   **BB**

ESSENTIAL REFERENCE – GIVENCHY

A pair of 1960s Givenchy pink oversized curving 'bug eye' frames, with original graduated violet lenses and wavy arms, marked "Givenchy L Unico-Frame France".

The haute couture house of Givenchy was founded in 1952 in Paris by Hubert Givenchy (b.1927). He worked with a number of influential haute couture fashion designers including Jacques Fath, Lucien Lelong and Esla Schiaparelli. After his retirement in 1995, he was succeeded by John Galliano, who was followed by Alexander McQueen and then Julien MacDonald. Famous patrons include Audrey Hepburn (notably for her films such as 'Sabrina') and the Kennedy family, some of whom wore Givenchy to John F. Kennedy's funeral. Part of the LVMH conglomerate, Givenchy continues to produce luxurious and elegant eyewear that reflects today's fashions.

5in (13cm) wide

$300-350   **VE**

A pair of 1970s American colorless and violet graduated plastic frames, with drop arms, inset 'WB' decal, and stamped "Satin Doll, American".

The 'drop' style of the arms is a typical feature of the 1970 styles.

6in (15cm) wide

$35-45   **BB**

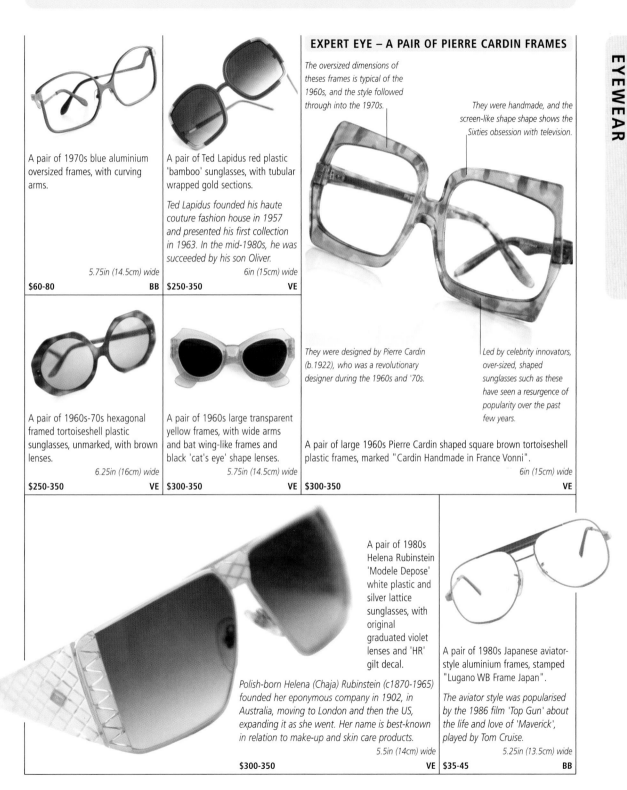

A pair of 1970s blue aluminium oversized frames, with curving arms.

5.75in (14.5cm) wide

$60-80   BB

A pair of Ted Lapidus red plastic 'bamboo' sunglasses, with tubular wrapped gold sections.

Ted Lapidus founded his haute couture fashion house in 1957 and presented his first collection in 1963. In the mid-1980s, he was succeeded by his son Oliver.

6in (15cm) wide

$250-350   VE

EXPERT EYE – A PAIR OF PIERRE CARDIN FRAMES

The oversized dimensions of theses frames is typical of the 1960s, and the style followed through into the 1970s.

They were handmade, and the screen-like shape shape shows the Sixties obsession with television.

A pair of 1960s-70s hexagonal framed tortoiseshell plastic sunglasses, unmarked, with brown lenses.

6.25in (16cm) wide

$250-350   VE

A pair of 1960s large transparent yellow frames, with wide arms and bat wing-like frames and black 'cat's eye' shape lenses.

5.75in (14.5cm) wide

$300-350   VE

They were designed by Pierre Cardin (b.1922), who was a revolutionary designer during the 1960s and '70s.

Led by celebrity innovators, over-sized, shaped sunglasses such as these have seen a resurgence of popularity over the past few years.

A pair of large 1960s Pierre Cardin shaped square brown tortoiseshell plastic frames, marked "Cardin Handmade in France Vonni".

6in (15cm) wide

$300-350   VE

A pair of 1980s Helena Rubinstein 'Modele Depose' white plastic and silver lattice sunglasses, with original graduated violet lenses and 'HR' gilt decal.

Polish-born Helena (Chaja) Rubinstein (c1870-1965) founded her eponymous company in 1902, in Australia, moving to London and then the US, expanding it as she went. Her name is best-known in relation to make-up and skin care products.

5.5in (14cm) wide

$300-350   VE

A pair of 1980s Japanese aviator-style aluminium frames, stamped "Lugano WB Frame Japan".

The aviator style was popularised by the 1986 film 'Top Gun' about the life and love of 'Maverick', played by Tom Cruise.

5.25in (13.5cm) wide

$35-45   BB

EYEWEAR

A pair of 1970s Prince Michel de Bourbon laminated light and dark blue plastic sunglasses with graduated lenses, stamped with a gilt shield motif and marked "12300 C 30".

The faux horn effect is created by selectively carving back the darker top layer, revealing the lighter color beneath.

5.75in (14.5cm) wide

$150-250   VE

A pair of 1970s French Balenciaga laminated red and clear plastic sunglasses, the corners overlaid with black cut with lines, together with the original tag marked "CR39" and "Handmade France".

Cristobal Balenciaga (1895-1972) opened his first boutique in 1914, and grew to be one of the most influential fashion designers of the mid-20thC. Described by Christian Dior as 'the master of all of us', he is particularly remembered for his tunic, chemise and Empire-style dresses of the late 1950s. His name continues today as part of the Gucci group.

6in (15cm) wide

$300-350   VE

A pair of French Emilio Pucci handmade faux tortoiseshell plastic frames, with gilt metal hinges and black lacquer panels, marked "Florence Made in France Fait Main EP274".

5.75in (14.5cm) wide

$250-350   VE

A pair of 1980s Playboy yellow, white and black laminated Optyl plastic sunglasses, with original graduated lenses, gold Playboy bunny motif, marked "Made in Austria Optyl Playboy".

Optyl is a cast-molded, thermo-setting plastic. It is used by Christian Dior, Dunhill and Paloma Picasso, among other, for their eyewear. Vintage licensed Playboy items are becoming increasingly collectable.

5.75in (14.5cm) wide

$250-350   VE

A pair of 1970s Occhi malachite green mottled laminated plastic over metal frames, with an applied metal stripe over one eye, the arms marked "Made in W.Germany".

$140-180   VE

A pair of 1980s Italian Zagato 'New Dimension' black, red and white plastic sunglasses, marked "Hand made Italy" and with original swing tag.

6in (15cm) wide

$300-350   VE

A pair of 1970s Christian Dior ivory-colored plastic curving sunglasses, with printed pattern, applied gilt shaped decal with 'CD' logo, and wide arms marked "Christian Dior", "Made in Germany" and "2346".

As with most frames, the addition of a designer's name, such as Dior's, from a classic period, such as the 1960s, indicates good quality and adds value.

5.75in (14.5cm) wide

$300-350   VE

A pair of American white plastic sunglasses, screen-printed with black and blue flag and circle motif, and with original sky blue lenses, marked "Cabana TS-1934".

The cat's eye shape is more typical of the 1950s, although the decoration indicates these are later.

5in (13cm) wide

$150-250   VE

A pair of aluminium frames, with matte 'glitter' effect to the top rim and protruding hinges, stamped "ALUM 46".

5.5in (14cm) wide

$50-80   BB

A pair of Bausch & Lomb 'Baluminum' gold-filled aluminium rimless frames, with inset rhinestones, the arms marked "Ballgrip 12KT GF.".

5in (13cm) wide

$350-450   VE

ESSENTIAL REFERENCE – VICTOR GROS

A pair of 1980s French 'Michele Lamy pour Victor Gros' Elisabeth black plastic asymmetric frames, with pearlized blue and gold plastic over one eye and arm.

Victor Gros was founded in 1872 by Edouard Gros to produce hair ornaments. They began producing glasses in 1930 when the company was being run by his son Victor Gros. Perhaps their most famous design was the oversized frame produced in 1968 for Jacqueline Kennedy Onassis, which became a hallmark of her look, and 20thC eyewear design. The design was exclusive to Onassis, who was a friend of the Gros family, until the 1980s but is now part of their Traction production range. Michele Lamy is a notable fashion consultant who once designed for Gros. Married to fashion designer Rick Owens, she is also is a backer behind fashion's avant garde ascending star Gareth Pugh.

6in (15.5cm) wide

$150-200   VE

A pair of 1960s purple and white woven fabric laminated in clear plastic frames, with 'VO' monogram.

5.75in (14.5cm) wide

$40-50   BB

A pair of 1960s French large tartan fabric and laminated plastic sunglasses, with graduated gray lenses, marked "Hand Made in France".

6in (15cm) wide

$250-350   VE

A pair of 1970s Ted Lapidus sunglasses, with original graduated UV lenses and wood-effect textured top rim, stamped "Paris Made in France" and "TL 63 02".

5.5in (14cm) wide

$250-350   VE

A pair of 1980s Nina Ricci 'Haute Couture' malachite green, white and clear cut and laminated plastic sunglasses, with applied gilt 'Nr' motif, stamped "Nina Ricci Paris", "Handmade" and "CR39" lenses, retaining original card.

The Nina Ricci fashion house was founded by Maria Ricci (1883-1970) in 1932. By the 1950s, she had retired from her active role in the company leaving it to her son Robert and, from 1954, the Belgian designer Jules-Francois Crahay.

5.5in (14cm) wide

$300-350   VE

A pair of 1980s French Alain Mikli gray pearlescent and black plastic laminated sunglasses, with original purple lenses, marked "Hand Made in France, C A.M. 88 706 366".

Alain Mikli (b.1955) founded his first eyewear design studio in 1978. Within a few years his innovative designs had attracted the attention of legendary collector Elton John.

5.75in (14.5cm) wide

$300-350   VE

EYEWEAR

A pair of curved rectangular tortoiseshell plastic gentleman's frames, marked "USA 5 3/4".

Striking low and wide rectangular forms such as these have seen a resurgence in popularity for men over the past few years.

5in (12.5cm) wide

$35-45   **BB**

A pair of American Optical laminated light blue over clear plastic small hexagonal frames.

5in (12.5cm) wide

$30-40   **BB**

A pair of transparent, pearlescent gray plastic gentleman's frames, with two inset metal star shaped screws, marked "Frame France".

5in (13cm) wide

$30-40   **BB**

A pair of 1970s American black plastic gentleman's frames, marked "U/Z 512 U.S.A."

Large, visually 'heavier' frames such as these have become fashionable for men over the past few years, particularly with the 'geek chic' trend.

5in (13cm) wide

$30-40   **BB**

A pair of 1970s deep blue plastic frames.

5.25in (13.5cm) wide

$30-35   **BB**

A pair of French Swank faceted black plastic gentleman's frames, marked "Frame France".

5.75in (14.5cm) wide

$30-35   **BB**

A pair of 1940s French handmade tortoiseshell plastic gentleman's sunglasses, the original blue lenses with rectangular "Fait Main Verres Filtrant" sticker and 'hockey stick' arms.

5.5in (14cm) wide

$150-200   **VE**

Four pairs of similar 1970s new-old stock frames.

The term 'new-old-stock' refers to vintage stock found in shops that was never sold or used. Old opticians are increasingly being used as exciting sources for vintage eyewear.

5.75in (14.5cm) wide

$40-50 (each)   **BB**

A pair of 1930s-40s light tortoiseshell plastic gentleman's frames, with half hexagonal top rims and 8mm thick arms.

This simple, curved style is known as 'hockey stick' and is desirable.

5.25in (13.5cm) wide

$150-200   **VE**

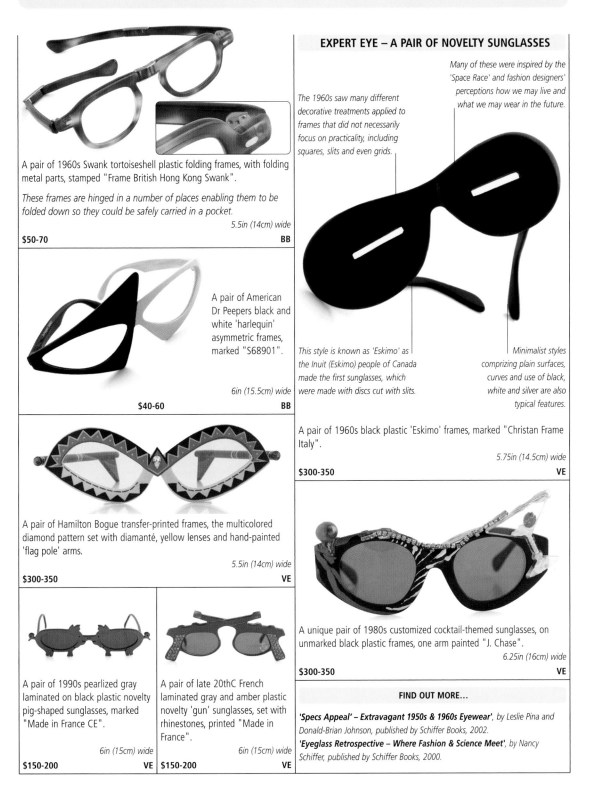

A pair of 1960s Swank tortoiseshell plastic folding frames, with folding metal parts, stamped "Frame British Hong Kong Swank".

These frames are hinged in a number of places enabling them to be folded down so they could be safely carried in a pocket.

5.5in (14cm) wide

$50-70   **BB**

A pair of American Dr Peepers black and white 'harlequin' asymmetric frames, marked "S68901".

6in (15.5cm) wide

$40-60   **BB**

A pair of Hamilton Bogue transfer-printed frames, the multicolored diamond pattern set with diamanté, yellow lenses and hand-painted 'flag pole' arms.

5.5in (14cm) wide

$300-350   **VE**

A pair of 1990s pearlized gray laminated on black plastic novelty pig-shaped sunglasses, marked "Made in France CE".

6in (15cm) wide

$150-200   **VE**

A pair of late 20thC French laminated gray and amber plastic novelty 'gun' sunglasses, set with rhinestones, printed "Made in France".

6in (15cm) wide

$150-200   **VE**

EXPERT EYE – A PAIR OF NOVELTY SUNGLASSES

The 1960s saw many different decorative treatments applied to frames that did not necessarily focus on practicality, including squares, slits and even grids.

Many of these were inspired by the 'Space Race' and fashion designers' perceptions how we may live and what we may wear in the future.

This style is known as 'Eskimo' as the Inuit (Eskimo) people of Canada made the first sunglasses, which were made with discs cut with slits.

Minimalist styles comprizing plain surfaces, curves and use of black, white and silver are also typical features.

A pair of 1960s black plastic 'Eskimo' frames, marked "Christan Frame Italy".

5.75in (14.5cm) wide

$300-350   **VE**

A unique pair of 1980s customized cocktail-themed sunglasses, on unmarked black plastic frames, one arm painted "J. Chase".

6.25in (16cm) wide

$300-350   **VE**

FIND OUT MORE...

'Specs Appeal' – Extravagant 1950s & 1960s Eyewear', by Leslie Pina and Donald-Brian Johnson, published by Schiffer Books, 2002.

'Eyeglass Retrospective – Where Fashion & Science Meet', by Nancy Schiffer, published by Schiffer Books, 2000.

ESSENTIAL REFERENCE

- Vintage fashion has moved into the mainstream over the past decade, a trend led by top models and celebrities such as Kate Moss and Sarah Jessica Parker. No longer just the preserve of costume or couture collectors, many buy vintage pieces to add an individual or classic look to an outfit. Although prices have risen, there is still plenty available to suit different budgets. Examples can be found at specialist auctions and costume dealers, and sometimes in charity shops.

- Designs by influential names such as Cristobal Balenciaga, Coco Chanel and Christian Dior will tend to be worth the most, particularly couture items made in limited quantities to exacting specifications. Pieces from notable collections will usually be the most sought-after, particularly if the collection is considered a classic of the designer's work or launched a new movement or style. The recent death of Yves Saint Laurent (1936-2008) may cause a surge of interest in his already iconic designs. Also consider lesser designers whose work is typical of a period.

- The 1950s and '60s, and the Disco era of the 1970s, have been collectible for a number of years and the High Street spawned many pieces copied or inspired by the work of leading designers, as it continues to do today. These are typically more affordable, but look out for the names of top retailers in prestigious locations, as these are often more desirable. Always consider the style of the label as many designers also produced diffusion ranges, which were considerably less expensive at the time and produced in greater numbers.

- Pieces from the 1980s are now rising strongly in value, particularly the work of innovative designers at the time, such as Gianni Versace and Thierry Mugler. A particularly notable example is the influential, and ever inventive, Vivienne Westwood, who became iconic for the Punk style of the 1970s, and went on to produce many important and sought-after collections during the 1980s and '90s.

- When buying, always consider the shape, construction, material, pattern and color. Finer quality pieces will be well-cut, using high grade materials and stitching. Avoid pieces that are stained or torn – unless this is intentional. Look at fashion books and learn how to recognize the key looks of a decade. Away from the work of leading designers, the more desirable pieces of any decade sum up the age perfectly and have eye appeal.

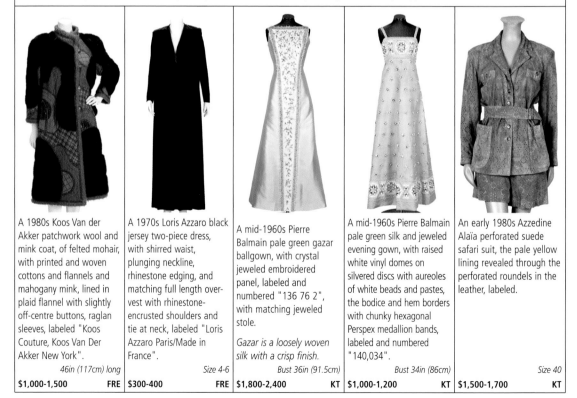

A 1980s Koos Van der Akker patchwork wool and mink coat, of felted mohair, with printed and woven cottons and flannels and mahogany mink, lined in plaid flannel with slightly off-centre buttons, raglan sleeves, labeled "Koos Couture, Koos Van Der Akker New York".

46in (117cm) long

$1,000-1,500   **FRE**

A 1970s Loris Azzaro black jersey two-piece dress, with shirred waist, plunging neckline, rhinestone edging, and matching full length over-vest with rhinestone-encrusted shoulders and tie at neck, labeled "Loris Azzaro Paris/Made in France".

Size 4-6

$300-400   **FRE**

A mid-1960s Pierre Balmain pale green gazar ballgown, with crystal jeweled embroidered panel, labeled and numbered "136 76 2", with matching jeweled stole.

Gazar is a loosely woven silk with a crisp finish.

Bust 36in (91.5cm)

$1,800-2,400   **KT**

A mid-1960s Pierre Balmain pale green silk and jeweled evening gown, with raised white vinyl domes on silvered discs with aureoles of white beads and pastes, the bodice and hem borders with chunky hexagonal Perspex medallion bands, labeled and numbered "140,034".

Bust 34in (86cm)

$1,000-1,200   **KT**

An early 1980s Azzedine Alaïa perforated suede safari suit, the pale yellow lining revealed through the perforated roundels in the leather, labeled.

Size 40

$1,500-1,700   **KT**

A late 1960s Geoffrey Beene jewel-tone metallic brocade A-line tunic evening dress, with Nehru collar, covered buttons, on-seam pockets, cuffs split and belled, labeled "Geoffrey Beene".

Size 10

$300-400   FRE

An early 1970s Biba cotton maxi dress, printed with large red and white ladybugs on a navy ground with an oversized pointed collar, red heart-shaped buttons on a fitted bodice with applied triangular breast pockets.

$250-350   FRE

A 1970s Bill Blass red chiffon evening gown, with attached scarf details, an under-column of rayon jersey and overlay and sleeves of sheer chiffon, labeled "Bill Blass".

Size 10

$150-250   FRE

EXPERT EYE – A BALENCIAGA DAY DRESS

Cristobal Balenciaga (1895-1972) was one of the most influential couturiers of his day, working for the house he founded until 1968. This piece was produced in 1965.

It is made from brocatelle, a comparatively heavy, woven patterned fabric typically of silk and linen, similar to brocade. The use of heavy fabrics was typical of Balenciaga's designs at the time.

During the late 1950s, Balenciaga abandoned the waisted hourglass form of the New Look, designing more linear tunic, chemise and sack dresses. Jacket capes were another common part of his designs.

His day wear was highly influential, and was worn by celebrities and personalities of the day, including Jackie Kennedy, the Duchess of Windsor and Diana Vreeland.

A Balenciaga ivory brocatelle day dress and cape, the simple sleeveless shift dress fastened by buttons down the front, invisible pockets inset into the front side seams, simple cape with single button to fasten, both pieces labeled and numbered "100656".

c1965   *Bust 32in (81cm)*

$2,500-3,500   KT

A 1990s Bill Blass sequined and feathered cocktail dress, covered in small black, grey and white sequins in a looping pattern, the skirt with 'salt and pepper' colored ostrich feathers, labeled "Bill Blass" and "Martha".

Size 4

$1,100-1,300   FRE

A Bob Bugnand embroidered tulle evening gown, of pale blue tulle, embelished with bands of smoke grey sequins, gold embroidery and bugle beads and pale blue pastes, labeled "Bob Bugnand, Paris".

c1955-60   *Bust 36in (91cm)*

$1,000-1,200   KT

A black moss crêpe wool evening gown, attributed to Pierre Cardin, the high neck with stand collar, V-shaped yoke to bodice echoing the pointed hem edged in streamers of fabric, black silk lining, unlabeled.

1970   Bust 34in (86cm)

$600-800   **KT**

A black moss crêpe mini dress, attributed to Pierre Cardin, with car-wash hem, and with gym-slip type bodice from which the bands fall and loop back into the Chinese lantern style skirt, unlabeled.

c1969-70   Bust 34in (86cm)

$1,000-1,200   **KT**

A contemporary Roberto Cavalli bias-cut silk gown, with spaghetti-straps and a naturalistically depicted snake and fruit motif, unlined, with a train and back zip closure, labeled "Roberto Cavalli".

Size small

$350-450   **FRE**

A 1990s bright coral-pink Chanel skirt suit, medium weight bouclé wool, with straight pencil skirt, double-breasted nipped-waist jacket with gold and velvet buttons, black velvet trim, labeled "Chanel Boutique".

Size 36-38

$800-1,000   **FRE**

A 1970s Chanel black silk chiffon metallic jacquard shirtwaist dinner dress, with bronze, gold and silver shaded dots, gold buttons, attached tie at the neckline, and calf-length gored-pleat skirt, labeled "Chanel Boutique".

$450-550   **FRE**

A Chanel white, pink and black tweed suit, with tousled edging to the short, boxy jacket, and matching skirt, labeled.

2005   Bust 38in (97cm)

$1,100-1,300   **KT**

An mid-1970s Ossie Clark/Celia Birtwell for Radley 'Floating Daisies' printed cream moss crêpe dress, with black and green printed bodice, and button front, labeled, with original shop tag.

Size 38

$800-1,000   **KT**

An Ossie Clark/Celia Birtwell printed muslin halterneck summer dress, with pale peach and black lily print overall, and wrap-around skirt, printed Ossie label.

c1970   Size 14

$650-750   **KT**

ESSENTIAL REFERENCE – OSSIE CLARK

A late 1960s Ossie Clark/Celia Birtwell 'Floating Daisies' printed chiffon dress, the cream chiffon ground printed overall in black and green, with Alice Pollock printed label.

Bust 36in (91cm)

$1,000-1,200 KT

An Ossie Clark/Celia Birtwell printed chiffon dress, printed with a green lattice and purple flowers on a primrose chiffon ground, with button front with handkerchief flounces to cuffs and hem, printed Ossie label.

This dress was inspired by fashions of the 1920s.

c1969   Size 12

$1,000-1,200 KT

An early 1970s André Courrèges cotton summer dress, the bodice of white honeycomb mesh edged in appliquéd embroidered cotton rope-twist banding, with matching belt, labeled and numbered "102216".

Bust 32in (81cm)

$700-900 KT

Ossie Clark (1942-96) was one of the most influential and popular designers of the 1960s, and was dubbed the 'King of King's Road'. A year after he graduated from the Royal College of Art in 1965, he produced a range for Quorum, owned by Alice Pollock. Within a year, the company had run into financial trouble due to Pollock and Clark's excessive lifestyles, and the company was acquired by Radley. In 1968, his diffusion range 'Ossie Clark for Radley' was released. He is known for his use of flowing chiffon and moss crepe to give a flamboyant, romantic and floaty feel to his dresses, which is backed up by the use of printed patterns of stylized natural motifs. These were designed by textile designer Celia Birtwell (b.1941), who first met Ossie in 1959 and became his wife in 1969. They worked together until just after their divorce in 1974, with Clark continuing to design, albeit on a lesser scale, until the 1980s when the Punk era dawned.

An Ossie Clark/Celia Birtwell black chiffon wrap-over dress, printed with cream and pink star-like florets in differing sizes, and with contrasting flounces to the neckline, printed Ossie label.

c1970   Size 12

$1,100-1,300 KT

A late 1960s/early 1970s André Courrèges couture purple velvet trouser suit, comprizing shaped, futuristic styled waistcoat with zip front, edged in purple vinyl, matching flared trousers, lined in white satin, labeled and numbered "122910".

Bust 36in (92cm)

$1,400-1,600 KT

A Marc Bohan for Christian Dior black and gold cocktail dress, with corseted inner bodice attached to the skirt, sleeveless brocade over-bodice, the fabric brocaded with tulips against a black ground in shades of gold, belt with large black jet-like stones, labeled and numbered "7521".

This dress was part of the Autumn/Winter 1962 collection. Bohan (b.1926) was the primary designer at Dior from 1958 to 1989, with his 1966 'Peter Pan' collection being particularly notable.

Bust 35in (89cm)

$1,200-1,400 KT

A 1960s Norman Norell taupe wool ensemble, A-line sleeveless dress with princess seams, wide leather belt, vertical welt pockets and silver fox trim with matching cropped three-button jacket, labeled "Norman Norell/New York" and "Marsal".

Size 6-8

$500-700   FRE

A 1960s Mollie Parnis gold-beaded cocktail dress, sleeveless round collared sheath lined in silk, back zip, heavily encrusted with glass beads and rhinestones and with beaded fringe at the hem and with a narrow matching belt, labeled "Mollie Parnis New York".

Size 4

$250-350   FRE

A 1970s Jean Patou pink metallic brocade tunic and pants, asymmetrical button-down closure with high neck and long sleeves, hip pockets, matching straight-leg slacks, labeled "Jean Patou Week End, Paris" and "Couture Boutique, Bergdorf Goodman" etc.

$150-250   FRE

A 1970s-80s Oscar de la Renta feather and sequin gown, silk chiffon bodice with sequin decoration and black cock feather ruff collar and cuffs, satin bow at waist and floor-length sequin-decorated velvet skirt, labeled "Oscar de la Renta" and "Marsal".

Size 4-6

$450-550   FRE

An Oscar de la Renta tweed cocktail dress, sleeveless black and white bouclé tweed cocktail-length sheath dress with bead, ostrich feather and rhinestone accents and with wool-fringed and tulle hem, labeled "Oscar de la Renta".

Size 6

$500-700   FRE

A 1970s Nina Ricci black silk tuxedo yoke bubble dress, jacquard tiny heart patterned silk with long sleeves and high neck, micro-pleated silk chiffon ruffled yoke and shirtsleeve cuffs, falling to below the knee in a gathered ruffle, labeled "Nina Ricci Boutique, Paris, Made in France".

Size 6

$400-600   FRE

A 1980s Yves Saint Laurent silk grosgrain twill party dress, geometric stars and symbols in bright primary and jewel-tone colors on black, deep scoop neckline and puffed-shoulder three-quarter length sleeves, pleated from the natural waist and falling to the calf, labeled "Yves Saint Laurent/Rive Gauche".

Size 40

$120-160   FRE

A 1980s-90s Yves Saint Laurent black cocktail dress, long sleeved with a pleated pouffed-out skirt in black silk-blend taffeta, with large faceted black glass buttons from the waist down, V-neck neckline with gored pleat forming a faux interior layer, hidden hooks to close at bust, labeled "Yves Saint Laurent/Rive Gauche".

Size 38

$350-450   FRE

A Vivienne Westwood 'Nostalgia of Mud' collection skirt, with Mudman print, of navy fleece fabric with textural grey 'mud' print, white stockinette waistband and side panels, World's End label.

1982-3   *Bust 26in (66cm)*

$1,000-1,200   **KT**

A Vivienne Westwood tracksuit ensemble, probably 'Punkature' collection, top printed with combination Keith Haring and Buffalo Gal motifs, white side panels to bodice, buttoned fly and hems of the trackpants, World's Ends label.

1983   *Chest 60in (152cm)*

$1,400-1,500   **KT**

EXPERT EYE – VIVIENNE WESTWOOD ENSEMBLE

The 'Nostalgia of Mud' collection was Westwood's third, and came after the sex-and-bondage inspired Punk fashions of the 1970s.

It examined both African, Indian and other cultures that were beginning to become a more visible part of multicultural British life.

The name was also used for a shop opened in London in 1982, which sold similarly styled clothes. It closed in 1984, a year after Westwood split from collaborator Malcolm McLaren.

Torn, disheveled and distressed fabric in muddy browns and beiges were typical, and her preference for unusual fabrics and cuts is clear.

A Vivienne Westwood 'Nostalgia of Mud' collection ensemble, comprizing cable knit sweater dress, the blue-grey flecked knitted skirt cut higher at the front, together with a pair of brown leather shoes with triple straps, with World's End label.

1982-83   *Chest 42in (102cm)*

$2,500-3,500   **KT**

A Vivienne Westwood Punkature collection printed 'big collar shirt', striped bib-front inset into a gold toile-de-Jouy style print on a mottled pink and brown ground, extra wide neck; together with a pair of slate grey cotton trousers, worn high on the chest with leather braces inset with metal springs, deep button flies, World's End label.

1983   *34in (86cm)*

$1,700-1,900   **KT**

A Vivienne Westwood Keith Haring designed 'Smiley Face' top, from the 'Witches' collection, woven in shades of light and dark grey, World's End label.

1983-84   *Chest 39in (96cm)*

$1,400-1,600   **KT**

A Vivienne Westwood 'Time Machine' collection black leather 'Armour' jacket, the waistcoat section with press-stud fastening detachable sleeves with open inner arms, segmented shoulder panels, red label.

1988-89   *Bust 40in (102cm)*

$1,400-1,600   **KT**

FIND OUT MORE...

'Miller's Collecting Fashion & Accessories', by Carol Harris, published by Miller's, 2000.

FASHION

ESSENTIAL REFERENCE

- Traditionally worn over the head as protection, the scarf as headwear gained further prominence during WWII when women wore them to keep their hair away from their work. During the 1950s, period colors and fashions drew designs away from more traditional and sober styles and patterns. Colors became brighter and motifs became light-hearted.
- The headscarf became an iconic form of headwear during the 1950s. Typical printed motifs included fashionable ladies, often walking their dogs, good luck symbols, polka dots and foreign places. As foreign travel also increased, souvenir scarves were produced. Notable names, such as

Hermés or Pucci, will also add value, particularly if the patterns are typical of the company.
- Look for bright colors and motifs that are typical of the period. Silk is usually valued higher than cotton or other materials, as it would have cost more originally, but it is generally the theme and eye-appeal that contributes most towards desirability. Examine edges carefully and look out for tiny holes. Although it is best to ask a specialist to clean vintage examples, cotton and man-made fibre scarves can be carefully washed at home.

A 1950s yellow printed cotton good luck themed scarf, with black cat motifs and 'good luck' in numerous European languages.

24.75in (63cm) wide

$40-60   **GCHI**

A 1950s-60s printed sky blue silk 'Superstition' scarf, with diamonds containing lucky activities.

19in (48cm) wide

$40-50   **GCHI**

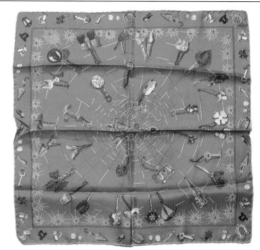

A 1950s printed red lucky charm scarf, with four-leaf clover, key, dog and horseshoe motifs.

19in (48cm) wide

$40-60   **GCHI**

A 1950s-60s printed fabric St Ives tourist souvenir scarf, with vignettes of scenes of St Ives, England.

16.25in (42cm) wide

$60-80   **GCHI**

A 1950s French RD Paris hand-painted silk scarf, with four scenes of stylized figures driving, taking a walk or undertaking other activities, and with frayed edges.

22.5in (57cm) wide

$40-60   **GCHI**

A 1950s American printed nylon 'Vermont – The Green Mountain State' tourist souvenir scarf.

29.5in (75cm) wide

$50-70   **GCHI**

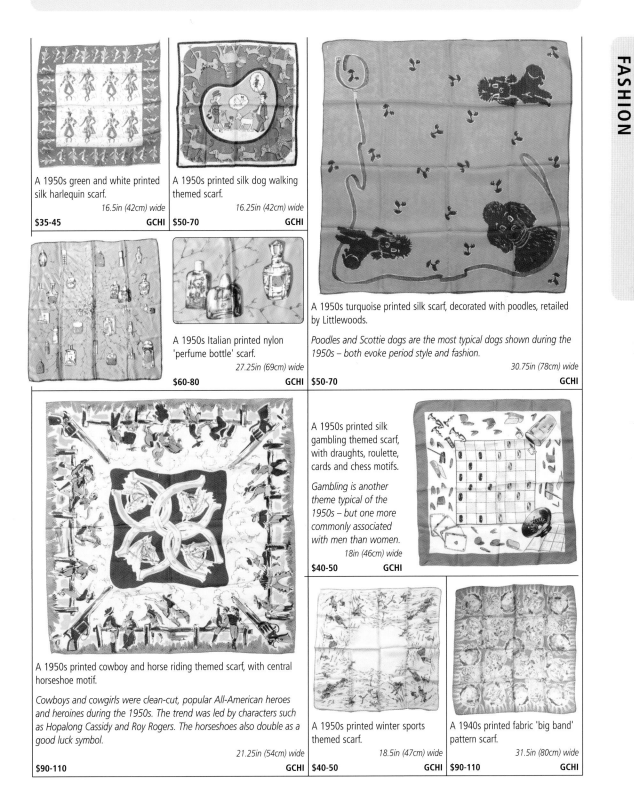

A 1950s green and white printed silk harlequin scarf.

16.5in (42cm) wide

$35-45   **GCHI**

A 1950s printed silk dog walking themed scarf.

16.25in (42cm) wide

$50-70   **GCHI**

A 1950s Italian printed nylon 'perfume bottle' scarf.

27.25in (69cm) wide

$60-80   **GCHI**

A 1950s turquoise printed silk scarf, decorated with poodles, retailed by Littlewoods.

Poodles and Scottie dogs are the most typical dogs shown during the 1950s – both evoke period style and fashion.

30.75in (78cm) wide

$50-70   **GCHI**

A 1950s printed silk gambling themed scarf, with draughts, roulette, cards and chess motifs.

Gambling is another theme typical of the 1950s – but one more commonly associated with men than women.

18in (46cm) wide

$40-50   **GCHI**

A 1950s printed cowboy and horse riding themed scarf, with central horseshoe motif.

Cowboys and cowgirls were clean-cut, popular All-American heroes and heroines during the 1950s. The trend was led by characters such as Hopalong Cassidy and Roy Rogers. The horseshoes also double as a good luck symbol.

21.25in (54cm) wide

$90-110   **GCHI**

A 1950s printed winter sports themed scarf.

18.5in (47cm) wide

$40-50   **GCHI**

A 1940s printed fabric 'big band' pattern scarf.

31.5in (80cm) wide

$90-110   **GCHI**

ESSENTIAL REFERENCE

- Even though men's clothes after WWII remained largely the same as those before the war, being somewhat sober and traditional, signs of brighter and more cheerful fashions began to appear. Much of these came from the US, where the teenager was becoming a force to be reckoned with, synthetic fibres were growing in popularity, and there was more freedom to experiment.

- One piece of clothing that changed dramatically was the tie. Designs became bolder, louder and more indicative of men's tastes at the time, moving away from traditional stripes and repeated motifs. Hawaii, gambling, drinking and naked or scantily clad pin-up girls, which gained

popularity with servicemen during the war, were key influences. Ties became wider to accommodate increasingly bold designs.

- Many were made on the West Coast of the US, and as well as being printed, a surprising number were hand-painted. Today, these have become immensely desirable once again as part of the trend for retro and vintage styles. Erotic or nude ties tend to be the most popular, but look out for any that show well-executed painted designs in a style typical of the period. Look carefully for holes, or minor tears. Ties should be taken to a specialist cleaner rather than washing them yourself.

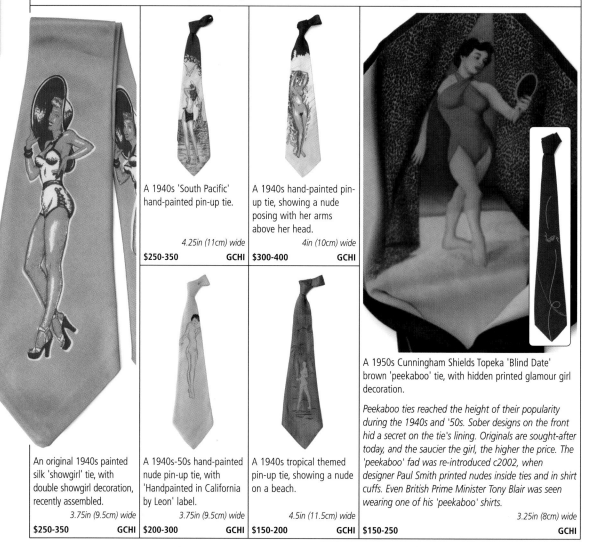

A 1940s 'South Pacific' hand-painted pin-up tie.

4.25in (11cm) wide

$250-350   **GCHI**

A 1940s hand-painted pin-up tie, showing a nude posing with her arms above her head.

4in (10cm) wide

$300-400   **GCHI**

An original 1940s painted silk 'showgirl' tie, with double showgirl decoration, recently assembled.

3.75in (9.5cm) wide

$250-350   **GCHI**

A 1940s-50s hand-painted nude pin-up tie, with 'Handpainted in California by Leon' label.

3.75in (9.5cm) wide

$200-300   **GCHI**

A 1940s tropical themed pin-up tie, showing a nude on a beach.

4.5in (11.5cm) wide

$150-200   **GCHI**

A 1950s Cunningham Shields Topeka 'Blind Date' brown 'peekaboo' tie, with hidden printed glamour girl decoration.

Peekaboo ties reached the height of their popularity during the 1940s and '50s. Sober designs on the front hid a secret on the tie's lining. Originals are sought-after today, and the saucier the girl, the higher the price. The 'peekaboo' fad was re-introduced c2002, when designer Paul Smith printed nudes inside ties and in shirt cuffs. Even British Prime Minister Tony Blair was seen wearing one of his 'peekaboo' shirts.

3.25in (8cm) wide

$150-250   **GCHI**

A 1950s hand-painted blue 'champagne' tie, with 'Made in California' label.

4.25in (10.5cm) wide

$150-200   **GCHI**

A 1950s French hand-painted silk 'Folies Bergere' tie.

3.75in (9.5cm) wide

$120-160   **GCHI**

A 1950s 'Desertones Marathon Cravat' hand-painted tie, made in San Francisco.

3.25in (8.5cm) wide

$200-300   **GCHI**

A 1950s Pilgrim hand-painted nylon tie, with a Mexican street scene.

4.5in (11.5cm) wide

$100-150   **GCHI**

A Pilgrim hand-painted marlin tie, with two fish and bands of brushstroke effects.

4in (10cm) wide

$100-150   **GCHI**

A 1950s Cutter Cravat Original 'Crooner' tie, showing a singer being applauded.

4in (10cm) wide

$150-200   **GCHI**

EXPERT EYE – A 'BILLIKIN' TIE

The pointy headed fat dwarf is a Billiken, an ancient Egyptian or Alaskan character associated with good luck and fun.

It was popularized from 1908 by US illustrator Florence Pretz after she received a patent for her drawn designs, and was the subject of a craze lasting until c1912.

As well as being printed and painted, his eyes and belly button are highlighted with small rhinestones.

The Billiken was also used by the Royal Order of Jesters, founded as part of the Freemasons in 1911. Membership is by invitation and unanimous vote only, and is limited to 13 new members annually.

A 1960s burgundy 'Royal Order of Jesters' tie, with painted Billiken and applied jewels.

3in (7.5cm) wide

$120-180   **GCHI**

FASHION

A 1940s pair of red leather shoes, in mint condition and unworn.

These are typical of the period with their solid, blocky form and sensible, practical heels.

$150-250   **GCHI**

A 1940s pair of Palizzio of New York black suede sling-backs, with red and black beads in the form of a poodle, and black sequin detail.

8in (20cm) long

$350-450   **GCHI**

A 1950s pair of Mackey Starr of New York handmade 'Countess' last sling-backs, with diamanté studded Lucite high heels and applied gilt metal 'buckles' inset with multi-colored rhinestones.

$250-350   **GCHI**

A 1950s pair of Dezario shoes, with multicolored assembled Lucite semi-circular heels, the black straps with holes and applied Lucite cabouchons.

8in (20cm) long

$50-70   **NOR**

A 1950s pair of wooden heeled mules, with woven straw uppers and clear Lucite heels containing raffia flowers, with very light wear.

6.5in (16.5cm) long

$400-500   **GCHI**

A 1950s pair of Italian carved and painted wood and woven raffia mules, with multicolored raffia trim and applied flowers, in mint and unworn condition.

The straps are lined with leather to prevent the raffia chafing the skin.

9in (23cm) long

$400-500 GCHI

A 1950s pair of Schiaparelli black patent leather shoes, with original ribbon, in excellent condition.

$450-550 GCHI

A 1950s pair of Gainsborough beige leather shoes, the silver leather and pink snakeskin toe decoration with three-leaf motif and applied metal circular decoration with inset rhinestones and turquoise enamel.

$200-300 GCHI

EXPERT EYE – A PAIR OF SHOES WITH INTERCHANGEABLE HEELS

Polish shoemaker Israel Miller began making shoes in 1892 for actresses in Broadway's theatrical productions. They were so beautiful and well-made that he was soon asked to make shoes for them personally.

In 1911, he opened a store on Broadway & 46th St in New York. In 1929, he adorned the building with sculptural wording by Alexander Sterling Calder concerning shoes, which can still be seen today.

The interchangeable heel system is rare and complex, and adds value, particularly as the three different heel styles are still together, and in mint condition.

Typical of Miller's shoes, they are finely constructed with black suede outers and pink kid leather linings.

A 1950s pair of I. Miller 'Beautiful' Perugia style black suede shoes, from the Paris collection, lined with pink kid leather, with three interchangeable heels, one set with diamanté, one set with beading and one set plain.

Interestingly, during the 1950s, Miller hired Andy Warhol to illustrate the company's advertising in an attempt to revamp the ailing brand.

9.5in (24cm) long

$400-600 GCHI

A 1950s pair of wedges, with iridescent sequins sewn with turquoise miniature beads, and applied floral motifs made up of miniature turquoise beads and with faux pearl centers.

$150-200 GCHI

A 1960s pair of stiletto sandals, with gold leather and clear plastic straps, gold leather lining and multicolored woven, striped decoration, in mint condition and unworn.

$150-250   **GCHI**

A 1950s pair of Dream Step Originals cream leather high-heeled shoes, the toes decorated with a hand-painted gold stylized foliate pattern highlighted with flowers and edged with metal studs with inset rhinestones.

The color and curving, yet pointed shape of these shoes make them extremely elegant.

$200-300   **GCHI**

A 1960s pair of pumps, with multicolored printed floral design overlaid with applied iridescent hexagonal glitter, together with matching purse, in mint condition, the shoes hardly worn.

$250-350   **GCHI**

A 1950s pair of cream leather sling-backs, decorated with gilt-edged hand-painted floral design, in unworn ,mint condition.

$200-300   **GCHI**

A 1950s-60s pair of Italian Mazerio hand-lasted stilettos, with woven gold thread and silver glitter, together with matching purse, in mint condition.

$100-150   **NOR**

A 1950s pair of Herbert Levine beige suede stilettos, with suede and 'jeweled' rhinestone tassels.

Size 6-61/2

$200-300 **GCHI**

EXPERT EYE – A PAIR OF HERBERT LEVINE SHOES

Herbert Levine shoes were designed by Herbert's wife, Beth Levine (1914-2006), who trained under Israel Miller and became his head designer.

Her shoes were worn by many celebrities and First Ladies, and she also invented the revolutionary Spring-O-Lator for mules.

She is best known for reintroducing boots to haute couture. Examples were famously worn by Nancy Sinatra when she sang "These Boots Are Made For Walkin'"

A 1970s pair of Vivaldi high heels, with silver reflective plastic heels and black suede straps inset with rhinestone triangles.

8in (20cm) long

$100-150 **NOR**

She is also known for her sculptural heels, fine quality construction, maverick designs and colorful patterns – her shoes have become hot collectors' items.

A 1950s pair of Herbert Levine blue and white printed polka dot slingbacks.

$150-200 **GCHI**

A pair of 1970s-80s Cover Girl 'Go Bananas' pink suede shoes, with cut holes in the plastic heels.

These holes would have added a spring to a girl's step, making them more comfortable to wear.

8.75in (22cm) long

$40-60 **NOR**

A 1970s pair of Italian Carber platform shoes, with wooden soles and printed green and white flower fabric straps, with original box.

8.5in (21.5cm) long

$100-150 **NOR**

A pair of 1980s Napoleon of London gold glitter-on-leather high-heels, with block heels.

These sparkling disco-tastic shoes would have looked great on the dancefloor.

8.25in (21cm) long

$150-200 **GCHI**

FASHION

A 1970s pair of yellow leather sandals, in very good condition.

$200-300   **GCHI**

A 1950s pair of Lady Studio patent yellow leather effect plastic open-toed high heels, with lace detailing.

8.75in (22cm) high

$30-50   **NOR**

A 1980s pair of The American Girl black, brown and white woven basketweave fabric high heels.

10.25 (26cm) long

$30-50   **NOR**

A 1950s pair of black fabric stilettos, with woven multicolored rectangles, in mint condition.

$80-120   **GCHI**

ESSENTIAL REFERENCE – CHARLES JOURDAN

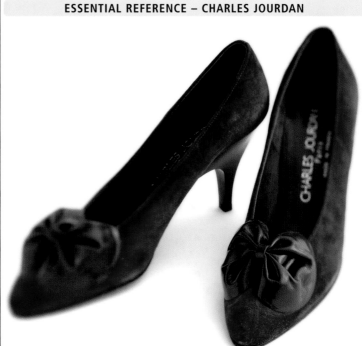

A 1980s pair of Charles Jourdan vivid purple suede shoes, with deep purple leather bows.

Charles Jourdan (1883-1976) is best known for his women's shoes, which he began producing in 1919. The 1950s saw expansion after great success, with a shop in Paris and sales to the UK. Along with Herbert and Beth Levine, they became notable for their use of unusual materials combined with fine construction and 'tailored' shapes and details. During the 1960s and '70s, their avant-garde advertising drew many to the brand, to which handbags were added in 1975. Although Charles died in 1976, the business continued to prosper under his sons into the 1980s. However, sales began to decline in the late 1980s, particularly after bad publicity in connection with Imelda Marcos, who owned many Jourdan shoes. In 2002, the company filed for bankruptcy despite the attempts of Patrick Cox as designer, but continues today under new ownership.

$200-300   **GCHI**

A 1950s pair of American Buster Brown black velvet children's 'Mary Jane' shoes, with transfer motif to the gilt interior.

6.75in (17cm) long

$50-70   **GCHI**

ESSENTIAL REFERENCE

- The 1950s saw an explosion in design following the restrictions of WWII. As well as serious new design movements, a sense of fun, color and frivolity pervaded designs. Themes included glamour, scantily clad girls, polka dots and playing card motifs, as well as geometric or abstract patterns that followed on from the Art Deco movement of the 1930s. Forms and patterns were frequently curving and asymmetric, and were often inspired by futuristic molecular or atomic motifs.

- New materials, many developed during the war, also took hold – plastics in particular. Plastic could be molded easily and economically into a range of forms, and could be brightly colored, matching the hopeful outlook of the decade. The material really took hold during the 1960s, when it was used to make furniture and other items. Many were molded into the space-age forms popular at the time. Formica offered similarly modern, affordable and easy to maintain pieces.

- The 1950s and '60s also saw the emergence of a 'throw away' culture, with many items being produced and sold inexpensively in fashionable styles. As styles changed, items were discarded and new ones bought. Young couples moved into new homes and decorated them in a colorful and modern way that rejected the styles of their parents. The teenager also emerged as a new and important part of society.

- The highest prices are reserved for those items by influential and important designers. However, representative pieces can be found at affordable prices. Always consider the style, pattern and color, as well as the condition. Many pieces were not made for long-term use and were worn and damaged over the years. A piece that is colorful, appealing and typical of the period in mint condition is likely to be a good investment.

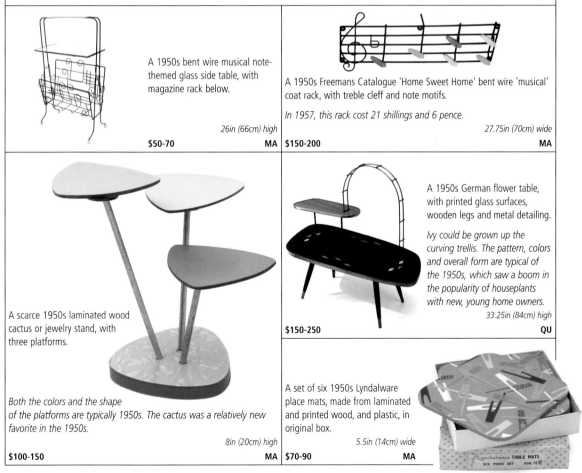

A 1950s bent wire musical note-themed glass side table, with magazine rack below.

26in (66cm) high

$50-70   **MA**

A 1950s Freemans Catalogue 'Home Sweet Home' bent wire 'musical' coat rack, with treble cleff and note motifs.

In 1957, this rack cost 21 shillings and 6 pence.

27.75in (70cm) wide

$150-200   **MA**

A scarce 1950s laminated wood cactus or jewelry stand, with three platforms.

Both the colors and the shape of the platforms are typically 1950s. The cactus was a relatively new favorite in the 1950s.

8in (20cm) high

$100-150   **MA**

A 1950s German flower table, with printed glass surfaces, wooden legs and metal detailing.

Ivy could be grown up the curving trellis. The pattern, colors and overall form are typical of the 1950s, which saw a boom in the popularity of houseplants with new, young home owners.

33.25in (84cm) high

$150-250   **QU**

A set of six 1950s Lyndalware place mats, made from laminated and printed wood, and plastic, in original box.

5.5in (14cm) wide

$70-90   **MA**

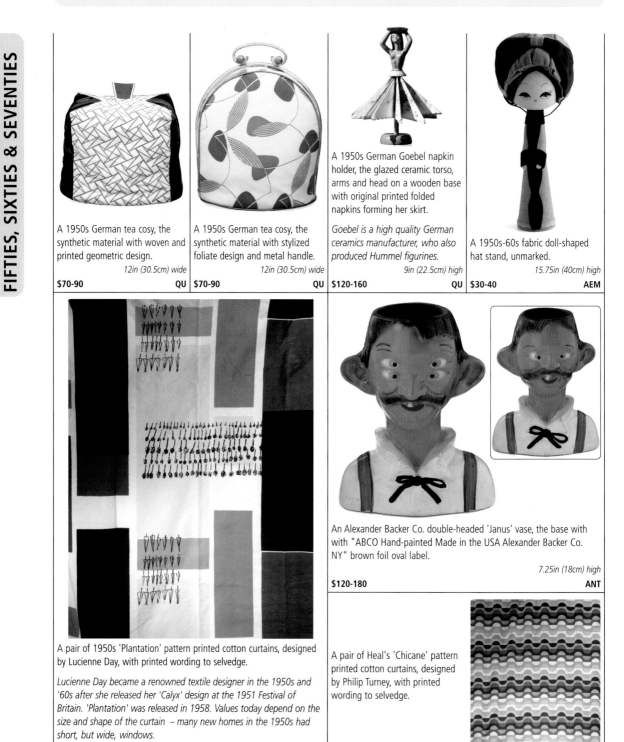

A 1950s German tea cosy, the synthetic material with woven and printed geometric design.

12in (30.5cm) wide

$70-90   **QU**

A 1950s German tea cosy, the synthetic material with stylized foliate design and metal handle.

12in (30.5cm) wide

$70-90   **QU**

A 1950s German Goebel napkin holder, the glazed ceramic torso, arms and head on a wooden base with original printed folded napkins forming her skirt.

Goebel is a high quality German ceramics manufacturer, who also produced Hummel figurines.

9in (22.5cm) high

$120-160   **QU**

A 1950s-60s fabric doll-shaped hat stand, unmarked.

15.75in (40cm) high

$30-40   **AEM**

A pair of 1950s 'Plantation' pattern printed cotton curtains, designed by Lucienne Day, with printed wording to selvedge.

Lucienne Day became a renowned textile designer in the 1950s and '60s after she released her 'Calyx' design at the 1951 Festival of Britain. 'Plantation' was released in 1958. Values today depend on the size and shape of the curtain – many new homes in the 1950s had short, but wide, windows.

91.75in (233cm) long

$600-800 (pair)   **WW**

An Alexander Backer Co. double-headed 'Janus' vase, the base with with "ABCO Hand-painted Made in the USA Alexander Backer Co. NY" brown foil oval label.

7.25in (18cm) high

$120-180   **ANT**

A pair of Heal's 'Chicane' pattern printed cotton curtains, designed by Philip Turney, with printed wording to selvedge.

81in (206cm) high

$80-120 (pair)   **WW**

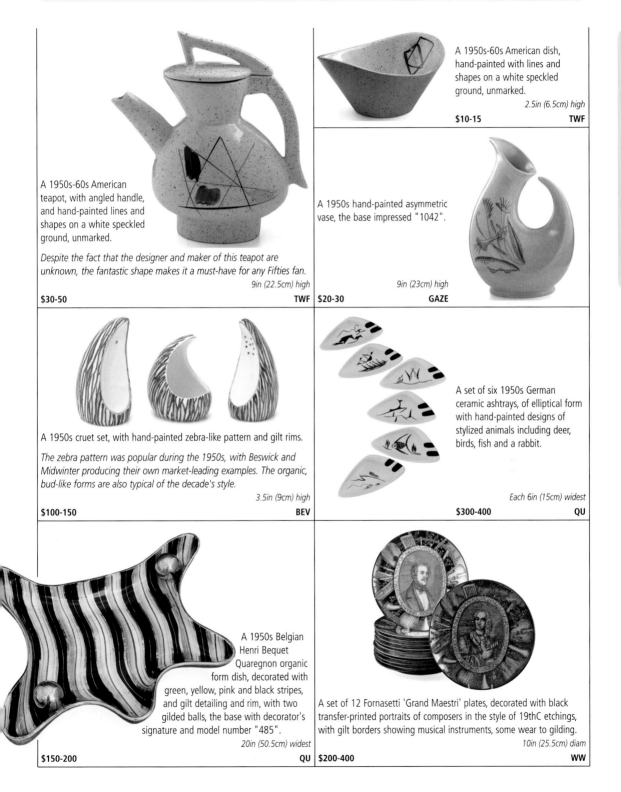

A 1950s-60s American teapot, with angled handle, and hand-painted lines and shapes on a white speckled ground, unmarked.

Despite the fact that the designer and maker of this teapot are unknown, the fantastic shape makes it a must-have for any Fifties fan.

9in (22.5cm) high

$30-50   TWF

A 1950s-60s American dish, hand-painted with lines and shapes on a white speckled ground, unmarked.

2.5in (6.5cm) high

$10-15   TWF

A 1950s hand-painted asymmetric vase, the base impressed "1042".

9in (23cm) high

$20-30   GAZE

A 1950s cruet set, with hand-painted zebra-like pattern and gilt rims.

The zebra pattern was popular during the 1950s, with Beswick and Midwinter producing their own market-leading examples. The organic, bud-like forms are also typical of the decade's style.

3.5in (9cm) high

$100-150   BEV

A set of six 1950s German ceramic ashtrays, of elliptical form with hand-painted designs of stylized animals including deer, birds, fish and a rabbit.

Each 6in (15cm) widest

$300-400   QU

A 1950s Belgian Henri Bequet Quaregnon organic form dish, decorated with green, yellow, pink and black stripes, and gilt detailing and rim, with two gilded balls, the base with decorator's signature and model number "485".

20in (50.5cm) widest

$150-200   QU

A set of 12 Fornasetti 'Grand Maestri' plates, decorated with black transfer-printed portraits of composers in the style of 19thC etchings, with gilt borders showing musical instruments, some wear to gilding.

10in (25.5cm) diam

$200-400   WW

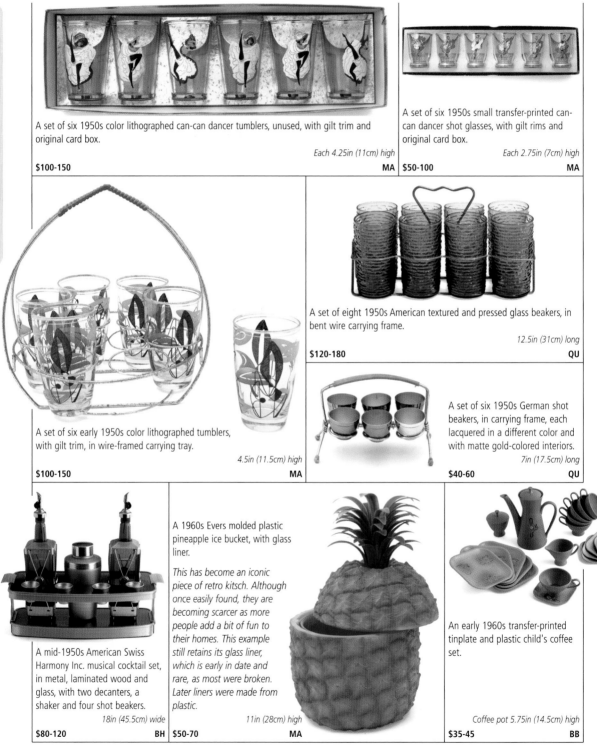

A set of six 1950s color lithographed can-can dancer tumblers, unused, with gilt trim and original card box.

Each 4.25in (11cm) high

$100-150   **MA**

A set of six 1950s small transfer-printed can-can dancer shot glasses, with gilt rims and original card box.

Each 2.75in (7cm) high

$50-100   **MA**

A set of eight 1950s American textured and pressed glass beakers, in bent wire carrying frame.

12.5in (31cm) long

$120-180   **QU**

A set of six early 1950s color lithographed tumblers, with gilt trim, in wire-framed carrying tray.

4.5in (11.5cm) high

$100-150   **MA**

A set of six 1950s German shot beakers, in carrying frame, each lacquered in a different color and with matte gold-colored interiors.

7in (17.5cm) long

$40-60   **QU**

A mid-1950s American Swiss Harmony Inc. musical cocktail set, in metal, laminated wood and glass, with two decanters, a shaker and four shot beakers.

18in (45.5cm) wide

$80-120   **BH**

A 1960s Evers molded plastic pineapple ice bucket, with glass liner.

This has become an iconic piece of retro kitsch. Although once easily found, they are becoming scarcer as more people add a bit of fun to their homes. This example still retains its glass liner, which is early in date and rare, as most were broken. Later liners were made from plastic.

11in (28cm) high

$50-70   **MA**

An early 1960s transfer-printed tinplate and plastic child's coffee set.

Coffee pot 5.75in (14.5cm) high

$35-45   **BB**

A 1950s Vogue large picture disc, no. R730, showing young couples jiving.

10in (25cm) diam

$70-90   BH

A pair of 1950s celluloid 'Kissing Dolls', made in Hong Kong, sold by Woolworths, mint and boxed.

These youthful and lusty bobble-heads have magnets inside the heads behind the mouths. When placed close together, the heads lean forward and lock to 'kiss'.

3.5in (9cm) high

$30-40   MTB

EXPERT EYE – A 1950s OLIVETTI TYPEWRITER

This typewriter was designed in 1969 by important and influential designer Ettore Sottsass (1913-2007), together with Olivetti design consultant Perry King.

It revolutionized typewriter design – the red plastic was typical of the period; fun, and also lightweight, meaning it could be easily carried.

Considered a design classic, it was also available in pink and grey. An example is in the Museum of Modern Art in New York.

Advertising for the typewriter featured people happily typing away outside cafés or on beaches. Many see both the typewriter and the advertising itself as a precursor to Apple's iMac.

An Olivetti Valentine typewriter, designed by Ettore Sottsass in 1969, red plastic fitted case, with molded factory marks.

16.25in (35cm) high

$250-350   WW

A 'Sun Kissed' lemon nodder, wearing a red and white striped bikini, with some chips.

6.25in (15.5cm) high

$15-25   BH

Two Peter Max covered vessels; one made of ceramic and shaped as a man wearing hat, signed "Max" in the print; the other as an ice bucket, the metal exterior stenciled with a man's face, with purple plastic sunglasses handle, dented.

8.25in (21cm) high

$700-900   SDR

A Peter Max 'Hello' blow-up plastic cushion, decorated with a Pop Art smile to each side, signed in the design.

15.75in (40cm) wide

$60-80   WW

ESSENTIAL REFERENCE

- Carnival glass is the name given to press molded glass sprayed with chemicals to give it an iridescent surface effect. It was first made during the 1900s, and reached the height of its popularity during the 1920s and 1930s. Mass-produced on mechanized factory production lines, it was bright, vividly colorful and inexpensive.
- The effect was inspired by Tiffany's expensive iridescent Favrile glass, and as a result it was often known as 'Poor Man's Tiffany'. It came to be called Carnival glass during the 1960s, probably because it was used for prizes at fairs. US factories dominated production until the late 1920s, when countries such as Scandinavia, Germany, Australia and the UK began to take the lead.
- Major US factories included Northwood (1902-25), Fenton Art Glass (est. 1904), the Imperial Glass Co. (1901-84) and Dugan (1904-13), which became known as the Diamond Glass Co. after 1913. Most Carnival glass is unmarked and factories are identified from the molded pattern. Northwood occasionally marked its glass with an 'N' in a circle.

- A number of criteria are used to value Carnival glass including pattern, the base color of the glass, shape and level of iridescence. To see the base color, shine a strong light through the piece. The orange 'marigold' is the most common color, with sky blue and red being much rarer.
- Examine patterns carefully as they can differ minutely, and factories frequently copied each other's designs. Patterns that were popular when produced are likely to have been made in large numbers, making them more common and therefore less valuable today. Ruffled bowls are the most common shape, with plates being much rarer.
- Sometimes the combination of a particular pattern, shape or color, even if each is individually common, can make a piece rare and desirable. Always examine edges for damage such as chips, which will appear shiny rather than silky matte. Carnival glass has been reproduced since the 1960s, particularly in the Far East, and Northwood's original designs are being used once again now the name has been revived.

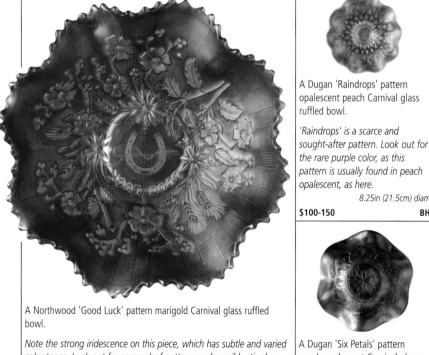

A Northwood 'Good Luck' pattern marigold Carnival glass ruffled bowl.

Note the strong iridescence on this piece, which has subtle and varied color tones. Look out for sparser leaf patterns and possibly stipples, which make this common pattern more desirable.

8.75in (22.5cm) diam

$180-220 BH

A Dugan 'Raindrops' pattern opalescent peach Carnival glass ruffled bowl.

'Raindrops' is a scarce and sought-after pattern. Look out for the rare purple color, as this pattern is usually found in peach opalescent, as here.

8.25in (21.5cm) diam

$100-150 BH

A Dugan 'Six Petals' pattern peach opalescent Carnival glass ruffled bowl.

8in (20.5cm) diam

$40-60 SAE

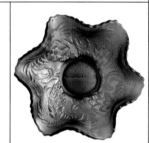

A Fenton 'Pine Cone' pattern green Carnival glass sweet dish.

Fenton originally called their Carnival glass 'Iridill'.

6in (15cm) diam

$200-300 BH

A Fenton 'Pine Cone' pattern blue Carnival glass sweet dish.

6in (15cm) diam

$150-200 BH

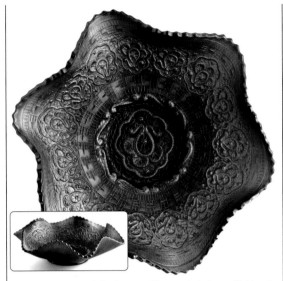

A Fenton 'Persian Medallion' pattern blue Carnival glass ruffled bowl.

This bowl has excellent iridescence all over, and extremely crisp molding. The pattern is heavily inspired by Oriental motifs.

10.5in (26cm) diam

$220-280 SAE

EXPERT EYE – PEACOCK & URN PATTERN

Seven variations of this classic and popular pattern were produced by Fenton, and from 1915 onwards by Northwood and Millersburg.

To distinguish them, pay close attention to the shape of the urn as well as the precise pattern of the leaves. Millersburg's version also has a bee near the peacock's beak.

With Fenton's version, the compote has a plain exterior while the bowl and plate are molded with the 'Bearded Berry' pattern.

This example has superb iridescence, making it more desirable.

A Fenton 'Peacock & Urn' pattern amethyst Carnival glass ruffled bowl, with 'Bearded Berry' pattern molded exterior.

9.25in (23cm) diam

$200-300 SAE

A Fenton 'Horses' Heads' pattern marigold Carnival glass bowl.

6.75in (17cm) diam

$60-90 SAE

A Fenton 'Butterfly & Berry' pattern marigold Carnival glass ball-and-claw footed bowl.

Footed forms are typical of this prolifically produced range. White is a very rare color.

1911-26   9.25in (23.5cm) diam

$100-150 BH

A Northwood 'Three Fruits' pattern marigold Carnival glass footed bon-bon dish.

This pattern is very similar to Northwood's 'Fruits & Flowers' pattern but without small flowers.

4in (10cm) high

$60-90 BH

A Dugan 'Wreathed Cherry' pattern amethyst Carnival glass banana bowl.

12.5in (30.5cm) long

$80-120 SAE

An Imperial 'Heavy Grape' pattern olive Carnival glass bowl.

6.75in (17cm) diam

$30-40 SAE

A Fenton 'Pinecone' pattern blue Carnival glass large bowl.

This pattern was produced in two sizes of bowl and one plate. Teal is the rarest color.

7.5in (18.5cm) diam

$40-50   SAE

A Fenton 'Kittens' pattern marigold Carnival glass saucer.

Kittens, a charming pattern intended for children, is both rare and sought-after, perhaps as so many were broken at meal times. This may explain the comparatively high value for such a small piece.

4.5in (11.5cm) diam

$70-100   SAE

MILLER'S COMPARES – SINGING BIRD PATTERN

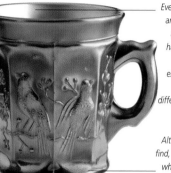

Even though these mugs are by the same maker, are the same size and have the same pattern, they are an excellent example of how values can vary based on different colors and levels of iridescence.

Although blue is hard to find, look out for 'smoke', which is the rarest color.

Marigold is a much more common color than blue, and the level of iridescence on the blue example is much stronger and considerably more desirable. Nevertheless, both are comparatively highly valued.

This is due to the fact that 'Singing Birds' is a popular pattern among collectors and is available in a wide range of shapes, making it an ideal pattern to focus on.

TOP: A Northwood 'Singing Birds' pattern blue Carnival glass mug.

3.75in (9.5cm) high

$200-250   BH

BOTTOM: A Northwood 'Singing Birds' pattern marigold Carnival glass mug.

3.75in (9.5cm) high

$80-120   BH

A Millersburg 'Mayan' pattern green Carnival glass ice cream bowl.

This example has very low levels of iridescence, and is in the most common color for this pattern. The rarest color is, surprisingly, marigold – only one example has been found to date.

8.5in (21.5cm) diam

$55-65   SAE

A Northwood 'Peacock at the Fountain' pattern blue Carnival glass tumbler.

Dugan produced some of the water sets found in this prolific pattern.

4in (10cm) high

$30-40   SAE

An English Sowerby 'Lea' pattern marigold Carnival glass creamer.

Along with the Thistle & Thorn pattern creamer to the right, this pattern is usually found in creamer, open sugar and bowl forms.

3.75in (9.5cm) high

$30-40   BH

An English Sowerby 'Thistle & Thorn' pattern marigold Carnival glass creamer.

4.25in (10.5cm) high

$20-30   SAE

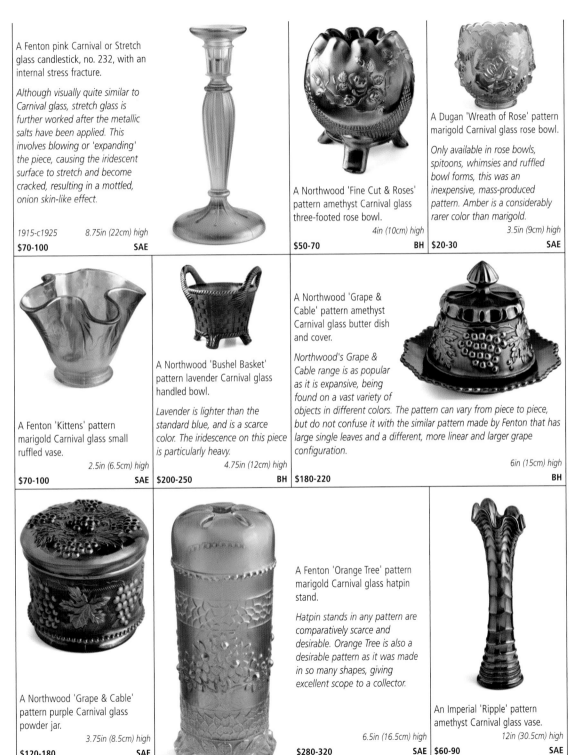

A Fenton pink Carnival or Stretch glass candlestick, no. 232, with an internal stress fracture.

Although visually quite similar to Carnival glass, stretch glass is further worked after the metallic salts have been applied. This involves blowing or 'expanding' the piece, causing the iridescent surface to stretch and become cracked, resulting in a mottled, onion skin-like effect.

1915-c1925   8.75in (22cm) high

$70-100   **SAE**

A Northwood 'Fine Cut & Roses' pattern amethyst Carnival glass three-footed rose bowl.

4in (10cm) high

$50-70   **BH**

A Dugan 'Wreath of Rose' pattern marigold Carnival glass rose bowl.

Only available in rose bowls, spitoons, whimsies and ruffled bowl forms, this was an inexpensive, mass-produced pattern. Amber is a considerably rarer color than marigold.

3.5in (9cm) high

$20-30   **SAE**

A Fenton 'Kittens' pattern marigold Carnival glass small ruffled vase.

2.5in (6.5cm) high

$70-100   **SAE**

A Northwood 'Bushel Basket' pattern lavender Carnival glass handled bowl.

Lavender is lighter than the standard blue, and is a scarce color. The iridescence on this piece is particularly heavy.

4.75in (12cm) high

$200-250   **BH**

A Northwood 'Grape & Cable' pattern amethyst Carnival glass butter dish and cover.

Northwood's Grape & Cable range is as popular as it is expansive, being found on a vast variety of objects in different colors. The pattern can vary from piece to piece, but do not confuse it with the similar pattern made by Fenton that has large single leaves and a different, more linear and larger grape configuration.

6in (15cm) high

$180-220   **BH**

A Northwood 'Grape & Cable' pattern purple Carnival glass powder jar.

3.75in (8.5cm) high

$120-180   **SAE**

A Fenton 'Orange Tree' pattern marigold Carnival glass hatpin stand.

Hatpin stands in any pattern are comparatively scarce and desirable. Orange Tree is also a desirable pattern as it was made in so many shapes, giving excellent scope to a collector.

6.5in (16.5cm) high

$280-320   **SAE**

An Imperial 'Ripple' pattern amethyst Carnival glass vase.

12in (30.5cm) high

$60-90   **SAE**

GLASS

ESSENTIAL REFERENCE

- The past few years have seen a rise in interest for postwar Czech glass design. As the country was behind the Iron Curtain until 1989, the major revolution in design has been largely ignored in favor of glass from countries, such as Italy and Scandinavia, despite the fact that exports were just as wide and prolific. As glass collectors and researchers have uncovered more information, prices have begun to rise and pieces have become harder to find.

- Complexity and rarity are currently the main indicators to value. The designer is also very important, but as the market is so new, many designers' names are not yet widely known. Hot-worked or enameled pieces, as well as unique cut and engraved examples, tend to make the highest sums. These often inspired ranges that were produced on a larger scale in factories, and are more affordable.

- Many of these are hot-worked or pressed glass designs,

with the most desirable being those that are in the modern, avant-garde style that was developed by designers from the late 1950s to the early 1970s. Leading designers whose work is sought-after include Adolf Matura, Frantisek Vízner, Milan Metelák, Jan Gabrhel and Frantisek Zemek, as well as influential names producing more unique works such as Stanislav Libensky, Pavel Hlava, René Roubícek and Jirí Harcuba.

- As much glass is unmarked, particularly away from unique art masterpieces at the higher end of the market, it is best to consult a reference book so you can learn how to recognise designs. Many are currently mistaken for the work of factories on Murano or in Scandinavia. A considerable amount of research is yet to be undertaken, and the area looks set to grow in importance and relevance over the next few years.

A Czechoslovakian Harrachov Glassworks Evening Blue colorless cased vase, designed by Milan Metelák in 1968.

7in (17.5cm) high

$150-250   **GC**

A Czechoslovakian Harrachov Glassworks Evening Blue colorless cased vase, designed by Milan Metelák in 1968, with pulled rim.

9.75in (24.5cm) high

$250-350   **GC**

A Czechoslovakian Harrachov Glassworks Green colorless cased vase, designed by Milan Metelák in 1968.

9.25in (23.5cm) high

$250-350   **GC**

A Czechoslovakian Harrachov Glassworks Topaz colorless cased vase, designed by Milan Metelák in 1968, with internal bubbles.

9.75in (24.5cm) high

$300-400   **GC**

A Czechoslovakian Harrachov Glassworks Evening Blue colorless cased vase, designed by Milan Metelák in 1968, with internal bubbles.

This range of vases, both with and without bubbles, were previously thought of as having been made by Schott Zweisel due to the similarity of the blue. Recent research has uncovered that they are Czech, not German. Evening Blue was the most successful color, and rare variations can be found with mica chips inside the bubbles.

9.75in (24.5cm) high

$400-500   **GC**

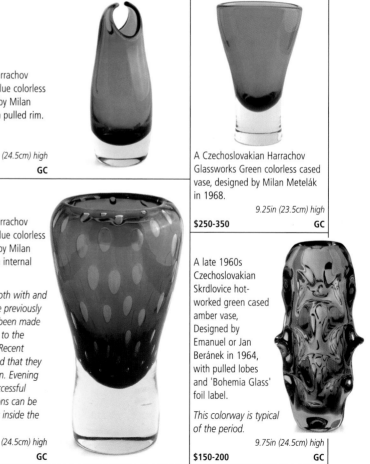

A late 1960s Czechoslovakian Skrdlovice hot-worked green cased amber vase, Designed by Emanuel or Jan Beránek in 1964, with pulled lobes and 'Bohemia Glass' foil label.

This colorway is typical of the period.

9.75in (24.5cm) high

$150-200   **GC**

A 1970s Czechoslovakian Chlum u Trebone Glassworks mold-blown bottle vase, designed by Jan Gabrhel after 1969, with textured surface.

7.75in (19.5cm) high

$300-500   **MHT**

A 1960s-70s Czechoslovakian Skrdlovice Glassworks light blue heart-shaped vase, designed by Vladimír Jelínek in 1965, with random pink and burgundy inclusions and a central well.

5.25in (14cm) high

$600-800   **QU**

A 1990s Czechoslovakian Exbor cased vase, designed by Jirí Suhajek c1974, with applied blue trailing and blue or sandy forms, on a mottled beige and opaque white ground.

9in (23cm) high

$1,500-2,000   **GC**

A Czechoslovakian Moser vase, designed by Jirí Suhajek in 1974, the colorless ovoid form with green casing to sides and central applied abstract flower and stalk motif.

8.25in (20.5cm) high

$900-1,100   **QU**

A Czechoslovakian Borské Sklo 'Large Olives' pattern green mold-blown optic ball vase, with machine-cut rim.

8.75in (22cm) high

$150-250   **GC**

A 1960s Czechoslovakian Borské Sklo luster painted mold-blown optic ball vase, designed by Max Kannegiesser in 1963, from the Nemo range.

4.25in (10.5cm) high

$30-40   **MHC**

A 1950s Czechoslovakian Borské Sklo gilded and painted grey mold-blown glass decanter, with stopper.

The amoebic painted forms are typical of the period, but are harder to find than more common, usually gilt, linear motifs. The angular form, reminiscent of a piston or machine part contrasts strongly with the organic pattern.

13.75in (35cm) high

$60-80   **MHC**

A Czechoslovakian Borské Sklo mold-blown smoked grey tapering vase, with thin white and gilt bands.

These can be found with clear and purple base glass, purple being the most desirable and valuable.

12in (30.5cm) high

$40-60   **GC**

GLASS

ESSENTIAL REFERENCE

- Depression glass is the term given by collectors to mechanically pressed glass, mass-produced from the 1920s onwards. It gained its name from its popularity during the Great Depression. Brightly and variously colored, durable, inexpensive and made in a huge variety of patterns, it brought cheer to those on hard times. As well as being retailed, Depression glass was given away as a premium in gas stations, cereal boxes and movie theaters.

- Some of the patterns introduced during this period, such as Whitehall, were still being made as functional tableware into the 1960s. Although many companies produced Depression glass, the majority found today was made by six of the larger companies including Anchor Hocking, Jeanette, Indiana, and Hazel Atlas.

- Green is one of the most common colors found, along with pink. Scarcer colors include cobalt blue, red and black. A colorless variety, known as Crystal was also very popular, particularly from the mid-1930s onwards. Many of the patterns found in Crystal imitated the more expensive cut lead crystal, offering buyers the look of luxury.

- Most collectors collect by pattern, and then perhaps by color. Natural themes predominate, often with complex patterns of stylized floral and foliate motifs. Each pattern has a name, often inspired by festive, historical, or natural themes. Pay close attention to the pattern, as some are very similar, but were produced by different companies, therefore having minor differences. 'Sandwich' is a good example.

- As well as color and pattern, consider the form as certain shapes are scarcer than others. Plates tend to be one of the most common forms, primarily as people tended to own more than one. Scarcer forms include cruet sets and butter dishes, as a single example was all a household was likely to require. Always examine pieces closely, to check for chips and deep scratches that devalue them. Bubbles and ripples are, however, more acceptable to collectors.

- Reproductions are also known, particularly in rare shapes. Handle as many originals as possible to become familiar with their feel and appearance. In general, reproductions are paler in color and the molded detailing may be less sharp. Consult a reference book to check the shape was made at the time.

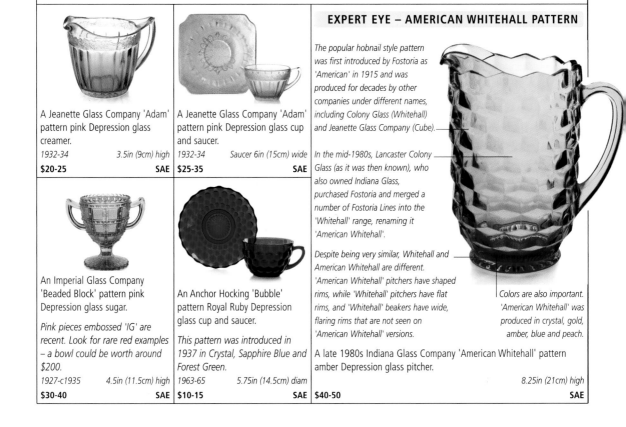

A Jeanette Glass Company 'Adam' pattern pink Depression glass creamer.

1932-34　　　　*3.5in (9cm) high*

$20-25　　　　　　　　　**SAE**

A Jeanette Glass Company 'Adam' pattern pink Depression glass cup and saucer.

1932-34　　*Saucer 6in (15cm) wide*

$25-35　　　　　　　　　**SAE**

An Imperial Glass Company 'Beaded Block' pattern pink Depression glass sugar.

Pink pieces embossed 'IG' are recent. Look for rare red examples – a bowl could be worth around $200.

1927-c1935　　*4.5in (11.5cm) high*

$30-40　　　　　　　　　**SAE**

An Anchor Hocking 'Bubble' pattern Royal Ruby Depression glass cup and saucer.

This pattern was introduced in 1937 in Crystal, Sapphire Blue and Forest Green.

1963-65　　*5.75in (14.5cm) diam*

$10-15　　　　　　　　　**SAE**

EXPERT EYE – AMERICAN WHITEHALL PATTERN

The popular hobnail style pattern was first introduced by Fostoria as 'American' in 1915 and was produced for decades by other companies under different names, including Colony Glass (Whitehall) and Jeanette Glass Company (Cube).

In the mid-1980s, Lancaster Colony Glass (as it was then known), who also owned Indiana Glass, purchased Fostoria and merged a number of Fostoria Lines into the 'Whitehall' range, renaming it 'American Whitehall'.

Despite being very similar, Whitehall and American Whitehall are different. 'American Whitehall' pitchers have shaped rims, while 'Whitehall' pitchers have flat rims, and 'Whitehall' beakers have wide, flaring rims that are not seen on 'American Whitehall' versions.

Colors are also important. 'American Whitehall' was produced in crystal, gold, amber, blue and peach.

A late 1980s Indiana Glass Company 'American Whitehall' pattern amber Depression glass pitcher.

8.25in (21cm) high

$40-50　　　　　　　　　**SAE**

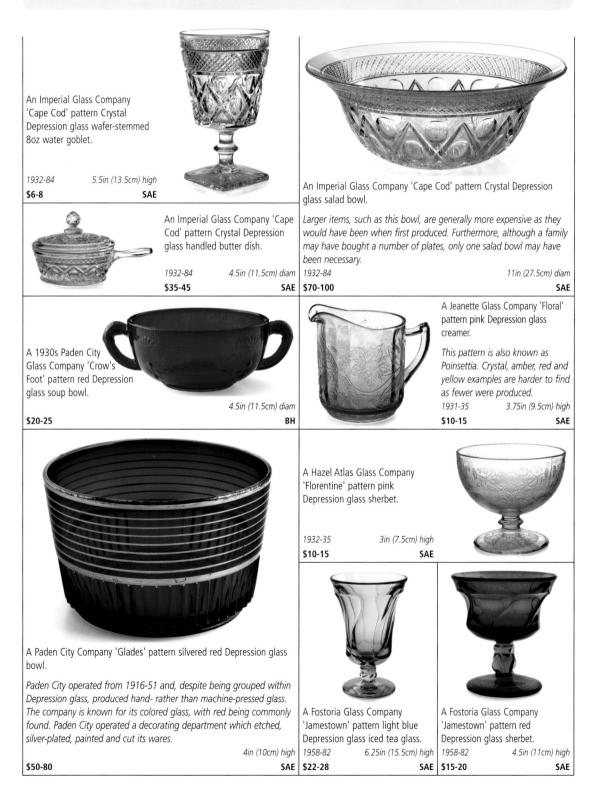

An Imperial Glass Company 'Cape Cod' pattern Crystal Depression glass wafer-stemmed 8oz water goblet.

1932-84   5.5in (13.5cm) high
$6-8   **SAE**

An Imperial Glass Company 'Cape Cod' pattern Crystal Depression glass handled butter dish.

1932-84   4.5in (11.5cm) diam
$35-45   **SAE**

An Imperial Glass Company 'Cape Cod' pattern Crystal Depression glass salad bowl.

Larger items, such as this bowl, are generally more expensive as they would have been when first produced. Furthermore, although a family may have bought a number of plates, only one salad bowl may have been necessary.

1932-84   11in (27.5cm) diam
$70-100   **SAE**

A 1930s Paden City Glass Company 'Crow's Foot' pattern red Depression glass soup bowl.

4.5in (11.5cm) diam
$20-25   **BH**

A Jeanette Glass Company 'Floral' pattern pink Depression glass creamer.

This pattern is also known as Poinsettia. Crystal, amber, red and yellow examples are harder to find as fewer were produced.

1931-35   3.75in (9.5cm) high
$10-15   **SAE**

A Hazel Atlas Glass Company 'Florentine' pattern pink Depression glass sherbet.

1932-35   3in (7.5cm) high
$10-15   **SAE**

A Paden City Company 'Glades' pattern silvered red Depression glass bowl.

Paden City operated from 1916-51 and, despite being grouped within Depression glass, produced hand- rather than machine-pressed glass. The company is known for its colored glass, with red being commonly found. Paden City operated a decorating department which etched, silver-plated, painted and cut its wares.

4in (10cm) high
$50-80   **SAE**

A Fostoria Glass Company 'Jamestown' pattern light blue Depression glass iced tea glass.

1958-82   6.25in (15.5cm) high
$22-28   **SAE**

A Fostoria Glass Company 'Jamestown' pattern red Depression glass sherbet.

1958-82   4.5in (11cm) high
$15-20   **SAE**

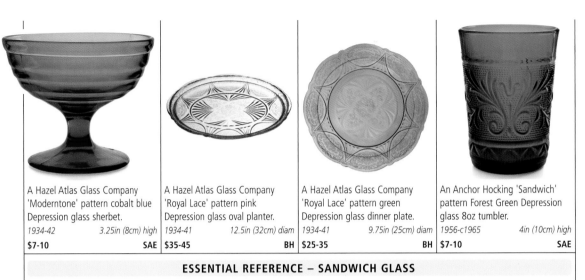

A Hazel Atlas Glass Company 'Moderntone' pattern cobalt blue Depression glass sherbet.

1934-42   *3.25in (8cm) high*

$7-10   **SAE**

A Hazel Atlas Glass Company 'Royal Lace' pattern pink Depression glass oval planter.

1934-41   *12.5in (32cm) diam*

$35-45   **BH**

A Hazel Atlas Glass Company 'Royal Lace' pattern green Depression glass dinner plate.

1934-41   *9.75in (25cm) diam*

$25-35   **BH**

An Anchor Hocking 'Sandwich' pattern Forest Green Depression glass 8oz tumbler.

1956-c1965   *4in (10cm) high*

$7-10   **SAE**

ESSENTIAL REFERENCE – SANDWICH GLASS

Sandwich glass refers both to the glass produced in the early 19thC by factories based around Sandwich, Massachusetts, such as the Boston & Sandwich Glass Company, and to a pressed glass pattern produced from the 1920s onwards. The most commonly found examples fall into the latter category. The pattern comprises a scrolling foliate motif on a background of stippled, slightly raised design, and was made by a number of factories. These include Anchor Hocking, Duncan & Miller, Indiana and Westmoreland. However, despite their similarities, each is slightly different. Duncan & Miller and Anchor Hocking are the most commonly found, with the former producing their version of the glass from 1924-55 and the latter from 1939-c1965. When building a collection, look closely at the designs of the scrolling form, the central pattern and particularly the flower to ensure you are adding the correct pieces to your collection. Duncan & Miller's flowers are more detailed, with lines through the centre of each raised relief petal, while Anchor Hocking's flowers have double outlines. Those by other makers tend to be less detailed.

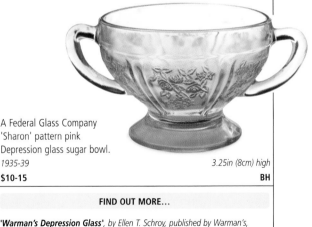

An Anchor Hocking 'Sandwich' pattern Forest Green Depression glass custard and liner.

1956-c1965   *Saucer 4.5in (11.5cm) diam*

$6-8   **SAE**

A Duncan & Miller 'Sandwich' pattern Crystal Depression glass sugar, creamer and tray.

Note the difference to Anchor Hocking's version. Colored examples by Duncan & Miller are harder to find than colorless Crystal.

1924-55   *Tray 8in (20cm) wide*

$22-35   **SAE**

A Federal Glass Company 'Sharon' pattern pink Depression glass sugar bowl.

1935-39   *3.25in (8cm) high*

$10-15   **BH**

FIND OUT MORE...

'Warman's Depression Glass', by Ellen T. Schroy, published by Warman's, 2003.

'Collectors' Encyclopedia of Depression Glass', by Gene & Cathy Florence, Collector Books, 2007.

ESSENTIAL REFERENCE

- Fenton was founded as a glass decorating company in 1905 in Martin's Ferry, Ohio. In 1907, the company moved to Williamstown, West Virginia and began to make its own glass. It became famous for its Carnival glass, and later for its mold-blown glass. Despite recent financial troubles, the company is still in existence and often re-issues popular past ranges and designs.
- Fenton's glass was largely affordable and most homes had an example. The most popular were inspired by Victorian styles and appealed to those who had no interest in the more avant-garde, modern designs being produced at the time. The same is true with collectors today, with Victorian styles fetching higher sums due to their desirability.
- The most popular designs include Coin Dot, Hobnail and Crest, with opaque milk glass also being popular, but much more affordable. All of these ranges were produced in a range of colors at different times. Some were only produced for a short period, making them rare today. However eye-appeal is important – vibrant and evocative colors like Cranberry tend to be the most desirable.
- As well as color, consider the shape. Large vases, which would have been expensive at the time, can be rare, as can unusual shapes such as lidded boxes. The handles of baskets were easily damaged, and intact examples are more desirable. Consult a reference book to learn how to spot rare shapes and unusual colorways.
- Fenton from the most popular period of the 1940s to '60s is usually unmarked, but may have a label. The company used over 12 types of label and, when present, they can help to date a piece to a period. After 1970, pieces were often marked on the base with the company name inside an oval. More modern pieces are rising in desirability, particularly unique pieces and those produced in limited amounts. Examine pieces, especially around the rim, for damage.

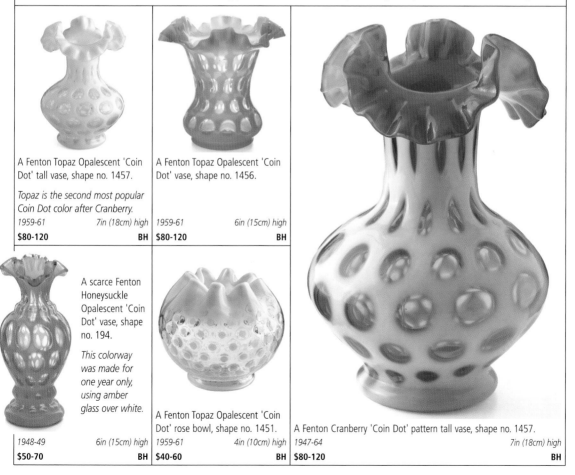

A Fenton Topaz Opalescent 'Coin Dot' tall vase, shape no. 1457.

Topaz is the second most popular Coin Dot color after Cranberry.

1959-61	7in (18cm) high
$80-120	**BH**

A Fenton Topaz Opalescent 'Coin Dot' vase, shape no. 1456.

1959-61	6in (15cm) high
$80-120	**BH**

A scarce Fenton Honeysuckle Opalescent 'Coin Dot' vase, shape no. 194.

This colorway was made for one year only, using amber glass over white.

1948-49	6in (15cm) high
$50-70	**BH**

A Fenton Topaz Opalescent 'Coin Dot' rose bowl, shape no. 1451.

1959-61	4in (10cm) high
$40-60	**BH**

A Fenton Cranberry 'Coin Dot' pattern tall vase, shape no. 1457.

1947-64	7in (18cm) high
$80-120	**BH**

GLASS

ESSENTIAL REFERENCE – FENTON PATTERNS

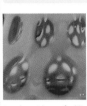

Coin Dot
Coin Dot was introduced in 1947 and is one of the company's most recognisable and popular ranges. It is covered in a thin translucent layer of white glass, and a textured 'spot' mold is used to create the dots. It can be found in Cranberry, blue, Honeysuckle yellow, Topaz yellow, Lime green and white 'French' Opalescent. Cranberry, French Opalescent and Blue Opalescent were the first to be made, with Cranberry being the most popular among collectors. Although the range was discontinued in 1964, it has been re-issued periodically since 1973.

Hobnail
The heavily textured Hobnail range was introduced in 1939 and was a key range until the 1970s. As such, it is commonly found today. It was made in a large number of colors including Cranberry, Emerald green, Lime green, Topaz Opalescent, Blue Opalescent, and the white French Opalescent. In the early 1960s, it was produced in overlay colors. From 1952 opaque pastel colored milk glass was introduced. From 1982 to 1983, the range was re-issued in three colors. Pieces were marked with the Fenton logo.

Crest
Also known as 'petticoat' glass, the Crest range was introduced in 1941, and comprised white or opaque colored bodies trimmed with a hand-applied differently colored rim. Crystal Crest was the first, and had an opaque white milk glass body trimmed with a clear, colorless rim and trimmed again with a further milk glass rim. As it was difficult and time consuming to make, it was discontinued in 1942. Crest was produced until the early 1980s with pink, blue, green, red, yellow, black and colorless rims, each at different times.

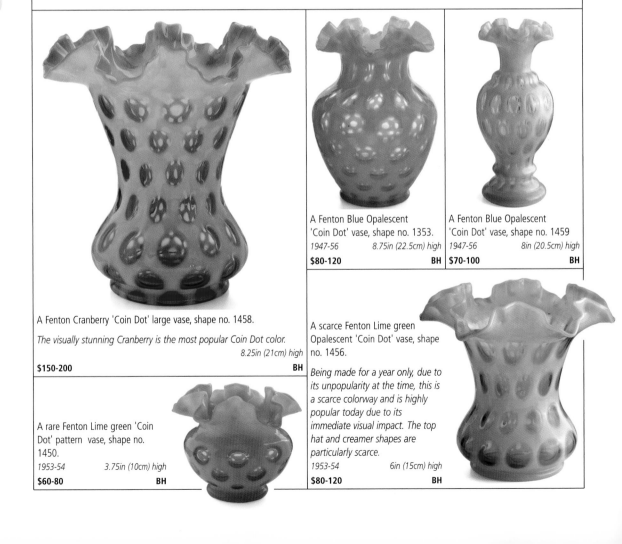

A Fenton Cranberry 'Coin Dot' large vase, shape no. 1458.

The visually stunning Cranberry is the most popular Coin Dot color.
8.25in (21cm) high

$150-200 BH

A Fenton Blue Opalescent 'Coin Dot' vase, shape no. 1353.
1947-56 8.75in (22.5cm) high

$80-120 BH

A Fenton Blue Opalescent 'Coin Dot' vase, shape no. 1459
1947-56 8in (20.5cm) high

$70-100 BH

A rare Fenton Lime green 'Coin Dot' pattern vase, shape no. 1450.
1953-54 3.75in (10cm) high

$60-80 BH

A scarce Fenton Lime green Opalescent 'Coin Dot' vase, shape no. 1456.

Being made for a year only, due to its unpopularity at the time, this is a scarce colorway and is highly popular today due to its immediate visual impact. The top hat and creamer shapes are particularly scarce.
1953-54 6in (15cm) high

$80-120 BH

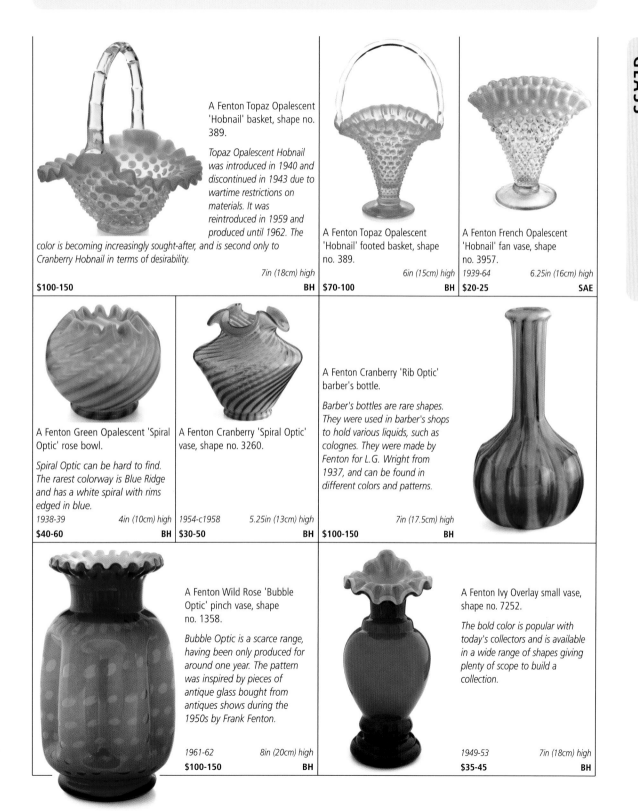

A Fenton Topaz Opalescent 'Hobnail' basket, shape no. 389.

Topaz Opalescent Hobnail was introduced in 1940 and discontinued in 1943 due to wartime restrictions on materials. It was reintroduced in 1959 and produced until 1962. The color is becoming increasingly sought-after, and is second only to Cranberry Hobnail in terms of desirability.

7in (18cm) high

$100-150   **BH**

A Fenton Topaz Opalescent 'Hobnail' footed basket, shape no. 389.

6in (15cm) high

$70-100   **BH**

A Fenton French Opalescent 'Hobnail' fan vase, shape no. 3957.

1939-64   *6.25in (16cm) high*

$20-25   **SAE**

A Fenton Green Opalescent 'Spiral Optic' rose bowl.

Spiral Optic can be hard to find. The rarest colorway is Blue Ridge and has a white spiral with rims edged in blue.

1938-39   *4in (10cm) high*

$40-60   **BH**

A Fenton Cranberry 'Spiral Optic' vase, shape no. 3260.

1954-c1958   *5.25in (13cm) high*

$30-50   **BH**

A Fenton Cranberry 'Rib Optic' barber's bottle.

Barber's bottles are rare shapes. They were used in barber's shops to hold various liquids, such as colognes. They were made by Fenton for L.G. Wright from 1937, and can be found in different colors and patterns.

7in (17.5cm) high

$100-150   **BH**

A Fenton Wild Rose 'Bubble Optic' pinch vase, shape no. 1358.

Bubble Optic is a scarce range, having been only produced for around one year. The pattern was inspired by pieces of antique glass bought from antiques shows during the 1950s by Frank Fenton.

1961-62   *8in (20cm) high*

$100-150   **BH**

A Fenton Ivy Overlay small vase, shape no. 7252.

The bold color is popular with today's collectors and is available in a wide range of shapes giving plenty of scope to build a collection.

1949-53   *7in (18cm) high*

$35-45   **BH**

An A.V. Mazzega 'Corroso' azure blue cased green vase, of teardrop form, the exterior corroded with acid to give a translucent mottled effect.

c1960   11in (28cm) high

$700-900   QU

An A.V. Mazzega dish, with violet, red and green bands and wide rim.

c1960   15.5in (39cm) diam

$800-1,000   QU

A Carlo Moretti vase, of teardrop form with applied random curving trails, and heavily iridescent surface.

The use of iridescence is unusual on Murano at this time, and is more commonly associated with the US, Central Europe and during the Art Nouveau period.

c1960   12in (30.5cm) high

$1,100-1,300   QU

A Nason & C. sommerso vase, the smoked glass core cased with a delicate layer of pink and then colorless glass, the exterior cut with wide facets, the base with a factory label.

c1960   10.75in (28cm) high

$300-400   QU

A Salviati & C. vase, designed by Claire Falkenstein in 1972, the amorphous cobalt blue body with three thickly applied opalescent trails forming the feet, the base engraved "Salviati" in diamond point.

Claire Falkenstein (1908-77) was an internationally renowned abstract expressionist sculptor. After studying, and building her career in the US, she went to Paris during the 1950s where she worked with Alberto Giacometti, Jean Arp and others. On her return to the US she met important American abstract expressionists including Sam Francis. Typical materials included shaped copper piping bonded to chunks of glass, themes echoed in this piece. Her 1981 spherical glass sculpture for Salviati, which this piece predates, is deemed a masterpiece of 1980s Murano glass.

17.25in (43.5cm) high

$2,500-3,500   QU

An Aureliano Toso 'Oriente' vase, designed by Dino Martens, of amorphous form with a wavy rim, overlaid with irregular panels of opaque powdered enamels in blue, dark violet, green, white, some with aventurine inclusions.

The Oriente range is typical of the design renaissance on Murano during the 1950s, with Dino Martens bringing his experience as a painter to the fore. Jugs and vases can be worth over $10,000, but beware of later reproductions, which lack the expression and finesse of his designs and use different color tones.

c1955   5.75in (14.5cm) high

$1,500-2,500   QU

An Aureliano Toso 'Oriente' small dish or ashtray, designed by Dino Martens, with pulled and curled rim, gold inclusions and multicolored enamel powder patches.

c1950   4.5in (11.5cm) long

$150-200   QU

A Fratelli Toso double-handled vase, the double gourd body decorated all over with alternating columns of millefiori murrines and murrines comprized of red flowers on an opaque white ground.

The form of the vase and the way the murrines are used are typically late 19thC in style. However, the use of white band of murrines containing highly complex flower bud motifs are different from the usual 'millefiori' style and are early examples of the company's individual, innovative and skilled approach to the creation of murrines.

c1915-20   4.25in (10.5cm) high

$800-1,000   QU

EXPERT EYE – A VISTOSI BIRD

This is one of a series of five bird sculptures designed by Alessandro Pianon (1931-84) in 1961.

Their whimsical appearance, stylized forms and bright colors make them highly appealing to collectors - they are also quite hard to find.

They are characterized by four simple abstract geometric shapes - the sphere, the wedge, the cube and the curve, and were revolutionary in their day.

It is decorated with circular murrines, others have trailed or applied chip decoration. This is one of the harder forms to find, the most common have an orange spherical body.

A Vistosi 'Pulcino' bird, designed by Alessandro Pianon in 1961, the petrol green blown body decorated with bands of red and blue circular murrines and impressed murrine eyes, mounted on colorless thighs with applied bent metal legs.

12.5in (31.5cm) high

$2,800-3,600   QU

An Aureliano Toso large yellow 'Filigrana' glass vase, designed by Dino Martens, with applied clear foot.

7.75in (19.5cm) wide

$1,000-1,200   SDR

A 1950s Turca free-form sommerso jug or vase, probably designed by Flavio Poli, with red, yellow and clear casing, pulled lip and handle, with 'Turca' silver foil label.

Flavio Poli is reputed to have produced designs for this company. The label reads "Murano Glass Turca Calle del Cristo 17 Tel: 39741".

9.75in (24.5cm) high

$120-180   P&I

A 1950s Turca free-form sommerso vase, probably designed by Flavio Poli, with red, orange and clear casing, pulled lip and 'Turca' silver foil label.

9.25in (23.5cm) high

$120-160   P&I

A pair of Vistosi stoppered bottles, designed by Alessandro Pianon in 1962, in red and cobalt blue glass, each with a spherical stopper with a contrastingly colored opaque band and factory paper label.

12in (30.5cm) high

$1,500-2,500   QU

A Vistosi cylindrical vase, designed by Peter Pelzel in 1962, with flared rim, the light blue body decorated with a band of red circular murrines with red centers.

8.75in (22cm) high

$550-650   QU

GLASS

ESSENTIAL REFERENCE – FACETED SOMMERSO

- From the 1960s onwards, a huge variety of vases, bowls and ashtrays were produced with sommerso bodies that were boldy cut with facets. Many factories copied each other making identification by shape or color nearly impossible. The sizes, shapes, colors and cuts vary widely, with each of the three factors affecting value considerably. Nevertheless, compared to much other Murano glass, these pieces are currently comparatively affordable.
- The combination of colors used is important to value. Some collectors will only collect a certain color, and more widely appealing colors and combinations will always be more valuable. Always examine edges and corners very carefully.

- Chips, and even small fleabites, can be very serious as facets are extremely hard to restore without cutting the facet back to below the chip, which is expensive and can affect the proportions of the piece. Chips can devalue a piece by well over 50 per cent.
- These designs were produced by a plethora of smaller glass factories, and are nearly always unmarked. Where they are marked, this is typically with a rare surviving label, which may include the factory name. Although a label may increase the desirability, it does not necessarily increase the value. Look out for large examples that have three layers of casing, or more complex cutting, as these are generally more valuable.

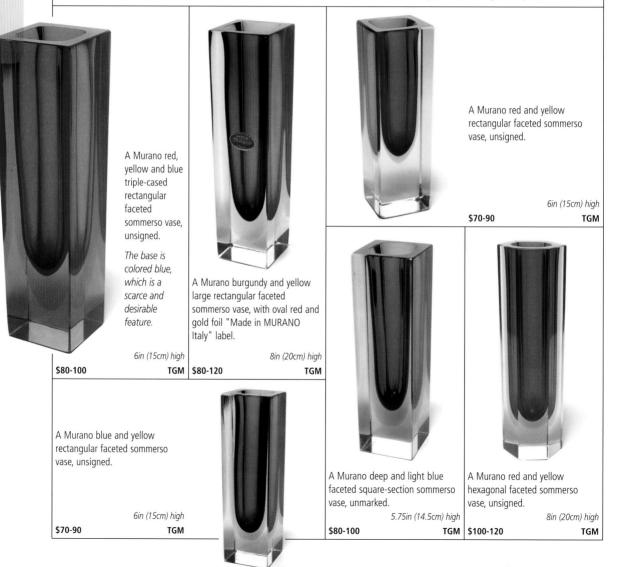

A Murano red, yellow and blue triple-cased rectangular faceted sommerso vase, unsigned.

The base is colored blue, which is a scarce and desirable feature.

6in (15cm) high

$80-100　　TGM

A Murano burgundy and yellow large rectangular faceted sommerso vase, with oval red and gold foil "Made in MURANO Italy" label.

8in (20cm) high

$80-120　　TGM

A Murano red and yellow rectangular faceted sommerso vase, unsigned.

6in (15cm) high

$70-90　　TGM

A Murano blue and yellow rectangular faceted sommerso vase, unsigned.

6in (15cm) high

$70-90　　TGM

A Murano deep and light blue faceted square-section sommerso vase, unmarked.

5.75in (14.5cm) high

$80-100　　TGM

A Murano red and yellow hexagonal faceted sommerso vase, unsigned.

8in (20cm) high

$100-120　　TGM

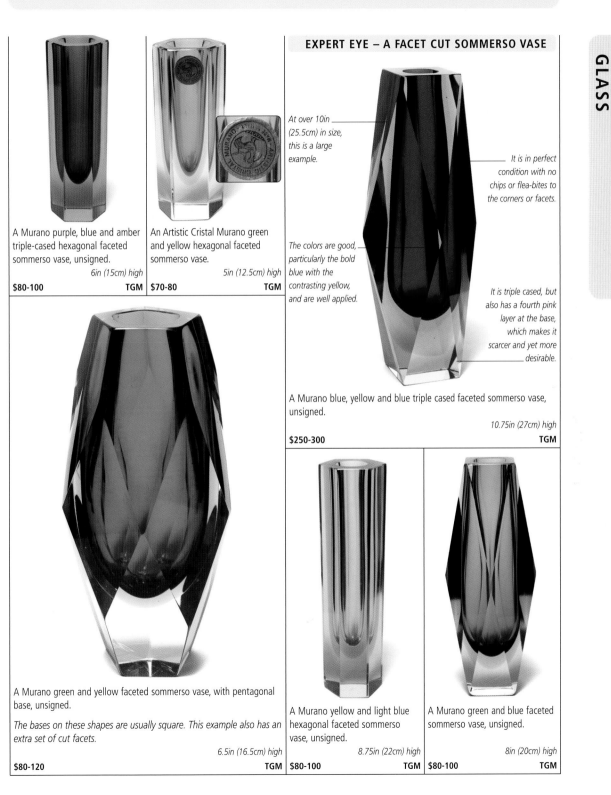

A Murano purple, blue and amber triple-cased hexagonal faceted sommerso vase, unsigned.

6in (15cm) high

$80-100   **TGM**

An Artistic Cristal Murano green and yellow hexagonal faceted sommerso vase.

5in (12.5cm) high

$70-80   **TGM**

EXPERT EYE – A FACET CUT SOMMERSO VASE

At over 10in (25.5cm) in size, this is a large example.

It is in perfect condition with no chips or flea-bites to the corners or facets.

The colors are good, particularly the bold blue with the contrasting yellow, and are well applied.

It is triple cased, but also has a fourth pink layer at the base, which makes it scarcer and yet more desirable.

A Murano blue, yellow and blue triple cased faceted sommerso vase, unsigned.

10.75in (27cm) high

$250-300   **TGM**

A Murano green and yellow faceted sommerso vase, with pentagonal base, unsigned.

The bases on these shapes are usually square. This example also has an extra set of cut facets.

6.5in (16.5cm) high

$80-120   **TGM**

A Murano yellow and light blue hexagonal faceted sommerso vase, unsigned.

8.75in (22cm) high

$80-100   **TGM**

A Murano green and blue faceted sommerso vase, unsigned.

8in (20cm) high

$80-100   **TGM**

A Murano red and yellow faceted sommerso vase, unmarked.

Note that the cut shoulders, usually in the middle of the vase, are applied lower down on this example. Red is also one of the most popular colors, particularly combined with yellow.

6in (15cm) high

$90-110   TGM

A Murano green yellow and blue triple cased faceted sommerso vase, with red and gold foil "Murano Glass Made In Italy" scroll label.

These shapes are comparatively hard to find, with this being a good example.

3.25in (8cm) high

$100-120   TGM

A Murano gray and blue faceted sommerso vase, with square-section base, unsigned.

This has the same cuts as the other vases on this page, but has been turned around, showing how different these vases can appear depending on the way they are viewed. This is an uncommon color combination.

8.75in (22cm) high

$120-140   TGM

A Murano faceted double-cased sommerso vase.

7in (18cm) high

$80-120   GC

A Murano red and yellow faceted sommerso rectangular vase, unsigned.

Note that the red well is slightly offset from the center, which detracts from the value. However, this is a comparatively scarce shape.

3in (7.5cm) high

$70-90   TGM

A Murano green and blue faceted sommerso ashtray, the outer layer tinged with violet.

5.25in (13cm) wide

$80-100   TGM

A 1960s Murano sommerso ashtray, with green, yellow and colorless faceted exterior layers.

5in (13cm) diam

$100-150   P&I

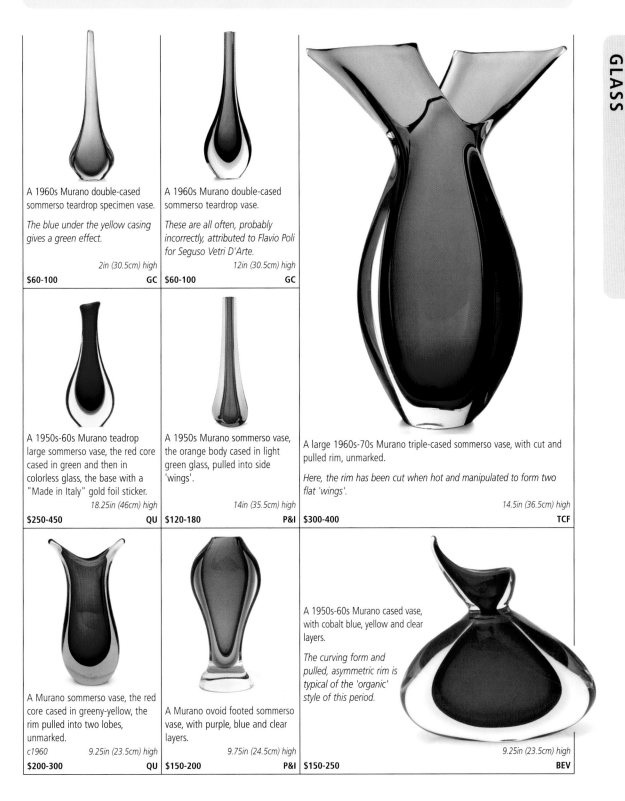

A 1960s Murano double-cased sommerso teardrop specimen vase.

The blue under the yellow casing gives a green effect.

2in (30.5cm) high

$60-100   **GC**

A 1960s Murano double-cased sommerso teardrop vase.

These are all often, probably incorrectly, attributed to Flavio Poli for Seguso Vetri D'Arte.

12in (30.5cm) high

$60-100   **GC**

A 1950s-60s Murano teadrop large sommerso vase, the red core cased in green and then in colorless glass, the base with a "Made in Italy" gold foil sticker.

18.25in (46cm) high

$250-450   **QU**

A 1950s Murano sommerso vase, the orange body cased in light green glass, pulled into side 'wings'.

14in (35.5cm) high

$120-180   **P&I**

A large 1960s-70s Murano triple-cased sommerso vase, with cut and pulled rim, unmarked.

Here, the rim has been cut when hot and manipulated to form two flat 'wings'.

14.5in (36.5cm) high

$300-400   **TCF**

A Murano sommerso vase, the red core cased in greeny-yellow, the rim pulled into two lobes, unmarked.

c1960   *9.25in (23.5cm) high*

$200-300   **QU**

A Murano ovoid footed sommerso vase, with purple, blue and clear layers.

9.75in (24.5cm) high

$150-200   **P&I**

A 1950s-60s Murano cased vase, with cobalt blue, yellow and clear layers.

The curving form and pulled, asymmetric rim is typical of the 'organic' style of this period.

9.25in (23.5cm) high

$150-250   **BEV**

GLASS

A Murano sommerso vase, the oval section tapering cylindrical green body cased in yellow.

This is very similar to designs by Seguso, showing how factories copied successful designs from each other.

c1960   9.5in (24cm) high

$700-900   **QU**

A 1960s Murano sommerso tapering cylindrical vase, with heavy colorless base.

9.25in (24.5cm) high

$60-100   **P&I**

A Murano trefoil form sommerso ashtray, with green and red layers, thick walls, and cut and polished rim.

5in (12.5cm) wide

$90-110   **P&I**

A 1960s Italian mold-blown lemonade set, the waisted jug and beakers with opaque white interiors cased in red, blue or yellow transparent glass, the jug with applied blue handle, unmarked.

The manufacturing process, choice of colors and almost 'plastic' appearance is similar to Per Lütken and Michael Bang's Carnaby and Palette ranges for Danish companies Holmegaard & Kastrup.

Jug 10.25in (26cm) high

$250-350   **QU**

A 1950s-60s Murano multicolored glass clown figure.

Highly fashionable in postwar Italy, these brightly colored clowns brought a feeling of cheer to a home. The largest and more finely made examples are worth the most, and some are decanters with the heads as stoppers.

8.25in (21cm) high

$60-100   **P&I**

A 1950s-60s Murano sommerso bird, the red core cased with uranium glass, unsigned.

Although unsigned, the way the tail and beak are handled is indicative of Seguso.

6in (15cm) long

$40-50   **TGM**

A 1950s-60s Murano large red blown glass bull figurine, with applied colorless hair, horns, head and legs, unmarked.

10in (25.5cm) high

$400-600   **FLD**

FIND OUT MORE...

'Venetian Glass 1890-1980', *by Rosa Barovier Mentasti, published by Arsenale Editrice, 1992.*

'Miller's Glass of the '50s & '60s', *by Nigel Benson, published by Miller's Publications, 2002.*

ESSENTIAL REFERENCE

- The Moor Lane Glasshouse at Brierley Hill, near Stourbridge, England, was renamed Stevens & Williams in 1819. During the 19thC it built up a strong reputation for its fine quality colored glass and cut glass. It then became known as Royal Brierley in 1931, after a visit from King George V.
- The 1960s saw the birth of handmade studio glass, which became highly fashionable. Many glass studios were producing ranges that were iridescent, often lightly textured or with random designs on the surface. Royal Brierley wished to appeal to this market, but produced a range on a larger factory-based scale.
- In 1986, they asked Michael Harris, founder of Isle of Wight Studio Glass, to design a range for them that gave the effect of studio glass, but could be produced on their factory production line. Harris and his family, who had experience of translating studio practices into a production line, adapted

one of their existing ranges, Lace.
- Royal Brierley applied the resulting design to a number of different forms including bowls, baluster-shaped and spherical vases, and perfume atomisers. Pieces would be molded before being sprayed with metallic salts to give the iridescent effect. Some molds were adapted from existing molds for light fittings. Vases and atomisers tend to be the most popular today, although large pieces in any form are harder to find and are desirable.
- To drive the point home, the range was called the Studio range, and a special acid mark was developed for the bases. Colors include black (actually a very deep blue), pink, green, white and blue. Rims are machine-cut and polished flat. Always examine the edge of rims for fleabites and chips. The range was comparatively expensive, and was only available for a few years, into the 1990s.

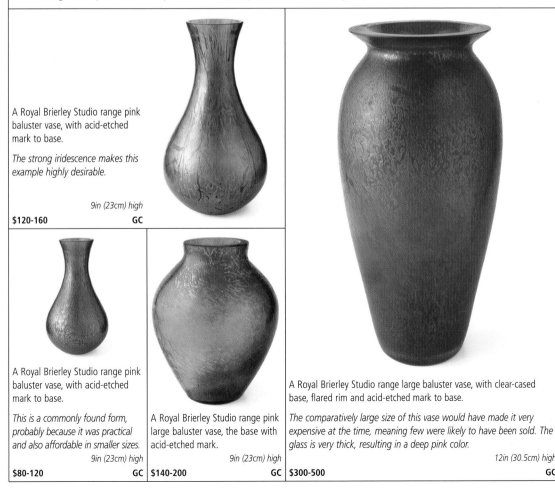

A Royal Brierley Studio range pink baluster vase, with acid-etched mark to base.

The strong iridescence makes this example highly desirable.

9in (23cm) high

$120-160   GC

A Royal Brierley Studio range pink baluster vase, with acid-etched mark to base.

This is a commonly found form, probably because it was practical and also affordable in smaller sizes.

9in (23cm) high

$80-120   GC

A Royal Brierley Studio range pink large baluster vase, the base with acid-etched mark.

9in (23cm) high

$140-200   GC

A Royal Brierley Studio range large baluster vase, with clear-cased base, flared rim and acid-etched mark to base.

The comparatively large size of this vase would have made it very expensive at the time, meaning few were likely to have been sold. The glass is very thick, resulting in a deep pink color.

12in (30.5cm) high

$300-500   GC

GLASS

A Royal Brierley Studio range small green baluster vase, with heavy iridescence, acid-etched mark to base.

6.75in (17cm) high

$120-160   GC

A Royal Brierley Studio range green squat globe vase, the base with acid-etched mark.

6in (15cm) high

$60-80   GC

A Royal Brierley Studio range white and cream mottled baluster vase, the base with acid-etched mark.

This mottled white tends to be scarcer than pink.

9in (23cm) high

$140-200   GC

A Royal Brierley Studio range white and cream mottled squat globe vase, the base with acid-etched mark.

6in (15cm) high

$60-80   GC

A Royal Brierley Studio range small black shouldered vase, with heavy iridescence and original foil label.

4in (10cm) high

$40-60   GC

A Royal Brierley Studio range small black baluster vase, with heavy iridescence and acid-etched mark to base.

6.75in (17cm) high

$100-140   GC

A Royal Brierley Studio range white mottled black baluster vase, with acid-etched mark to base.

This is a very scarce color combination.

6in (15cm) high

$120-160   GC

A Royal Brierley Studio range peacock blue tapering cylinder vase, with clear casing and acid-etched mark to base.

Cylinder vase forms tend to be harder to find than the more common baluster form and its variants. This blue is also comparatively hard to find, as is the casing, seen at the base.

10.25in (26cm) high

$160-240   GC

ESSENTIAL REFERENCE

- Holmegaard was founded in Zealand, Denmark, in 1825 and initially produced bottles and pressed glass tablewares. A second factory was established at Kastrup in 1847, but was sold in 1873. Glass from the post-WWII period is representative of the 20thC Scandinavian modern style and has become highly collectable in recent years.
- The most important designer was Per Lütken (1916-98), who joined Holmegaard in 1942 and is best known for his organic vases and bowls, with curving, often asymmetric, forms that are typical of the 1950s. Colors tend to be cool, classical grays and light blues, although stronger greens are known.
- Lütken was also responsible for the brightly colored Carnaby range of the late 1960s and '70s. The polar opposite of his earlier work, the range is typified by opaque vibrant reds and yellows, and is strongly geometric in nature. He also produced tableware and other inventive art glass ranges, some being close to studio glass.
- Michael Bang (1968-2002) was another important designer. Son of Jacob Bang (1899-1965), who also designed for the factory, Michael produced the Palet range that is often confused with the similar Carnaby range. He was also responsible for other ranges, including the 'Hole' vase.
- When buying Holmegaard, always examine the piece carefully. Minor production flaws, and even tiny internal bubbles, will mean the piece was a second. This is backed up by the fact that seconds are not signed on the base. Signatures can help to date the manufacture of a piece, but the company discontinued dates in 1961. Avoid pieces that are scratched, chipped or deeply limed with water deposits as they detract from the form and clarity of the glass.

A Danish Holmegaard Smoke gray 'Heart' vase, designed by Per Lütken in 1955, from the Minuet range, the base inscribed "Holmegaard PL 15732".

1961-76   3.5in (8.5cm) high
$70-90   TGM

A Danish Holmegaard May green 'Heart' vase, designed by Per Lütken in 1955, from the Minuet range, the base inscribed "Holmegaard PL 18119".

Although designed in 1955, this vase was only available in this color from 1963.

1963-76   2.75in (7cm) high
$55-65   TGM

A Danish Holmegaard gray-green rounded vase, designed by Per Lütken, with thick rounded walls and offset well, the base inscribed "19PL57".

1957   4in (10cm) high
$180-260   UCT

A Danish Holmegaard blue ovoid vase, no. 15469, designed by Per Lütken in 1955, the base inscribed "19PL61".

Available in a number of sizes, the largest is 15-16in high and is quite scarce. It is among the most valuable of Lütken's designs and can be worth over $2,000.

1961   9.5in (24cm) high
$450-600   UCT

A Danish Holmegaard colorless cased purple ovoid vase, designed by Per Lütken in 1955, the base inscribed "19PL55".

1955   5.75in (14.5cm) high
$250-300   UCT

A Danish Holmegaard red cased opaque white vase, no. 390245, designed by Per Lütken in 1968, from the Carnaby range.

1969-76   6in (15cm) high
$250-300   **UCT**

A Danish Holmegaard red cased opaque white vase, designed by Per Lütken in 1968, from the Carnaby range.

Michael Bang designed a very similar form, but with a shorter neck, for use as a storage jar in 1970. It was produced as part of the Palet range until 1975.

1969-76   4in (10cm) high
$100-150   **UCT**

A Danish Holmegaard mold-blown opaque yellow bottle vase, designed by Per Lütken in 1968, from the Carnaby range, cased in clear glass.

The appearance of this 'unglass-like' bottle follows the 1960s and '70s Pop Art obsession with plastic.

1969-76   10.5in (26.5cm) high
$150-200   **GC**

A Danish Holmegaard red cased opaque white 'Gulvas' bottle vase, designed by Otto Brauer in 1962.

Produced in a number of colors, the opaque cased variations are the most sought-after. Be aware of reproductions produced during the 1980s and '90s, which were made in different sizes and colors. Made in China or Central Europe, they are of slightly different proportions and are lighter in weight – always compare color and form to known examples to ensure that you are buying the real deal.

1962-80   12.25in (31cm) high
$280-360   **UCT**

A Danish Holmegaard blue cased opaque white vase, designed by Per Lütken in 1968, from the Carnaby range.

1969-76   9in (23cm) high
$280-360   **UCT**

A Danish Holmegaard olive green and white cased Napoli vase, designed by Michael Bang in 1969, with applied dark trail.

This range was produced in other colors, including white and blue, and shapes including bulbous vases and candlesticks.

1969-71   6.25in (16cm) high
$150-200   **GC**

ESSENTIAL REFERENCE

- Post-WWII Scandinavian glass has risen enormously in both popularity and value recently. Glass collectors have re-appraised its importance to 20thC design over the past decade. Popular attention has also been drawn to the area by the increasing amounts of media coverage outside specialist publications. New information is being found each year, widening knowledge.
- The 1950s saw an asymmetric style, with curving forms and cool colors inspired by natural forms such as buds and leaves. This gave way in the 1960s to a clean-lined, geometric Modern style that is typically found in bright colors. Towards the end of the decade and into the 1970s, textured forms became popular. There was also great innovation in terms of technique from the early 20thC onwards.
- Look on the base for engraved marks to help with identification – the factory and the designer count considerably towards value. However, with a little experience, the designer and the maker can also be identified from the overall style of a piece, the color, and the way it is made. The most popular factories include Orrefors, Kosta Boda, Iittala, Riihimäen Lasi Oy and Holmegaard.

- Look for the work of leading designers who defined the movement and influenced others, such as Vicke Lindstrand, Simon Gate, Tapio Wirkkala, Sven Palmqvist, Per Lütken, Tamara Aladin and Nanny Still. Some, such as Lindstrand, moved between factories, and factories themselves were frequently merged with others. However, it is often the eye appeal of a piece that draws attention.
- Stylish pieces by Riihimäen Lasi Oy and Holmegaard are currently particularly popular, and look to remain so, for their modern Pop forms and bright colors. Keep an eye out for secondary factories, designers or ranges that are still being researched, as now may be the time to buy. These include Strömbergshyttan, John Orwar Lake for Ekenas, and Erik Höglund for Boda.
- Always consider how a piece was made, and its color, as some techniques and colors can be rare. A unique Orrefors Graal vase will always be worth more than a Riihimäki mold-blown production line piece, although both have their fans. Examine pieces closely, avoiding those with chips, cracks, scratches or lime marks from water. These detract from the purity of color and form so typical of this type of glass.

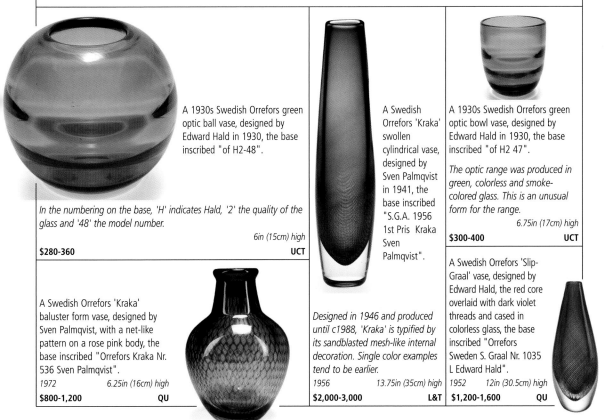

A 1930s Swedish Orrefors green optic ball vase, designed by Edward Hald in 1930, the base inscribed "of H2-48".

In the numbering on the base, 'H' indicates Hald, '2' the quality of the glass and '48' the model number.

6in (15cm) high

$280-360   **UCT**

A Swedish Orrefors 'Kraka' baluster form vase, designed by Sven Palmqvist, with a net-like pattern on a rose pink body, the base inscribed "Orrefors Kraka Nr. 536 Sven Palmqvist".

1972   6.25in (16cm) high

$800-1,200   **QU**

A Swedish Orrefors 'Kraka' swollen cylindrical vase, designed by Sven Palmqvist in 1941, the base inscribed "S.G.A. 1956 1st Pris Kraka Sven Palmqvist".

Designed in 1946 and produced until c1988, 'Kraka' is typified by its sandblasted mesh-like internal decoration. Single color examples tend to be earlier.

1956   13.75in (35cm) high

$2,000-3,000   **L&T**

A 1930s Swedish Orrefors green optic bowl vase, designed by Edward Hald in 1930, the base inscribed "of H2 47".

The optic range was produced in green, colorless and smoke-colored glass. This is an unusual form for the range.

6.75in (17cm) high

$300-400   **UCT**

A Swedish Orrefors 'Slip-Graal' vase, designed by Edward Hald, the red core overlaid with dark violet threads and cased in colorless glass, the base inscribed "Orrefors Sweden S. Graal Nr. 1035 L Edward Hald".

1952   12in (30.5cm) high

$1,200-1,600   **QU**

GLASS

A Swedish Orrefors 'Ariel' vase, designed by Ingeborg Lundin, with a cased geometric design, the base inscribed "Orrefors, Ariel nr 136B Ingeborg Lundin".

c1968   6.25in (16cm) high

$2,400-3,600   **WW**

A Swedish Orrefors 'Ariel' technique footed bowl, designed by Sven Palmqvist, the bowl with internal spiralling pattern of burgundy columns and colorless air bubbles, with full engraved signature and number to base.

5.25in (13cm) diam

$600-700   **FLD**

A Swedish Orrefors large 'Fiskegraal' vase, no. 2513, designed by Edward Hald in 1937, cased glass internally decorated with green fish, with incized marks and original retailers label.

Like Ariel, the core is decorated with a three-dimensional pattern, but with Graal it is carved using a spinning tool rather than sandblasted. This technique was developed in 1917. This celebrated design was made from 1937 until 1988, but earlier examples tend to be more complex with more elements and finer detail.

1946   5in (12.5cm) high

$800-1,200   **WW**

EXPERT EYE – AN ORREFORS ARIEL VASE

The complex and innovative Ariel technique was developed in 1937 by Vicke Lindstrand at Orrefors. Later, the technique was also used by other glassmakers, such as Ronald Stennett-Willson, see page 259 for an example.

The pattern is sandblasted onto a pre-made blank, with the pattern masked out using 'resists' to protect the underlying glass.

It is then reheated, blown and cased in colorless glass that magnifies the design and captures air bubbles underneath it, resulting in a more fluid design than the similar Graal.

This is a comparatively more common form. It also has a stylized portrait of a lady on one side and a dove in a frame on the other – both are inspired by modern art of the time.

A Swedish Orrefors 'Ariel' vase, designed by Edvin Öhrström, of tear-drop form, the base with engraved signature and numbered "147-F".

7.5in (19cm) high

$4,000-6,000   **FLD**

A Swedish Orrefors small 'Fiskegraal' vase, designed by Edward Hald, internally decorated with fish, the base etched with marks.

6in (15cm) high

$600-800   **WW**

A 1950s Swedish Orrefors 'Selina' small opalescent vase, designed by Sven Palmqvist, with swung-out neck and rim, the base inscribed "Orrefors".

c1955   7in (17.5cm) high
$120-200   **UCT**

A 1950s Swedish Orrefors 'Selina' opalescent bowl, designed by Sven Palmqvist, with a curving, asymmetric rim, the base inscribed "Orrefors".

2.25in (5.5cm) high
$100-150   **UCT**

EXPERT EYE – AN ORREFORS SELINA VASE

Palmqvist said that the silvery-white color with very pale blue tinges was similar to that of moonbeams.

Opalescent glass by Orrefors is extremely rare. It is fully signed on the base.

Selina was produced in a wide range of shapes. This organic vase was swung when molten to create the elegantly long neck and bud-like asymmetric rim.

It was developed from 1948 by Orrefors' Sven Palmqvist and the influential glass technologist W.E.S. Turner (1881-1963), who worked with a number of major glass factories.

A Swedish Orrefors Selina opalescent vase, designed by Sven Palmqvist in 1954, the base inscribed "Orrefors PU3090/5" and with museum catalogue style numbering "UB.214.HL.14" around the base rim.

c1955   13in (33cm) high
$100-150   **TGM**

A Swedish Orrefors colorless cased smoky gray 'Dusk' vase, designed by Nils Landberg in 1956, the base inscribed "Orrefors 352219".

This color of cellophane sticker was used from 1960 until 1998, with paper examples being slightly earlier.

8in (20cm) high
$150-250   **UCT**

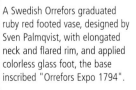

A Swedish Orrefors graduated ruby red footed vase, designed by Sven Palmqvist, with elongated neck and flared rim, and applied colorless glass foot, the base inscribed "Orrefors Expo 1794".

8.75in (22cm) high
$300-400   **UCT**

A Swedish Kosta dark green footed vase, designed by Elis Bergh, with ball knop, the base inscribed with an "EB" monogram and numbered "158".

This is an unusual and well-proportioned shape, as well as a large size.

1930   13.75in (33.5cm) high

$350-450   **UCT**

A Swedish Kosta blue optic goblet vase, designed by Elis Bergh, the foot inscribed with an "EB" monogram and "594".

1934   8.5in (21.5cm) high

$250-350   **GC**

A Swedish Kosta Dark Magic range dark blue-gray cased vase, designed by Vicke Lindstrand, the base inscribed "Kosta LH1606".

c1956   6.75in (17cm) high

$500-600   **UCT**

A Swedish Kosta colorless cased purple vase, with offset well and concave machine-cut and polished rim, the base inscribed "Kosta 441889".

3.25in (8.5cm) high

$150-200   **UCT**

A 1960s Swedish Kosta colorless cased blue tapering vase, designed by Mona Morales-Schildt, with heavy base, the base inscribed "Kosta SH224".

Mona Morales-Schildt (1908-99) trained as a glass designer at Venini on Murano and then worked at Kosta from 1958 until 1970. As such, her designs often have a southern, rather than northern, European feel to them.

6.5in (16.5cm) high

$150-200   **UCT**

A Swedish Kosta glass vase, model no. 1590, designed by Vicke Lindstrand, internally decorated in green and blue, cased in clear, etched "Kosta LH 1590".

Internal threads were frequently used as design motifs by Lindstrand during the 1950s and '60s.

c1958   8.75in (22cm) high

$500-600   **WW**

A unique Swedish Kosta Boda glass ship sculpture, designed by Bertil Vallien, the colorless cast form decorated on the underside with colored enamels, the top side cut and polished, mounted on a black basalt base with two pegs, engraved "Kosta Boda Unique 130390363 B. Vallien".

Vallien has created a series of these cast glass boat sculptures that carry mythological themed cargoes, although each is unique.
c1988   19.25in (48.5cm) long
$3,500-4,000   QU

A Swedish Kosta glass decanter and stopper, the amber glass body with ruby stopper, with applied paper label, etched "Kosta".

9in (23cm) high
$150-200   WW

A Swedish Kosta colorless glass bowl, with internal fine lines of purple powder curling at the top, and thick asymmetric wavy rim, the base inscribed "Kosta LH1212".

3.5in (9cm) high
$200-250   UCT

A Swedish Kosta bowl, designed by Vicke Lindstrand, the colorless core with an applied blue powder enamel pattern in the form of overlapping leaves with deep blue edges, cased in colorless glass and with an asymmetric curving rim, the base engraved "Kosta LH 1138/49".
c1954   3.5in (9cm) high
$150-250   UCT

A Swedish Kosta leaf-shaped dish, designed by Vicke Lindstrand, with internal purple threads and machine-cut rim, inscribed "Kosta LH 1387".
1958   13in (33cm) long
$250-350   UCT

A Swedish Boda Afors cast and blown candle-holder or vase, designed by Bertil Vallien, the base inscribed "V511-140 B.Vallien".

6in (15cm) high
$90-110   UCT

A Swedish Boda Afors cast and blown candle-holder or vase, designed by Bertil Vallien, the base inscribed "V451-190 B.Vallien".

7.25in (18.5cm) high
$100-120   UCT

GLASS

A Finnish Iittala mold-blown 'Lichen' vase, no. 3515, designed by Tapio Wirkkala in 1950, with acid-etched exterior, the base signed "Tapio Wirkkala 3515".

1950-64   3.5in (9cm) high
$350-450   **UCT**

A Finnish Iittala mold-blown 'Pinus' vase, designed by Tapio Wirkkala, with textured surface, the base inscribed "Tapio Wirkkala 3729".

If this were unsigned, the value would fall to around $60-80. The texture was inspired by ice and tree bark in Scandinavia's rugged landscape.

6.75in (17cm) high
$100-120   **TGM**

EXPERT EYE – AN IITTALA FOAL'S FOOT VASE

The curving form, with its asymmetric rim, is typical of the organic movement of 1950s Scandinavian design.

The elongated shape is meant to represent the delicate leg of a new-born foal.

In 1948, an example was acquired for the collection of the Museum of Modern Art, New York.

The exterior is skillfully cut by hand with a spinning copper wheel leaving very fine lines of an even depth, which are faultless and perfectly spaced.

A Finnish Iittala 'Foal's Foot' vase, no. 3215, designed by Tapio Wirkkala in 1947, cut with fine vertical lines and with a pulled asymmetric rim, the base inscribed "Tapio Wirkkala 3215".

1947-59   6in (15cm) high
$150-250   **UCT**

A rare Finnish Iittala 'Q Color' cased milky glass bowl, designed by Tapio Wirkkala, with etched signature.

4.5in (11.5cm) high
$600-800   **WW**

A Finish Iittala 'Boletus' sculptural vase, designed by Tapio Wirkkala in 1953, with flared, down-turned rim and cut with fine vertical lines, the base signed "Tapio Wirkkala - Iittala 55".

Large sizes over 7in (18cm) in height can be worth over $2,000. Do not confuse this form with the rarer and more valuable 'Chanterelle', which has a thinner body and rim, part of which is turned up.

1953-59   3.5in (9cm) high
$550-650   **UCT**

A Finnish Iittala free-form 'Orchid' sculptural vase, no. 3568, designed by Timo Gchianeva in 1953, the base inscribed "Timo Sarpaneva Iittala-57".

This piece, that crosses the boundary between sculptural art object and functional vase, won the Grand Prix at the Milan Triennale in 1954. It was also named 'Object of the Year' by House Beautiful magazine in the US, in the same year. It was produced from 1953 until 1973, being revised in 1985 and produced from then to the present. Even though earlier examples tend to be more sought-after, values do not depend solely on age – it is more important that the piece is signed, otherwise it is a second.

11in (28cm) high
$600-1,000   **UCT**

A Finnish Iittala cased blue vase, no. 3529, designed by Tapio Wirkkala, with tall neck and flared rim, the base inscribed "Tapio Wirkkala 3529".

7in (17.5cm) high

$280-340   **UCT**

A Finnish Iittala blue 'Bird' bottle, no. i-400, designed by Timo Gchianeva in 1956, from the i-line range, the base inscribed "Timo Gchianeva Iittala-57".

The i-line range was produced as a cross between art glass and functional tableware. It was only sold in design and leading department stores, and was not inexpensive. It was available in four colors; blue, green, gray and lilac, as well as colorless. The range also spawned the 'i' logo the company uses today – originally designed for this range only, its simple design and popularity meant it was soon extended across the entire range.

1957-66   *7.5in (19cm) high*

$150-250   **UCT**

EXPERT EYE – AN IITTALA FINLANDIA VASE

Finlandia was developed in 1961 by Timo Gchianeva, and used textured molds made from wood.

As the hot, molten glass was blown into the mold it burnt the wood, and took on a bark-like texture.

As the wooden mold was damaged each time, the effect on each piece was unique. As molds were ultimately destroyed through use, metal molds soon took over.

The Finlandia name was also used for textured vodka bottles and drinking glasses. However, these were designed by Tapio Wirkkala in 1969 and were all mass-produced using industrial metal molds.

A Finnish Iittala Finlandia vase, shape no. 3356, designed by Timo Gchianeva, of molded cylindrical form with everted rim, the base with etched marks.

8in (20cm) high

$500-600   **WW**

A Finnish Iittala blue 'Bird' bottle, no. i-401, designed by Timo Gchianeva in 1956, from the 'i-line' range, the base inscribed "Timo Gchianeva Iittala-57".

1957-68   *6in (15cm) high*

$150-250   **UCT**

An Iittala 'Jääpuikko' colorless cased blue-gray jug, designed by Timo Gchianeva, of conical form with a pulled spout, the base inscribed '"Timo Gchianeva 2388".

Jääpuikko is Finnish for icicle.

1958   *10.25in (26cm) high*

$350-400   **QU**

A Finnish Iittala mold-blown purple decanter or vase, no. 2518, designed by Timo Gchianeva in 1961.

These vases were made until recently, and the only way to tell the age is from the label – if one is still there. Pieces from before 1980 use a water transfer (shown here), later labels are self-adhesive plastic stickers.

9.5in (24cm) high

$240-320   **UCT**

A Finnish Riihimäen Lasi Oy cased red mold-blown 'Tuulikki' vase, designed by Tamara Aladin in 1972.

1972-76   7in (18cm) high
$70-90   **UCT**

A Finnish Riihimäen Lasi Oy cased blue vase, the design attributed to Tamara Aladin.

8in (20cm) high
$70-90   **UCT**

A Finnish Rihiimäen Lasi Oy green 'Pompadour' vase or candlestick, shape no. 1405, designed by Nanny Still in 1967.

1967-73   11in (28cm) high
$200-300   **QU**

A Finnish Rihiimäen Lasi Oy cased green vase, by an unidentified designer.

10in (25cm) high
$40-60   **GC**

A Finnish Rihiimäen Lasi Oy cased blue spindle-shaped vase, the base engraved "Riihimäen Lasi Oy Finland 1360".

6.5in (16.5cm) high
$30-40   **QU**

ESSENTIAL REFERENCE – RIIHIMÄEN LASI OY

Riihimäki was founded in Finland, in 1910, and was known as Riihimäen Lasi Oy from 1937. From the 1930s onwards, the company held competitions to recruit new talent to their design team. These included Helena Tynell in 1946, Nanny Still in 1949 and Tamara Aladin in 1959. During the 1960s and '70s, these three were primarily responsible for a wide range of mold-blown vases, which are typified by their vibrant colors and often geometric forms. Some, such as the pieces from the Country House range, were inspired by the countryside. They are now sought-after for their visual impact and representation of the period's design. In general, the more unusual and outlandish the form, the more desirable it is. Large sizes tend to be the most valuable, and red is the most popular color with many collectors.

A Riihimäen Lasi Oy 'Piironki' glass vase, designed by Helena Tynell in 1968, from the Vanha Kartano (Country House) series.

1968-74   8.25 (21cm) high
$150-200   **WW**

MILLER'S COMPARES – TWO SCANDINAVIAN MOLD-BLOWN VASES

Most of these mold-blown pieces are unmarked, making identification difficult – consider shape, size and color.

The bright green is not a Finnish color, but was used by other Scandinavian factories.

Reijmyre examples tend to have bases molded with concentric circles like this one on a similar purple vase.

Although this design is in Riihimäki's catalogues, the name of the designer has not been confirmed. It is from a range that was imported into the UK for sale in retailers such as Boots The Chemist, after the closure of a number of British glass factories.

A Swedish Reijmyre cased green tapering vase, with concentric circle molded base.

10.25in (26cm) high

$80-100 **UCT**

A Finnish Riihimäen Lasi Oy cased petrol blue tapering vase, no. 1939, attributed to Tamara Aladin.

11in (28cm) high

$80-100 **UCT**

A 1970s Swedish Riihimäen Lasi Oy mold-blown colorless 'Dice' vase, designed by Nanny Still.

Red is the most desirable color in this range, and examples can be worth over $300

6.75in (17m) high

$160-240 **UCT**

A Swedish Riihimäen Lasi Oy mold–blown 'Pala' vase, designed by Helena Tynell in 1964, with textured surface.

1964-76 *4.5in (11.5cm) high*

$70-90 **UCT**

A Swedish Riihimäen Lasi Oy mold-blown burgundy 'Pala' small posy vase, designed by Helena Tynell in 1964, with textured exterior.

1964-76 *2.5in (6.5cm) high*

$20-30 **UCT**

A 1970s Swedish Riihimäen Lasi Oy mold-blown orange footed bowl, designed by Nanny Still, with molded prunts, surface texture and machine-cut rim.

This bowl can be seen in the 'Make Love Not War' catalogue, and also on page 214 of 'Miller's 20th-Century Glass' by Andy McConnell, where a grinning Still is shown holding an example before the excess glass is cut away, leaving only the bowl. Interestingly, the form has somewhat collapsed here, making one flat side.

7.75in (1.5cm) high

$300-400 **UCT**

A Finnish Nuutajärvi Nöstjo 'Helminauha' (String of Pearls) vase, designed by Gunnel Nyman in the late 1940s, with a stream of controlled internal air bubbles, the base with illegible etched marks.

Although Nyman died in 1948, this vase continued to be produced into the 1950s and appears in two sizes in the company's 1953 and 1958 catalogues. It is one of the company's scarcer and more prized designs, and is widely regarded as a masterpiece of Scandinavian glass design of the period.

9in (23cm) high

$800-1,200 UCT

A Finnish Nuutajärvi Nöstjo bird, designed by Oiva Toikka, the orange body with internal bubbles, and applied head with colorless beak, the base with "Nuutajärvi O. Toikka" acid stamp.

Toikka's wide range of bird figures was introduced in 1981, and at least one has been released each year since. In 1988, Iittala and Nuutajärvi merged, so birds can be found with both Nuutajärvi acid marks and Iittala labels. The range continues to be produced by Iittala today, although some shapes have been discontinued.

2002 *8in (20cm) long*

$150-200 UCT

A Finnish Nuutajärvi Nöstjo tapering vase, designed by Gunnel Nyman, the amber bowl with trails of controlled internal bubbles, and a heavy cased colorless foot, the base etched "G.Nyman Nuutajärvi Nöstjo".

7.75in (19.5cm) high

$500-600 UCT

A Finnish Nuutajärvi Nöstjo mold-blown cobalt blue 'Hourglass' vase, no. KF245, designed by Kaj Franck in 1956.

This design is multifunctional and can be used as a goblet, vase or even a candle-holder. Colors included yellow, violet, lilac, green, and light and dark blue.

1956-69 *6.75in (17cm) high*

$100-200 UCT

A Finnish Nuutajärvi Nöstjo bird, designed by Oiva Toikka, the green body with applied colored chips, the applied head with colorless beak, the base with "Nuutajarvi O. Toikka" acid stamp.

9in (23cm) long

$150-250 UCT

A Finnish Nuutajärvi Nöstjo 'Northern Duck' bird, designed by Oiva Toikka, with iridescent swirled body. the applied head with colorless beak, the base with "Nuutajärvi O. Toikka" acid stamp.

1991 *6.75in (17cm) long*

$150-200 UCT

A Finnish Nuutajärvi Nöstjo 'Whip-Poor-Will' blown bird, designed by Oiva Toikka, with applied head and spiralling green stripes to body, the base with acid stamp "O.Toikka Nuutajärvi.

This model is currently still being sold by Iittala.

5.75in (14.5cm) long

$80-120 TGM

A Swedish Strömbergshyttan large glass vase, engraved with deer grazing in a glade, the base engraved "Strömbergshyttan 1664 = 1168" and with an artist's signature.

The deer are engraved on one side and the trees on the other, giving a sense of perspective. The technique used for the bark on the trees is interesting, as the glass has been chipped away to give the almost sparkling effect of early morning, dew-laden trunks.

12in (30.5cm) high

$600-800   GC

A 1950s-60s Swedish Strömbergshyttan clear glass vase, unsigned, probably designed by Gerda Stromberg, with thick, cut rim.

6.75in (17cm) high

$20-40   AEM

A Swedish Strömbergshyttan colorless cased brown vase, possibly designed by Gunnar Nyland, with offset well and asymmetric curving pulled rim, the base inscribed "Strömberg B775".

4.25in (10.5cm) high

$150-200   UCT

A Swedish Strömbergshyttan brown torpedo vase, designed by Gunnar Nylund in 1955, the base signed "Strömbergshyttan".

10in (25.5cm) high

$100-150   TGM

A Swedish Strömbergshyttan brown-toned vase, designed by H.J. Dunne-Cooke, of flower-like form.

8.25in (21cm) high

$140-180   GC

A Swedish Strömbergshyttan hollow blown bird figurine, with applied eyes, beak, neck and wings, and with plastic label to base, the machine-cut base rim inscribed "AB 7405 Strömbergshyttan".

Strömberg was taken over by Orrefors in 1976 and closed in 1979, meaning this bird must have been made during the 1960s or '70s, or else Orrefors used the name later.

6.75in (17cm) high

$120-160   UCT

A Swedish Afors colorless cased purple glass vase, designed by Ernest Gordon, the base inscribed "5H 3130 E.Gordon Lila".

Ernest Gordon (b.1926) worked for Afors from 1954 to 1961, and his designs followed the organic Scandinavian Modern movement, but also conformed to more Modernist lines. Unless signed, his designs are difficult to attribute.

7in (17.5cm) high

$200-300   UCT

A Swedish Aseda colorless cased mottled deep blue vase, designed by Bo Borgstrom, with powder inclusions, heavy base and 'folded' rim.

Although they appear black, the powder inclusions are in fact a very dark blue. The rim, which has been tightly folded down over the neck, is one of the most interesting features of this vase – it is a challenging technique requiring skill and experience.

7in (17.5cm) high

$100-150   UCT

A Swedish Björkshult mold-blown figural decanter, by an unknown designer, with original paper label.

The original blown stopper typically fits loosely in the neck.

9.5in (24cm) high

$150-200   GC

A Swedish Boda cast orange paperweight, designed by Erik Höglund, with impressed deer.

The strong color and chunky, comparatively unrefined, form and motif are typical of Höglund's designs. Among other themes, he was also inspired by cave paintings, an inspiration that can be clearly seen in the animal motif.

4.5in (11.5cm) high

$80-100   UCT

A Swedish Boda cast green paperweight, designed by Erik Höglund, with impressed stylized walking deer.

4in (11.5cm) diam

$70-90   UCT

A Swedish Boda cast colorless glass paperweight, designed by Erik Höglund, with impressed stylized boy's head and shoulders.

4in (11.5cm) high

$70-90   UCT

A Swedish Boda cast orange paperweight, designed by Erik Höglund, with impressed stylized face.

4.5in (11.5cm) wide

$70-90   UCT

A Swedish Boda cast green paperweight, designed by Erik Höglund, with impressed stylized bust of a busty woman.

4in (11.5cm) diam

$70-90   UCT

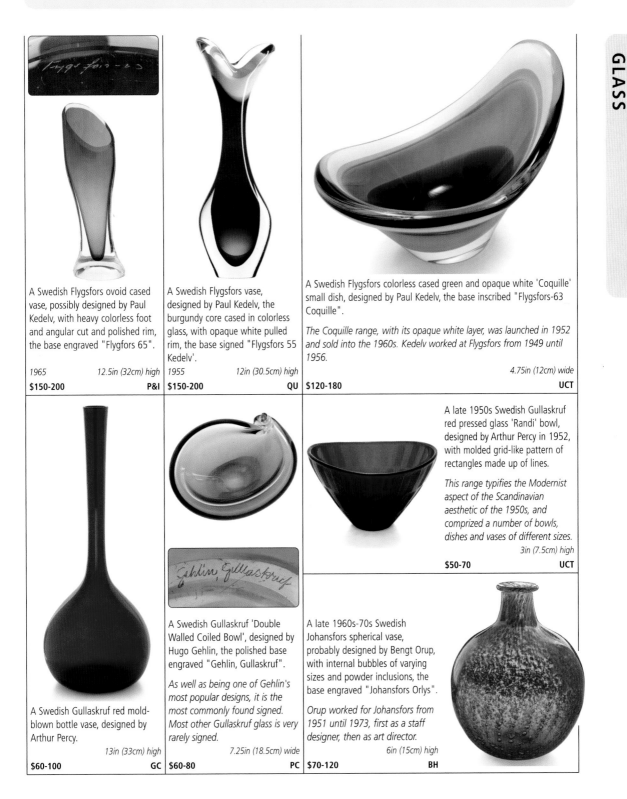

A Swedish Flygsfors ovoid cased vase, possibly designed by Paul Kedelv, with heavy colorless foot and angular cut and polished rim, the base engraved "Flygfors 65".

1955   12.5in (32cm) high

$150-200   P&I

A Swedish Flygsfors vase, designed by Paul Kedelv, the burgundy core cased in colorless glass, with opaque white pulled rim, the base signed "Flygsfors 55 Kedelv'.

1955   12in (30.5cm) high

$150-200   QU

A Swedish Flygsfors colorless cased green and opaque white 'Coquille' small dish, designed by Paul Kedelv, the base inscribed "Flygsfors-63 Coquille".

The Coquille range, with its opaque white layer, was launched in 1952 and sold into the 1960s. Kedelv worked at Flygsfors from 1949 until 1956.

4.75in (12cm) wide

$120-180   UCT

A late 1950s Swedish Gullaskruf red pressed glass 'Randi' bowl, designed by Arthur Percy in 1952, with molded grid-like pattern of rectangles made up of lines.

This range typifies the Modernist aspect of the Scandinavian aesthetic of the 1950s, and comprized a number of bowls, dishes and vases of different sizes.

3in (7.5cm) high

$50-70   UCT

A Swedish Gullaskruf red mold-blown bottle vase, designed by Arthur Percy.

13in (33cm) high

$60-100   GC

A Swedish Gullaskruf 'Double Walled Coiled Bowl', designed by Hugo Gehlin, the polished base engraved "Gehlin, Gullaskruf".

As well as being one of Gehlin's most popular designs, it is the most commonly found signed. Most other Gullaskruf glass is very rarely signed.

7.25in (18.5cm) wide

$60-80   PC

A late 1960s-70s Swedish Johansfors spherical vase, probably designed by Bengt Orup, with internal bubbles of varying sizes and powder inclusions, the base engraved "Johansfors Orlys".

Orup worked for Johansfors from 1951 until 1973, first as a staff designer, then as art director.

6in (15cm) high

$70-120   BH

A Norwegian Randsfjord translucent white and mottled blue spherical vase, designed by Torbjörn Torgersen, with flared rim, the base with embossed paper and gilt label.

4.25in (10.5cm) high

$60-80   TGM

A 1960s Swedish Skruf cut glass vase, designed by Bengt Edenfalk, with stylized sunburst design, the base etched "Edenfalk Skruf".

8.25in (21cm) high

$200-300   GC

EXPERT EYE – A SCANDINAVIAN GLASS VASE

It is hard to be sure which factory made this vase, but the form suggests Johansfors or, more probably, Lindshammar.

Swards decorated pieces from Gullaskruf, hence the name on the label, but also bought pieces from other factories such as Johansfors and Lindshammar.

The decoration is extremely unusual and contrasts with the organic form. Gilt bands are more commonly associated with Czechoslovakian glass design of the same period.

The label bears the names 'Swards' and 'Gullaskruf'. Edvin and Freda Sward were originally glass decorators at Gullaskruf, before leaving to found their own glass decorating company.

A very rare 1960s Swedish Lindshammar or Johansfors shouldered vase, possibly designed by Sixten Wennerstrand, the applied gilt and white enameled banding by Swards, with asymmetric, pulled rim, and gold and silver foil Swards label.

With thanks to members of the Glass Message Board for the above information (see www.glassmessages.com).

10.75in (27cm) high

$150-250   PC

A 1970s Swedish Skruf Glasbruk mold-blown full lead crystal vase, designed by Lars Hellsten in c1970, with scrolling design, the base engraved "Hellsten Skruf H 18 2".

Lars Hellsten (b1933) worked as a designer at Skruf Glasbruk from 1964 to 1972, before moving to Orrefors.

6.5in (16.5cm) high

$200-300   GC

A 1960s Swedish Skruf Glasbruk bottle vase, designed by Bengt Edenfalk, the red body cased in colorless glass, the base marked "Edenfalk Skruf Inka 6".

10.5in (26.5cm) high

$150-250   QU

FIND OUT MORE...

'Miller's 20th-Century Glass', *by Andy McConnell, published by Miller's, 2006.*

'Scandinavian Ceramics & Glass In The Twentieth Century', *by Jennifer Opie, published by V&A Publications, 1989.*

'20th Century Factory Glass', *by Leslie Jackson, published by Mitchell Beazley, 2000.*

ESSENTIAL REFERENCE

- Stuart (founded 1787) produced a wide range of brightly colored enameled table and decorative wares from 1928 until 1939. Over 600 patterns were designed, including geometric, figural, floral and foliate motifs. The majority were designed by the company's leading cutter and designer, Ludwig Kny. Geoffrey Stuart also produced designs after 1933.
- Outlines were applied by transfer, with teams of women and girls filling them in with color. As these paintresses were less costly to pay than glass cutters, the enameled wares could be sold for less than cut glass.

- Geometric designs typically followed the prevalent Art Deco style of the day, and reached the peak of their popularity in the mid-1930s.
- Look out for complex decoration. Decorative ware is usually worth more than tableware. Cocktail shakers are the exception as they attract interest from cocktail shaker collectors and those buying for use. Scarce and desirable designs include 'Red Devil', introduced in 1933, and the spider web pattern produced from c1935. Similar pieces were produced by other companies and in other countries, so always look on the base for Stuart's acid stamp.

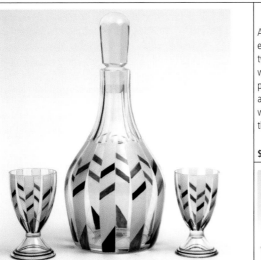

A 1930s Art Deco Stuart enameled conical decanter and two matching goblets, decorated with a yellow and black wavy line pattern and alternating frosted and plain columns, the decanter with slice-cut neck and stopper, the base with acid stamp.

Decanter 12in (30.5cm) high

$850-950　　　　**FLD**

A 1930s Stuart decanter and set of six matching glasses, enameled with a mounted huntsman, the decanter with slice-cut neck and spire form stopper, the bases with acid marks.

Decanter 12.25in (31cm) high

A 1930s Stuart enameled decanter and pair of matching glasses, decorated with a blue and black geometric pattern in alternating acid-etched and plain columns, the decanter with facet-cut stopper.

Decanter 10.5in (26.5cm) high

$900-1,100　　　　**FLD**　**$600-800**　　　　**FLD**

A 1930s Art Deco Stuart enameled footed posy vase, decorated with a stylized floral garland and green curl border, the base with acid stamp.

5.5in (14cm) high

$250-350　　　　**FLD**

A pair of Art Deco Stuart enameled candle-holders, decorated with an abstract geometric pattern of cogs and flashes, the base with acid stamp.

3.25in (8cm) high

$300-400　　　　**FLD**

A 1930s Art Deco Stuart enameled preserve pot, decorated with clover flowers and bees, the base with acid stamp.

4in (10cm) high

$120-160　　　　**FLD**

GLASS

ESSENTIAL REFERENCE

- Studio glass is the name given to glass produced by individual artists working outside of the confines of a factory environment. The movement as it is known today began in the US, in the early 1960s, when Harvey Littleton and Dominick Labino developed a process that allowed individuals to melt, form and blow glass themselves. Glassmakers in other countries had also made similar developments, and soon the movement spread.
- Although there are no new techniques in glass, which has been made since Roman times, skills have developed enormously over the past 20 years. Pieces are now generally more finely made, using increasingly complex techniques. Glass has also been seen increasingly as an art form, rather than a craft, and since the 1980s leading museums and galleries have been adding studio glass to their collections.
- The work of major names, such as Dale Chihuly and Marvin Lipofsky, already make high sums on the secondary market. However, works by those they taught, or lesser known makers, can be more affordable. The market for second and third generation artists is lively. Some have attracted, or are attracting, large groups of fans and collectors – a factor that has caused demand, and thus prices, to rise.

- Learn about an artist's background to see who they studied with, and build up an eye for their style and work. Many pieces are signed, but signatures can be hard to read, and some are not signed at all. Also learn a little about how glass is made as this will help you spot complex pieces, which were time-consuming to make, and so were probably expensive at the time, and may be rare today.
- Also learn about the key movements and styles of any given period. Date is not always an indicator of value, and some early examples are crudely formed, although they do represent this important development in glass-making history. Large pieces, and those by makers who already have a large following could be good investments as interest in this vibrant area is developing every year.

A Sarah Cable large vase, the matte green body with iridescent, low relief mottles, and pink petal rim, the base signed "Sarah Cable".

New studio glass artist Sarah Cable first blows a colored body. This is then overlaid with another layer of dark glass that is iridized to make it opaque. The petal-like pink lobes are added by hand. She then applies protective decals in the forms of the mottles and sandblasts any unprotected areas away. These vases are produced in a number of sizes, colors and patterns.

c2007   15in (38cm) high

$150-250   **TGM**

A Sarah Cable large vase, the matte beige-yellow body with iridescent, low relief stripes, and blue petal rim, the base signed "Sarah Cable".

c2007   8.75in (22cm) high

$120-140   **TGM**

A Sarah Cable large vase, the matte blue body with iridescent, low relief mottles, and lime green petal rim, the base signed "Sarah Cable".

c2007   8.75in (22cm) high

$120-140   **TGM**

An Adam Aaronson ball vase, covered with a layer of fragmented silver foil, the base signed "The Handmade Glass Co 1998 Adam Aaronson Design".

1998   5in (12cm) high

$60-100   **TGM**

A Jane Charles ribbed footed ball vase, the blue and green mottled body with short neck and flat rim, the base signed "Jane Charles".

3.75in (9.5cm) high

$65-75   **TGM**

A Norman Stuart-Clarke vase, with mottled beige effect, applied cane and chips to form a tree motif, and iridescent surface, the base with broken pontil mark and signed "Norman Stuart Clarke 86".

Norman Stuart-Clarke's hot-worked designs, inspired by the Cornish landscape around him, have become increasingly sought-after over the past few years.

1986   8in (20cm) high

$280-320   **TGM**

A Norman Stuart-Clarke bowl, the lower half covered with colored chips to represent the ground and with applied iridescent moon, the base signed "Norman Stuart Clarke 88".

1988   6.5in 16.5cm (high)

$240-320   **TGM**

A Julia Donnelly cylinder vase, with flared rim, with applied shards of glass, and mottled and veiled decoration, the base signed "Julia Donnelly 1998".

Donnelly studied under Peter Layton and worked with Siddy Langley, but no longer makes glass.

1998   6.25in (15.5cm) high

$70-90   **TGM**

A Julia Donnelly flattened oval vase, the mottled surface with colored chips, signed "Julia Donnelly 1995".

1995   4.25in (10.5cm) high

$60-80   **TGM**

A Carin von Drehle ovoid vase, the exterior with randomly applied trails and heavy iridescence, the base signed "Carin von Drehle 1990".

US glass artist Carin von Drehle trained under Peter Layton at the London Glassblowing Studios, which were then in Rotherhithe, during the mid-late 1980s. Designs with iridescence and applied trails were typical of production at the time. Unlike her colleagues Siddy Langley and Norman Stuart-Clarke, von Drehle gave up glassmaking in the early 1990s.

4.75in (12cm) high

$150-250   **TGM**

A Carin von Drehle bottle vase, the light blue body decorated with a random pattern of colored trails, canes and chips, with an iridescent surface effect, the base signed "Carin von Drehle"

8in (20cm) high

$150-200   **TGM**

A Carin von Drehle disc vase, the tapered translucent white body with applied mottled brown-black bands, the base signed "Carin von Drehle 1986".

This is similar to designs produced by Layton at the time, such as the piece shown on page 306, however, it has an outer layer of colorless glass.

3in (7.5cm) high

$150-200   **TGM**

A Dominick Labino deep ruby red vase, with applied swirling prunts, the base inscribed "Labino 1973".

Dominick Labino (1910-87) is one of the founding fathers of the studio glass movement. Along with Harvey Littleton, he developed the glass formula and small furnace that allowed glassmaking to move out of the factory and become economical and viable for individual artists. His students went on to become the first studio glass artists. As such, his work is highly sought-after, particularly in the US. This is typical of his free-formed works, which appear in many museums around the world.

1973   6.25in (16cm) high

$1,800-2,200   **ANT**

A Peter Layton cylinder vase, with flared rim, the opaque white body overlaid with black powdered enamels in a random geometric pattern. signed "Peter Layton 1983" in one of the black areas.

1983   8.75in (22cm) high

$280-320   **TGM**

An Isgard Moje-Wohlgemuth bowl, with melted colored enamels in triangular and dripped patterning giving the effect of ink staining, engraved "MOJE 1972".

1972   6.25in (15.5cm) diam

$400-600   **QU**

A William Walker mold-blown bowl, the spiralling optic opaque white body with a brown randomly applied streak, and with a coiled rim cased in colorless glass, the base signed 'William Walker'.

The applied and tightly folded down rim requires great skill to achieve successfully.

3.25in (8.5cm) high

$70-80   **TGM**

An early 1980s David Wallace vase, the heavy colorless body overlaid with randomly applied pink striped canes and cased in an outer layer of colorless glass, the base signed "David Wallace".

3.75in (9.5cm) high

$100-120   **TGM**

A David Wallace perfume bottle, with applied black arms, central disc and matching black stopper, the base signed "David Wallace".

4in (10cm) high

$70-90   **TGM**

A David Wallace perfume bottle, the colorless body with applied canes twisted into a spiral, the base signed "David Wallace 1988".

1988   5.25in (13cm) high

$60-70   **TGM**

ESSENTIAL REFERENCE

- Powell & Sons was founded in 1680, in London, England. The original site was once a monastery, and the company became more commonly known as Whitefriars. In 1923, the company moved to Wealdstone, Middlesex and in 1962 the name Whitefriars was officially adopted. The company grew to prominence during the late 19thC producing art glass, some inspired by Venetian and European styles.

- In 1954, Royal College of Art, London, graduate Geoffrey Baxter (1922-95) was employed as designer, and produced the most important Whitefriars designs of the late 20thC. His designs are also the most collectible and in many instances the most valuable, and some have become icons of 20thC glass design. His designs were strongly modern, and were inspired by Scandinavian glass of the same period. Other important designers include Peter Wheeler and William Wilson.

- Baxter's most characteristic output was the Textured range, designed in 1966 and introduced the following year. All pieces were handmade, being blown into textured molds, and were produced in bright colors with inventive, abstract shapes drawing inspiration from many sources including the natural world and geometry.

- Consider the form, color and size of pieces, as these factors affect value considerably. New colors were introduced in 1969, and dates shown represent a combination of the colors and shapes. Prices for iconic designs such as the 'Banjo' and 'Drunken Bricklayer' have reached a plateau over the past few years, but are still very strong. Look for examples with good levels of sharp detail, as molds tended to wear down over time, leaving lower levels of texture.

- Look out for organically knobbly and lobed cased pieces from the 1950s, designed in association with William Wilson, and pieces from the Late Textured range of the 1970s, as these are possibly under-priced. Most were free-formed, so exact sizes and colors will differ, making each piece unique. Similarly unique are the pieces from the Studio ranges, which continue to rise in price and popularity.

A 1960s Whitefriars Ruby red 'Molar' lobed vase, no. 9410, designed by William Wilson.

c1955   7.25in (18cm) high

$120-140   TGM

A Whitefriars Sea green 'Twisted Molar' vase, no. 9386, designed by William Wilson.

c1953   8in (20cm) high

$80-120   GC

A Whitefriars cased Emerald green 'Knobbly' vase, no. 9611 designed by Harry Dyer in 1963.

1964-72   7in (17cm) high

$100-120   TGM

A Whitefriars cased Kingfisher blue five-lobed bowl, no. 9407, designed by Geoffrey Baxter in 1957.

1957-70   5.5in (14cm) high

$100-140   TGM

A Whitefriars cased Meadow green 'Knobbly' thin vase, no. 9612, designed by Harry Dyer in 1963.

Meadow green is a desirable color.

1964-72   9.5in (24cm) high

$100-120   TGM

A Whitefriars Kingfisher blue 'Ribbon Trailed' vase, no. 9706, designed by Geoffrey Baxter in 1969, with green ribbons.

1969-c1971   *10.25in (26cm) high*

$140-200   **TGM**

A Whitefriars orange baluster vase, no. 9803, designed by Geoffrey Baxter in 1972, from the New Studio range, with flared rim, the body overlaid with randomly trailed orange streaks highlighted with silver chloride.

All items in the Studio ranges were relatively highly priced and made in comparatively small quantities. As Whitefriars was also going through a decline in sales, at this time, examples are rare today.

1972-80   *7in (18cm) high*

$400-600   **GC**

EXPERT EYE – A WHITEFRIARS STUDIO VASE

The Studio range was introduced in 1969 in answer to the growing interest in, and the influence of, the Studio glass movement that had sprung up at that time.

There were three designs within it – an opaque white core cased in orange streaks, created in silver chloride. The final casing makes it appear as if the design is floating above the core. This was produced in 1969 only.

Some designs were produced by Geoffrey Baxter, but the specific 'Studio Range' was designed by art school graduate Peter Wheeler, who worked with Baxter during 1969.

Shapes are simple and solid, providing a monumental feel, and the design was also available in 'Old Gold' with a silvery cream ground and gold-brown stripes.

A Whitefriars Studio vase, no. S6, designed by Peter Wheeler, with opaque white glass cased in brown lined orange.

c1969   *10.25in (26cm) high*

$450-550   **WW**

A Whitefriars Sapphire blue jug, no. M104, designed by William Wilson.

Geoffrey Baxter produced cut designs for this jug the following year. Cut examples are scarce. The jug was also sold as part of a water set with tapering drinking glasses.

c1958   *9.25in (23cm) high*

$60-80   **GC**

A Whitefriars cut and polished glass vase, of tapering cylindrical form with an asymmetric rim and cut with a shoal of small fish and a larger fish.

Whitefriars' cut glass is relatively hard to find. A production date for this unique piece is unknown as it was never catalogued.

9in (22.5cm) high

$500-600   **WW**

A Whitefriars Sky blue bubbled paperweight, no. 9303, designed by Geoffrey Baxter.

1980   *3in (7.5cm) diam*

$40-50   **TGM**

MILLER'S COMPARES – FAKE & AUTHENTIC DRUNKEN BRICKLAYERS

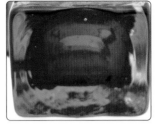

The base is different to originals, with a less well executed polished concave pontil mark. There is also no sign of wear through use, such as small criss-crossing scratches.

The green vase is a recent fake – the color is intended to mimic Meadow Green, but is the wrong tone. A dark cobalt blue and a strong amber can also be found and again, were never used by Whitefriars.

The texture on the original is slightly sharper and better defined. Although textures differ depending on the age of the mold, they are usually crisper and in higher relief than on reproductions.

The authentic vase is cased all over the body, whereas the green vase is not, and the casing on the base is different.

A fake Whitefriars green 'Drunken Bricklayer' vase.

c2007   8.5in (21.5cm) high
$40-60   **PC**

A Whitefriars aubergine 'Drunken Bricklayer' small vase, no. 9673, designed by Geoffrey Baxter in 1966.

1972   8in (20cm) high
$500-600   **GC**

A Whitefriars Kingfisher blue small 'Drunken Bricklayer' vase, no. 9673, designed by Geoffrey Baxter in 1966.

This popular form was produced in two sizes, and this is the smallest. This color was available from 1969 to 1974, even though the shape was introduced in 1966.

1969-74   8.25in (21cm) high
$440-520   **TGM**

A Whitefriars Kingfisher blue 'Banjo' vase, no.9861 designed by Geoffrey Baxter in 1966.

The iconic 'Banjo' was available in Kingfisher blue from 1969.

1969-c1973   12.5in (32cm) high
$1,200-1,600   **MAX**

A Whitefriars Tangerine 'Banjo' vase, no. 9681, designed by Geoffrey Baxter in 1966.

1966-c1973   13in (33cm) high
$1,200-1,600   **GC**

GLASS

ESSENTIAL REFERENCE – AMBERINA

Amberina is the name given to a type of heat-sensitive glass patented by John Locke for the New England Glass Co. in 1883, and popular until the 1920s. The glass mix includes colloidal gold, which turns the glass transparent yellow. When it is cooled slightly and then re-heated in the furnace, the yellow turns to a deep ruby red. Most pieces were free-blown or mold-blown to give form and molded pattern, but some were pressed. As pieces were re-heated at the top, they had to be mounted on a rod from the base, leaving a pontil mark. Mt Washington also made a version, as did Boston and the Sandwich Glass Co. Collectors do not distinguish between the factories, and it can be hard to identify them, unless pieces are marked. The piece shown here is rare as it is 'Reverse Amberina', where the base is red, rather than the top. Rarer still is 'Plated Amberina', which has an interior lined with opaque white glass.

A rare reverse Amberina mold and free-blown hobnail waisted vase.

7in (18cm) high

$300-400   BH

An Amberina nine-sided vase, with flower-form flared rim.

The form of this vase is quite modern, perhaps indicating it was made during the early 20thC.

8in (20cm) high

$150-200   BH

A late 19thC Amberina attenuated vase, with ruffled rim.

7.75in (19.5cm) high

$70-100   BH

A Mt Washington Amberina 'Diamond Quilted' pattern pitcher.

8in (20cm) high

$300-400   BH

An Amberina 'Diamond Quilted' pattern tumbler.

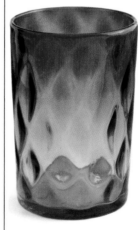

3.75in (9.5cm) high

$60-80   BH

A 1930s-40s Cambridge Glass Co. tazza, the amber bowl in a Farber Bros. chrome-plated stand, with stamped mark to the base.

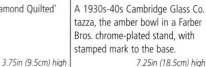

7.25in (18.5cm) high

$18-22   AEM

A 1930s Daum large amber glass stepped vase, with flared rim and acid-cut low relief tessellated block pattern, with wheel-cut signature and cross of Lorraine mark.

14.5in (36.5cm) high

$700-800   **FLD**

A Heisey mold-blown purple ball vase, with optic columns and machine-cut rim.

5.75in (14.5cm) high

$80-120   **GC**

A 1960s Higgins large slump glass ashtray, with molded cigarette rests, internal gold applied star transfers and signature, one corner with original foil label.

13.75in (35cm) wide

$300-500   **TCF**

A Lauscha or Bimini snake shaped solifleur vase, with orange stripes and applied opaque white eyes with applied black pupils.

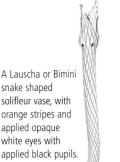

Thin and delicate lampworked pieces such as this are often attributed to Austrian company Bimini, founded by Fritz Lampl during the 1930s. However, a number of factories continued to produce these designs after WWII, many around Lauscha in Germany.

8.5in (21.5cm) high

$10-15   **PAS**

A Leerdam attenuated bottle, designed by Floris Meydam in 1970, the body of orangey-brown opaque glass and the neck of transparent cobalt blue.

17in (43cm) high

$250-350   **QU**

A 1930s Dutch Leerdam 'Ariel' sea-green glass ovoid vase, designed by Andreas Dirk Copier, with internal seaweed and fish pattern, the base inscribed "W 1618".

This vase uses the complex Ariel technique developed at Orrefors in Scandinavia, in 1937, for more information, see page 288.

13.75in (35cm) high

$2,500-3,500   **FLD**

A 1950s Dutch Leerdam 'Unica' vase, designed by Floris Meydam, the compressed ovoid body with crescent rim decorated with internal cased bands of blue and green, the base with inscribed signature and numbered "1-133".

7.5in (19cm) high

$600-800   **FLD**

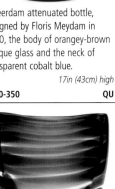

A Loetz corseted vase, designed by Michael Powolny, the flared rim in semi-opaque white glass with cobalt trailing, the base engraved "Prof Powolny Loetz".

5in (12.5cm) high

$1,500-2,000   **SDR**

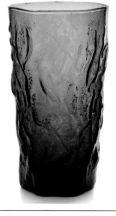

A Morgantown purple 'Crinkle' iced tea glass.

Crinkle was released during the 1940s and produced until Morgantown closed in 1971. The range can be found in over 25 different colors and tones, with Bristol Blue and White being the hardest to find.

5.75in (14.5cm) high

$8-12   **AEM**

EXPERT EYE – A PHOENIX GLASS VASE

Phoenix Glass was founded in Monaca, Pennsylvania, in 1880 and is best known for its lighting wares, although it did produce a limited number of decorative wares.

The Sculpted Art Ware range was released in 1933 and produced until 1958. Some designs were produced by Kenneth Haley.

Opaque white glass was blown into a textured mold to give a high relief design, which was then picked out in colors before it was treated to give a matte surface. Natural themes are typical.

Some pieces in single, solid colors were made in strictly limited quantities by other companies using original molds during the 1960s, and again in 1976 for employees only.

A Phoenix Glass 'Sculpted Art Ware' vase, the low relief molded decoration with brown stems, green leaves and yellow flowers.

12in (30.5cm) high

$300-400   **ANT**

An Italian Opalina Fiorentina mold-blown opaque blue vase, with molded stylized flower design.

These vases are often mistakenly attributed to Dartington due to the flower motif. Opalina Fiorentina was based in Empoli, Italy. This vase is one of their most common, and can be found in beige, green, yellow, orange and blue. Many are lined with an opaque white layer, making the colors vibrant, although transparent examples are also known.

12in (30.5cm) high

$60-80   **GC**

A Paden City 'Spring Orchard' pattern Glades pressed glass vase, with acid-etched floral pattern.

8.25in (20.5cm) high

$40-60   **AEM**

A Phoenix Glass 'Sculpted Art Ware' vase, with low relief molded leaves and cherries, painted over mold-blown matte opaque glass.

9.5in (24cm) high

$280-320   **ANT**

ESSENTIAL REFERENCE – SATIN GLASS

Satin glass is a term used to describe any late 19thC or early 20thC glass with a satin finish. The idea was developed in the UK by Benjamin Richardson in 1858. Patents were issued in the US, in 1886 to Frederick Shirley of Mt Washington and Joseph Webb of Phoenix Glass. It was also reproduced in large numbers during the mid-20thC. Satin glass was produced by dipping the body into acid, which ate away the glossy finish. Sometimes a wax-resist was applied to mark out a design that would remain glossy, protected by the wax-resist. Nearly all satin glass was cased over an opaque white core, with graduated or solid pink, yellow or blue being the most common colors. Transparent, colorless satin glass is also known. Designs, such as the 'Diamond Quilted' pattern here, were created by blowing the piece into a textured mold, leaving indentations marking out the pattern. Air was then trapped in this pattern under the final outer layer.

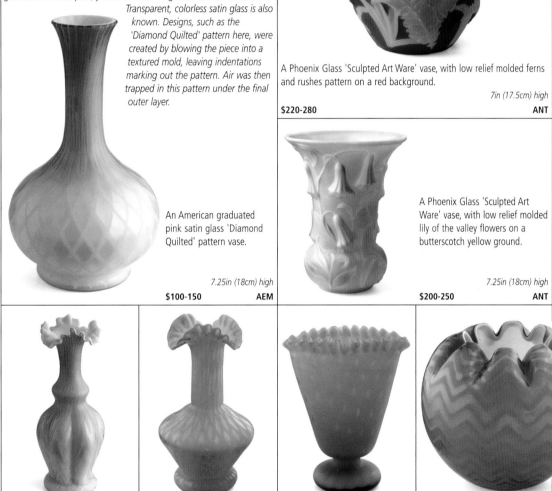

A Phoenix Glass 'Sculpted Art Ware' vase, with low relief molded ferns and rushes pattern on a red background.

7in (17.5cm) high

$220-280   **ANT**

An American graduated pink satin glass 'Diamond Quilted' pattern vase.

7.25in (18cm) high

$100-150   **AEM**

A Phoenix Glass 'Sculpted Art Ware' vase, with low relief molded lily of the valley flowers on a butterscotch yellow ground.

7.25in (18cm) high

$200-250   **ANT**

A Mt Washington satin glass herringbone pattern vase.

8.75in (22cm) high

$80-120   **AEM**

An American satin glass graduated blue and white 'Diamond Quilted' pattern vase, with internal bubbles and frilled rim.

5.25in (13cm) high

$70-100   **BH**

A blue quilted satin vase, with trapped air bubbles and frilly rim.

6.5in (16cm) high

$70-100   **BH**

A Mother of Pearl pink satin glass herringbone pattern rose bowl.

4.75in (12cm) high

$100-150   **BH**

GLASS

An American graduated pink satin glass rose bowl, with purple and red color tones.

3.25in (8cm) high

$60-90   **BH**

A Belgian Val St Lambert green cased cut glass vase, inscribed with factory name on base.

11in (28cm) high

$200-300   **BH**

A Belgian Val St Lambert dish, the champagne colored glass pulled into four lobes.

Always examine the forms, colors and bases of these dishes carefully as many of this type were also made in France and on Murano. These tend to be worth less than this example.

c1960   *16.5in (42cm) long*

$200-300   **QU**

A 1960s Belgian Val St Lambert bowl, of dynamic form, the pink core cased in colorless glass, with factory gilt label.

13.5in (34cm) long

$200-300   **QU**

EXPERT EYE – A CUT GLASS VASE

Glass designed by architect and ceramics designer Keith Murray is both of high quality and rare, as it was only produced for a few years before WWII.

Although this shape was designed by Keith Murray, the strongly Art Deco cut design does not appear to be, as it is not in the company's pattern book of Murray's designs.

However, the pattern book starts at 100, possibly indicating that the first 99 designs by him may be missing.

If further research, or the discovery of any missing designs by Murray, show that this design is indeed by him, the value of this large vase could rise to over $5,000.

A 1930s (Stevens & Williams) Royal Brierley cut glass vase, shape no. 716A or 725A, designed by Keith Murray, and cut with Art Deco chevron design bands and lenses.

The dark green color is typical of Royal Brierley at this time.

12in (30.5cm) high

$800-1,200   **PC**

A Vedar enameled glass vase, decorated with brightly colored buildings, on square glass foot, painted "Vedar VII", chip to foot rim.

Perhaps surprisingly, this enameled vase was made in Milan, Italy, by Vetri D'Arte Fontana. 'Vedar' was taken from the first two letters of the first two words of the company's name. The range was introduced by Dr Carlo Vezzoli in 1925 and produced until 1930. Like most, this is signed and dated in Roman numerals 'VII' for the year 1927.

1927   *8.75in (22.5cm) high*

$150-250   **WW**

A 1930s Art Deco Westmoreland pressed glass pink ice bucket, cut with a trail of flowers.

6.25in (15.5cm) high

$50-80   AEM

A 1960s Viking Persimmon 'Epic Drape' floor vase, with three molded curving drips and swung asymmetric rim.

23in (58cm) high

$20-25   AEM

A 1960s Viking Bluenique 'Epic Three Foil' tall vase, with free-form swung rim.

19in (48cm) high

$30-40   AEM

A 1960s Kingfisher blue molded large art glass vase, possibly by Viking, with free-form, swung rim.

17.5in (44.5cm) high

$25-35   AEM

A 1960s opaque graduated glass footed pitcher, with swung-out asymmetric rim and pulled handle.

16.25in (41cm) high

$20-30   AEM

A 1960s opaque graduated glass molded footed vase, with swung out asymmetric rim.

13in (33cm) high

$20-30   AEM

A Peach Blow ruffled vase, possibly by Mt Washington.

Peach Blow, fading from creamy white to pink, was made in different ways by a number of companies including Mt Washington, Gunderson-Pairpoint, and New England Glass Co., who introduced their range in 1885. As this is not cased, and is lighter in weight than Pairpoint examples, it is likely to have been made by Mt Washington.

5in (12.5cm) high

$60-90   BH

HANDBAGS

A 1920s-30s French beaded and embroidered purse, the gold-tone frame set with white glass cabochons, and with gold tone chain handle.

Always examine beaded purses carefully. Tears and missing beads are almost impossible to repair satisfactorily thereby reducing values by over 75 percent.

5in (12.75cm) high

$60-100   PC

A 1930s Art Deco beaded purse, with a metal internal frame, and white and clear glass beads in a floral design.

6in (15cm) wide

$20-30   PC

A 1930s French handmade beaded evening purse, with gilt metal frame.

9.25in (23.5cm) wide

$140-200   GCHI

A 1950s black velvet purse, with applied fabric flowers and beaded designs, the purse with a rigid frame.

11.75in (30cm) high

$160-240   GCHI

A black 1950s woven straw purse, with applied fabric and beaded decoration, and "Made in Japan" label.

15.5in (39cm) high

$140-200   GCHI

A 1950s navy blue fabric purse, with all-over beaded decoration in the form of a sleeping Mexican.

As well as a funky pattern, the beads glow in the dark.

12in (30.5cm) wide

$50-70   GCHI

A black fabric and tapestry purse, with rigid frame and beaded details, and black plastic handle.

13in (33cm) high

$200-280   GCHI

A 1960s Art Deco-style leather clutch purse, printed and stamped with a geometric design in light brown over a burgundy-brown background.

10in (25cm) long

$20-40   PC

A 1950s Koret alligator purse, rich golden brown leather with hinged top frame opening, single top loop handle, brass hardware and sable leather interior with multiple pockets and coin purse.

$360-440   FRE

A 1960s Roger Vivier umber patent leather purse, with an oversized faux-tortoiseshell link handle, snap-top closure, lined in kid leather, embossed "Roger Vivier Paris".

$200-300   FRE

A Chanel chevron-quilted red leather purse, rectangular bright red top-zip purse with double-chain handle shoulder straps, exterior pockets on each side.

$360-440   FRE

A 1980s Judith Leiber suede leather gold charm evening purse, with removable chain handle and applied gold Asian-themed designs.

Judith Leiber is particularly notable for her rhinestone encrusted metal-bodied purses, often in the form of animals, known as minaudières. She shot to fame after a number of celebrities and notable personalities, including many of America's First Ladies, were seen with her creations.

$400-600   FRE

EXPERT EYE – A HERMÈS PURSE

This design has enormous classic appeal. With its double handles and flap it recalls the more valuable and iconic Birkin.

The attention to detail is also high. Note the H-shaped clasps and the way the leather has been cut to create a symmetrical pattern.

All Hermès purses are hand made using quality materials including leather linings and fully stamped metalware.

This leather is farmed in Australia and is considered by many to be the premier Hermès leather. Its fine sheen is gained by repeated buffing with a smooth stone.

A Hermès chocolate brown 'Drage' purse, covered with 'Crocodylus porosus' crocodile skin and lined in soft brown leather, the gilt brass 'H' closures with maker's name and also stamped in gold to the front panel under the closure flap.

12in (30cm) long

$4,000-6,000   KT

A Whiting & Davis Co. gilt mesh 'miser's purse', with pink satin interior, the expandable neck closing with a lid.

Whiting & Davis, founded in 1876, are renowned for their metal mesh purses. During the 1930s, they collaborated with designers such as Paul Poiret and Elsa Schiaparelli. Although their purses went out of fashion in the 1950s, their sparkle ensured a comeback during the Disco era of the 1970s and '80s, and they are highly collectable.

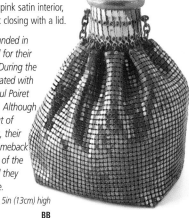

5in (13cm) high

$65-75   **BB**

An American Lin Bren aqua suede slouch purse, with Lucite circular handle and gold-colored compact clasp.

11in (28cm) high

$300-400   **GCHI**

A 1950s woven bent-wood box purse, with red plastic banding, and cherry and leaf decoration to lid.

8in (20cm) wide

$160-240   **GCHI**

An Edwardian brown crocodile leather suitcase, with canvas 'storm' cover monogrammed "BJ", and gilt brass locks.

c1910   *18in (46cm) wide*

$240-360   **ROS**

An early 20thC leather-bound traveling case, the interior with fitted compartments, and with oval plaque to lid above lock.

$200-300   **BRI**

EXPERT EYE – AN EMILIO PUCCI PURSE

Italian nobleman and flying ace Emilio Pucci (1914-92) rose to prominence during the 1960s with his printed fabrics and easy-to-wear dresses that typified the decade.

Vintage Pucci is always in vogue. It has seen a further surge in popularity since Bernard Arnault's LVMH group relaunched the brand in 2000.

This is typical of his printed designs, with its bright, psychedelic colors, and asymmetric geometric and abstract pattern.

Due to Pucci's success and the high cost of vintage and new pieces, imitations are known. Always look closely, as authentic examples bear the 'Emilio' name repeated within the design.

An Emilio Pucci printed silk purse, bright canary yellow printed with gray and earth tone geometric designs, with black leather single strap and brass loops at the side, hidden snap at the front flap closure, lined in black leather and embossed "Emilio Pucci".

$400-600   **FRE**

ESSENTIAL REFERENCE

- The most desirable and valuable pieces of Christmas memorabilia were made in Germany during the early 20thC. Most were made from composition or papier-mâché / pressed pulp, which was then hand-painted. The larger or more complex a piece is, the more valuable it is likely to be. Clothes and accessories are similarly handmade. Makers' names do not generally appear, with most being simply marked 'Germany'.

- Also look out for rare variations in terms of color, or the accessories the figure may be holding, as these can add value. The same goes for later molded plastic memorabilia made from the 1950s and '60s onwards, which is rising in value. Nevertheless, a great many examples can still be found for under $50, with prices rarely rising above $300.
- Condition is important for both areas, with examples in truly mint condition being worth a premium.

EXPERT EYE – A 1920S GERMAN SANTA FIGURINE

At nearly 15in high, this is a very rare large example of a figurine.

He is in near mint condition and is complete with a fur beard and all of his accessories.

The mottled green, brown and tan woven mohair coat is both unusual and extremely rare.

His wicker backpack still contains its rare original gifts, which are individually wrapped.

A 1920s-30s German painted plaster Santa Claus sweets container, with rare moss green felt coat and fur beard, holding a brass basket and feather tree.

11in (28cm) high

$2,000-2,500   **SOTT**

A very rare 1920s-30s large Santa Claus figurine, with painted plaster face, fur beard and multicolored mohair coat, holding a stocking and a wire-and-feather tree, with a wicker pack on his back containing separately made gifts.

14.75in (37cm) high

$3,200-3,800   **SOTT**

An early German painted plaster stooped Santa Claus figurine, with red mohair coat, holding a feather tree and a gift-filled bag, and a gift-filled wicker basket on his back.

c1910   10in (25.5cm) high

$1,500-2,000   **SOTT**

A 1920s-30s German Santa Claus figurine, with long coat, feather Christmas tree, in a woven wicker car with wooden wheels.

7.25in (18cm) long

$800-1,200   **SOTT**

HOLIDAY MEMORABILIA

An early German blue painted plaster Belsnickle figurine, decorated with glass chips, red chenille trim and a feather tree.

8.5in (21.5cm) high

$1,000-1,500   **SOTT**

A 1920s-30s German painted plaster Belsnickle figure, with wire-and-feather tree, red chenille trim and applied clear Venetian glass or Coralene beads.

Coralene are tiny glass beads that are glued onto the surface of an object. Wear and loss of the beads is common, and reduces value.

10.5in (26.5cm) high

$800-1,200   **SOTT**

A 1920s-30s German painted plaster Santa Claus sweets container, opening at the waist.

4.25in (10.5cm) high

$150-200   **SOTT**

A 1920s-30s German composition 'Santa on a log' figure, with a pack of toys on his back, the base painted "Germany".

2.75in (7cm) high

$100-150   **SOTT**

A large Annalee Christmas poseable reindeer soft toy.

4in (10cm) high

$12-18   **AEM**

An American Schoenhut hand-painted composition smiling Santa Claus 'Roly Poly' toy, with weighted bottom, repair to top of head.

9in (23cm) high

$600-800   **BER**

A set of 12 Santa Claus picture blocks, the wooden cubes with color lithographed images of Santa Claus in different scenes.

2.25in (5.5cm) wide

$500-700   **BER**

A 'Santa Claus In Africa Picture Puzzle' box, published by McLoughlin Bros., New York, with color lithographed label showing children riding ostriches followed by Santa on his sleigh, lacks contents.

10.25in (26cm) high

$300-400   **BER**

ESSENTIAL REFERENCE

- Halloween memorabilia is the second most popular area of holiday collecting after Christmas memorabilia, particularly in the US. Much reflects the holiday's rural origins in 18thC Scotland, as the custom was brought to the US by Scottish settlers during the 1880s. Despite this, most of the earliest pieces from the 1900s to '30s were made in Germany and exported.
- Pumpkin-shaped jack-o-lanterns or candy containers are the most common form, but figurines, skulls and other related items can also be found. The majority are made from card, which was pressed into molds when wet, before being painted. Papier–mâché, pressed pulp, crêpe paper, lithographed tinplate and plaster-of-Paris were also used. Most pieces were decorated in typical oranges and blacks.

- As the materials used were fragile, many items did not survive the rigours of play and use over the years. Always look for the original paper inserts in jack-o-lanterns as these add value. Damage, such as tears or wear to the paint, can reduce values by 50 percent or more. Large pieces tend to be rare, partly as they were expensive to begin with. They were also more easily damaged through use.
- Look out for novelty or amusing forms and unusual colorways, as they can add value. During the 1950s and '60s, plastic was increasingly used as it was more robust, cheaper, and easier to produce in quantity. Although values still don't match earlier pieces, rare forms, such as those with moving parts or unusual poses, can fetch hundreds of dollars. As earlier pieces become harder to find and therefore more expensive, these are rising in desirability.

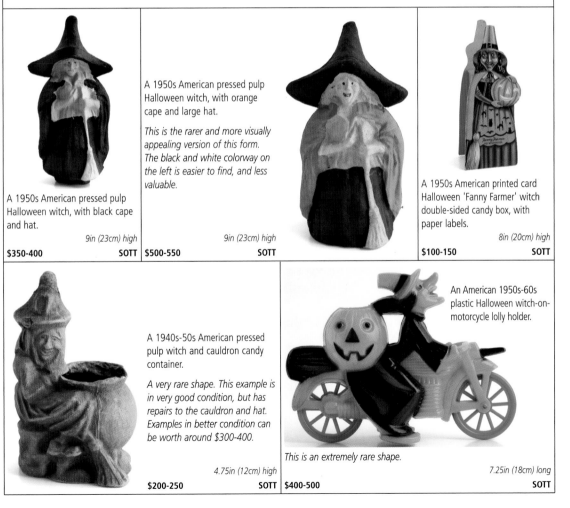

A 1950s American pressed pulp Halloween witch, with orange cape and large hat.

This is the rarer and more visually appealing version of this form. The black and white colorway on the left is easier to find, and less valuable.

A 1950s American pressed pulp Halloween witch, with black cape and hat.

9in (23cm) high

$350-400　　　　　　**SOTT**

9in (23cm) high

$500-550　　　　　　**SOTT**

A 1950s American printed card Halloween 'Fanny Farmer' witch double-sided candy box, with paper labels.

8in (20cm) high

$100-150　　　　　　**SOTT**

A 1940s-50s American pressed pulp witch and cauldron candy container.

A very rare shape. This example is in very good condition, but has repairs to the cauldron and hat. Examples in better condition can be worth around $300-400.

4.75in (12cm) high

$200-250　　　　　　**SOTT**

An American 1950s-60s plastic Halloween witch-on-motorcycle lolly holder.

This is an extremely rare shape.

7.25in (18cm) long

$400-500　　　　　　**SOTT**

A rare pair of 1950s-60s American plastic Halloween pastry cooks-on-wheels lolly holders.

5in (13cm) high

$450-550   **SOTT**

A 1920s-30s German painted plaster miniature Halloween veggie man candy box, with removable card base printed "Made in Germany".

This more commonly found shape is not a nodder, which explains why the value is lower.

3.25in (8cm) high

$320-380   **SOTT**

A 1920s-30s German painted plaster Halloween boy-eaten-by-pumpkin nodder candy container, with removable card disc base.

This is a valuable container, despite its diminutive size. Nodders are easily damaged, making complete examples rarer and more desirable.

2.75in (7cm) high

$400-450   **SOTT**

A 1920s-30s German painted plaster and card Halloween child-riding-pumpkin nodder candy container.

3.75in (9.5cm) high

$500-600   **SOTT**

A 1920s-30s German painted plaster and card Halloween child-riding-pumpkin nodder candy container.

3.75in (9.5cm) high

$500-600   **SOTT**

A very rare and early pair of German painted plaster Halloween old woman and old man nodders.

c1910-15   *7in (17.5cm) high*

$1,800-2,200   **SOTT**

A 1920s-30s German painted plaster Halloween red devil nodder.

6in (15cm) high

$400-500   **SOTT**

A rare German Halloween clicker, with composition head and felt clothes, the back of one trouser leg printed "D.R.G.M. 18284".

The clicker works by holding the handle and shaking the body, causing the figure to bend at the waist and make a clicking sound.

c1910-20   *10in (25.5cm) high*

$550-650   **SOTT**

A 1930s-40s American pressed pulp large Halloween roly-poly pumpkin man lantern.

Always look at the top of the head, as this area is usually damaged by being pushed in and broken. Although this example shows some signs of pressing, it is not broken.

9.25in (23cm) high

$500-600 **SOTT**

EXPERT EYE – A HALLOWEEN DEVIL

The head was also produced separately and is rare. On its own, it can be worth over $1000.

Figures are hard to find, but examples of this size and level of detail are almost once-in-a-lifetime finds, particularly when complete.

This (probably) unique piece was most likely to have been a special commission from a wealthy client, or made as a shop display.

It is incredible to think that the delicate crêpe paper clothes have survived in this condition for over 80 years – this accounts for a large part of the value.

A 1920s-30s German large Halloween devil, constructed from card, papier-mâché, crêpe paper and wire, complete with original paint, paper insert, clothes, base and fork.

20.75in (52.5cm) high

$3,500-4,000 **SOTT**

A 1920s-30s German double-sided printed card and crêpe paper Halloween squeaky toy, the crêpe tube printed "Germany".

The crêpe paper tube and printed card surfaces in particular are easily damaged. This example is in excellent condition.

4.5in (11cm) high

$250-350 **SOTT**

A 1950s American pressed pulp Halloween black cat candy container.

7.25in (18cm) high

$400-450 **SOTT**

A 1950s American painted pressed pulp Halloween cat candy container, with rare heavy gloss finish.

6.75in (17cm) high

$450-500 **SOTT**

A 1930s-40s American pressed pulp Halloween owl lantern.

10in (25cm) high

$180-220 **SOTT**

HOLIDAY MEMORABILIA

EXPERT EYE – A HALLOWEEN JACK-O-LANTERN

The pulped paper, eggbox-like material used here is typical of American production of the 1950s.

This double-faced form is very rare, and the singing 'choir boy' expression is both scarce and desirable.

During the 1930s-40s, the color was added to the pulp mix as a dye, but during the 1950s, the surface was painted with color, as here.

German factories pressed wet card into molds, which was then covered in a layer of strengthening plaster, before being painted. US factories did not use these materials.

A 1950s American pressed pulp Halloween double-faced jack-o-lantern, with 'choir boy' expression and original printed paper inserts.

4.5in (11.5cm) high

$150-200   SOTT

A large 1920s-30s German Halloween jack-o-lantern, with original printed paper insert and card base.

7.5in (19cm) high

$500-600   SOTT

A German card oversized Halloween jack-o-lantern, with original printed paper insert.

1910-20   10.75in (27cm) wide

$1,800-1,900   SOTT

A 1930s-40s American sprayed pressed pulp Halloween jack-o-lantern, with original insert and black 'wrinkle' lines.

5.25in (13cm) high

$220-280   SOTT

A 1950s American pressed pulp Halloween jack-o-lantern, with spray painted decoration and black outlined features.

3.5in (9cm) high

$75-85   SOTT

A 1920s-30s German spray painted pressed card Halloween skull jack-o-lantern.

This was produced using the more common pumpkin mold, but was sprayed white to resemble a skull.

5in (13cm) high

$350-400   SOTT

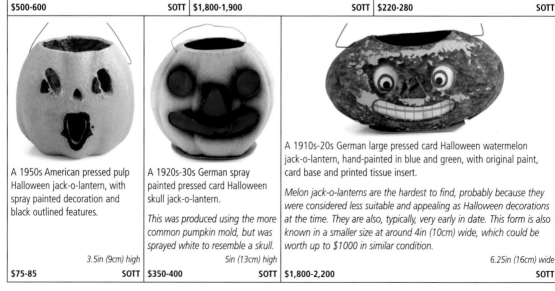

A 1910s-20s German large pressed card Halloween watermelon jack-o-lantern, hand-painted in blue and green, with original paint, card base and printed tissue insert.

Melon jack-o-lanterns are the hardest to find, probably because they were considered less suitable and appealing as Halloween decorations at the time. They are also, typically, very early in date. This form is also known in a smaller size at around 4in (10cm) wide, which could be worth up to $1000 in similar condition.

6.25in (16cm) wide

$1,800-2,200   SOTT

A German sprayed and painted composition Halloween skull jack-o-lantern.

This is a rare size and is in surprisingly good condition for such an easily damaged material.

1910-15   4.25in (11cm) high
$900-1,100   SOTT

An early German heavy plaster-over-card Halloween simian skull jack-o-lantern, with original printed paper insert.

1910-20   3.25in (8cm) high
$500-600   SOTT

An early German heavy plaster Halloween small skull jack-o-lantern, with original red paper insert.

1910-20   3.25in (8cm) high
$400-500   SOTT

A German painted pressed card and plaster-coated Halloween skull jack-o-lantern, with original rosette crêpe paper base.

Note how detailed and well executed the expression is.

1910-20   5.5in (14cm) high
$750-850   SOTT

An extremely rare and large 1920s-30s German hand-painted papier-mâché Halloween devil's head jack-o-lantern, with original paint and printed paper insert for eyes and mouth.

This would have been made for display, possibly in a shop, or as a table centerpiece. Its size and high cost meant that few would have been sold and even fewer would have survived in this condition.

11.25in (28.5cm) high
$2,200-2,400   SOTT

A German plaster-coated papier-mâché Halloween devil's head jack-o-lantern, with replaced printed paper insert.

1910-20   2.75in (7.5cm) high
$400-500   SOTT

A 1930s-40s American pressed pulp Halloween devil's head jack-o-lantern, with original paper insert.

This form, with its strongly molded and deep features, is very rare.

6.5in (16.5cm) high
$400-450   SOTT

A dark soapstone Inuit woman, by an unidentified artist, signed in syllabics, dated "'72".

1972   *10in (25cm) high*
$3,000-4,000   **WAD**

A soapstone 'Man Playing Accordian' figure, by an unidentified artist.

8in (20.5cm) high
$1,000-1,500   **WAD**

A soapstone figure, by Mathew Aqigaaq, E2-350, signed in syllabics.

Born in 1940 into the Qamani'tuaq community, Aqigaaq's work has been included in many publications and exhibitions, including 'Sculpture/Inuit: Masterworks of the Canadian Arctic', organised by the Canadian Eskimo Arts Council. He was also mentioned in an article by James Houston.

c1972   *12in (33cm) high*
$6,500-7,500   **WAD**

A stone figure of a seated woman, by Leonie Qunnut (b.1941), E5-417, from Igloolik, signed in Roman, with disc number.

15in (6cm) wide
$1,000-1,200   **WAD**

A soapstone 'Woman With Kudlik' figure, by Timothy Naralik (b.1942), signed in Roman.

5in (12.5cm) high
$1,000-1,200   **WAD**

A stone figure of a mother and child, by Mathew Aqigaaq, E2-350, from Baker Lake, signed in syllabics.

9in (23cm) high
$1,500-2,500   **WAD**

A soapstone, ivory and wood 'Hunter' figure, by an unidentified artist.

c1967   *13in (33cm) high*
$1,200-1,600   **WAD**

An antler, skin and stone figure of a hunter, by Judas Ullulaq, E4-342, from Gjoa Haven.

13in (33cm) high

$4,000-6,000   **WAD**

EXPERT EYE – JUDAS ULLULAQ

Judas Ullulaq (1937-98) began by carving ivory miniatures, later moving to larger soapstone sculptures – most include details made from other materials, such as inset bone, ivory, or antler eyes.

He was heavily influenced by his nephew, Karoo Ashevak, who is one of the most desirable artists in today's market. Both focused on spirits and the supernatural in their abstracted figural works.

His forms are typically bulging and exaggerated with bizarre distorted or grotesque faces, often with open mouths with teeth, which give a highly expressive appearance to his work.

Ullulaq was a founder of the important Netsilik school, known for its asymmetrical styles inspired by mysticism. His work is more humorous and whimsically amusing.

A soapstone and antler 'Mother and Child' figure, by Judas Ullulaq, E4-342, from Gjoa Haven, signed in syllabics.

17in (43cm) high

$8,000-10,000   **WAD**

A dark soapstone shaman, by Judas Ullulaq, E4-342, from Gjoa Haven, with inset eyes and teeth, being attacked by a bone creature and holding an antler axe, signed in syllabics.

12in (30cm) high

$7,000-8,000   **WAD**

A soapstone and antler 'Hunter' figure, by Judas Ullulaq, E4-342, from Gjoa Haven.

16in (40.5cm) high

$5,000-10,000   **WAD**

A soapstone and antler 'Shaman' figure, by Judas Ullulaq, E4-342, from Gjoa Haven, signed in syllabics.

16in (40.5cm) high

$6,000-10,000   **WAD**

A stone, figure of a demon collecting eggs, by Abraham Kingmiatuq (b.1933), E4-329, from Spence Bay, signed in syllabics.

14in (35.5cm) high

$5,000-6,000   **WAD**

A stone figure of a dancing polar bear, by Paulassie Pootoogook (b.1927), E7-1176, from Cape Dorset.

13in (33cm) high

$2,500-3,500   **WAD**

ESSENTIAL REFERENCE – THE POLAR BEAR

Sharing the Arctic circle with the Inuit people, polar bears are both admired and feared. Known as 'Nanuk', they are considered to be wise, dangerous and powerful, being able to outrun, outswim and outfight a man. They are also considered 'man-like' as they could walk on two legs. When hunted and killed, great respect is paid to their skins and bodies, nearly all parts of which are used for survival in harsh conditions. The bear's power and mystical nature has led it to be depicted in Inuit and pre-Inuit sculpture and art for many centuries. During the 20thC, one of the most notable artists of polar bear sculptures was Pauta Saila (b.1916). He became known for his monumental, heavily stylized dancing bears that poked gentle fun at the animal, yet drew attention to its great strength and power. Born in Cape Dorset in 1977, Pootoogook works in a similar style to Saila, and manages here to convey a superb sense of movement. Dancing polar bears have become one of the most desirable types of Inuit sculpture in recent years.

A carved soapstone figure of an acrobatic polar bear, by Mosesie Pootoogook from Cape Dorset, signed in Roman.

2in (5cm) high

$3,500-4,500   **WAD**

A stone figure of a dancing polar bear, by George Arluk (b.1949), E3-1049, from Arviat, signed in Roman.

1995   *12.5in (32cm) high*

$700-1,000   **WAD**

A stone figure of a polar bear, by David Ruben Piqtoukun (b.1950), W3-1119, signed in Roman and dated "1986".

1986   *9in (23cm) wide*

$1,000-1,500   **WAD**

A soapstone 'Polar Bear' figure, by Mannumi Shaqu (b.1917), signed in syllabics.

11in (28cm) long

$2,500-3,500   **WAD**

A carved and polished black soapstone polar bear, by Joe Kovik (b.1950), E9-188, signed with syllabics and disc number.

8in (20.5cm) high

$800-1,200   **THG**

A soapstone 'Exhausted Polar Bear' figure, by Kananginak Pootoogook (b.1935), signed in Roman.

5in (12.5cm) long

$400-600   **WAD**

A stone and antler musk ox figure, by Lucassie Ikkidluak (b.1947), E7-765, from Lake Harbor, signed in syllabics, dated "1992".

1992   *16in (40.5cm) wide*

$8,000-10,000   **WAD**

A stone and antler musk ox figure, by Seepee Ipellie (b.1940), E7-511, from Iqaluit, signed in syllabics.

13in (33cm) wide

$2,500-3,500   **WAD**

A stone and ivory floating walrus figure, by Markoosie, E7-647, signed in Roman and with disc number.

c1970   *4in (10cm) high*

$550-650   **WAD**

A carved light gray soapstone perching bird, probably by Mary Sanguvia Qumala (b.1946) from Povungnituk, the base inscribed "1346".

7.25in (19cm) high

$250-350   **THG**

A soapstone 'Musk Ox' figure, by Nuveeya Ipellie, with antler horns.

6.5in (16.5cm) long

$1,000-1,500   **WAD**

A stone figure of a bird, by Abraham Etungat (1911-99), E7-809, from Cape Dorset.

9in (23cm) long

$1,700-1,900   **WAD**

A stone bird figure, by Abraham Etungat, E7-809, from Cape Dorset, signed in syllabics.

3in (7.5cm) high

$1,600-2,000   **WAD**

A dark soapstone otter, by an unidentified artist.

c1960   *20cm (8in) wide*

$1,000-1,500   **WAD**

INUIT ART

A stone Sedna, by Gideon Qauqjuaq, E4-392, Spence Bay.

6in (15cm) high

$350-450   **WAD**

A stone bird woman figure, by Tivi Anasuga, signed in syllabics.

6.5in (16.5cm) high

$350-450   **WAD**

A gray soapstone animal figure, by Andy Miki, E1-436, from Arviat.

Like Pangnark, Miki (1918-83) is known for his simplification of form and strong stylization that recalls ancient and primitive sculpture. His work is similarly sought-after.

7in (18cm) high

$10,000-15,000   **WAD**

A stone caribou figure, by Andy Miki, E1-436, from Arviat, signed in syllabics.

6in (15cm) high

$3,500-4,500   **WAD**

EXPERT EYE – JOHN PANGNARK

Pangnark (1920-80) is known for his highly abstracted forms that are reminiscent of hills, mountains, rocky outcrops or even Inuit huddled together.

The simplest of facial features, consisting of mere lines, are lightly carved or inscribed on a small part of the sculptures.

Although typically tiny in size, the simple forms make them appear massive and monumental, and recall the other tribal statues like the Moai statues on Easter Island.

His work enjoys enormous popularity with values varying, depending on the size, sense of weight and form, and visual appeal of the piece..

A stone figure, by John Pangnark, E1-104, from Arviat.

9in (23cm) long

$10,000-15,000   **WAD**

A stone figure, by John Pangnark, E1-104, from Arviat, signed in syllabics.

2.75in (7cm) high

$800-1,000   **WAD**

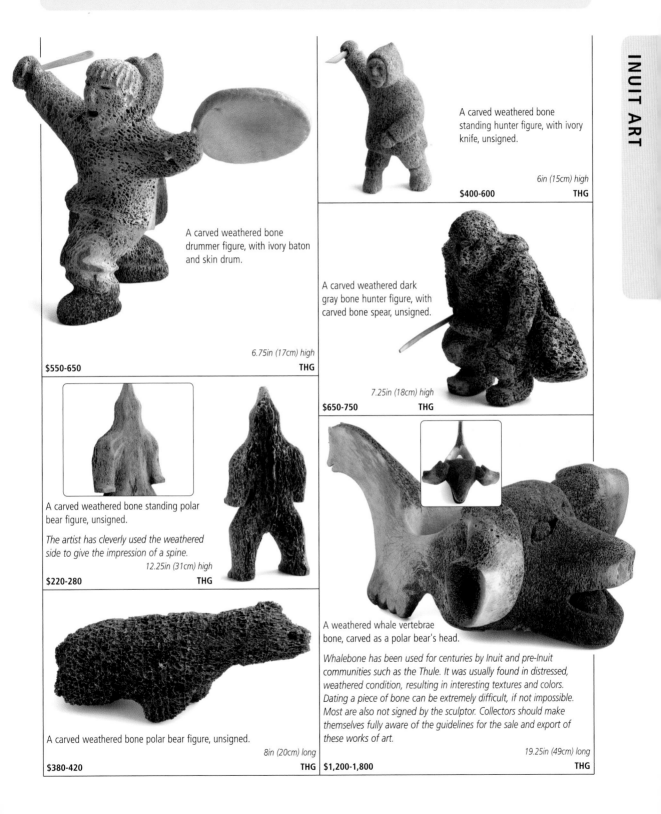

A carved weathered bone drummer figure, with ivory baton and skin drum.

6.75in (17cm) high

$550-650   **THG**

A carved weathered bone standing hunter figure, with ivory knife, unsigned.

6in (15cm) high

$400-600   **THG**

A carved weathered dark gray bone hunter figure, with carved bone spear, unsigned.

7.25in (18cm) high

$650-750   **THG**

A carved weathered bone standing polar bear figure, unsigned.

The artist has cleverly used the weathered side to give the impression of a spine.

12.25in (31cm) high

$220-280   **THG**

A weathered whale vertebrae bone, carved as a polar bear's head.

Whalebone has been used for centuries by Inuit and pre-Inuit communities such as the Thule. It was usually found in distressed, weathered condition, resulting in interesting textures and colors. Dating a piece of bone can be extremely difficult, if not impossible. Most are also not signed by the sculptor. Collectors should make themselves fully aware of the guidelines for the sale and export of these works of art.

19.25in (49cm) long

A carved weathered bone polar bear figure, unsigned.

8in (20cm) long

$380-420   **THG** | $1,200-1,800   **THG**

INUIT ART

A limited edition engraving of a bird, untitled, by Pauta Saila (b.1916), from an edition of 50.

1962   *11.75in (30cm) wide*
$700-1,000   **WAD**

A limited edition 'Geese With Hawk' engraving, by Kenojuak Ashevak (b.1927), from an edition of 50.
1963   *11.75in (30cm) wide*
$550-650   **WAD**

EXPERT EYE – A LUKE ANGUHADLUQ INUIT PRINT

Anguhadluq was in his late sixties when he was inspired to become an artist by his cousin Jessie Oonark, who was becoming increasingly successful.

His first drawings were made between 1960 and 1961, and by 1970 his work had become part of the Baker Lake Annual Print Collection, to which he contributed until 1982.

His style of small figures in a large area of blank white paper reflects the focus and experience of the hunter in the vast expanse of the frozen, white Arctic.

His work has appeared in over 70 exhibitions in Canada and around the world. His strictly limited edition prints are highly sought-after.

A limited edition 'Muskox' stonecut and stencil print, by Luke Anguhadluq (1895-1982), from an edition of 50.
1977   *37in (94cm) wide*
$2,500-3,000   **WAD**

A limited edition 'Young Owls' stonecut print, by Lucy Qinnuayuak (1915-82), E7-1068, from Cape Dorset, from an edition of 50, unframed.

24.5in (62.5cm) wide
$1,700-1,900   **WAD**

A limited edition 'Caribou Hunters' engraving, by Kiakshuk (1886-1966), from an edition of 50, signed in syllabics.
1963   *12in (31cm) wide*
$500-700   **WAD**

A limited edition 'Geese With Hawk' engraving, by Kenojuak Ashevak (1927-), from an edition of 50.
1963   *11.75in (30cm) wide*
$900-1,100   **WAD**

FIND OUT MORE...

The Inuit Art Center: www.ainc-inac.gc.ca/art/index_e.html
'Inuit Art: An Introduction', by Ingo Hessel, Dieter Hessel and George Swinton, published by Douglas & McIntyre, 2003.
'Sculpture of the Inuit', by George Swinton, published by McLelland & Stewart, 1999.

ESSENTIAL REFERENCE

- Much like 19th and early 20thC kitchenalia, post-WWII domestic and kitchen accessories and equipment is primarily collected for its decorative appeal. The 1950s in particular saw an explosion in design, and the production of labour-saving devices to make looking after a home easier. Look out for pieces that represent the dominant styles of the period. Major manufacturers often employed important designers, and these will usually fetch a premium.

- Solid teak kitchen and tablewares have seen a rise in interest and values recently. Forms are usually very simple, with the style leaders being Scandinavian, primarily Danish. The most notable name is Dansk, founded in 1954 by US entrepreneur Ted Nierenberg. The company's main designer until the 1980s was Jens Quistgaard, who produced innovative designs in teak, iron and steel. These have become hotly sought-after today.

- Not all of Dansk's designs were by Quistgaard – look at the base for stamped marks including an 'IHQ' monogram. His most famous design was an ice bucket inspired by the prow of a Viking longboat. Other countries also producing teak wares included Italy and South America. As teak is now an endangered wood, it cannot be used to make solid items, and only limited supplies exist. Always consider style and condition, looking for typically modern forms.

A pair of 1950s-60s Danish solid teak candlesticks, unmarked.

11.5in (29cm) high

$90-110   **UCT**

A pair of Danish solid teak candlesticks, with curving asymmetric rims, unmarked.

These are said to be by Jens Quistgaard (b.1919), but this cannot be confirmed as they they are typically unmarked.

9in (23cm) high

$90-100   **UCT**

A pair of Danish solid teak salt and pepper shakers, with inset metal 'S' and 'P', unmarked.

4.75in (12cm) high

$50-70   **UCT**

A 1960s Dansk solid teak pepper grinder, designed by Jens Quistgaard, with stamped marks to base.

3.5in (9cm) high

$90-130   **UCT**

A Danish Woodline solid teak cylindrical ice bucket, with double-ringed handles, hinged lid and metal liner, the base impressed "Woodline Denmark".

6.5in (16.5cm) high

$150-200   **UCT**

A Danish Anri Form solid teak ice bucket, with two shaped handles and a metal liner, the base with inset factory metal medallion.

9in (23cm) high

$80-120   **UCT**

KITCHENALIA

A 1950s-60s Danish solid teak bowl, with asymmetric curved rim, unmarked.

4in (10cm) high

$60-80   **UCT**

A Danish solid teak three-legged candle-holder, with brass insert, unmarked.

4.5in (12cm) high

$50-70   **UCT**

A Danish Digsmed carved solid teak meat cutting tray, with impressed mark to base.

As well as having a decorative central boss that grips the joint of meat, the surface is sloped so the meat juices drain away.

c1964   *17in (43cm) diam*

$70-90   **UCT**

A 1950s Gotthilf Singer 'Type T.V.E. 20' desk fan, with turquoise rubber blades, and maker's mark to base.

10.75in (28cm) high

$100-150   **QU**

EXPERT EYE – A TEAK ICE BUCKET

The form is similar to a Shaker 'dipper', used for getting water from a barrel or stream, or a cylindrical folk art candle box.

The simple, almost geometric form is typical of its day and is similar to those produced in Denmark at the time.

The design and placement of the handle also allows it to be hung on the wall.

It is built from slats of wood like a barrel, with the vertical lines and different color tones and grains adding interest.

An Italian Anri Form solid teak ice bucket, with single handle and metal liner, the base with inset factory metal medallion.

15in (38cm) high

$100-150   **UCT**

A 1950s Spanish '125 Hurricane' desk fan, with mottled green bakelite body, three red blades and chromed metal stand.

The mottled green body and red blades make this an unusually colorful piece. The form and stand also suggest a rocket or a airplane's propeller engine, which is another attractive feature.

6.75in (17cm) high

$400-600   **QU**

A 1950s-60s hand-painted 'Granny' utensil holder.

10.25in (26cm) high

$8-12 AEM

A 1950s-60s hand-painted 'Grated Cheese' chef cheese sprinkler.

8in (20cm) high

$8-12 AEM

A seated teddy bear chocolate mold, numbered "40" but otherwise unmarked.

The teddy bear is a desirable subject, and the seated bear is much harder to find. Additionally, as he is seated, the resulting chocolate is more three-dimensional.

4.75in (12cm) high

$200-300 SOTT

An American 'Man With Flowers' cast iron doorstop, painted in colors.

Depicted in 18thC clothing, this is a very well detailed stop.

9in (23cm) high

$600-800 BER

A 1950s-60s Wilton Prod. painted cast iron bottle opener.

Intended for opening beer bottles, the double-eye effect gives the impression of being drunk.

3.75in (9.5cm) high

$60-80 BH

A Japanese Holt Howard hand-painted cat's head string dispenser, dated "1958".

1958 *5.25in (13cm) wide*

$20-30 AEM

A 1950s American Ice-o-Mat ice crusher, by Rival Manufacturing Co. Kansas City 289, Missouri, in Wood Tone with Sandalwood, mint condition together with original box.

Boxed 10.75in (27cm) high

$30-50 MA

A late 1950s German AEG KMEG offee bean grinder, designed by Hans Krebs in 1954, in white and brown plastic, with maker's plaque to base.

6.25in (15.5cm) high

$160-240 QU

MARBLES

ESSENTIAL REFERENCE

- Vintage collectible marbles fall into one of two distinct categories: handmade marbles and machine-made marbles. Handmade marbles were produced primarily in Germany from the 1860s to the 1920s. Machine-made marbles were produced in the US after 1905 when M.F. Christensen developed a marble-making machine. Production reached a peak in the 1920s and '30s. In the 1950s and '60s machine-made marbles began to be produced in large numbers in the Far East and South America, but these are generally of little interest to collectors.
- Handmade marbles can be distinguished by the presence of rough pontil marks, where they were broken away from the glass rod to be formed into a sphere. Although traditionally the most sought after, the scarcity of fine hand-made

examples has meant that collectors' interest in the best machine-made marbles is now almost as fervent.
- Machine-made marbles have no pontil mark. Notable manufacturers include the short-lived Christensen Agate Company, which operated between 1905 and 1917, and Akro Agate, that produced marbles from 1910 until the factory's closure in 1951.
- The type of marble can affect value considerably. Patterns, colors and sizes are all important. Symmetry in design and unusual or very bright colors have proved consistently popular. Chips, scuffs, marks and play wear will reduce value, particularly of machine-made marbles, or if the marble's pattern is affected. Marbles in truly mint condition can be worth up to double the value of a worn example.

A German handmade Joseph's Coat marble.

This type of marble has many tightly packed thin multicolored strands under a very thin surface layer of clear glass.

c1880-1920   0.75in (2cm) diam

$100-150   **AB**

A German handmade pink Onionskin marble.

c1880-1920   0.75in (2cm) diam

$40-60   **AB**

A German handmade Custard Swirl marble.

c1880-1920   0.75in (2cm) diam

$70-100   **AB**

A German handmade Latticinio Core Swirl marble, with an alternating color core.

c1880-1920   1in (2.5cm) diam

$80-120   **AB**

A German handmade Latticinio Core Swirl marble.

c1880-1920   1.25in (3cm) diam

$100-150   **AB**

A German handmade Solid Core Swirl marble.

c1880-1920   1in (2.5cm) diam

$50-60   **AB**

A German handmade Divided Core marble.

c1880-1920   1.75in (4.5cm) diam

$200-300   **AB**

A German handmade Coreless Swirl marble.

c1880-1920   *0.75in (2cm) diam*

$15-25   AB

A German handmade Banded Swirl marble.

c1880-1920   *0.5in (1.5cm) diam*

$10-20   AB

A German handmade Indian Swirl marble, with white, green, blue and purple bands.

Indian marbles have black bases. The greater the variety of colors in the swirls, the more valuable it is likely to be.

c1880-1920   *0.75in (2cm) diam*

$40-60   AB

EXPERT EYE – A MICA MARBLE

The glass rod used to make the marbles was rolled in mica chips, which give a glittering effect, before being coated in another layer of glass.

The mica chips usually run through the marble, with distinct sections, known as 'panels', being very rare.

Red is a very rare color, most are colorless.

The spread of the mica chips within the panels, and the panels themselves, are even and symmetrical, which makes this example appealing.

A German floating paneled Mica Onionskin marble.

c1880-c1920   *1.25in (3cm) diam*

$4,000-5,000   AB

Three German handmade 'End of Day' Onionskin marbles.

Rather than indicating they were made at the end of a glassmaker's day, as the term usually implies, 'End of Day' here indicates that the marble was made with stretched flecks of left-over glass rather than rods.

c1880-1920   *0.75in (2cm) diam*

$100-150 (each)   AB

A German or American handmade Transitional Oxblood marble.

c1880-1910   *0.75in (2cm) diam*

$500-750   AB

An American Christensen Agate Company 'Cobra' marble.

With its tornado-like interior swirl, this is a very rare marble.

1927-29   *0.5in (1.5cm) diam*

$2,000-3,000   AB

A German or American handmade Clearie marble.

c1880-1920   *0.5in (1.5cm) diam*

$15-25   **AB**

An American handmade Melted Pontil Transition marble.

c1880-1910   *0.75in (2cm) diam*

$80-120   **AB**

EXPERT EYE – A GUINEA MARBLE

Guineas are among the most desirable and rarest machine-made marbles.

Bases are usually transparent, with colorless being very common, amber and blue being less so, and green and red being the rarest.

They are characterized by their random stretched flecks and blotches of multicolored glass that cover the surface. The manufacturers named them for the colors on the Guinea cocks roaming around the factory yard.

Reproductions are known, so always compare to an original or seek professional advice.

An American Christensen Agate Company machine-made Guinea marble.

c1927-29   *0.75in (2cm) diam*

$300-450   **AB**

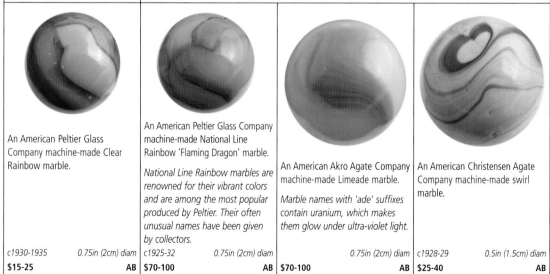

An American Peltier Glass Company machine-made Clear Rainbow marble.

c1930-1935   *0.75in (2cm) diam*

$15-25   **AB**

An American Peltier Glass Company machine-made National Line Rainbow 'Flaming Dragon' marble.

National Line Rainbow marbles are renowned for their vibrant colors and are among the most popular produced by Peltier. Their often unusual names have been given by collectors.

c1925-32   *0.75in (2cm) diam*

$70-100   **AB**

An American Akro Agate Company machine-made Limeade marble.

Marble names with 'ade' suffixes contain uranium, which makes them glow under ultra-violet light.

0.75in (2cm) diam

$70-100   **AB**

An American Christensen Agate Company machine-made swirl marble.

c1928-29   *0.5in (1.5cm) diam*

$25-40   **AB**

ESSENTIAL REFERENCE

- Waterman, Parker, Montblanc and Dunhill Namiki remain the most sought-after brands, with large pens and early precious metal-covered examples being particularly valuable. Fine examples of Dunhill's 1930s maki-e lacquer models occupy the pinnacle of the market. Pens from lesser known companies that now no longer exist, such as Conklin, De La Rue and Mabie Todd are also collectible, although these generally attract lower prices.

- Collectors have traditionally been most interested in pens produced in their own countries, yet with a maturing market and increasing prices, this has recently changed. Those interested in pens are now looking further afield and, with the help of Internet trading, are adding formerly less appreciated brands to their collections. England's Conway Stewart, for example, is now proving popular on both sides of the Atlantic. More modern pens, such as the Parker 75, are also receiving greater attention.

- Modern limited editions are often produced in large numbers and are only of value if kept in pristine condition with their boxes and paperwork. Used examples are less desirable and collectors should look for early editions, such as Parker's 'Spanish Treasure' and 'Hall of Independence', or editions produced in smaller numbers, ideally under 1,000.

- Condition and completeness are paramount. As many collectors use their pens, they should be in working order. Avoid cracked or chipped examples and try to ensure that replaceable parts, such as nibs and clips, are correct.

- Fountain pens were mass-produced before the ballpoint became universal and many standard pens are worth under $40, even with original gold nibs. However, those at the lower end of the market can still make useful and interesting writing instruments.

An exceptionally rare American Parker 51 Blue Diamond 'Red Band' button-filling pen, with red housing and medium nib, in mint condition with a used gold-filled Custom cap.

The 'Red Band' 51 is extremely rare as it was only made between July 1946 and late 1947. It used a new, supposedly quick, button-filling mechanism attached to the barrel by a red collar – hence its nickname. However, this collar tended to split with use and any other problems with the pen (such as a nib replacement) required its removal, as the nib hood was fixed to the barrel.
1946-47

$1,000-1,200   BLO

An American Parker 51 Blue Diamond Vacumatic-filling pen, Buckskin body with gold-filled Custom cap, 'jewel' clip screw and barrel tassie and medium nib, in very good condition.

1945

$360-440   BLO

A mid-1940s American Parker 51 Blue Diamond Classic De Luxe Vacumatic-filling pen, burgundy body with brushed stainless steel 'wedding ring' cap and fine nib.

$120-180   BLO

A 1950s English Parker 51 Custom pen, burgundy body with rolled gold Insignia design cap and fine nib, in 'inked mint' condition, with remains of chalk marks.

In used condition, particularly with any signs of wear, this pen is usually worth around $40-60.

$200-300   BLO

An American Parker Demi-51 Custom pen, Plum Lucite body with gold-filled Custom cap and medium nib, in very good condition.

Plum is by far the rarest of the standard 51 colors and was only produced in the USA for a couple of years.
1949

$240-360   BLO

A new-old-stock 1970s American Parker 51 Custom MkIII pen and ballpoint duo set, black body with gold-filled Insignia design cap, metal clip screw and fine nib, in mint condition, with tag on the pen.

$200-300   BLO

An English Parker 61 Custom pen, black body with gold-filled Insignia design cap and medium nib, in excellent condition with remains of chalk marks on barrel.

1962-67

$120-160   **BLO**

An English Parker 61 'Heirloom' capillary action-filling pen, Vista Blue body with pink and green rolled-gold 'Rainbow' cap and medium nib, in near mint condition with chalk marks.

c1964-67

$200-300   **BLO**

An American Parker 61 'Legacy' capillary action-filling pen, gray body with nickel and silver 'Rainbow' cap and medium nib, assembled from mint new-old-stock parts, but later Classic barrel with chalk marks.

Parker's three Rainbow caps are hard to find, particularly in good condition, as they were easily scratched and worn. The Legacy is by far the rarest of the three, as it was only produced for two years.

1957-59

$140-180   **BLO**

An English Parker 61 Custom Insignia duo pen set, rolled gold barrel and cap with Insignia design, and medium nib, together with matching push-cap ballpoint, in mint condition, with swing tag on pen.

Examine these pens all over for engraved names, serious scratches or dents, as these will reduce this value.

1966-68

$140-200   **BLO**

An English Parker 61 Presidential 9ct gold 'Waterdrop' pattern ballpoint pen and propelling pencil, in Parker duo Presidential presentation box, in near mint condition, London hallmarks for 1965.

$800-1,000   **BLO**

A 1960s English Parker 61 Custom Heirloom capillary action-filling pen, dark gray body with yellow and brown rolled gold Rainbow cap, fine nib, in excellent condition.

While only being worth around $40-60 on its own, this style of Parker 61 presentation box is very rare.

$160-240   **BLO**

A rare English Parker 61 Consort cartridge/convertor-filling pen trio set, black body with rolled gold Consort pattern (horizontal and vertical line) cap, fine nib, and with matching push-cap ballpoint and rotary pencil, in Parker trio hard box, in near mint condition, box excellent.

1967-69

$360-440   **BLO**

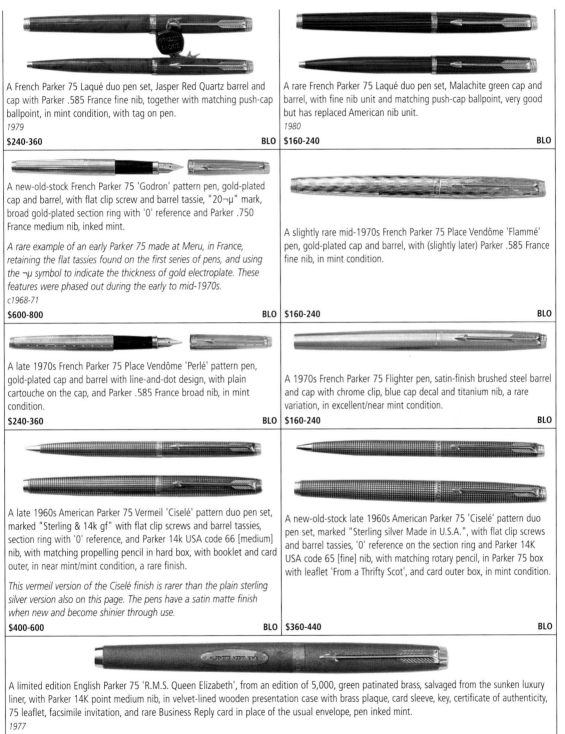

A French Parker 75 Laqué duo pen set, Jasper Red Quartz barrel and cap with Parker .585 France fine nib, together with matching push-cap ballpoint, in mint condition, with tag on pen.
1979
$240-360   **BLO**

A rare French Parker 75 Laqué duo pen set, Malachite green cap and barrel, with fine nib unit and matching push-cap ballpoint, very good but has replaced American nib unit.
1980
$160-240   **BLO**

A new-old-stock French Parker 75 'Godron' pattern pen, gold-plated cap and barrel, with flat clip screw and barrel tassie, "20¬µ" mark, broad gold-plated section ring with '0' reference and Parker .750 France medium nib, inked mint.

A rare example of an early Parker 75 made at Meru, in France, retaining the flat tassies found on the first series of pens, and using the ¬µ symbol to indicate the thickness of gold electroplate. These features were phased out during the early to mid-1970s.
c1968-71
$600-800   **BLO**

A slightly rare mid-1970s French Parker 75 Place Vendôme 'Flammé' pen, gold-plated cap and barrel, with (slightly later) Parker .585 France fine nib, in mint condition.
$160-240   **BLO**

A late 1970s French Parker 75 Place Vendôme 'Perlé' pattern pen, gold-plated cap and barrel with line-and-dot design, with plain cartouche on the cap, and Parker .585 France broad nib, in mint condition.
$240-360   **BLO**

A 1970s French Parker 75 Flighter pen, satin-finish brushed steel barrel and cap with chrome clip, blue cap decal and titanium nib, a rare variation, in excellent/near mint condition.
$160-240   **BLO**

A late 1960s American Parker 75 Vermeil 'Ciselé' pattern duo pen set, marked "Sterling & 14k gf" with flat clip screws and barrel tassies, section ring with '0' reference, and Parker 14k USA code 66 [medium] nib, with matching propelling pencil in hard box, with booklet and card outer, in near mint/mint condition, a rare finish.

This vermeil version of the Ciselé finish is rarer than the plain sterling silver version also on this page. The pens have a satin matte finish when new and become shinier through use.
$400-600   **BLO**

A new-old-stock late 1960s American Parker 75 'Ciselé' pattern duo pen set, marked "Sterling silver Made in U.S.A.", with flat clip screws and barrel tassies, '0' reference on the section ring and Parker 14K USA code 65 [fine] nib, with matching rotary pencil, in Parker 75 box with leaflet 'From a Thrifty Scot', and card outer box, in mint condition.
$360-440   **BLO**

A limited edition English Parker 75 'R.M.S. Queen Elizabeth', from an edition of 5,000, green patinated brass, salvaged from the sunken luxury liner, with Parker 14K point medium nib, in velvet-lined wooden presentation case with brass plaque, card sleeve, key, certificate of authenticity, 75 leaflet, facsimile invitation, and rare Business Reply card in place of the usual envelope, pen inked mint.
1977
$1,200-1,400   **BLO**

An American Mabie, Todd & Bard half-overlaid Swan eyedropper-filling pen, marked "Sterling" on the 'Scroll Chased' pattern overlay, with hard rubber over/underfed Swan nib, in Mabie, Todd & Bard hard presentation case, in very good/excellent condition.

An unusual variation of this attractive pattern, with 'C' scrolls rather than 'snail' whorls.
1890s-1906
$1,400-2,000   **BLO**

A rare 1920s English Mabie, Todd & Co Swan Eternal 444B/61 lever-filling pen, mottled red and black hard rubber with Swan Eternal 4 medium nib, in very good condition.

$300-400   **BLO**

A rare English Mabie, Todd & Co. Swan 9ct rose-gold 'Rosette' pattern [265/19] Self-Filler, with gold section and Swan 2 broad nib, three initials and seam split in cap, London hallmark, in leather case.

A rare example of a precious metal Self-Filler made in England; most lever-fillers were made in the USA, with metal overlay production in the UK concentrating on the top-line Leverless filling system introduced in 1934.
1933
$300-400   **BLO**

An English Mabie, Todd & Co. Blackbird Self-Filler BB2/46 lever-filling pen, 'Oriental Blue' light blue and dark blue with bronze-gold marble celluloid, with Blackbird 14ct medium nib, in excellent condition.
1934-37
$400-500   **BLO**

A Mabie, Todd & Co Swan Leverless L112/49 pen, with 'Mother O' Pearl' celluloid barrel and cap, and Swan No.1 broad nib.

This is a rare pen, however the usual darkening to the plastic and two engraved initials, reduces the value.
1937-40
$60-80   **BLO**

An English Mabie, Todd & Co Blackbird BB2/45 lever-filling pen, with greenish silver and black marbled celluloid, and Blackbird medium-oblique nib, in near mint condition.

c1937
$140-200   **BLO**

A Mabie, Todd & Co Swan Leverless L312/88 twist-filling pen, with green lizardskin celluloid with later Swan 3G medium nib, excellent, restored.

This attractive celluloid is prone to opening up along the seams, particularly on the cap, so always inspect examples carefully.
c1937
$240-360   **BLO**

An English Mabie, Todd & Co. un-numbered pearl gray snakeskin and green veined celluloid Self-Filler, with chrome trim and narrow cap band, with Swan No.1 fine nib, mint new-old stock.

c1937
$60-80   **BLO**

A Mabie, Todd & Co 'Le Merle Blanc' pen, with silver and black marbled celluloid with chrome trim, and Warranted 14ct broad nib, in mint condition.

This pen was produced for export to the French market, as indicated by the partially French barrel imprint. This is the same form as Mabie Todd's 'Big Blackbird' series, which is very hard to find, particularly in multicolored celluloid.
c1937
$300-400   **BLO**

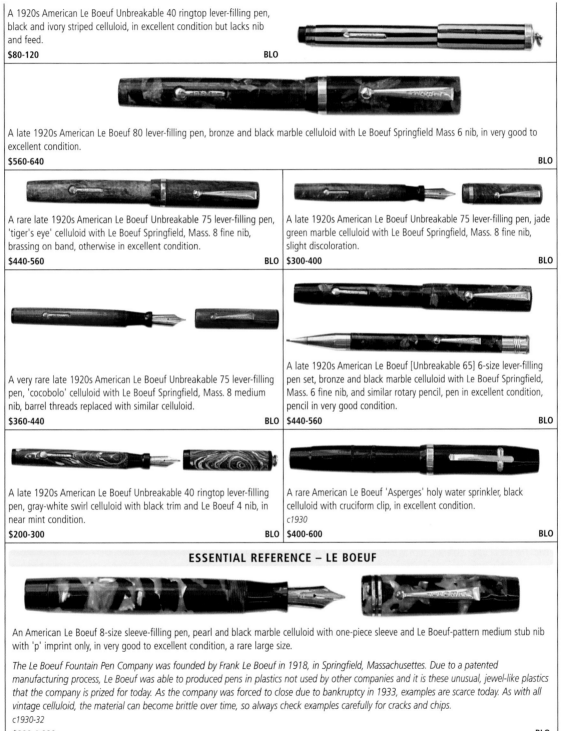

A 1920s American Le Boeuf Unbreakable 40 ringtop lever-filling pen, black and ivory striped celluloid, in excellent condition but lacks nib and feed.

$80-120   BLO

A late 1920s American Le Boeuf 80 lever-filling pen, bronze and black marble celluloid with Le Boeuf Springfield Mass 6 nib, in very good to excellent condition.

$560-640   BLO

A rare late 1920s American Le Boeuf Unbreakable 75 lever-filling pen, 'tiger's eye' celluloid with Le Boeuf Springfield, Mass. 8 fine nib, brassing on band, otherwise in excellent condition.

$440-560   BLO

A late 1920s American Le Boeuf Unbreakable 75 lever-filling pen, jade green marble celluloid with Le Boeuf Springfield, Mass. 8 fine nib, slight discoloration.

$300-400   BLO

A very rare late 1920s American Le Boeuf Unbreakable 75 lever-filling pen, 'cocobolo' celluloid with Le Boeuf Springfield, Mass. 8 medium nib, barrel threads replaced with similar celluloid.

$360-440   BLO

A late 1920s American Le Boeuf [Unbreakable 65] 6-size lever-filling pen set, bronze and black marble celluloid with Le Boeuf Springfield, Mass. 6 fine nib, and similar rotary pencil, pen in excellent condition, pencil in very good condition.

$440-560   BLO

A late 1920s American Le Boeuf Unbreakable 40 ringtop lever-filling pen, gray-white swirl celluloid with black trim and Le Boeuf 4 nib, in near mint condition.

$200-300   BLO

A rare American Le Boeuf 'Asperges' holy water sprinkler, black celluloid with cruciform clip, in excellent condition.
c1930

$400-600   BLO

ESSENTIAL REFERENCE – LE BOEUF

An American Le Boeuf 8-size sleeve-filling pen, pearl and black marble celluloid with one-piece sleeve and Le Boeuf-pattern medium stub nib with 'p' imprint only, in very good to excellent condition, a rare large size.

The Le Boeuf Fountain Pen Company was founded by Frank Le Boeuf in 1918, in Springfield, Massachusettes. Due to a patented manufacturing process, Le Boeuf was able to produced pens in plastics not used by other companies and it is these unusual, jewel-like plastics that the company is prized for today. As the company was forced to close due to bankruptcy in 1933, examples are scarce today. As with all vintage celluloid, the material can become brittle over time, so always check examples carefully for cracks and chips.
c1930-32

$800-1,000   BLO

'Holland-Amerika Lijn, S.S. Statendam', designed by Reyn Dirksen, printed by Kunstdruk Luii & Co., Amsterdam.
c1956   *37.5in (95.5cm) high*
$1,400-1,600   **VSA**

'Holland-America Line', designed by Frans Mettes.
c1955
95.5in (242.5cm) high
$1,000-1,200   **VSA**

'American President Lines, Bombay', lithographed in the US.
1960   *101.5in (258cm) high*
$250-350   **VSA**

'American President Lines Bangkok', designed by J. Clift, lithographed in the US.
1958   *86in (218.5cm) high*
$400-600   **VSA**

'American President Lines Singapore', designed by J. Clift, lithographed in the US.
1958   *86in (218.5cm) high*
$500-700   **VSA**

'Europe-Canada Linie M.S. Seven Seas', designed by Reyn Dirksen.
c1955   *96in (244cm) high*
$700-900   **VSA**

'SAL – Svenska Amerika Linien', designed by Rittmark, printed on japan paper by Isacsons, Göteborg, Sweden.
c1935   *100in (254cm) high*
$7,500-8,500   **VSA**

'Royal Interocean Lines', designed by Teyn Dirksen, printed in Holland.

c1955 92in (233.5cm) high

$1,100-1,300 **VSA**

'United States Lines', designed by Charles Shepherd, printed in England.

c1930 101.5in (258cm) high

$2,500-3,500 **VSA**

EXPERT EYE – A QUEEN MARY II POSTER

Despite having only been produced four years ago, this poster is already making healthy prices on the secondary market, partly due to the fame of the liner and the recently renewed interest in cruising.

Razzia is the pseudonym for Gerard Courbouleix, who is lauded as one of the finest living poster artists. He does not use a computer for designing, instead painting the original image traditionally.

He has produced work for a number of clients including Louis Vuitton, L'Oreal, Harrod's and Macy's, and may be a hot collecting tip for the future.

His designs are inspired by Surrealism and Cubism, but also the best poster designs from the pre-war golden age. The large ship, angular design, and colors are reminiscent of designs by Adolphe Mouron (Cassandre).

'Cherbourg, Le 14 April 2004, Queen Mary II', designed by Razzia.

2004 176in (447cm) high

$200-300 **VSA**

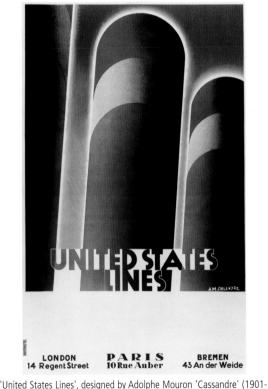

'United States Lines', designed by Adolphe Mouron 'Cassandre' (1901-68), and printed by Hachard, Paris, restoration to folds and edges.

Cassandre's designs draw the attention of collectors, as well as high prices. For more information about this notable poster designer, see the railway poster on P.342.

1928 39.5in (100.5cm) high

$15,000-20,000 **SWA**

'Fascinating South America', designed by Mark von Arenburg.

c1955 89in (226cm) high

$300-400 **VSA**

'Ireland Overnight, Dublin via Holyhead – Belfast via Heysham', by Claude Buckle, printed for BR(LMR) by Haycock Press Ltd.

50in (127cm) wide

$550-650 **ON**

'L'Europe voyagez par BOAC', by an unknown designer, printed in Great Britain, mounted on linen.

1957   *30in (76cm) high*
$100-150   **ON**

'Far Better Travel By BOAC', by Abram Games, printed in Great Britain, mounted on linen.

1952   *30in (76cm) high*
$700-900   **ON**

'Air France', designed by Edmond Maurus, printed by Goossens Publicité, France, losses and repaired tears to margins.

'Jet Your Way by B.O.A.C. Around the World', designed by Adelman.

1958   *101in (256.5cm) high*
$600-700   **VSA**

'British European Airways – The Key to Europe', by Lee-Elliott, printed by Curwen, dry mounted.

1946   *40in (102cm) high*
$120-160   **ON**

Air France is a popular airline with a global reputation, and released a large number of well-designed posters that are sought-after today. Maurus was one of their best designers, and is known for his images of planes flying over buildings or locations symbolic of the destination. Africa, shown here was, and continues to be, an important destination for the airline. The bold colors that recall the African desert, and a dizzying feel of perspective and speed also make this a desirable poster.

1947   *39.5in (100.5cm) high*
$3,000-4,000   **SWA**

'Swissair', designed by Carlo L. Vivarelli, printed by Fretz Bros. Ltd Zürich.

c1950   *102in (259cm) high*
$700-800   **VSA**

'Swissair Coca-Cola OK', printed in Switzerland.

1987   *102in (259cm) high*
$150-250   **VSA**

'American Airlines to Boston', by Edward McKnight Kauffer, lithograph in colors, in near mint condition, linen-backed.

1953	40in (102cm) high

$700-900   **BLNY**

'New York – Capital Airlines', by an unknown designer, lithograph in colors, in near mint condition, not linen-backed.

c1960	35in (89cm) high

$1,100-1,300   **BLNY**

'New Orleans – Delta Air Lines'.

c1960	71.5in (181.5cm) high

$300-500   **VSA**

'Pan American – The Philippines', designed by A. Amspoker, screen-processed in the US.

1960	89in (226cm) high

$400-600   **VSA**

'Fly TWA – New York', designed by David Klein.

c1955	63.5in (161cm) high

$700-900   **VSA**

'Western Airlines – New York', printed on linen.

c1985	93.5in (237.5cm) high

$200-300   **VSA**

EXPERT EYE – A PAN AMERICAN AIRLINE POSTER

Jean Carlu (1900-97) was a leading French poster designer during the 1920s and '30s, along with Adolphe Mouron Cassandre and Paul Colin.

He trained as an architect, turning to poster design in 1919. He was heavily influenced by Surrealism and Cubist art – inspirations that can be clearly seen in this poster.

He went to the US in 1939 and remained there until 1953, producing a series of posters for Pan Am. He also worked for Air France, Larousse and Firestone.

Posters for the now defunct Pan Am are popular for their typically stylish corporate branding. Combined with the designer and appeal of the design, this is a valuable poster.

'To Paris via Pan American', by Jean Carlu, lithographed in colors, linen-backed.

1954	42.5in (106cm) high

$2,000-3,000   **BLNY**

'Disputed Passage', US one-sheet poster, linen-backed and in very good condition.

1939   *41in (104cm) high*

$120-160   **RTC**

'Doctor Blood's Coffin', US insert poster.

1961   *36in (91.5cm) high*

$50-80   **AAC**

EXPERT EYE – A DR STRANGELOVE POSTER

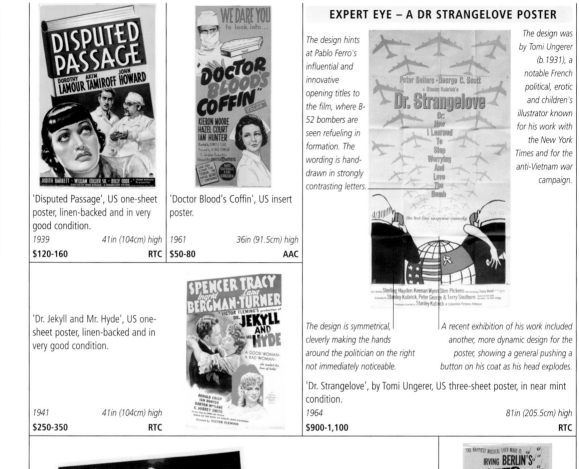

The design hints at Pablo Ferro's influential and innovative opening titles to the film, where B-52 bombers are seen refueling in formation. The wording is hand-drawn in strongly contrasting letters.

The design was by Tomi Ungerer (b.1931), a notable French political, erotic and children's illustrator known for his work with the New York Times and for the anti-Vietnam war campaign.

'Dr. Jekyll and Mr. Hyde', US one-sheet poster, linen-backed and in very good condition.

1941   *41in (104cm) high*

$250-350   **RTC**

The design is symmetrical, cleverly making the hands around the politician on the right not immediately noticeable.

A recent exhibition of his work included another, more dynamic design for the poster, showing a general pushing a button on his coat as his head explodes.

'Dr. Strangelove', by Tomi Ungerer, US three-sheet poster, in near mint condition.

1964   *81in (205.5cm) high*

$900-1,100   **RTC**

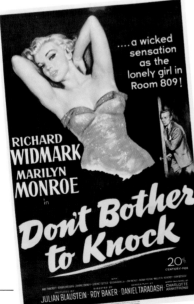

'Don't Bother to Knock', US one-sheet poster, linen-backed and in very good condition.

Ravaged dames were the favoured subject matter of paperback cover artists such as Reginald Heade and F.W. Perle. This particular dame and the positioning of the title echo the covers of these popular books.

'Easter Parade', US insert card, in near mint condition.

1952   *41in (104cm) high*

$600-800   **RTC**

1948   *36in (91.5cm) high*

$400-600   **RTC**

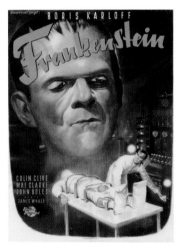

'Frankenstein', German A1 one-sheet poster, linen-backed and in near mint condition.

This is a postwar release of the enduringly popular poster showing Boris Karloff. Posters for horror and science fiction films are among the most sought-after genres, with some originals being worth vast sums. In 1993, an original 1931 Frankenstein film poster, one of only five known, sold for a then record price of $198,000. In 2007, an original Universal lobby card from 1931 fetched over $23,000.

1947   33in (84cm) high
$3,500-4,500   RTC

'How Green Was My Valley', US one-sheet poster, linen-backed and in near mint condition.

1941   41in (104cm) high
$500-700   RTC

'Ringaren I Notredame' [The Hunchback of Notre Dame], Swedish one-sheet, in near mint condition.

1939   41in (104cm) high
$3,000-4,000   RTC

'Far from The Madding Crowd', US half sheet.

1967   28in (71cm) wide
$150-200   AAC

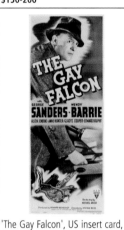

'The Gay Falcon', US insert card, in very good condition.

1941   36in (91.5cm) high
$250-350   RTC

'Heaven Can Wait', US insert card, in very good condition.

1942   36in (91.5cm) high
$250-350   RTC

'The Karate Killers', US insert poster for a Man from U.N.C.L.E. film.

1967   36in (91.5cm) high
$300-500   AAC

'Délicieuse' [Mad About Music], Belgian one-sheet poster, linen-backed and in near mint condition.

1938   33in (84cm) high
$150-200   RTC

'Ocho Sentencias de Muerte' [Kind Hearts and Coronets], Spanish one-sheet, linen-backed and in near mint condition.

1949   39in (99cm) high

$250-350   RTC

'King Solomon's Mines', US insert card, in near mint condition.

1935   36in (91.5cm) high

$800-1,000   RTC

'Kon-Tiki', US insert poster for the Norwegian film.

So far, this is the only Norwegian film to win an Oscar.

1950   36in (91.5cm) high

$40-60   AAC

'Lady in the Dark', US one-sheet poster, linen-backed and in near mint condition.

1944   41in (104cm) high

$250-350   RTC

'Laughing Sinners', US one-sheet poster, linen-backed and in near mint condition.

As well as featuring a stern looking Joan Crawford, the film also starred Clark Gable, further adding to the attraction of this early poster with its bold and striking artwork.

1931   41in (104cm) high

$1,000-1,200   RTC

'The Littlest Rebel', US one-sheet poster, linen-backed and in very good condition.

As well as the strongly patriotic design, this poster shows Shirley Temple, a highly collectable name, who is noted for her dancing in this film. However, the film has since been criticized for its overt racism.

1935   41in (104cm) high

$1,700-2,000   RTC

'Licence To Kill', US insert poster.

1989   36in (91.5cm) high

$60-80   AAC

'The Lost Weekend', US one-sheet poster, linen-backed and in near mint condition.

1945   41in (104cm) high

$800-1,000   RTC

'A Man for All Seasons',
US three-sheet poster,
linen-backed and in near
mint condition.

*This is a rare pre-Oscar
version. The film won six
Oscars including Best
Actor for Paul Schofield,
Best Director and Best
Film and was nominated
for a further two.*

1966   81in (205.5cm) high

$700-1,000   RTC

'Monster On The Campus', US
insert poster.

*Also known as 'Stranger on The
Campus', this low-budget film
was the last of Universal's science
fiction/monster films released
before 'Island of Terror' in 1966.*

1958   30in (76cm) high

$50-70   AAC

'Marie Antoinette', Belgian poster,
in near mint condition.

1938   33in (83.5cm) high

$400-600   RTC

'The Misfits', US one-sheet poster,
linen-backed and in near mint
condition.

1961   41in (104cm) high

$350-450   RTC

'My Gal Sal', US one-sheet poster,
linen-backed and in near mint
condition.

1942   41in (104cm) high

$700-800   RTC

'Night has a Thousand Eyes', US
insert card, in near mint condition.

1948   36in (91.5cm) high

$400-600   RTC

'The Night of the Hunter', US one-
sheet poster, linen-backed and in
near mint condition.

1955   41in (104cm) high

$500-700   RTC

'Personal Property', US one-sheet poster, linen-backed and in near mint
condition.

1937   41in (104cm) high

$1,000-1,200   RTC

POT LIDS

ESSENTIAL REFERENCE

- Pot lids are decorative, usually colored, ceramic lids used on pots of products such as food, hair preparations and toothpaste.
- Blue and white pot lids were produced during the 1820s and in bulk from the 1830s. The first colored lids appeared in the early 1840s and often featured bears, as bear's grease was used as a popular hair preparation for men at the time. Manufacturers were based in Staffordshire, England, and include F. & R. Pratt, who were granted a related patent in 1848, T.J. & J. Mayer and J. Ridgway.
- It is not possible to date the majority of pot lids with any accuracy as they are usually undated and were often produced for long periods of time. Examples that commemorate a specific event, such as 'The Interior of the Grand International Building 1851' (below), can be dated to

c1851, as production was unlikely to have taken place much after that date. Otherwise, registration dates, changes in design and some maker's marks can date lids to a period.
- Before 1860, lids were flat and lightweight and often had a screw thread. As the quality at this time was so high, these are usually the most desirable. Between 1860 and 1875 lids became heavier and more convex and, after 1875, became even heavier but with flat tops once again.
- Collectors have sought pot lids almost since they were first introduced, and they first appeared at auction in 1924. Today collectors look for examples in excellent condition and those with unusual variations in the main design or borders.
- The numbers given in the description are those used in K.V. Mortimer's "Pot-Lids Reference & Price Guide", the standard reference for pot lids.

A Staffordshire 'The Interior of the Grand International Building 1851' pot lid, no. 143, produced by the Mayer factory, with title and other wording around the rim.

The version without the wording around the rim can be worth twice as much.

5.25in (13cm) diam

$550-650 SAS

EXPERT EYE – A STAFFORDSHIRE POT LID

This pot lid was produced to mark the opening of the Exhibition of the Industry of All Nations that opened in New York City in 1853. It was inspired by the success of the Great Exhibition of 1851, held in London, England. The fair even had its own Crystal Palace, but this was destroyed by fire in 1858.

This is the first version issued for this pot lid. A version with a gold band around the rim is much rarer and can be worth twice as much.

Due to the subject matter, this pot lid would also be of interest to collectors of exhibition memorabilia.

A number of later re-issues were made into the 20thC, but these are of significantly less interest to collectors.

A Staffordshire 'New York Exhibition 1853' pot lid, no. 154, produced by the Mayer factory, with oak leaf border, minor hairline crack to rim.

c1853   5.25in (13cm) diam

$1,200-1,400 SAS

A Staffordshire 'L'Exhibition Universelle de 1867' pot lid, no. 152, produced by the Pratt factory.

c1867   4.75in (12.5cm) diam

$140-200 SAS

A Staffordshire 'Albert Memorial' pot lid, no. 240, probably produced by Bates, Brown-Westhead, Moore & Co., without carriage in the foreground.

4in (10cm) diam

$160-240 SAS

A Staffordshire 'The New Blackfriars Bridge' pot lid, no. 244, produced by the Pratt factory.

4.5in (11cm) diam

$45-55 SAS

A Staffordshire 'Thames Embankment' pot lid, no. 245, produced by the Pratt factory.

4.25in (10.5cm) diam

$90-110 SAS

ESSENTIAL REFERENCE – PEGWELL BAY POT LIDS

A Staffordshire 'Pegwell Bay, Established 1760' pot lid, no. 32, with sandy road and pathway.

Pegwell Bay in Kent, England, was a tourist resort from the 1760s, peaking in popularity between 1847 and 1875, and competing with its larger and more popular neighbor, Ramsgate. It was noted for the fresh shrimp teas served at the Belle Vue tavern and pots of shrimp paste sold to tourists as souvenirs. The pot lids were decorated with scenes of the village and surrounding countryside as well as shrimping and fishing scenes. Today, collectors group these seemingly disparate lids together to form a small collecting area of their own. They would also appeal to historians of the local area.

4in (10cm) diam

$90-110   SAS

A Staffordshire 'Belle Vue Tavern, Pegwell Bay' pot lid, no. 37, with flat lid, dark cliffs, no name on tavern.

3.5in (9cm) diam

$2,000-3,000   SAS

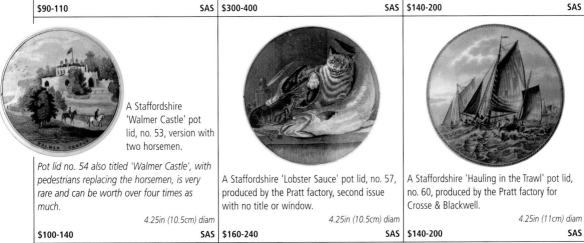

A Staffordshire 'Pegwell Bay, Ramsgate, Still Life Game' pot lid, no. 43, produced by the Mayer factory, hairline crack.

4.25in (10.5cm) diam

$90-110   SAS

A Staffordshire 'Pegwell Bay, Ramsgate (Farmyard Scene)' pot lid, no. 45, produced by the Mayer factory.

4in (10cm) diam

$300-400   SAS

A Staffordshire 'Royal Harbour, Ramsgate' pot lid, no. 50, probably produced by the Cauldon factory.

4in (10cm) diam

$140-200   SAS

A Staffordshire 'Walmer Castle' pot lid, no. 53, version with two horsemen.

Pot lid no. 54 also titled 'Walmer Castle', with pedestrians replacing the horsemen, is very rare and can be worth over four times as much.

4.25in (10.5cm) diam

$100-140   SAS

A Staffordshire 'Lobster Sauce' pot lid, no. 57, produced by the Pratt factory, second issue with no title or window.

4.25in (10.5cm) diam

$160-240   SAS

A Staffordshire 'Hauling in the Trawl' pot lid, no. 60, produced by the Pratt factory for Crosse & Blackwell.

4.25in (11cm) diam

$140-200   SAS

A Staffordshire 'Alas Poor Bruin' pot lid, no. 1, produced by the Pratt factory, with lantern on tavern sign, and double line-and-dot border.

3.5in (8.5cm) diam

$240-360   **SAS**

A very early Staffordshire 'Bear's Grease Manufacturer' advertising pot lid, no. 3, attributed to the Mayer factory, no lettering, restored.

Some versions of this rare pot lid carry advertising for Clayton & Co., Bears Grease, 58 Watling Street, London and these can be worth about 20 percent more.

3.25in (8cm) diam

$6,000-8,000   **SAS**

A Staffordshire 'Bear Hunting' pot lid, no. 4, produced by Pratt factory, with "119 & 120 Bishopsgate" wording, blue checkered border, hairline crack.

There are a number of variations of this pot lid. While the picture stays the same, the border changes. The most desirable version features the "119 & 120 Bishopsgate" address and additional gold line border.

3.5in (9cm) diam

$1,100-1,300   **SAS**

A Staffordshire 'Shooting Bears' pot lid, no. 13, produced by the Pratt factory, no lettering.

3.25in (8cm) diam

$200-300   **SAS**

A very early Staffordshire 'Bear in Ravine' advertising pot lid, no. 14, probably produced by the Ridgway factory, flange restored.

2.5in (6.5cm) diam

$3,000-4,000   **SAS**

EXPERT EYE – BEAR POT LID

This is probably the first colored pot lid produced, as it is recorded, as early as 1846.

Pot lids with bear subject matter are generally early in date.

There is another version with a moon in the sky and a more overall blue tone, which can be worth about double this version.

While black or brown bears are a much more common subject matter, polar bears also appear on 'Arctic Expedition in search of Sir John Franklin', which refers to an incident in 1848, dating it with some certainty.

A Staffordshire 'Polar Bears' pot lid, no. 18, without moon, gold border.

3.25in (8cm) diam

$650-750   **SAS**

A Staffordshire 'The Ins' pot lid, no. 15, with fancy lettering, flange restored.

'The Ins' and 'The Outs' (below) were produced as a pair. The producer is unknown but it has been suggested that it could be Pratt or possibly Ridgway. Examples of either pot lid with a fancy ribbon border will be worth slightly more.

3.5in (8.5cm) diam

$700-900   **SAS**

A Staffordshire 'The Outs' pot lid, no. 16, with fancy border, restored.

3.5in (9cm) diam

$1,400-1,600   **SAS**

A Staffordshire 'The Queen God Bless Her' pot lid, no. 269, produced by the Pratt factory, with fancy border.

5in (12.5cm) diam

$90-110   SAS

A Staffordshire 'Deerhound Guarding Cradle' or 'Fidelity' pot lid, no. 270, with marbled border.

3.25in (8cm) diam

$140-200   SAS

A Staffordshire 'Deer Drinking' pot lid, no. 277, produced by the Pratt factory, hairline crack.

A larger version with a seaweed surround can be worth about double this version.

4.25in (10.5cm) diam

$90-110   SAS

A Staffordshire 'The Shepherdess' pot lid, no. 279, produced at the Cauldon factory by Bates, Brown-Westhead Moore & Co.

4in (10cm) diam

$70-90   SAS

A Staffordshire 'The Boar Hunt' pot lid, no. 288, produced by the Mayer factory, without border.

This pot lid was reissued by Kirkhams up to 1960. The version with a decorative border can be worth half as much again.

4.25in (10.5cm) diam

$900-1,100   SAS

A Staffordshire 'The Master of the Hounds' pot lid, no. 295, produced by the Pratt factory.

Later examples have a line and dot border and a title, they are usually worth much less.

4.25in (10.5cm) diam

$200-300   SAS

A Staffordshire 'The Fair Sportswoman' pot lid, no. 297, produced at the Cauldon factory by Bates, Brown-Westhead Moore & Co.

4.25in (10.5cm) diam

$90-100   SAS

A Staffordshire 'Summer' pot lid, no. 335, produced by Bates, Elliot & Co.

Look for early examples with a registration mark on the underside, as these can be worth twice as much. 'Autumn' also exists as a pot lid and 'Spring' can be found on a plaque, however 'Winter' has yet to be seen.

4.5in (11cm) diam

$70-90   SAS

POT LIDS

A Staffordshire 'The Packman' pot lid, no. 103, probably produced by J. Ridgway & Bates, restored.

The most desirable version of this pot lid is the one with 'Bandoline Pomade' advertising around the rim. It can be worth ten times as much as this.

3.25in (8cm) diam

$100-140 SAS

A Staffordshire 'Letter from the Diggings', no. 131, produced by the Pratt factory, with fancy border.

The Australian gold rush of the early 1850s was the inspiration for this pot lid. The version with the seaweed surround can be worth about twice the value.

5in (13cm) diam

$100-140 SAS

A Staffordshire 'Queen Victoria and Prince Consort' pot lid, no. 167, probably produced by the Pratt factory, with oak leaves and acorn border.

This pot lid would also appeal to collectors of Royal memorabilia.

5in (13cm) diam

$400-600 SAS

A Staffordshire 'Windsor Castle' or 'Prince Albert (Hare Coursing)' pot lid, no. 176, produced by the Mayer factory, minor hairline crack.

4.25in (10.5cm) diam

$240-360 SAS

A Staffordshire 'Wellington with Cocked Hat' pot lid, no. 183, with lettering, restored.

5.25in (13.5cm) diam

$1,000-1,200 SAS

A Staffordshire 'Wellington with Clasped Hands' pot lid, no. 184, produced by the Mayer factory.

One of four variations of this design. The values do not differ greatly, but the version with a blue bow below the title is slightly more desirable.

4.75in (12cm) diam

$1,400-1,600 SAS

A Staffordshire 'The Blue Boy' pot lid, no. 196, produced by the Pratt factory.

Based on Thomas Gainsborough's famous painting of Master Jonathan Butall, this pot lid was produced for many years by Pratt and very early examples are scarce. Look for examples with a seaweed border and flange, and a gold border as these can be worth much more.

4.75in (12cm) diam

$120-160 SAS

A Staffordshire 'Little Red-Riding Hood' pot lid, no. 200, produced by the Pratt factory.

Unsurprisingly, this design is also found on nursery plates.

3in (7.5cm) diam

$200-300 SAS

A Staffordshire 'A Fix' pot lid, no. 302, produced by the Mayer factory, no border.

4.25in (11cm) diam

$300-400 SAS

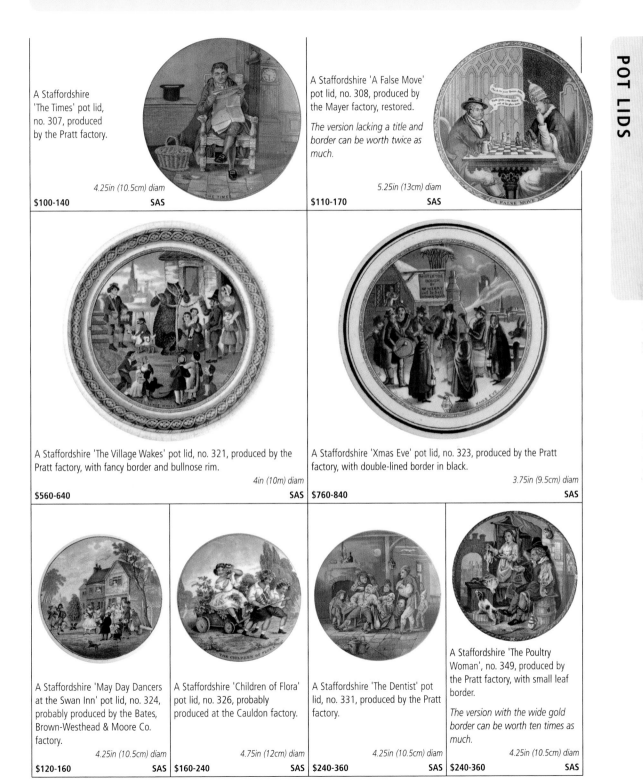

A Staffordshire 'The Times' pot lid, no. 307, produced by the Pratt factory.

4.25in (10.5cm) diam

$100-140   SAS

A Staffordshire 'A False Move' pot lid, no. 308, produced by the Mayer factory, restored.

The version lacking a title and border can be worth twice as much.

5.25in (13cm) diam

$110-170   SAS

A Staffordshire 'The Village Wakes' pot lid, no. 321, produced by the Pratt factory, with fancy border and bullnose rim.

4in (10m) diam

$560-640   SAS

A Staffordshire 'Xmas Eve' pot lid, no. 323, produced by the Pratt factory, with double-lined border in black.

3.75in (9.5cm) diam

$760-840   SAS

A Staffordshire 'May Day Dancers at the Swan Inn' pot lid, no. 324, probably produced by the Bates, Brown-Westhead & Moore Co. factory.

4.25in (10.5cm) diam

$120-160   SAS

A Staffordshire 'Children of Flora' pot lid, no. 326, probably produced at the Cauldon factory.

4.75in (12cm) diam

$160-240   SAS

A Staffordshire 'The Dentist' pot lid, no. 331, produced by the Pratt factory.

4.25in (10.5cm) diam

$240-360   SAS

A Staffordshire 'The Poultry Woman', no. 349, produced by the Pratt factory, with small leaf border.

The version with the wide gold border can be worth ten times as much.

4.25in (10.5cm) diam

$240-360   SAS

ROYAL MEMORABILIA

A Royal Doulton King George V 'A Royal Exemplar' in memoriam loving cup.

1936   *4.75in (12cm) high*

$100-150   **SAS**

A Royal Doulton George VI & Elizabeth Coronation porcelain beaker, printed with superimposed profiles in gray on a blue ground, with gilt highlights.

1937

$350-450   **SAS**

EXPERT EYE – A GEORGE V TOBY JUG

They were designed by Sir Francis Carruthers Gould (1888-1925), a famous and important political cartoonist of the time.

This is from a set of 11 toby jugs that included other military and political leaders during WWI, such as Lord Kitchener.

Produced from 1915-20, only limited numbers of each were made meaning some characters, and full sets in particular, are very rare today.

The colors are rich and strong, and the facial modeling is true to the character of the individual.

A Wilkinson Ltd 'George V' naval character jug, designed by Sir Francis Carruthers Gould, the base with printed marks.

                                          12.5in (31cm) high

$800-1,200   **FLD**

A limited edition Minton King George VI & Queen Elizabeth Coronation beaker, from a limited edition of 2,000, enameled with super-imposed profiles within a gilt starburst.

1937

$250-350   **SAS**

A John Maddock & Sons 'Royal Ivory' commemorative transfer-printed plate, commemorating the visit of George VI & Queen Elizabeth to the Dominion of Canada in 1939, and showing the coats-of-arms for the nine different dominions of Canada.

c1939   *8.75in (22cm) wide*

$35-45   **TCF**

A Grimwade's Royal Winton commemorative transfer-printed ashtray, commemorating the visit of George VI & Queen Elizabeth to Canada and the US in 1939.

c1939   *4in (10cm) wide*

$70-100   **TCF**

A Paragon London Pride Princess Elizabeth & the Duke of Edinburgh commemorative ashtray, with sepia transfer-printed image of the British Houses of Parliament, with border reading 'HRH Princess Elizabeth Canada HRH Duke of Edinburgh Oct 1951'.

This commemorates the first visit Queen Elizabeth II (then Princess Elizabeth) made to Canada with her husband, in October 1951.

c1951   4.75in (12cm) diam

$35-45   **TCF**

EXPERT EYE – A POOLE POTTERY CHARGER

The bright colors and swirling linear pattern are typical of Poole's 'Contemporary' range that was being produced at this time.

It was produced in a very limited edition of 25. Demand from both Poole Pottery collectors and royal memorabilia collectors means examples are scarce and valuable.

It is a large piece, and chargers are popular as they make a superb display.

It is fully signed on the back.

The design was produced by Alfred Read, the pottery's designer at the time, and is part of a number of designs he produced to commemorate the Coronation, all including either the Royal coat of arms, EIIR monogram or celebratory phrases.

A limited edition Poole Pottery Queen Elizabeth II Coronation charger, designed by Alfred Read and decorated by Ruth Pavely, from an edition of 25, the reverse with impressed and painted marks.

1953   15in (38cm) diam

$1,200-1,500   **WW**

A Wedgwood Queen Elizabeth II Golden Jubilee mug, with hand-painted gilt pattern, based on a design by Eric Ravilious.

2002   4in (10.5cm) high

$100-200   **WW**

A Doulton for Whiteley Prince George, Duke of York & Mary of Teck Royal Wedding commemorative pottery mug, printed in brown and decorated in colors, with gilt rim.

1893

$120-150   **SAS**

A Doulton for Mortlocks Prince George, Duke of York & Mary of Teck Royal Wedding stoneware jug, with applied molded foliate decoration, date and monogrammed oval.

John Mortlock & Co. was a distillery, which explains the grape and hop motifs in the decoration.

1893

$50-70   **SAS**

A Royal Worcester kidney-shaped plate from the Royal Household, with ER monogram surmounted by a crown printed in blue, the reverse with printed Royal coat-of-arms, ribboned inscription and dated 1905.

This plate was sold with a copy of a letter from Reverend Cannon F.A.J. Hervey, formerly the chaplain to King Edward VII at Sandringham.

c1905   8.25in (21cm) wide

$300-400   **SAS**

A 1930s Dutch earthenware commemorative charger, titled 'Prinses Juliana 30 April 1909-1934' and bearing heraldic crest, inscribed verso "Juliana bord no. 270 Schoonhoven Holland".

12.25in (31cm) diam

$150-250   **BIG**

SCIENTIFIC INSTRUMENTS

ESSENTIAL REFERENCE

- Although they have been produced for centuries, it is instruments from the 19thC, and possibly from the late 18thC, that are most likely to be found today. Many are made from lacquered brass, although other materials were also used, including mahogany, and occasionally precious metals. Collectors tend to focus on one category, such as navigational or optical instruments, or one type such as microscopes.
- The period and maker are two of the most important factors

that count towards value. Although a piece may look similar, the presence of a notable maker's name such as Cuff, Powell & Lealand or Dollond indicates quality and accounts for the value. Similarly, complex, finely made examples will be worth more. The presence of a complete set of original accessories, including a box, will add value. Values have fallen somewhat as the area has become largely unfashionable, so now may be a good time to buy.

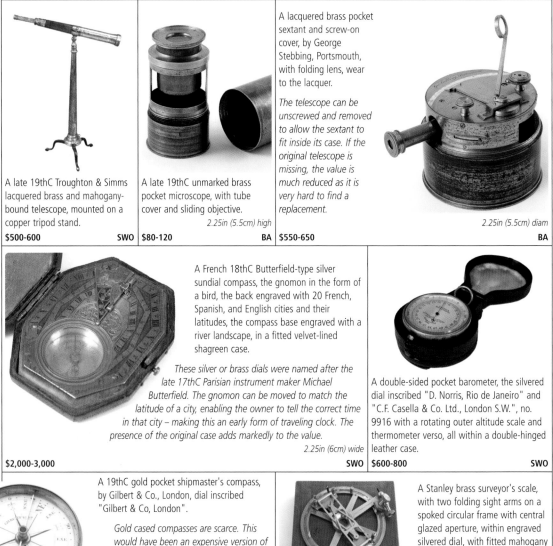

A late 19thC Troughton & Simms lacquered brass and mahogany-bound telescope, mounted on a copper tripod stand.

$500-600   **SWO**

A late 19thC unmarked brass pocket microscope, with tube cover and sliding objective.

2.25in (5.5cm) high

$80-120   **BA**

A lacquered brass pocket sextant and screw-on cover, by George Stebbing, Portsmouth, with folding lens, wear to the lacquer.

The telescope can be unscrewed and removed to allow the sextant to fit inside its case. If the original telescope is missing, the value is much reduced as it is very hard to find a replacement.

2.25in (5.5cm) diam

$550-650   **BA**

A French 18thC Butterfield-type silver sundial compass, the gnomon in the form of a bird, the back engraved with 20 French, Spanish, and English cities and their latitudes, the compass base engraved with a river landscape, in a fitted velvet-lined shagreen case.

These silver or brass dials were named after the late 17thC Parisian instrument maker Michael Butterfield. The gnomon can be moved to match the latitude of a city, enabling the owner to tell the correct time in that city – making this an early form of traveling clock. The presence of the original case adds markedly to the value.

2.25in (6cm) wide

$2,000-3,000   **SWO**

A double-sided pocket barometer, the silvered dial inscribed "D. Norris, Rio de Janeiro" and "C.F. Casella & Co. Ltd., London S.W.", no. 9916 with a rotating outer altitude scale and thermometer verso, all within a double-hinged leather case.

$600-800   **SWO**

A 19thC gold pocket shipmaster's compass, by Gilbert & Co., London, dial inscribed "Gilbert & Co, London".

Gold cased compasses are scarce. This would have been an expensive version of the instrument in its day.

2in (5cm) diam

$1,200-1,500   **L&T**

A Stanley brass surveyor's scale, with two folding sight arms on a spoked circular frame with central glazed aperture, within engraved silvered dial, with fitted mahogany case.

7in (18cm) wide

$300-400   **ROS**

ESSENTIAL REFERENCE

- Balls, bats, uniforms and cards have traditionally been very popular items with collectors. Paper ephemera, publications and advertisements can be more affordable. Many of these show interesting period details, such as uniforms and equipment and those featuring famous players or notable teams tend to be of more interest to collectors and fetch higher sums. Yearbooks, kit catalogs and souvenir books are all popular items, examples from the first few decades of the 20thC are particularly sought-after. Condition is very important, examples should be clean, bright and undamaged, whilst programs should not be annotated with scores or other information.

- Signed baseballs should be official American or National League balls and also bear the name of either the League President, if dating from before 1999, or the Commissioner,

if after 1999. Consult specialist sources for a full list of Presidents and Commissioners. Uniforms are particularly desirable if signed, or if they have been worn by a well-known player during a game. Game-used bats are similarly highly sought after, with examples signed by famous individuals, or by members of a successful team, being of special interest to collectors. It is important to buy from reputable sources to ensure the authenticity of these items.

- Gloves are a highly collectible area. Value is generally dependent on the name of the player featured on the glove, the maker and its age and condition. Pre-war gloves can be recognized by their shape, and often, in the case of fielder's gloves, by their laced fingers. Gloves were often sold in boxes, and an original box in good condition can add to the value of a glove significantly.

A Topps Henry Aaron rookie baseball card, no. 128.

Aaron (b.1934) held the record for most career home runs, until Barry Bonds overtook him in 2007. He took the record from Babe Ruth in 1974. There were death threats and also hatemail from those who did not wish to see an African American take Ruth's record. This card is considered one of the most important post-WWII baseballs cards.

1954   3.75in (9.5cm) high

$800-1,200   **AEM**

A Topps Yogi Berra baseball card, no. 110, with facsimile signature.

1956   3.75in (9.5cm) wide

$60-80   **AEM**

A Mordecai Brown 'T206' cigarette card, with Brown wearing a 'Chicago' shirt.

This is from the famous T206 set of cards, which includes the world record holding Honus Wagner card; it sold on eBay in 2000 for $1.27 million. Brown appeared in three different cards, one with a 'Cubs' shirt and a portrait shot.

1909-11   2.5in (6.8cm) high

$200-250   **AEM**

A Ty Cobb 'T206' cigarette card, with red background.

1909-11   2.5in (6.8cm) high

$400-600   **AEM**

A Play Ball 'Joe DiMaggio' signed baseball card, no. 71, graded with PSA/DNA rating of 'Mint 9'.

$1,300-1,700   **MAS**

SPORTING MEMORABILIA

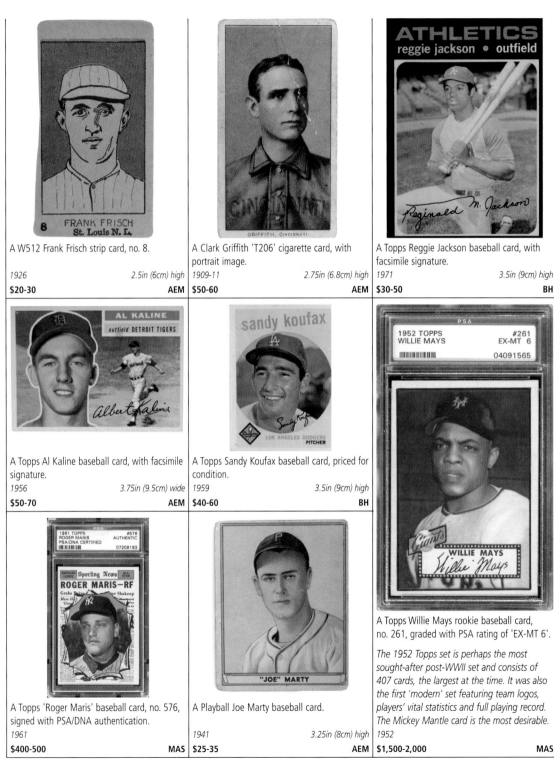

A W512 Frank Frisch strip card, no. 8.

1926   2.5in (6cm) high
$20-30   **AEM**

A Clark Griffith 'T206' cigarette card, with portrait image.

1909-11   2.75in (6.8cm) high
$50-60   **AEM**

A Topps Reggie Jackson baseball card, with facsimile signature.

1971   3.5in (9cm) high
$30-50   **BH**

A Topps Al Kaline baseball card, with facsimile signature.

1956   3.75in (9.5cm) wide
$50-70   **AEM**

A Topps Sandy Koufax baseball card, priced for condition.

1959   3.5in (9cm) high
$40-60   **BH**

A Topps 'Roger Maris' baseball card, no. 576, signed with PSA/DNA authentication.

1961
$400-500   **MAS**

A Playball Joe Marty baseball card.

1941   3.25in (8cm) high
$25-35   **AEM**

A Topps Willie Mays rookie baseball card, no. 261, graded with PSA rating of 'EX-MT 6'.

The 1952 Topps set is perhaps the most sought-after post-WWII set and consists of 407 cards, the largest at the time. It was also the first 'modern' set featuring team logos, players' vital statistics and full playing record. The Mickey Mantle card is the most desirable.

1952
$1,500-2,000   **MAS**

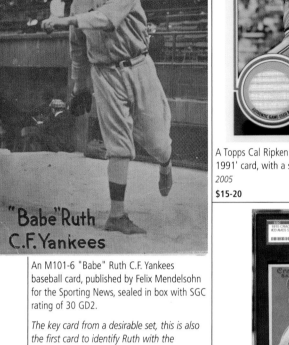

A Topps Cal Ripken 'Most Valuable Player in 1991' card, with a slice of Ripken's bat.

2005   *3.5in (9cm) high*

$15-20   **BH**

A Topps Frank Robinson baseball card, priced for condition.

1959   *3.5in (9cm) high*

$20-30   **BH**

An M101-6 "Babe" Ruth C.F. Yankees baseball card, published by Felix Mendelsohn for the Sporting News, sealed in box with SGC rating of 30 GD2.

The key card from a desirable set, this is also the first card to identify Ruth with the Yankees. The card was initially produced with Ruth playing for the Red Sox but he was sold just prior to the end of the card's production and the title was changed accordingly. However, the same photograph, with Ruth in a Red Sox uniform, is used on both versions.

1920

$2,800-3,200   **MAS**

A Cracker Jack Amos Strunk baseball card, no. 33, sealed in box with SGC grading of '88 NM/MT 8'.

1915

$600-700   **MAS**

A W513 Paul Waner strip card, no.70.

1928   *2.25in (5.5cm) high*

$30-40   **AEM**

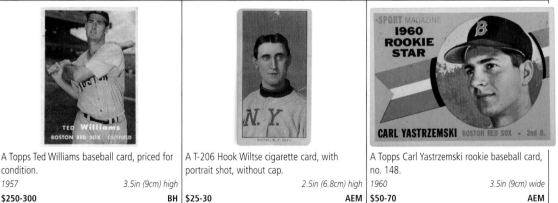

A Topps Ted Williams baseball card, priced for condition.

1957   *3.5in (9cm) high*

$250-300   **BH**

A T-206 Hook Wiltse cigarette card, with portrait shot, without cap.

2.5in (6.8cm) high

$25-30   **AEM**

A Topps Carl Yastrzemski rookie baseball card, no. 148.

1960   *3.5in (9cm) wide*

$50-70   **AEM**

A Ty Cobb Auto Racing news photograph.
1911
$220-280   MAS

A Mickey Mantle, Ted Williams and Joe DiMaggio signed photograph.
$850-950   MAS

A Walter Johnson News Service photograph.
1925
$750-850   MAS

A Connie Mack signed photograph.
$500-600   MAS

A Babe Ruth News Service photograph.

1922
$280-320   MAS

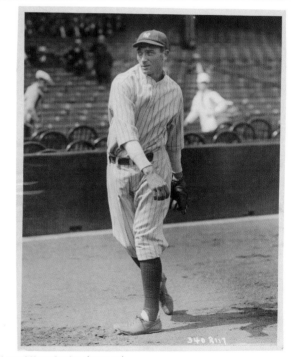

A Tony Lazzeri News Service photograph.
1927
$850-950   MAS

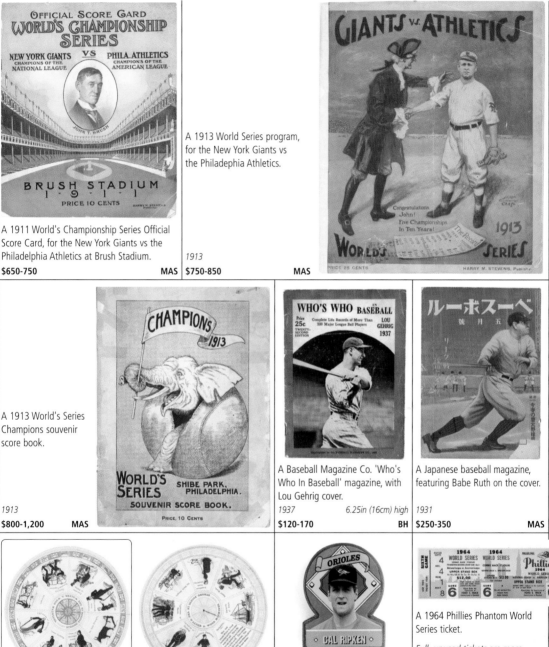

A 1911 World's Championship Series Official Score Card, for the New York Giants vs the Philadelphia Athletics at Brush Stadium.

$650-750   MAS

A 1913 World Series program, for the New York Giants vs the Philadelphia Athletics.

1913

$750-850   MAS

A 1913 World's Series Champions souvenir score book.

1913

$800-1,200   MAS

A Baseball Magazine Co. 'Who's Who In Baseball' magazine, with Lou Gehrig cover.

1937   6.25in (16cm) high

$120-170   BH

A Japanese baseball magazine, featuring Babe Ruth on the cover.

1931

$250-350   MAS

An agriculture-themed advertising piece, featuring Hall of Famer John Clarkson.

1881

$180-220   MAS

A very rare box of Topps test-issue Cal Ripken sweets, with Baltimore Orioles banner, unopened and complete with contents.

1991   2.75in (6.5cm) high

$30-40   BH

A 1964 Phillies Phantom World Series ticket.

Full, unused tickets are more desirable than ticket stubs. Stubs will generally not command high prices unless they are from very significant games.

1964   7.5in (19cm) long

$40-50   BH

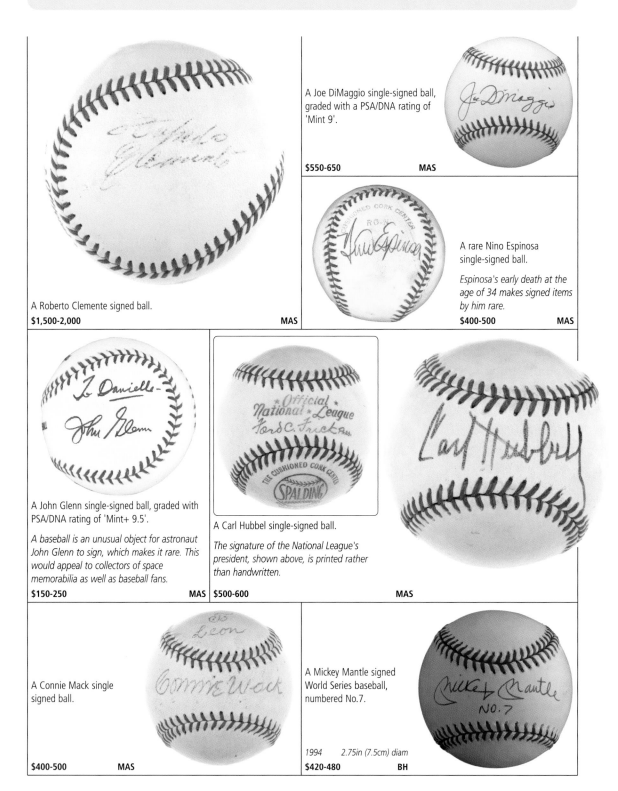

A Joe DiMaggio single-signed ball, graded with a PSA/DNA rating of 'Mint 9'.

$550-650   MAS

A rare Nino Espinosa single-signed ball.

Espinosa's early death at the age of 34 makes signed items by him rare.

$400-500   MAS

A Roberto Clemente signed ball.

$1,500-2,000   MAS

A John Glenn single-signed ball, graded with PSA/DNA rating of 'Mint+ 9.5'.

A baseball is an unusual object for astronaut John Glenn to sign, which makes it rare. This would appeal to collectors of space memorabilia as well as baseball fans.

$150-250   MAS

A Carl Hubbel single-signed ball.

The signature of the National League's president, shown above, is printed rather than handwritten.

$500-600   MAS

A Connie Mack single signed ball.

$400-500   MAS

A Mickey Mantle signed World Series baseball, numbered No.7.

1994   2.75in (7.5cm) diam

$420-480   BH

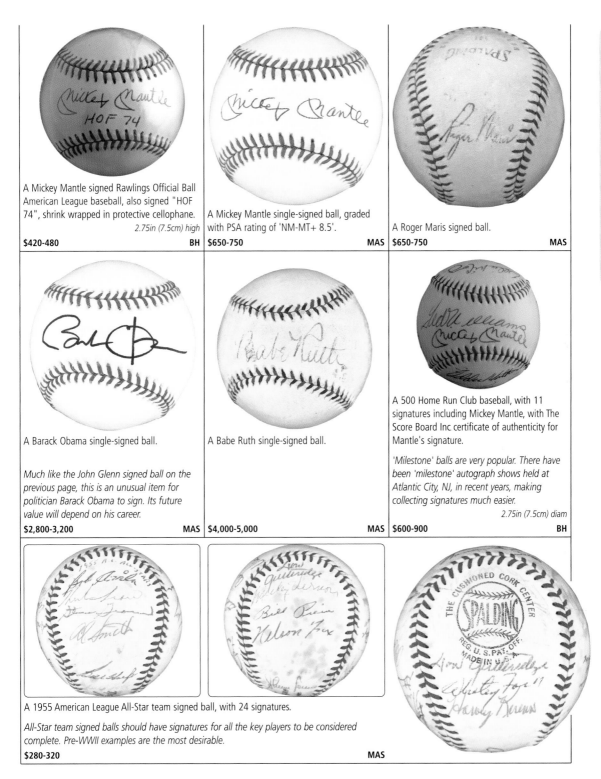

A Mickey Mantle signed Rawlings Official Ball American League baseball, also signed "HOF 74", shrink wrapped in protective cellophane.

2.75in (7.5cm) high

$420-480   **BH**

A Mickey Mantle single-signed ball, graded with PSA rating of 'NM-MT+ 8.5'.

$650-750   **MAS**

A Roger Maris signed ball.

$650-750   **MAS**

A Barack Obama single-signed ball.

Much like the John Glenn signed ball on the previous page, this is an unusual item for politician Barack Obama to sign. Its future value will depend on his career.

$2,800-3,200   **MAS**

A Babe Ruth single-signed ball.

$4,000-5,000   **MAS**

A 500 Home Run Club baseball, with 11 signatures including Mickey Mantle, with The Score Board Inc certificate of authenticity for Mantle's signature.

'Milestone' balls are very popular. There have been 'milestone' autograph shows held at Atlantic City, NJ, in recent years, making collecting signatures much easier.

2.75in (7.5cm) diam

$600-900   **BH**

A 1955 American League All-Star team signed ball, with 24 signatures.

All-Star team signed balls should have signatures for all the key players to be considered complete. Pre-WWII examples are the most desirable.

$280-320   **MAS**

A David Ortiz Boston Red Sox game-worn home jersey.

Given the potentially high value of jerseys, particularly game-worn examples, fakes are on the market, so ensure you buy from a reputable dealer and ask for provenance. In recent years, teams have begun to sell their game-worn jerseys in bulk directly to dealers which provides a guarantee of authenticity.

2007

$1,500-2,000   MAS

A New York Mets World Champions team replica road jersey, with 25 signatures, including Nolan Ryan and Tom Seaver.

1969

$800-1,000   MAS

A pair of Dave Winfield Minnesota Twins signed game-worn road pants.

1993

$400-500   MAS

A 1980s pair of Ryne Sandberg game used cleats, signed.

$550-650   MAS

A New Era Chicago Cubs blue baseball cap, game used and signed by Sammy Sosa, with foil label, together with certificate of authenticity and photograph of him signing it.

2002   *7.75in (19.5cm) wide*

$600-800   BH

A limited edition 1949 Hall of Fame Induction commemorative Louisville Slugger bat, from an edition of 500, with facsimile signatures for inductees Mordecai Brown, Kid Nichols and Charlie Gehringer.

1949   *33.5in (85cm) long*

$100-150   BH

A Rawlings 2131 baseball glove, signed by Cal Ripken Jr, with certificate of authenticity from The Score Board Inc.

10.75in (27cm) high

$400-500   BH

A Kelly Heath 1984 Columbus Clippers International League Champions League player's ring.

1984

$1,700-2,000   MAS

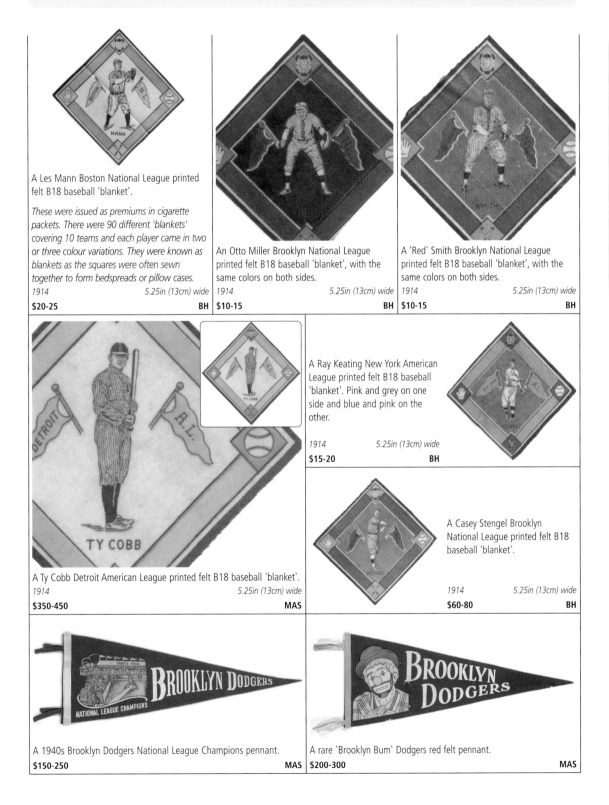

A Les Mann Boston National League printed felt B18 baseball 'blanket'.

These were issued as premiums in cigarette packets. There were 90 different 'blankets' covering 10 teams and each player came in two or three colour variations. They were known as blankets as the squares were often sewn together to form bedspreads or pillow cases.

1914   *5.25in (13cm) wide*
$20-25   **BH**

An Otto Miller Brooklyn National League printed felt B18 baseball 'blanket', with the same colors on both sides.

1914   *5.25in (13cm) wide*
$10-15   **BH**

A 'Red' Smith Brooklyn National League printed felt B18 baseball 'blanket', with the same colors on both sides.

1914   *5.25in (13cm) wide*
$10-15   **BH**

A Ray Keating New York American League printed felt B18 baseball 'blanket'. Pink and grey on one side and blue and pink on the other.

1914   *5.25in (13cm) wide*
$15-20   **BH**

A Ty Cobb Detroit American League printed felt B18 baseball 'blanket'.
1914   *5.25in (13cm) wide*
$350-450   **MAS**

A Casey Stengel Brooklyn National League printed felt B18 baseball 'blanket'.

1914   *5.25in (13cm) wide*
$60-80   **BH**

A 1940s Brooklyn Dodgers National League Champions pennant.
$150-250   **MAS**

A rare 'Brooklyn Bum' Dodgers red felt pennant.
$200-300   **MAS**

A Babe Ruth celluloid scorer, in near mint condition.

1935

$220-280 MAS

A Roberto Clemente commemorative coin, marked '1934-1972' and '30003'.

1972 *2in (5cm) diam*

$20-25 BH

A Babe Ruth Champion commemorative coin.

1.5in (3.5cm) diam

$15-20 BH

A 1950s Mickey Mantle souvenir ring, with inset photographic image.

$150-200 MAS

A 1930s Babe Ruth hand-painted doll, with original wooden bat.

$600-700 MAS

A limited edition Gartlan USA Michael Jack Schmidt cold cast figurine, commemorating his 500th home run hit on April 18 1987, from an edition of 1,987, signed by Mike Schmidt on the plinth, with removable wooden bat, with certificate of authenticity.

Gartlan also released 20 artist's proofs, which are also signed by the artist. These are worth about twice the value of this limited edition.

1988 *7.75in (19.5cm) high*

$180-220 BH

A Starting Lineup Kirby Puckett action figure, by Kenner, mint and carded.

Kenner began making these figures in 1988. In 2001 Hasbro, which now owns Kenner, announced the discontinuation of the line.

1988 *Card 9in (23cm) high*

$25-35 BH

A Starting Lineup Ozzie Smith action figure, by Kenner, mint and carded.

1988 *Card 9in (23cm) high*

$35-45 BH

ESSENTIAL REFERENCE

- Very early pieces of golf memorabilia from the early to mid-19thC are rare and can be extremely valuable. Examples from the late 19thC and early 20thC are more readily available and generally more affordable. Golf clubs and balls form the basis of many collections and these items are consistently highly sought-after. Early, rare or high-quality examples made by renowned manufacturers tend to occupy the upper echelons of the market. As most equipment was used in play, items in good condition will generally fetch the largest sums.

- The on-going popularity of the sport across the world has ensured that a huge amount of golfing-themed items are available to collectors, including metalware, glass, artwork and books, some of which are easily affordable. Ceramics celebrating the game were also produced by a number of factories, including Doulton, Shelley and Spode, these are of interest to collectors of both sporting and ceramic items. Ephemera related to games and tournaments, such as programmes and tickets, are also popular and often more affordable. Those related to important games or players, and in good condition, will tend to attract the most interest.

- Although golf is one of the oldest sports still played today, it was not until the early 20thC that women began to participate. Memorabilia associated with female players is therefore rare and can command a premium, particularly as interest in the women's game is still increasing. Specialist auctions are quite common, with a number taking place in July, around the time of the Open Championship.

A 'Gyro' bramble pattern gutty ball, retaining much of its original paint, several hack marks.

$400-600   L&T

A Haskell bramble gutty ball, retaining much of the original finish, some light hack marks.

$500-700   L&T

A Goodrich 'Haskell Bramble 10' bramble pattern gutty ball.

$550-650   L&T

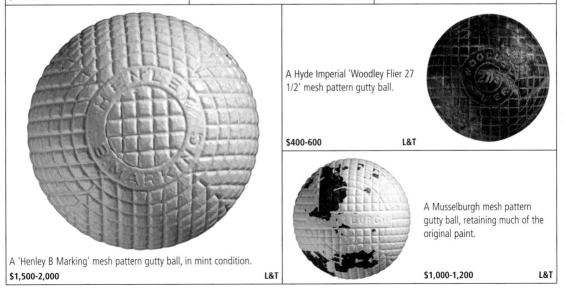

A 'Henley B Marking' mesh pattern gutty ball, in mint condition.

$1,500-2,000   L&T

A Hyde Imperial 'Woodley Flier 27 1/2' mesh pattern gutty ball.

$400-600   L&T

A Musselburgh mesh pattern gutty ball, retaining much of the original paint.

$1,000-1,200   L&T

A Silvertown mesh pattern gutty ball, with large letters, retaining most of its original paint.

$500-700   **L&T**

A Wilsden's Rocket mesh pattern gutty ball, retaining much of the original paint.

$500-700   **L&T**

EXPERT EYE – A HAND-HAMMERED GUTTY BALL

Gutta percha balls were introduced in 1848. Gutta percha is a hard latex-like natural plastic made from the resin of a tree.

Balls were hand-hammered until molds were introduced in the 1860s.

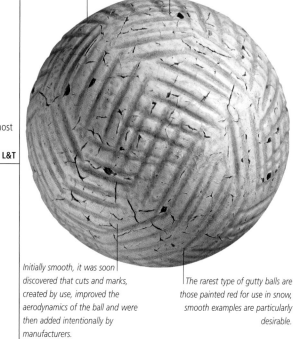

Initially smooth, it was soon discovered that cuts and marks, created by use, improved the aerodynamics of the ball and were then added intentionally by manufacturers.

The rarest type of gutty balls are those painted red for use in snow, smooth examples are particularly desirable.

A hand-hammered gutty ball, in virtual mint condition, with only slight paint loss.

$2,800-3,600   **L&T**

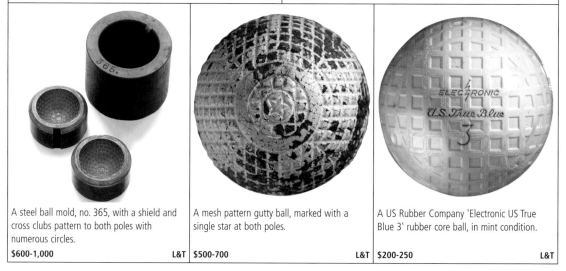

A steel ball mold, no. 365, with a shield and cross clubs pattern to both poles with numerous circles.

$600-1,000   **L&T**

A mesh pattern gutty ball, marked with a single star at both poles.

$500-700   **L&T**

A US Rubber Company 'Electronic US True Blue 3' rubber core ball, in mint condition.

$200-250   **L&T**

A MacSmith aluminum-headed putter, the hickory shaft with channeled huntly grip, hosel cracked.

$400-600   L&T

A Robert Black Wilson 'OK Special A1' putter, lacks hosel, with hickory shaft.

$1,100-1,300   L&T

A longnose putter, with horn insert to sole, lead counterweight, hickory shaft, the scared beech head stamped "H. Philip".

$1,500-1,700   L&T

A Grosse Ile Putter Co. patent brass-headed putter, with alignment flange, hickory shaft.

$1,600-1,800   L&T

A Jack Randall of Sundridge Park patent mallet head putter, the face of the aluminum head fitted with 13 plugs of lead weight, the sole stamped with patent no. 186522, with unusual oval section hosel, hickory shaft and leather-covered grip.

$150-250   GBA

A 'Bennie no. 2 Putter', the aluminum head with unusual circular projection for striking the ball, hickory shaft.

$1,100-1,300   L&T

A Carston Mfg. Corp. Ping Anser putter, steel shaft, the head stamped "Phoenix Ariz." and numbered "85029".

$500-700   L&T

An Otto G.A. Hackbarth aluminum-headed putter, with forked hosel, hickory shaft.

$800-1,200   L&T

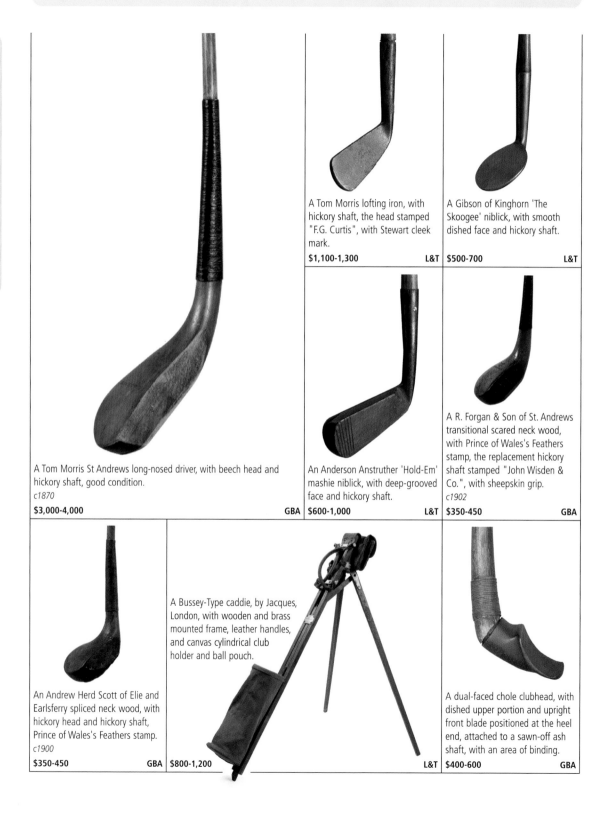

A Tom Morris lofting iron, with hickory shaft, the head stamped "F.G. Curtis", with Stewart cleek mark.

$1,100-1,300   **L&T**

A Gibson of Kinghorn 'The Skoogee' niblick, with smooth dished face and hickory shaft.

$500-700   **L&T**

A Tom Morris St Andrews long-nosed driver, with beech head and hickory shaft, good condition.
c1870

$3,000-4,000   **GBA**

An Anderson Anstruther 'Hold-Em' mashie niblick, with deep-grooved face and hickory shaft.

$600-1,000   **L&T**

A R. Forgan & Son of St. Andrews transitional scared neck wood, with Prince of Wales's Feathers stamp, the replacement hickory shaft stamped "John Wisden & Co.", with sheepskin grip.
c1902

$350-450   **GBA**

An Andrew Herd Scott of Elie and Earlsferry spliced neck wood, with hickory head and hickory shaft, Prince of Wales's Feathers stamp.
c1900

$350-450   **GBA**

A Bussey-Type caddie, by Jacques, London, with wooden and brass mounted frame, leather handles, and canvas cylindrical club holder and ball pouch.

$800-1,200   **L&T**

A dual-faced chole clubhead, with dished upper portion and upright front blade positioned at the heel end, attached to a sawn-off ash shaft, with an area of binding.

$400-600   **GBA**

A National Open Championship gilt metal and enamel contestant's badge, by the Whitehead & Hoag Company, Newark, NJ, dated "June 23 to 25, 1932", centrally with the initials of the "USGA", lacking pin to the reverse.

1.25in (3cm) wide
$800-1,200   **L&T**

A Club Professional Championship Contestant money clip, from The Professional Golfers Association of America.

1968
$400-600   **L&T**

A 33rd National Open Golf Championship Marshal's medal, made by The Whitehead & Hoag Company, Newark, NJ, the yellow ribbon inscribed 'Winged-Foot Golf Club, June 27-28-29, 1929', the medal of ball pattern with superimposed club crest, the pin inscribed 'Marshal' within a chased-gilt metal border.

3.5in (9cm) high
$1,700-2,000   **L&T**

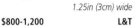

A Professional Golfer's Association of America member white metal badge.

1916
$350-450   **MAS**

A Blackheath Royal Golf Club 'The Calcutta Cup' white metal medal, the obverse relief decorated with a trophy and inscribed 'The Calcutta Cup', the reverse with the crest and motto of the Blackheath Royal Golf Club, with blue suspension silk ribbon and white metal clasp, in a Baddeley Bros. case.

c1900
$1,400-1,600   **L&T**

A silver golfing medal, of Maltese Cross form, Birmingham, centrally engraved with a golfer at the top of his swing, ring suspension, cased, the lid inscribed "Ruthwell Golf Club 1895".

1894   *1.25in (3cm) wide*
$700-900   **L&T**

An English Searle & Co. silver golfing trophy, the front engraved 'Presented to the Ottawa Golf Club by Cleveson-Gower 1910', the sides engraved with winners' names and years, with maker's marks and London hallmarks for 1907.

1907   *9.25in (23.5cm) high*
$2,000-3,000   **TCF**

A Ladies' Amateur Championship silver-plated golfing trophy, from Manitou Beach, Saskatoon, mounted on a wooden base with applied plaques.

15.5in (39cm) high
$900-1,300   **TCF**

FIND OUT MORE...

'Golf Memorabilia', by Sarah Fabian-Baddiel, published by Miller's, 1994.

ESSENTIAL REFERENCE

- The popularity of soccer has ensured that memorabilia connected with the sport has long been in great demand. Items connected to famous teams, popular players or important matches, tend to gain the most interest and the highest values.
- Past stars, including Pelé, George Best, Bobby Charlton and Bobby Moore, remain popular today and items associated with these men are in high demand. Nevertheless, the enormous popularity of today's soccer stars and teams ensures that memorabilia associated with them can also attract equally significant sums. Shirts, boots and other equipment used or worn by well-known players are highly sought-after and some can demand very large sums, particularly if worn during an important match or signed by the player and their team mates.
- Programs are another popular area of collecting. There is a large variety available, and values vary widely.

- Modern programs are printed in large numbers, and many fans store them in good condition, meaning that these can be an affordable entry into collecting. Programs from FA and European Cup finals, international and early, pre-WWI games generally fetch larger sums. Nevertheless, the enormous significance of some matches ensured that programs were kept in large enough numbers to keep values relatively modest. A large amount of programs from the 1966 World Cup final, for example, were kept as souvenirs. Programs should be in clean condition. Annotated examples will fetch lower sums than those in mint condition.
- Caps are also popular. Those that date from before WWII were traditionally made from a velvet-like material and have the date of the match on the narrow peak, and often the location, tour or organisation. Those from after the war have both teams' names and the date embroidered onto them.

David Beckham's match-worn L.A. Galaxy no. 23 long-sleeved jersey, with MLS flash, the reverse lettered 'Beckham', unwashed.

This jersey was released from within the club as match-worn. The particular match was not stipulated but the August 2007 release date, points towards the Superliga match against DC United .

2007

$3,500-4,500   **GBA**

Wayne Rooney's match-worn Manchester United no. 8 short-sleeved jersey, for the 2005-06 season, with F.A. Premier League flashes, the reverse lettered 'Rooney'.

This jersey was worn by Rooney in the Premier League match at Tottenham Hotspur in season 2005-06. The jersey was gained in a swap by a Spurs player.
2005-06

$600-800   **GBA**

Alan Shearer's match-worn Newcastle United short-sleeved jersey and captain's armband, from the F.A. Cup semi-final against Tottenham Hotspur played at Old Trafford 11th April 1999, the reverse lettered 'Shearer'; together with a signed handwritten note of authenticity from Shearer.

Newcastle United won this game 2-0 with Alan Shearer scoring both goals during extra-time.

$2,500-3,500   **GBA**

Patrick Vieira's match-worn France no. 4 short-sleeved jersey, worn in the international match against England at the Stade de France on 2nd September 2000, inscribed 'France, Angleterre, 02-09-2000', the reverse lettered 'Vieira', together with a note of authenticity.

$1,100-1,300   **GBA**

An F.A. Cup final program for Aston Villa v Newcastle United, played on 26th April 1924, with original color pictorial covers preserved, areas of professional restoration.

This is considered one of the rarest Wembley Cup final programs, for two reasons. Firstly, it rained on the day of the match, ruining many examples, which had thin paper covers. The Football Association had also doubled the price of the program that year making it too expensive for many fans during the economically depressed 1920s.
1924

$1,400-1,600 GBA

An F.A. Cup final program for Aston Villa v Huddersfield Town, played at Stamford Bridge Chelsea on 24th April 1920.
1920

$4,000-5,000 GBA

An F.A. Cup final program Bolton Wanderers v Manchester City, played on 24th April 1926.
1926

$2,500-3,500 GBA

An F.A. Cup final program for Arsenal v Cardiff City, played on 23rd April 1927.

$4,000-6,000 GBA

An F.A. Cup final program Blackburn Rovers v Huddersfield Town, played on 21st April 1928.

$1,500-2,000 GBA

An F.A. Cup final program for Bolton Wanderers v Portsmouth 27th April 1929.

1929

$2,000-3,000 GBA

An F.A. Cup final program for Birmingham v West Bromwich Albion, played on 25th April 1931.
1931

$1,400-1,800 GBA

A Charlton Athletic official home program, vol. III, from the 1934-35 season.

$250-350 GBA

An England v Spain international match program, played at Highbury on 9th December 1931.
1931
$800-1,000   GBA

An England v Wales international program, played at Ayresome Park on 17th November 1937.
1937
$600-800   GBA

An England v Ireland international program, played at Bloomfield Road, Blackpool on 17th October 1932.

1932
$2,500-3,500   GBA

A Germany v England international program, played at the Olympic Stadium, Berlin on 14th May 1938.

$1,000-1,2000   GBA

An England v Norway international program, played at St James' Park on 9th November 1938.
1938
$1,400-1,800   GBA

An England v Ireland international program, played at Old Trafford on 16th November 1938, tied with a green ribbon.
1938
$600-800   GBA

A very rare England v Wales wartime international program, played at the City Ground, Nottingham 26th April 1941.
1941
$1,400-1,600   GBA

A Belgium v England international program, played at the Heysel Stadium, Brussels on 21st September 1947.
1947
$700-900   GBA

A Football Association steward's badge for the F.A. Cup final between Bury and Derby County, at Crystal Palace 18th April 1903.

1903

$1,100-1,300   GBA

A Football Association steward's enameled badge for the 1929 F.A. Cup final at Wembley Stadium.

1929

$400-600   GBA

A Football Association steward's enameled badge for the 1932 F.A. Cup final at Wembley Stadium.

1932

$400-600   GBA

A Football League 9ct gold medal for the 1935-36 season, inscribed 'The Football League, Champions, Division 3, Northern Section, Chesterfield F.C., Season 1935-36, M.Dando'.

This medal was awarded to the Spireites' Maurice 'Mick' Dando (1905-49) who scored 29 goals in just 27 games. Dando played for Bath City and Bristol Rovers before moving north in the summer of 1933 to join York City where he scored 46 goals in two seasons. He joined Chesterfield in June 1935 and finished his career at Crewe. Dando suffered from ill-health and died prematurely, aged 44, in 1949.

$1,700-1,900   GBA

A silver medallion presented to Sir Stanley Matthews by the French Football Federation on the occasion of their 75th anniversary, sold with a certificate of authenticity signed by Sir Stanley Matthews' daughter.

$700-900   GBA

Mal Donaghy's Manchester United 1991 European Super Cup winner's gold metal medal, inscribed "UEFA, Super Competition 1991", in original fitted case.

Manchester United beat Red Star Belgrade 1-0 at Old Trafford. The away leg was never played due to political unrest in the former Yugoslavia. Malachy Donaghy was signed by Alex Ferguson from Luton Town for $130,000 in October 1988. The Northern Ireland international repaid the manager's faith with consistent performances at center-back and at full-back in his four year spell at United.

$2,500-3,500   GBA

A miniature gold-plated replica of the FIFA World Cup trophy, by Bertoni of Milan, set on a square marble base with a plaque inscribed 'FIFA World Cup, Germany 2006'.

6.25in (16cm) high

$1,000-1,500   GBA

An Art Deco style Royal Winter Fair Horse Show silver-plated trophy, mounted on a black finished wooden base, engraved 'Royal Winter Fair Horse Show, 1937, Class 39 Pony Four In Hands 1st Prize Won By'.

c1936   *6in (15cm) high*

$500-700   **TCF**

An piece of original artwork depicting ice hockey center Bobby Clarke, in his Philadelphia Flyers uniform.

$120-150   **MAS**

A salesman's sample of Wayne Gretzky's Edmonton Oilers 1984 Stanley Cup Champions ring.

c1984

$1,300-1,500   **MAS**

An Adidas sports shoe, signed by Heide Rosendahl and other athletes at the 1972 Olympic Games.

Rosendahl competed in and won the 4 x 100m women's relay race for West Germany.

c1972

$250-350   **QU**

A pair of Carl Lewis Seoul Summer Olympics signed race-used track spikes.

Canada's Ben Johnson came first in the 100m final but later tested positive for steroid abuse. Second place Lewis was awarded gold and his time of 9.92 seconds was recognized as an Olympic and world record time.

1988

$800-1,000   **MAS**

A Muhammad Ali signed 1986 Olympics commemorative gold basketball.

This would appeal to collectors of Ali memorabilia as well as those of Olympics memorabilia.

$400-600   **MAS**

A 1950s German transfer-printed tinplate Dunlop Tennis Balls tin.

8in (20cm) high

$120-150   **QU**

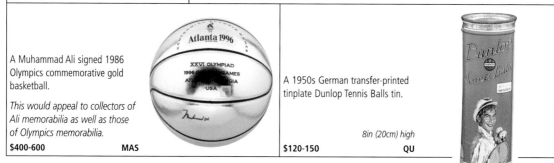

ESSENTIAL REFERENCE

- Teddy bears were named after President Theodore (Teddy) Roosevelt, who refused to shoot a bear on a hunting trip in 1902. The media picked up on his act of kindness and a cartoon was published. Entrepreneur Morris Michtom produced a soft toy teddy bear to commemorate the event, starting a craze that is still with us today.

- Despite the teddy's origins in the US, German company Steiff (founded 1886) are considered the best maker, with their bears being the most desirable and valuable. Gebruder Hermann, Bing, and Schreyer & Co. (Schuco), are other notable German names to look out for. British companies include Farnell (1908-60s) who are often called the 'English Steiff', Merrythought (1920-2006) and Chad Valley (1915-78). In the US, bears were produced by a large number of factories including Ideal, Gund and Knickerbocker.

- Bears from before WWII tend to have long limbs with large, upturned paw pads, pronounced snouts and humped backs. They are usually made from mohair and solidly stuffed with wood shavings or wool known as kapok. After the war,

limbs became shorter, bodies became plumper and snouts less pronounced, on more rounded heads. Other, largely synthetic, materials were used from the 1960s onwards.

- Bears can be identified and dated from labels, if they are still present, or from the materials, color and overall form. Consult reference books and handle as many as possible so you can build up an eye for the different styles. Always consider condition as tears, stains, replaced pads and particularly worn fur, reduces value considerably. However, apart from fur, bears can be restored professionally, giving new life to old friends.

- Modern limited edition bears by major names, such as Steiff, are beginning to make good prices on the secondary market, as are bears made by contemporary bear artists. Many are replicas of older bears, so do not confuse these with original versions, which can be worth many times more. When buying a modern replica or limited edition, always retain the box and paperwork with the bear, keeping everything in mint condition.

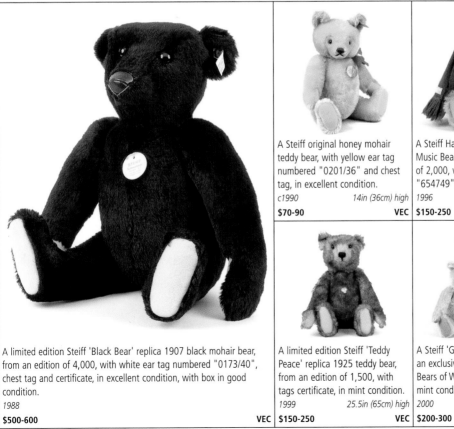

A limited edition Steiff 'Black Bear' replica 1907 black mohair bear, from an edition of 4,000, with white ear tag numbered "0173/40", chest tag and certificate, in excellent condition, with box in good condition.

1988

$500-600   VEC

A Steiff original honey mohair teddy bear, with yellow ear tag numbered "0201/36" and chest tag, in excellent condition.

c1990   *14in (36cm) high*

$70-90   VEC

A Steiff Harrods golden mohair Music Bear, from a limited edition of 2,000, with ear tag numbered "654749", label and certificate.

1996   *17in (44cm) high*

$150-250   VEC

A limited edition Steiff 'Teddy Peace' replica 1925 teddy bear, from an edition of 1,500, with tags certificate, in mint condition.

1999   *25.5in (65cm) high*

$150-250   VEC

A Steiff 'George' teddy bear, from an exclusive edition for Teddy Bears of Witney, with ear tag, in mint condition, with felt bag.

2000   *12in (30cm) high*

$200-300   VEC

A limited edition Steiff British Collectors honey golden mohair teddy bear, from an edition of 4,000, with white ear tag numbered "660728", card tag and certificate.

2000   13.75in (35cm) high
$150-250   **VEC**

A limited edition Steiff British Collectors honey golden mohair teddy bear, from an edition of 4,000, with tags and certificate, in mint condition and with near mint condition box.

2002   13.75in (35cm) high
$150-250   **VEC**

A limited edition Steiff replica 1909 'Rolly Polly' beige mohair bear, from an edition of 3,000, with white ear tag numbered "406652", chest tag, certificate and box, in mint condition.

2003   6.25in (16cm) high
$150-200   **VEC**

A 1950s German Steiff pull-along bear on wheels, with metal frame and tinplate wheels.

    23.75in (60cm) long
$350-450   **QU**

EXPERT EYE – A STEIFF CENTER SEAM TEDDY BEAR

The term 'center seam' applies to the sewn seam that runs down the center of his head.

To enable the factory to use the mohair economically, every seventh bear was made by joining two pieces of fabric. This meant the bear had a seam down his nose and makes them rarer than standard bears.

The center seam also gives bears a typically appealing and charming facial expression, which makes them popular with collectors.

This early example is large in size and in superb condition, also retaining his early button and original pads.

A Steiff blond mohair 'center seam' teddy bear, with original boot button eyes, stitched nose, paw pads, and early blank ear button.

c1905   16in (40.5cm) high
$4,500-5,500   **SOTT**

A rare limited edition Steiff Club Members 'Haute Couture' teddy bear, from an edition of 500, made with pastel woven fabric embellished with silver metallic sequins, with stainless steel 'edition' button to ear, black embroidered tag to side seam, book and boxes, in mint condition.

As well as being from a very small edition, recipients were chosen by a prize draw at Steiff. The unusual sparkling, tweedy fabric was designed at the Jakob Schlaepfer studio in St. Gall and was woven in Northern Italy, the eyes are made from Murano glass, and the pads are covered with Indian silk.

2004-05   12.25in (31cm) high
$800-1,000   **VEC**

A 1960s Merrythought 'Cheeky' golden mohair teddy bear, with amber and black plastic eye, velvet inset muzzle, black vertically stitched nose, bells within ears, fully jointed, with worn areas and losses and damage to stitching, and with one eye missing.

A 1950s-60s Farnell 'Alpha' blond mohair teddy bear, with amber and black plastic eyes, black vertically stitched nose, fully jointed rexine pads, label to torso, paw pad covering worn.

10in (25cm) high

$120-180   **VEC**

A 1960s Farnell 'Alpha' blond mohair teddy bear, amber and black plastic eyes, black plastic nose, fully jointed, rexine pads, remains of label to side seam, paw pads with cracked surface.

20in (51cm) high

$100-150   **VEC**

Had it been in better condition, it may have been worth twice as much. However, despite the wear, its fur is in good condition, so it is likely that it could be restored professionally.

13in (33cm) high

$100-150   **VEC**

An American Ideal blond mohair teddy bear, with original eyes, stitched nose and paw pads.

This bear shows a number of features typical of Ideal bears, including a triangular head with widely spaced apart ears set on the sides of the head. Arms set low on the body are another typical feature.

c1910   13in (33cm) high

$550-650   **SOTT**

A 1930s German golden mohair musical bear, by an unknown maker.

Squeezing his body activates the musical mechanism which, was obviously a popular amusement for the original owner, judging by the wear on his back.

15in (38cm) high

$400-600   **SOTT**

A 1970s Gabrielle Design beige plush Paddington Bear, unjointed, wearing an orange hat, red duffle coat, blue Dunlop rubber boots, label to rear seam, in very good condition.

18in (46cm) high

$150-200   **VEC**

A 1990s Channel Island Toys Miller's Books promotional teddy bear, with woven navy blue jumper with embroidered logo.

These bears were produced for bookstore displays in the early 2000s.

8.25in (21cm) high

$15-20   **PC**

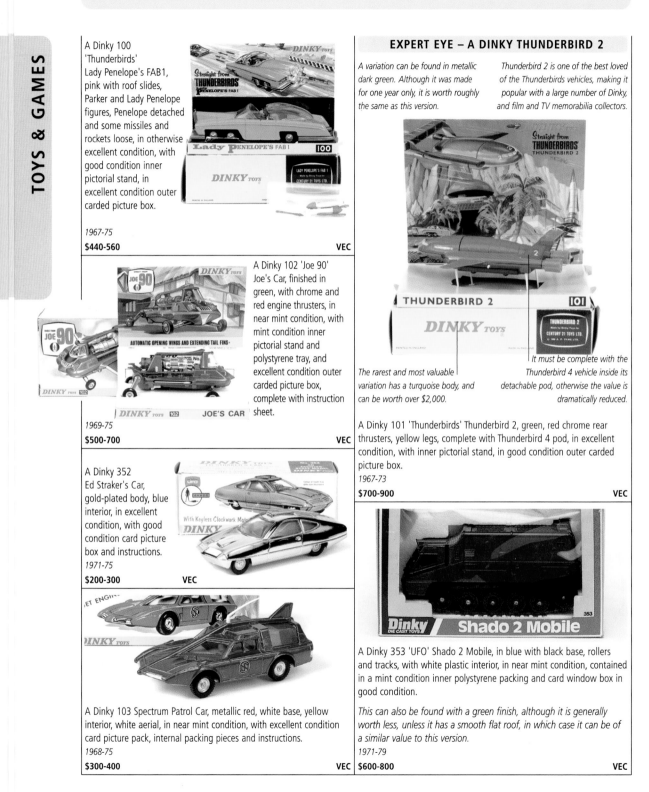

A Dinky 100 'Thunderbirds' Lady Penelope's FAB1, pink with roof slides, Parker and Lady Penelope figures, Penelope detached and some missiles and rockets loose, in otherwise excellent condition, with good condition inner pictorial stand, in excellent condition outer carded picture box.

1967-75

$440-560   **VEC**

A Dinky 102 'Joe 90' Joe's Car, finished in green, with chrome and red engine thrusters, in near mint condition, with mint condition inner pictorial stand and polystyrene tray, and excellent condition outer carded picture box, complete with instruction sheet.

1969-75

$500-700   **VEC**

A Dinky 352 Ed Straker's Car, gold-plated body, blue interior, in excellent condition, with good condition card picture box and instructions.

1971-75

$200-300   **VEC**

A Dinky 103 Spectrum Patrol Car, metallic red, white base, yellow interior, white aerial, in near mint condition, with excellent condition card picture pack, internal packing pieces and instructions.

1968-75

$300-400   **VEC**

EXPERT EYE – A DINKY THUNDERBIRD 2

A variation can be found in metallic dark green. Although it was made for one year only, it is worth roughly the same as this version.

Thunderbird 2 is one of the best loved of the Thunderbirds vehicles, making it popular with a large number of Dinky, and film and TV memorabilia collectors.

The rarest and most valuable variation has a turquoise body, and can be worth over $2,000.

It must be complete with the Thunderbird 4 vehicle inside its detachable pod, otherwise the value is dramatically reduced.

A Dinky 101 'Thunderbirds' Thunderbird 2, green, red chrome rear thrusters, yellow legs, complete with Thunderbird 4 pod, in excellent condition, with inner pictorial stand, in good condition outer carded picture box.

1967-73

$700-900   **VEC**

A Dinky 353 'UFO' Shado 2 Mobile, in blue with black base, rollers and tracks, with white plastic interior, in near mint condition, contained in a mint condition inner polystyrene packing and card window box in good condition.

This can also be found with a green finish, although it is generally worth less, unless it has a smooth flat roof, in which case it can be of a similar value to this version.

1971-79

$600-800   **VEC**

ESSENTIAL REFERENCE

- Corgi toys were first introduced in 1956 by the UK toy company, Mettoy. The company has produced model cars, aircraft, farm vehicles, commercial vehicles and boats, and continues to produce limited editions today.
- Corgi toys were released to compete with Dinky's Supertoys series. They were the first toys to have plastic windows, a feature which was copied by competitors. Doors and trunks that opened were also included, as was sprung suspension, which was marketed as Glidamatic and introduced in 1959.
- As with other die-cast models, condition is paramount when determining value. Collectors look for examples in very good, or excellent condition, with top prices going to examples in mint condition. Never attempt to paint over any scuffs or chips, as this will reduce value. Models should ideally be accompanied by their original boxes, which should also be in good condition.
- Variations are similarly important to value. Look for models

with rare colors or interiors as these are generally worth more. Superdetailing kits were sold in the 1960s and included stickers with which to decorate a Corgi. The addition of these stickers to a model will usually decrease value. For a complete guide to colors, variations and models, consult a dedicated reference book, such as Ramsay's British Die-cast Model Toys Catalogue.
- A number of models were produced during the 1960s and 1970s to tie-in with popular TV programs and films. These included James Bond vehicles, Batman's Batmobile and Batboat and the Chitty Chitty Bang Bang car. These were very popular when released, and have remained so with collectors. Other popular special models include the range of Chipperfield Circus vehicles. Boxed gift sets are also of great interest to collectors. These should still have their original internal packaging to be considered complete and to make the highest prices.

A Corgi 236 'Motor School' Austin A60, in pale blue with red interior and roof turning disk, and spun hubs, in near mint condition, with correct issue folded instruction sheet, and good condition outer blue and yellow carded box.
1964-68

$160-240   **VEC**

A Corgi 229 Chevrolet Corvair, in mid-blue with lemon interior and spun hubs, in mint condition, with mint condition blue and yellow carded box complete with Collectors Club folded leaflet.
1961-66

$240-360   **VEC**

A Corgi 233 Heinkel Trojan Economy car, the orange body with lemon interior and cast hubs, in near mint condition, with near mint condition blue and yellow carded box with Collectors Club folded leaflet.

Metallic blue, turquoise or fawn bodies are rarer and can be worth at least 50 percent more in this condition.
1962-72

$140-200   **VEC**

A Corgi 240 Fiat Ghia 600 Jolly, in blue with red and silver plastic canopy, two figures, and spun hubs, in near mint condition, with good condition blue and yellow carded box.
1963-64

$160-240   **VEC**

A Corgi 213 'Fire Service' Jaguar 2.4, in orangey-red with flat spun hubs, gray plastic aerial and roofbox, in near mint condition, with excellent condition blue and yellow carded box.

Look out for the rarer, and slightly more valuable, version produced from 1961 until 1962, with suspension and shaped spun wheels.
1959-61

$300-500   **VEC**

A Corgi 247 Mercedes Benz 600 Pullman, in maroon with cream interior, spun hubs and chrome trim, in mint condition, with mint condition correct instruction sheet and folded collectors leaflet, with outer blue and yellow carded box in excellent condition.
1964-69

$140-200   **VEC**

TOYS & GAMES

A Corgi 327 MGB GT, the red body with pale blue interior with gold steering wheel, black baggage case and wire wheels, complete with Collectors Club folded leaflet and unapplied racing number 6 decal sheet, in near mint condition, with mint condition blue and yellow carded box.

1967-69

$200-300   VEC

A Corgi 349 Morris Mini-Minor 'Pop-Art Mostest', in orangey-red with psychedelic roof, side and hood decals, lemon interior and cast hubs, in mint condition.

This is one of the rarest versions of the popular Mini. It was only made for one year in 1967, and few examples were produced. It is also in mint condition.

1967

$1,600-2,400   VEC

A Corgi 237 'County Sheriff' Oldsmobile Super 88, in black and white with red interior and roof-light, in near mint condition, with near mint condition inner packing card and Collectors Club folded leaflet, and excellent condition outer blue and yellow carded box.

1962-67

$200-300   VEC

A Corgi 219 Plymouth Sports Suburban Station Wagon, the cream body with beige roof, red interior and flat spun hubs, in near mint condition, with Collectors Club folded leaflet excellent condition blue and yellow carded box.

1959-63

$200-300   VEC

A Corgi 445 Plymouth Sports Suburban Station Wagon, the pale lilac body with red roof, lemon interior and spun hubs, in mint condition, with near mint condition blue and yellow carded box complete with Collectors Club folded leaflet.

1963-66

$300-400   VEC

A Corgi 205 Riley Pathfinder Saloon, in red with flat spun hubs and silver trim, in good condition, with near mint condition all-carded blue box with correct issue folded color leaflet.

1956-62

$300-400   VEC

A Corgi 506 'Police' Sunbeam Imp, in blue and white with brown interior with figure driver, cast hubs and blue roof-light, in mint condition, with excellent condition blue and yellow carded picture box with Collectors Club folded leaflet.

1968-69

$240-360   VEC

A Corgi 926 'James Bond' Stromberg Helicopter, in black and yellow, lacks missiles, otherwise mint condition, with excellent condition striped window box.

This is the Stromberg helicopter taken from the 1977 Bond film "The Spy Who Loved Me".
1978-80

$140-200 VEC

A Corgi 929 Superman 'Daily Planet' Jetcopter, in red and white, the missile still attached to sprue, in mint condition, with mint condition striped window box, ex-store stock.
1979-80

$120-160 VEC

EXPERT EYE – A CORGI JAMES BOND LOTUS ESPRIT

This was based on the Lotus in the 1977 James Bond film 'The Spy Who Loved Me'. The scene where it emerges from the sea onto the beach is a much-loved classic.

In 1977, 10 gold plated models were produced with special mountings and boxes, these can be worth over $4,000.

The earlier versions had instruction manuals inside, which must be present, rather than having instructions printed on the base of the box.

Collectors prefer the missiles to be still attached to the sprue and all components to be in mint condition, as with this model.

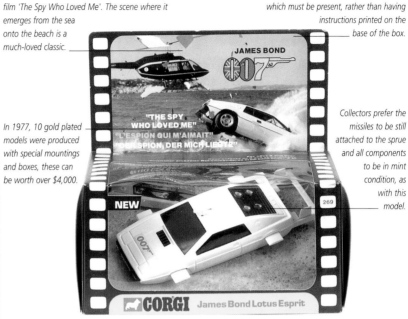

A Corgi 269 'James Bond' Lotus Esprit, in white and black, the missiles still attached to sprue, in mint condition, with mint condition inner carded display, and excellent condition outer film strip window box with 'Hammer & Sickle' logo.
1977-83

$240-360 VEC

A Corgi 342 'The Professionals' Ford Capri, in metallic silver, complete with three figures, in mint condition, with mint condition inner carded tray, and excellent condition outer striped window box.
1980-82

$200-300 VEC

A Corgi 292 'Starsky & Hutch' Ford Torino, in red and white with two figures, in excellent condition, with excellent condition inner plastic tray and carded display, and good condition outer striped window box.
1977-82

$160-240 VEC

A Corgi 805 'The Hardy Boys' 1912 Rolls Royce Silver Ghost, in yellow, red, blue with gold trim, in excellent condition, with mint condition figures in dome, with good condition outer window box.
1970-71

$160-240 VEC

A Corgi 804 Noddy's Car, in yellow and red with chrome trim, complete with Noddy figure, in near mint condition, with excellent condition later issue window box.
1975-78

$200-300 VEC

ESSENTIAL REFERENCE

- The US toy manufacturer Mattel released its Hot Wheels range of model vehicles in 1968. The eye-catching models were designed to appeal to boys looking for more exciting toys than those offered by competing UK manufacturers Corgi, Dinky and Matchbox.
- Hot Wheels specialized in producing models of 'muscle cars' and hot rods, some of which were decorated with a special metallic finish called Spectraflame, developed to make their cars look different from the competition. Cars finished in Spectraflame were produced in a number of different colors with pink and purple generally the rarest, as these were considered too 'feminine' by many boys and bought in fewer numbers.

- Redline models, featuring red stripes around the wheels, were made between 1968 and 1977 and tend to be popular with collectors. Hot Wheels models are still produced by Mattel and the company currently produces a range of toys aimed at both children and older collectors.
- As with all die-cast models, condition has a great affect on value. But, unlike the toys from most other manufacturers, Hot Wheels were packaged in blister packs, rather than boxes, which were usually badly damaged and then discarded when opened. As a result, it is much more difficult to find Hot Wheels models still with their packaging. Those that have their complete and intact packaging will generally command a significant premium.

A Mattel Hot Wheels 'red line' purple Custom Fleetside, no. 6213.

1967   3.25in (8cm) long
$30-40   SOTT

A Mattel Hot Wheels 'red line' metallic lime Deora with surfboards, no. 6210.

1968   2.75in (7cm) long
$80-100   SOTT

A Mattel Hot Wheels gold 'red line' Custom Mustang, no. 6206, with brown interior, open hood scoops, in excellent condition, with excellent condition tin pin.

1968
$560-640   VEC

A Mattel Hot Wheels 'red line' bronze Twinmill, with stickers.
1968   3in (7.5cm) long
$45-65   SOTT

A Mattel Hot Wheels 'red line' green Silhouette, no. 6209.
1968   2.75in (7cm) long
$30-40   SOTT

A Mattel Hot Wheels 'red line' orange Splittin' Image, no.6261.
1969   3in (7.5cm) long
$45-55   SOTT

A Mattel Hot Wheels 'red line' purple Sand Crab, no. 6403, with chipped windshield and Crane Arms decal.
1970 *2.5in (6cm) long*
$25-35 **SOTT**

A Mattel Hot Wheels 'red line' turquoise Stripteaser, no. 6188, with 'Firestone' transfer.
1971 *3.25in (8cm) long*
$80-120 **SOTT**

A Mattel Hot Wheels 'red line' blue Cement Mixer, no. 6452, from The Heavyweights range.
1970 *3.5in (9cm) long*
$40-60 **SOTT**

A Mattel Hot Wheels 'red line' burgundy Snorkel, no. 6020, from the The Heavyweights range, with broken platform rail.
1971 *3.5in (8.5cm) long*
$70-100 **SOTT**

A Mattel Hot Wheels green Ranger Rig, with replaced wheels.
1975 *3in (7.5cm) long*
$45-55 **SOTT**

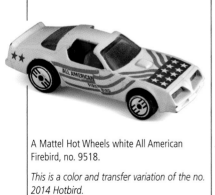

A Mattel Hot Wheels white All American Firebird, no. 9518.

This is a color and transfer variation of the no. 2014 Hotbird.
1977 *3in (7.5cm) long*
$40-60 **SOTT**

A Mattel Hot Wheels T-Bird, no. 2013, with pink and green side streaks and plastic base.
1978 *3in (7.5cm) long*
$6-10 **SOTT**

A Mattel Hot Wheels purple Turboa, no. 2061, made in Malaysia, from the 'Speed Demons' series.
1986 *3in (7.5cm) long*
$10-15 **SOTT**

TOYS & GAMES

ESSENTIAL REFERENCE

- Model trains were first produced in the 1850s, but they were stylized, bulky and rather unrealistic. By the 1890s, German makers such as Märklin (est. 1859) and Gebruder Bing (1863-1933) had introduced more realistic tinplate models, with clockwork or steam mechanisms. Many of these were exported to the US, and other European countries. Production and exports ceased during the two world wars.
- Märklin introduced gauge sizes in 1891, with the larger gauges of I, II and III being eclipsed in 1910 by the smaller I and 0, as demand for smaller trains and sets grew. Gauge I was discontinued by 1938, and gauge 0 itself was replaced in 1935 with the even smaller 00-gauge. The H0-gauge appeared in 1948.
- Hornby, a UK company, began making trains in 1920 and the name has since become synonymous around the world

with model trains. Their pre-WWII gauge 0 trains are widely collected. Postwar examples tend to be of poorer quality, which led to the range being discontinued in 1969.
- Their Dublo range, introduced in 1938, was designed to compete with small gauge sets by Märklin and Trix, and is highly collectable. Nationalized livery trains from 1953-1957 tend to be less desirable, but after this date, the range was refreshed. The company was taken over by Tri-ang in 1964.
- Condition is paramount for value, as trains were made to be played with, and usually were. The precise model, date and livery are also important factors with regard to price, and a premium is paid for rarer models. Sets from the 1950s to '60s, such as those by Tri-ang, are now worth looking out for, particularly if in mint and complete condition with their boxes. These are still reasonably priced, but may rise in the future.

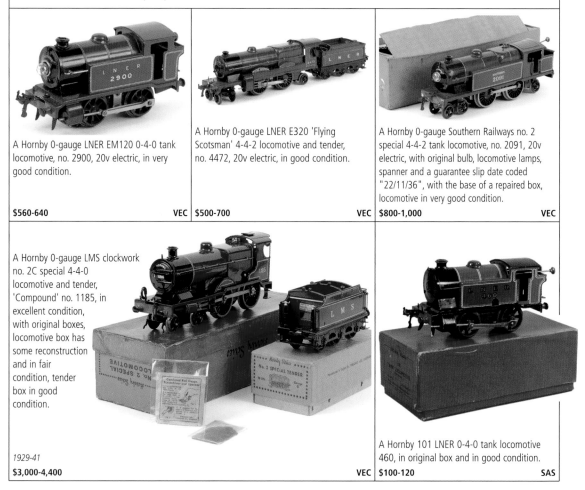

A Hornby 0-gauge LNER EM120 0-4-0 tank locomotive, no. 2900, 20v electric, in very good condition.

$560-640   VEC

A Hornby 0-gauge LNER E320 'Flying Scotsman' 4-4-2 locomotive and tender, no. 4472, 20v electric, in good condition.

$500-700   VEC

A Hornby 0-gauge Southern Railways no. 2 special 4-4-2 tank locomotive, no. 2091, 20v electric, with original bulb, locomotive lamps, spanner and a guarantee slip date coded "22/11/36", with the base of a repaired box, locomotive in very good condition.

$800-1,000   VEC

A Hornby 0-gauge LMS clockwork no. 2C special 4-4-0 locomotive and tender, 'Compound' no. 1185, in excellent condition, with original boxes, locomotive box has some reconstruction and in fair condition, tender box in good condition.

1929-41

$3,000-4,400   VEC

A Hornby 101 LNER 0-4-0 tank locomotive 460, in original box and in good condition.

$100-120   SAS

EXPERT EYE – A HORNBY DUBLO TRAIN

This was made in 1947 only, with a pre-war body but an electric motor and automatic couplings.

As with all early models, it has the the usual gold block on the bunker back – later models have a silver block.

With its green Southern livery, it is the most valuable variation of the EDL7 models, which were made at various times from 1947 to 1954.

It is in excellent condition, retaining its dated instruction booklet and its box, which are both in very good condition.

A Hornby Dublo three-rail EDL7 Southern olive green 0-6-2 tank locomotive, no. 2594, with gold decal to bunker rear and fitted with a horseshoe-type motor, with instruction booklet dated "9/47", minor paint loss to smokebox door, in otherwise excellent condition, with a pale blue box in good condition dated "6/48".
1947

$1,700-1,900   VEC

A Hornby Dublo three-rail GWR green EDG7 tank locomotive, no. 6699, with gold decal to bunker rear and fitted with horseshoe-type motor and complete with instruction booklet dated "8/49", in excellent condition and with good condition pale blue box with GW sticker to one end and dated "6/48".
c1949

$1,400-1,600   VEC

A Hornby Dublo three-rail LNER green EDG7 N2 class 0-6-2 tank locomotive, no. 9596, with silver decal to bunker rear and fitted with horseshoe-type motor, in excellent condition, with repair box with repair label "14955" to both ends and complete with blue end packing pieces and printed cover strip.

$200-300   VEC

A Hornby Dublo three-rail LMS black EDG7 0-6-2 tank locomotive, with Sheriff lettering, damage to gold decal on bunker rear and some paint chips to body, in good condition and with good condition pale blue box with some fading and dated "5/49".

$240-360   VEC

A Hornby Dublo three-rail LNER black EDL7 N2 class 0-6-2 tank locomotive, no. 9596, with gold decal to bunker rear and fitted with horseshoe-type motor, some minor damage to gold decal and paint loss to smokebox door, unboxed, in good condition.

$360-440   VEC

A Hornby Dublo three-rail GWR EDL7 0-6-2 tank locomotive, no. 6699, with BR-type totem applied to both tank sides, unboxed, in good condition.

$300-400   VEC

A Hornby Dublo three-rail LNER blue 'Sir Nigel Gresley' EDL/D1 A4 class 4-6-2 locomotive and tender, no. 7, fitted with a horseshoe-style motor, locomotive in near mint condition, tender in excellent condition but plastic coal section has minor distortion, both contained in pale blue boxes in excellent condition, locomotive box dated "6/48" and complete with all inner packing sections, printed cover strips and complete with spanner, tender box dated "1/49".

Early models in the earlier light blue boxes are more desirable and are therefore valuable.
c1949

$1,200-1,400   VEC

A Hornby Dublo three-rail LNER blue 'Sir Nigel Gresley' EDL1 A4 class 4-6-2 locomotive, no. 7, marked "EDL1" to inside of cab roof, slight distortion to plastic tender top, in good condition, unboxed.

$160-240   VEC

A rare Canadian issue Hornby Dublo three-rail BR green class 20 L30/3230 Bo-Bo diesel locomotive, no. D8000, some marks to roof, in otherwise good condition, with picture box in good condition with instruction booklet dated "11/58", guarantee slip dated "1/59", Meccano Magazine order form and yellow test tag.

The Canadian models are identical to the standard models, with molded plastic bodies, but have no buffers.

$360-440   VEC

A Hornby Dublo two-rail BR green 'Cardiff Castle' 2221 4-6-0 locomotive, no. 4075, with instruction booklet dated "8/60", in excellent condition and with excellent condition box.

$200-300   VEC

A Hornby Dublo two-rail BR green 'Golden Fleece' A4 class 2211 4-6-2 locomotive, no. 60030, with instruction booklet dated "9/60", also including metal talisman head board, in excellent condition and with excellent condition box with two surface tears where adhesive tape has been removed.

$360-440   VEC

A Hornby Dublo two-rail BR green 'Barnstaple' West Country class 2235 4-6-2 locomotive, no. 34005, with instruction booklet dated "3/61", amended instruction flyer dated "June/1961" and purple guarantee slip, two small paint chips to tender front left side and minor lining loss to left side cylinder, otherwise in excellent condition and with excellent condition box, base torn to one side.

$240-360   VEC

A Hornby Dublo two-rail BR maroon 'City of London' Princess Coronation class 2226 4-6-2 locomotive, no. 46245, with instruction booklet dated "10/59", in excellent condition and with excellent condition box but some minor scuffing to lid.

$200-300   VEC

A Hornby Dublo BR black 8F class two-rail 2224 2-8-0 locomotive, no. 48073, with instruction booklet dated "8/60", in very good condition and with excellent condition box.

$240-360   VEC

EXPERT EYE – A HORNBY DUBLO 'GREEN ARROW' TRAIN

This is from a limited edition of only 210 models, and is numbered '11'. Its ticket is glued to the inside of the box lid.

It retains its certificate and special reproduction picture box, which is also in mint condition.

It was produced to celebrate the Golden Jubilee of Hornby's Dublo trains in 1988.

This item is in truly mint condition, a common feature of many limited edition toys. The edition was very small, hence the high value.

A limited edition Hornby Dublo two-rail BR green 'Green Arrow' V2 class 2240 2-6-2 locomotive, no. 60800, from an edition of 210, with numbered certificate, in mint condition with mint condition box.

$1,600-2,000   **VEC**

A Hornby Dublo two-rail BR green class 20 2231 0-6-0 diesel shunter, no. D3302, split-rod type, complete with instruction booklet dated "7/60" and purple guarantee slip, in excellent condition and with excellent condition box with Tri-ang/Hornby sticker to left side of lid and with unused tube of oil.

$200-300   **VEC**

A Hornby Dublo three-rail Southern malachite green EDL7 0-6-2 tank locomotive, no. 2594, fitted with horseshoe-type motor and having gold decal to bunker rear, in excellent condition, with pale blue box in good condition dated "6/48" and with Southern Railways sticker to one end.

$800-1,000   **VEC**

A Hornby Dublo two-rail BR green 2232 Co-Co diesel locomotive, with instruction booklet dated "7/60" and purple guarantee slip, in excellent condition and with excellent condition box.

$120-160   **VEC**

A Hornby Dublo two-rail 2006 tank goods train set, consisting of 0-6-0 BR green R1 class tank locomotive, no.31340, three Superdetail goods wagons, brown steel open, United Glass & Bottle Co. open and BR (WR) gray brake van, track, instruction booklet dated "11/59" and guarantee slip, rolling stock appears unrun, small paint loss to rear buffer beam on tank loco, in excellent condition and with very good condition box but with some minor graffiti to lid.

$140-200   **VEC**

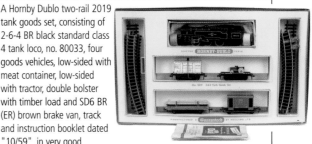

A Hornby Dublo two-rail 2019 tank goods set, consisting of 2-6-4 BR black standard class 4 tank loco, no. 80033, four goods vehicles, low-sided with meat container, low-sided with tractor, double bolster with timber load and SD6 BR (ER) brown brake van, track and instruction booklet dated "10/59", in very good condition and with good condition box with excellent condition inserts for goods wagons, locomotive insert missing.

$200-300   **VEC**

A rare Hornby 0-gauge 'Coleman's Mustard' private owner van, finished in yellow with "Colemans Mustard", "Royal Appointment" and bull's head figure transfers to both sides, sides in good condition, roof in fair condition.

This is a very rare van, and was only produced for one year. Coleman's advertising memorabilia is also popular with collectors. There is a Coleman's museum in Norwich, England.

$1,200-1,400   **VEC**

A Hornby 0-gauge 'Fyffes' private owner van, with black base and red roof, sides in excellent condition, roof in good condition, with a box dated "3/40" in excellent condition.

$300-400   **VEC**

A Hornby 0-gauge 'Cadburys' private owner van, with a green base and a white roof, sides in excellent condition, with box in excellent condition.

$800-1,000   **VEC**

A Hornby 0-gauge 'Fyffes' private owner van, with red base and roof, sides in excellent condition, roof in near mint condition, with box in excellent condition.

It is the excellent to near mint condition of this model, which also has an undamaged roof, that makes it more valuable than the other example shown above right.

$700-900   **VEC**

A Hornby 0-gauge 'Power Ethyl' petrol tank wagon, in excellent condition, with a good condition box date coded "6/38".

$600-800   **VEC**

A Hornby 0-gauge 'Redline–Glico' petrol tank wagon, in excellent condition, with a fair condition box date coded "12/39".

$400-600   **VEC**

A Hornby 0-gauge Southern Railways breakdown van and crane, with small gold SR lettering to van sides, finished in green and blue with black chassis, in excellent condition with a box in excellent condition.

$360-440   **VEC**

A Hornby Series LMS gunpowder van, in original box, with 'LMS' roundel, over-painted roof, and some white letter embellishment, lacks two tabs, one end flap detached, some damage.

$200-300   **SAS**

A Wrenn LNER blue 'Mallard' A4 class W2110 4-6-2 locomotive, no. 4468, in excellent condition with very good condition box.

$160-240   VEC

A Wrenn LNER blue 'Sir Nigel Gresley' A4 class W2212 4-6-0 locomotive, no. 7, fitted with plastic bogie, pony truck and tender wheels, with instruction booklet, in excellent condition with excellent condition Tri-ang Wrenn box.

$140-200   VEC

A Wrenn BR maroon 'City of London' Princess Coronation class 2226 4-6-2 locomotive, no. 46245, fitted with plastic bogie, pony truck and tender wheels, in excellent condition with good condition Tri-ang Wrenn box without 'W' prefix to end number.

$120-160   VEC

A Wrenn BR green 'Dorchester' West Country class W2236 4-6-2 locomotive, no. 34042, fitted with plastic bogie, pony truck and tender wheels, in excellent condition with very good condition Tri-ang Wrenn box.

$120-200   VEC

A Wrenn BR green 'City of Birmingham' Princess Coronation class W2228 4-6-2 locomotive, no. 46235, with instruction booklet, in excellent condition with very good condition box.

$300-400   VEC

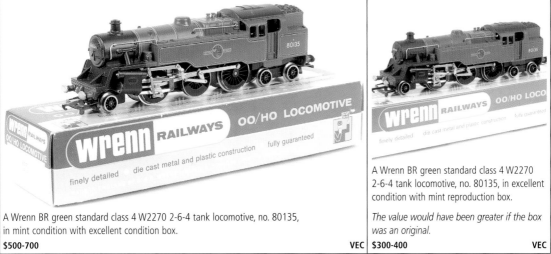

A Wrenn BR green standard class 4 W2270 2-6-4 tank locomotive, no. 80135, in mint condition with excellent condition box.

$500-700   VEC

A Wrenn BR green standard class 4 W2270 2-6-4 tank locomotive, no. 80135, in excellent condition with mint reproduction box.

The value would have been greater if the box was an original.

$300-400   VEC

TOYS & GAMES

A kit-built BR black Z class 00-gauge 0-8-0 tank locomotive, no. 30954, professionally built and painted, in excellent condition.

$360-440   VEC

A kit-built Royal Scot class 'The Royal Artilleryman' 00-gauge 4-6-0 BR green parallel boiler locomotive, no. 46157, constructed from brass, missing footstep to tender right side front, well-built and painted, in excellent condition.

$140-200   VEC

A kit-built BR Clan class 'Clan Stewart' 00-gauge DJH 4-6-2 locomotive, no. 72009, professionally built and detailed with paintwork by Larry Goddard, signed under right side running plate, in excellent condition.

2000

$1,000-1,200   VEC

A kit-built LMS crimson 'Queen Victoria's Rifleman' Royal Scot class 00-gauge F131 parallel boiler 4-6-0, no. 6160, mounted on proprietary chassis with scale driving wheels, in very good condition.

$100-160   VEC

A kit or scratch-built LMS parcels coach, running no. 31059, in mint condition.

$360-440   VEC

Two kit-built 00-gauge steam locomotives, comprising 4-6-0 Great Central lined black livery Class 1A no. 4 'Glenalmond', and 0-6-0 GWR green Dean opencab saddle tank no. 1853.

$160-240   VEC

Two kit-built LNER black 00-gauge steam locos, comprising 0-8-0 class Q1 ex-Great Central hump shunter, no. 9929 mounted on Hornby Dublo chassis, and 0-6-0 J15 no. 5393, in very good condition.

Two kit-built LNER green 00-gauge steam locomotives, comprising 4-4-0 class D49 Shire no. 246 'Morayshire' and 2-6-2 class L1 no. 9000, both of brass construction, well painted and in excellent condition.

$500-700 (pair)   VEC   **$240-360**   VEC

ESSENTIAL REFERENCE

- Tinplate toys were made from the mid-19thC as toymakers started to appreciate the material's advantages over wood. Manufacturers produced toys with finer details as tinplate can be fashioned and decorated more intricately and economically. By the late 19thC tinplate toys were being produced in large quantities.
- Germany became the epicentre of 19thC and early 20thC tinplate toy manufacture. A number of famous German tinplate manufacturers were founded and flourished during this period, including Märklin (founded 1856), Gebrüder Bing (1863-1933) and Schreyer & Co. (1912-78), known as Schuco. Toys bearing these names are keenly collected. Note that toys from German manufacturers were not exported during wartime.
- Tinplate toy manufacturing also took place in the US from the 1880s onwards. Toys by makers such as Marx (1896-c1982) and Ferdinand Strauss (c1914-42), particularly cars and airplanes, are avidly collected.
- Early tinplate toys were generally hand-painted. To identify these, look closely at the surface of the decoration for signs of brush marks. Later examples were transfer-printed; the decoration on these toys tends to be shinier, more detailed and more uniformly smooth.
- After WWII the centre of production moved to Japan and tinplate toys became more novelty in theme. Developments during this period included the addition of battery-operated features, which saw tinplate toys adorned with lights and able to produce electronic sounds. Robots from the 1960s are popular, and notable Japanese manufacturers include Yoshiya, and Horikawa who produced toys under the SH Toys brand. Extra detailing and features usually add value.
- Value is dependent upon the type of toy, the maker, size, date and condition. Toys by major manufacturers such as Märklin are very desirable. Large ships, aircraft and early cars tend to fetch high prices, as do smaller penny toys, if rare and in excellent condition.
- Be aware that modern reproductions of a number of original toys have been produced. Check colors with reference books to ensure you are buying an original. Reproduction boxes, aimed at collectors, are also currently available. Beware of rust and scratched lithography, as this is almost impossible to restore.

A German Tipp & Co. clockwork two-door saloon, with permanent key, red, cream with tinplate wheels, chauffeur to interior, some wear to edges of roof, otherwise in good condition.

8.75in (22cm) long

$400-500   VEC

A Wells, or similar tinplate Citroen car, four-door sedan in red, with cream upper, opening rear trunk, clockwork operation with permanent key, tin-printed balloon wheels, some wear to edges of roof and hood, otherwise in good condition.

11.5in (29cm) long

$300-400   VEC

A Mettoy tinplate clockwork two-door car, red, with cream tin-printing, tinplate wheels, clockwork operation with permanent key, some wear to rear trunk and slight fading to plated parts, otherwise in good condition.

9in (23cm) long

$300-400   VEC

A Chad Valley tinplate clockwork two-door coupé, in red, with black trim and running boards, tin-printed wheels, nut and bolt assembly from the Ubilda Series, in good condition.

10.25in (26cm) long

$160-240   VEC

A pre-war French tinplate fire car, with hinged roof, possibly used as a cookie tin, red, black, with detailed tin-printing including fireman, with 'SP9' license plate to rear and "Fabrication Francaise" to base, in good condition,

6.75in (17cm) long

$100-160   VEC

A rare German Arnold Lizzie tinplate novelty car, yellow with opening dickey seat, steerable front wheels, lacks front headlights and windshield but includes four composition passengers, with novelty graffiti to car bodywork, otherwise in fair condition.

10in (25cm) long

$360-440   VEC

TOYS & GAMES

A German Tipp & Co. tinplate four-door car, dark green, plated parts including plastic hubs, black plastic wheels, in near mint condition.

7.5in (19cm) long

$140-200   VEC

A rare German Distler tinplate Jaguar XK120, blue, with detailed tin-printing, rubber tires with steerable front wheels, plated parts, battery operation, very light scratches to roof and hood, otherwise in excellent condition.

8.75in (22cm) long

$240-360   VEC

A German Arnold tinplate Mercedes four-door saloon, cream, clockwork operation, detailed interior, plated parts, includes motif to radiator grille, in excellent condition.

9.5in (24cm) long

$240-360   VEC

A Japanese ATC Subaru tinplate car, friction-drive model in brick red, with detailed tin-printed interior and hub caps, plated parts, in near mint condition.

Made by the Asahi Toy Company (ATC), this is a rare model and is in near mint condition.

6.25in (16cm) long

$700-900   VEC

A 1950s Japanese Asahi Toy transfer-printed tinplate battery operated 'Musical Car', with original card box and maker's mark.

9in (23cm) long

$360-440   QU

A rare Japanese Yonezawa tinplate Opel Olympic, large scale battery operated car in light blue, with cream roof, detailed tin-printed interior, with operating switch to driver's door, wired for illuminated headlights, rubber tires with steerable front wheels, plated parts, in excellent condition.

c1954   11.75in (30cm) long

$500-700   VEC

A Japanese tinplate Ford Thunderbird, by an unknown maker, large scale battery operated tinplate model in orange, with detailed interior and hub caps, plated parts, opening driver's door, clear plastic windshield, in excellent condition.

11in (28cm) long

$160-240   VEC

A Japanese tinplate 'James Bond' no. M101 Aston Martin DB5, with remote control, finished in silver with black base, some slight loss of chrome around bumpers, otherwise in excellent condition, in fair condition lift-off lid box.

$360-440   VEC

EXPERT EYE – A GERMAN TINPLATE MOTORCYCLE

The presence of the 'US Zone' wording allows this to be dated to between 1945 and c1949, when Germany was divided into four zones for administrative purposes.

It retains its original card box in good condition, which is a rare survivor. The artwork on the box is also excellent, being detailed and suggesting a sense of excitement and speed.

The toy itself is also well-detailed in terms of the molding and the transfer-printed design and is in near mint condition.

This model is also rare, and is harder to find than the other Technofix model shown on this page.

A rare US Zone German Technofix no. 258 clockwork motorcyclist, red bike, light brown and gray rider with "4" to his back, "Technofix" and "GE258" in brown on white, clockwork mechanism with fixed key, in near mint condition, with good condition illustrated card box.

$440-560   **VEC**

A 1930s Spanish Rico clockwork touring rider-on-motorcycle, mechanism with fixed key, red bike, brown and blue rider, plain brown tinplate wheels, stabilisers, "RSA" to tank sides, clockwork mechanism requires some attention, in good condition.

6.5in (16.5cm) long

$440-560   **VEC**

A Russian Touring clockwork motorcyclist, with red and yellow bike, green and blue rider with brown helmet, tinplate tires with small outriders, in working order and in near mint condition, unboxed.

$80-120   **VEC**

A French SFA motorcyclist and sidecar, red bike and sidecar, blue rider, "SFA-Paris" to tank sides and sidecar, registration no. "2139-RP9", in near mint condition.

$140-200   **VEC**

A 1950s German Technofix no. 255 clockwork trick motorcycle, light brown bike, red and blue Rider with "2" to his back and rear wheels and "Technofix" and "GE255" to front in white on red, in good condition, unboxed.

$160-240   **VEC**

A Japanese MT clockwork police rider, mechanism driven with fixed key, on green bike with eagle logo to tank sides, rider in silver suit with green helmet and "PD" to helmet and on arm, meant for variable cable action, in near mint condition, unboxed.

$120-200   **VEC**

TOYS & GAMES

A 1950s-60s Japanese TM Modern Toys transfer-printed tinplate and plastic battery powered 'Space Explorer Ship', marked "Made in Japan TM", with original card box.

10in (25.5cm) diam

$700-900   **QU**

EXPERT EYE – A LI'L ABNER MECHANICAL TOY

Unique Art Manufacturing Co. of Newark, New Jersey, were known for their mechanical tinplate character toys, which also included 'Gertie The Goose'.

This toy was produced for Christmas 1945, and was based on a popular comic strip of the time.

The movement is superb. When wound and set off, every character moves with Abner dancing, Daisy Mae playing the piano, Mammy Yokum keeping time, and Pappy Yokum playing the drums.

The form is complex, involving many separate components, and the transfer-printed decoration is detailed and colorful, covering all parts of the toy.

A 1950s American Unique Art Manufacturing Co. 'Li'l Abner and his Dogpatch Band' tinplate mechanical lithographed toy, with attached figures of Daisy Mae, Abner, Mammy and Pappy Yokum, in good condition.

12in (30cm) wide

$440-560   **VEC**

A 1950s-60s Japanese Nogura transfer-printed tinplate and plastic robot, marked "Made in Japan".

This robot is modeled after the iconic robot Robby, first seen in the 1956 film 'Forbidden Planet'.

12in (31cm) high

$1,000-1,200   **QU**

A US Zone German Schuco Turn Miki 881 mouse toy, gray felt body, green trousers, yellow neck ribbon, gray wire arms with brown felt hands, black tail, in near mint condition, with good condition box and instruction leaflet.

5.5in (14cm) high

$360-440   **VEC**

A US Zone German Schuco Solisto 985/1 clockwork monkey drummer, green jacket, blue pants, red beret, brown hair, tin drum, yellow bow tie, slight discoloration to felt, tiny marks to face of drum, otherwise in good condition, with fair condition box.

4.5in (11cm) high

$200-300   **VEC**

A 1950s Japanese Haji transfer-printed tinplate and wood clockwork mother and child in pram, the pram sides printed with a detailed childhood scene, with maker's mark.

6.25in (16cm) long

$600-800   **QU**

ESSENTIAL REFERENCE

- Cast and painted lead figures saw their golden age from the late 19thC until the late 1950s, when cheaper plastic took over. Soldiers are the most popular category, although domestic and pastoral themes such as farming and zoos were produced, particularly after WWI. There are a number of makers, with Britains (founded 1845) being the largest and most popular. Other names include Charbens, Taylor & Barrett, and John Hill Co.

- Look for fine detailing and original paint. Paint which is completely opaque, overly bright or has unusual color tones may indicate a repainted figure. These, or figures that have had parts replaced, re-attached or customized, should be avoided. If buying a set, ensure that it is complete and does not contain incorrectly duplicated figures. Original boxes will add value, particularly in excellent condition, as they were often thrown away or became damaged.

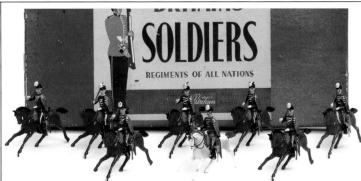

A Britains Royal Scots Greys set 32, comprising five mounted troopers, in scarlet dress uniform, in original box tied to stringing card.

c1953   *3.25in (8.5cm) high*

$150-200   **W&W**

A scarce Britains Danish Guard Hussar regiment set 2018, comprising of six men with swords and an officer, all on brown horses, and a trumpeter on a gray horse, in original box.

3.25in (8.5cm) high

$700-900   **W&W**

A Britains Greek Army Evzones set 196, containing seven marching soldiers with shouldered rifles, some wear and paint chips.

3in (7.5cm) high

$200-300   **W&W**

A rare Britains 1937 Coronation state coach set 1470, with seated figures of George VI & Elizabeth pulled by Windsor grey horses, in original box.

Box 22in (56cm) wide

$250-350   **W&W**

A rare Britains metal knights in armour set 1307, in original box.

$150-250   **W&W**

A Britains US Airmen set 334, comprising six Marching Airmen in service dress with peak caps, brown belts and boots, all very good, rare figures to find in this condition.

$450-550   **VEC**

A Britains Farmers Gig, no. 20F, one shaft damaged, boxed.

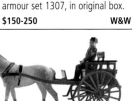

4.75in (12cm) wide

$120-180   **GAZE**

TOYS & GAMES

ESSENTIAL REFERENCE

- While Star Wars memorabilia covers such diverse areas as film props, posters, clothing, breakfast cereal boxes and Christmas ornaments, it is the toys, and especially the 3.75in action figures, that most fans associate with the subject and therefore tend to make the highest prices.
- The merchandising license was initially offered to Mego Corp., but they declined and it was eventually taken up by Kenner in the US and Palitoy in the UK.
- Before Star Wars, the standard size for action figures was 8 to 12in. Kenner chose to produce the figures at around 3.75in so spaceships like the Millennium Falcon could be in scale with the figures, something that would have been prohibitively expensive with the large figures. This also meant they could be sold more cheaply than the larger versions, making them a popular choice with parents as well as children.
- The first 12 figures were released in 1978 and were sold mounted on cards illustrating the 12 figures in the range.

These cards are known as '12-backs' and are generally the most sought-after today. As more figures were released, the card backs were updated. More toys were issued to coincide with each new film in the original trilogy but following the release of Return of the Jedi in 1983, the toy franchise was beginning to tire. The line was retired in 1985 but then resurrected in 1990. The recent prequel trilogy has resulted in a huge number of new toys being released.

- Today, the market for vintage toys has now leveled off as older collectors have mature collections, younger fans have little interest in the older characters, and a number of large collections have come to the market. Toys produced for the new trilogy are unlikely to reach the high prices of vintage examples today. While the films are aimed at the juvenile market, the toys are geared towards the collectors market where mint and boxed pieces are the norm, rather than the exception.

"Star Wars", issue 1, published by Marvel Comics, 1 July 1978, with 30¢ cover price.

Look for the edition of the first issue with the 35¢ cover price. It is possible as few as 1,500 copies where printed and it can be worth over 10 times as much as the regular 30¢ edition.

1978   10.25in (26cm) high

$25-35   KNK

A "Star Wars Punch Out and Make It" activity book, published by Random House.

1977   12in (30cm) high

$8-12   KNK

A "Star Wars Intergalactic Passport", first edition, by Ballantine Books, designed by Charles R. Bjorklund.

450 Intergalactic Passports were originally produced for visitors to the Empire Strikes Back set and can be worth over $600. This example was on release to the general public in far greater numbers.

1983   6in (15cm) high

$15-20   KNK

A Star Wars themed first day cover commemorating the Viking Mission to Mars, post dated 20th July 1978.

This card is dated five days before the Viking 2 orbitor failed due to a fuel leak. The lander continued to operate on the surface of Mars until 11th April, 1980.

1978   7in (17.5cm) wide

$20-25   KNK

A Star Wars: The Empire Strikes Back printed card party centerpiece, produced by Designware, unopened and unused.

c1980   14in (35.5cm) high

$25-35   KNK

A Star Wars: The Empire Strikes Back themed Puffs facial tissue box, illustrated with a scene from Bespin Cloud City, with 'cut-out and color' Luke Skywalker on the back.

Boxes with scenes from Hoth and Dagobah were also produced and each had one of two 'cut-out and color' scenes on the back.

1980   13.5in (34cm) high

$15-25   KNK

A Canadian Star Wars: Droids – The Adventures of R2-D2 and C-3PO 'R2-D2' action figure, by Kenner, mounted on dual language card with collectors coin.

The figures in this range are the same as those produced for the original movies, but are painted in 'cartoon' colors.

c1985   *Card 9in (23cm) high*

$100-150   **KNK**

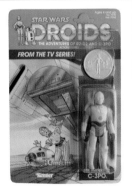

A Star Wars: Droids 'C-3PO' action figure, by Kenner, mounted with collectors coin.

Droids was a short-lived cartoon series, which aired with its companion series 'Ewoks'. A series of figures was released for the first series, of which Boba Fett (always a fan favourite) and Vlik, produced only in Brazil, are the most desirable.

c1985   *Card 9in (23cm) high*

$100-150   **KNK**

EXPERT EYE – AN UNLICENSED STAR WARS FIGURE

As official Star Wars figures were not licensed to Communist Europe, local toy manufacturers made molds from licensed figures.

Moving parts such as limbs were removed during the molding process and were often reassembled incorrectly. For example, this figure has the correct torso for an AT-AT Commander, but the limbs are from another figure.

Figures were also produced with differing details and colorings and this can make them sought-after by collectors. The Polish 'Stormtrooper' figure is bright blue and can be worth up to $800.

The card would appear to have been used for a number of different figures. While the 'AT-AT Commander' is an Imperial character, the card is illustrated with an Alliance Y-Wing starfighter.

An unlicensed Polish Star Wars: Return of the Jedi 'AT-AT Commander' action figure, unopened and mounted on a Polish language card with an illustration of an Y-Wing starfighter.

c1985   *Card 8.25in (21cm) high*

$300-400   **KNK**

A Star Wars 'Holographic Princess Leia' carded transparent action figure, by Hasbro, sold exclusively at the San Diego Comic-Con 2005, in mint condition.

The figure is taken from the 1998 Power of the Force II action figure.

2005   *9in (22.5cm) high*

$5-10   **MTB**

A Star Wars: Episode I 'Darth Sidious' carded action figure, by Hasbro, with 'Com Talk' chip, in mint condition.

9in (22.5cm) high

$4-8   **MTB**

A Star Wars: Episode I 'Watto' carded action figure, by Hasbro, with 'Com Talk' chip, mint and carded.

9in (22.5cm) high

$4-8   **MTB**

A Star Wars 'Imperial Cruiser' diecast ship, by Kenner, with sliding cargo bay doors to base, containing removable 'Rebel Blockade Runner' ship.

If the Rebel Blockade Runner is not present, the value falls to well below $10. The condition of the paintwork also affects the value considerably.

c1979   7in (18cm) long

$25-35   **KNK**

A Star Wars: Return of the Jedi '"Battle Damaged" Imperial TIE Fighter' vehicle, by Kenner, with decals and TIE fighter pilot.

These mid-sized models are hard to find, especially complete with the 'damage' decals and pilot. A button on the back of the cockpit collapses the 'wings'.

c1983   4.75in (12cm) high

$25-30   **KNK**

A scarce Star Wars: The Empire Strikes Back '"Battle Damaged" X-Wing Fighter' vehicle, by Kenner, with decals and pilot.

A button on the back of the cockpit collapses the nose.

c1982   7.75in (20.5cm) long

$25-30   **KNK**

A Star Wars: Return of The Jedi 'Laser Rifle Carry Case' action figure carrying case, by Kenner, with original card packaging.

This case was the last one produced by Kenner from their first range of cases. Compared to others in the range, such as 'C-3PO' and 'Darth Vader', this case held fewer figures and was also rather large for a child to carry, making it less popular. Its shape also meant it was often played with as a gun and suffered damage as a result. While this example is discolored, it does retain its cardboard base adding to the value.

c1984   25.5in (64.5cm) long

$80-100   **KNK**

EXPERT EYE – A STAR WARS DIECAST SHIP

The TIE Bomber was originally intended to feature in the original Star Wars film, but instead made its first, brief, appearance in The Empire Strikes Back.

An example with the original box could be worth nearly three times as much.

The white plastic wings have yellowed with age, while the diecast body has stayed white.

Planned for the second series of diecast ships by Kenner, a limited number of TIE Bombers were produced to test the market. Little interest was shown and the ship was never put into general production, making it scarce today.

A rare Star Wars: The Empire Strikes Back diecast 'TIE Bomber' ship, by Kenner.

c1979   5.25in (13cm) wide

$200-250   **KNK**

A Star Wars: The Empire Strikes Back 'Switcheroo' Darth Vader shaped lightswitch cover, by Kenner.

The eyes show red for 'on' and white for 'off'.

1980   6.25in (15.5cm) high

$15-25   **KNK**

A Star Wars: Return of the Jedi 'Wicket W. Warrick the Ewok' soft toy, by Kenner, with original head-dress, fabric tag and card tag, in near mint condition.

Kenner made five Ewok plush soft toys and Wicket is the most easily found as he was the most popular character. The value drops to $12-16 without head-dress and tags.
1983   14.75in (37.5cm) high
$20-25   **KNK**

A scarce Star Wars: Return of the Jedi 'Wiley' Wokling plush soft toy, by Kenner, with fabric tag, in excellent condition.

Wiley is Latara's little brother. Both characters featured in the ABC animated TV series 'Ewoks'.
1983
$8-12   **KNK**

A scarce Star Wars: Return of the Jedi 'Latara' Ewok plush soft toy, with head-dress and fabric tag, in excellent condition.

$20-25   **KNK**

A rare Star Wars: Return of the Jedi Ewoks plush soft toy shop display box, by Kenner.

As these boxes were usually thrown away by shops after use, they are rare today.
c1984   21in (53.5cm) wide
$150-200   **KNK**

A Star Wars: Return of the Jedi yellow vinyl child's raincoat, by Adam Joseph, with Yoda transfer to back.

A version with Darth Vader and the Imperial Guard on the back was also made.
1983   22.5in (57cm) long
$25-35   **KNK**

A Star Wars blue and white satin jacket, by Bright Red Group, with Greg and Tim Hildebrandt iron-on artwork to the back, and with woven badge to front, size 2.
c1977
$80-120   **NOR**

A pair of Star Wars: Return of the Jedi 'Darth Vader' roller skates, by Brookfield Athletic, with original box.

c1983
$40-60   **W&W**

A Star Wars: Return of the Jedi bag, by Frankel & Roth, with Jabba the Hutt and Bib Fortuna on one side and a hanger bay scene on the other.

c1983   12in (30.5cm) wide
$6-10   **W&W**

TOYS & GAMES

An A-Team 'Off Road Attack Cycle' molded plastic toy, by Galoob, mint and boxed.

Only the early pieces from this range are desirable to collectors.
c1983   5.5in (14cm) high
$90-110   MTB

A 1970s Alice in Wonderland 'Alice' doll, by Pedigree, based on the 1951 Walt Disney film, mint and boxed.

The doll is based on Pedigree's Sindy doll but with a slightly altered head. This makes it popular with collectors of Sindy dolls and Alice in Wonderland.
     Box 12in (30.5cm) high
$40-60   MTB

A World of Annie 'Annie' poseable figure, by Knickerbocker, modeled on the characters from the 1982 'Annie' musical film, mint and boxed.

The most popular figure from the full range of characters, Annie originally cost $2.
c1982   *Box 8.25in (21cm) high*
$15-25   MTB

A World of Annie 'Daddy Warbucks' poseable figure, by Knickerbocker, modeled on the characters from the 1982 'Annie' musical film.

c1982   *Box 8.25in (21cm) high*
$15-25   MTB

A World of Annie 'Punjab' poseable figure, by Knickerbocker, modeled on the characters from the 1982 'Annie' musical film.

This figure originally retailed for $2.97.

c1982   *Box 8in (20.5cm) high*
$15-25   MTB

A Battlestar Galactica 'Imperious Leader' action figure, by Mattel, mint and carded.

A range of 3.5in action figures were made, based on the Battlestar Galactica series, and the 'bad guys' were a popular subject. While Starbuck and Adama were recreated in miniature form, other popular characters such as Apollo and Boomer were curiously overlooked.
c1978   *9in (23cm) high*
$35-45   MTB

A Battlestar Galactica 'Ovion' action figure, by Mattel, mint and carded.
c1978   *9in (23cm) high*
$35-45   MTB

A Battlestar Galactica 'Cylon Raider' plastic toy, by Mattel, mint and boxed.

Initially the toy spaceships were produced with firing missiles but safety concerns lead to these missiles being removed.
c1978   *Box 9.75in (25cm) high*
$100-120   MTB

A 'Battlestar Galactica' spiral-bound notebook, by The Mead Corporation, with photographic cover showing Starbuck, Apollo, Boomer and a Colonial Viper firing.

c1978   10.75in (27cm) high

$7-10   BH

A Bionic Woman 'Jamie Sommers' action figure, by Denys Fisher and licensed by Universal Studio Inc., complete with clothes, in mint condition in factory sealed box.

c1975   Box 14in (15.5cm) high

$160-240   MTB

EXPERT EYE – A BUCK ROGERS ACTION FIGURE

Despite being well-made, figures from the Buck Rogers range did not prove popular. This may be partly due to the figures being based solely on the pilot movie, aired several months before the series began, and many of the characters did not become series regulars or were re-cast for the series.

Mego figures are prone to 'plastic melt', as can be seen by Buck's gray face. As the plastic degrades, a gas is released that discolors the plastic and, in bad cases, can freeze joints when the gas cannot escape from the packaging. If this example was not discolored it could be worth around $180.

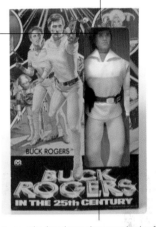

Perhaps due to their poor sales, boxed examples are not hard to find. A loose figure with all its clothing and accessories would be worth about $40. As Buck is one of the most popular characters from the series, his figure is one of the easiest to find.

A Buck Rogers in the 25th Century 'Buck Rogers' action figure, by Mego Corp., mint and boxed.

1979   Box 13.5in (34cm) high

$80-120   MTB

A Buck Rogers in the 25th Century 'Dr. Huer' action figure, by Mego Corp., mint and boxed with no discoloration.

Dr. Huer was less popular at the time, making him harder to find today.

13.5in (34cm) high

$140-180   MTB

A Buck Rogers in the 25th Century 'Draco' action figure, by Mego Corp., mint and boxed with no discoloration.

13.5in (34cm) high

$140-180   MTB

A Buck Rogers in the 25th Century 'Killer Kane' action figure, by Mego Corp., mint and boxed with no discoloration.

13.5in (34cm) high

$140-180   MTB

A Buck Roger in the 25th Century 'Walking Twiki' battery operated plastic figure, by Mego Corp., mint and boxed.

Box 8.25in (21cm) high

$60-100   **MTB**

A Charlie's Angels 'Sabrina' action figure, by Hasbro, licensed by Spelling Goldberg Productions, mint and carded.

c1977   12in (30.5cm) high

$90-110   **MTB**

A Charlie's Angels 'Jill' action figure, UK-issue by Hasbro, licensed by Spelling Goldberg Productions, mint and carded.

c1977   12in (30.5cm) high

$110-130   **MTB**

A Charlie's Angels boxed gift set, US-issue by Hasbro, comprizing 'Sabrina', 'Kris' and 'Kelly', mint and boxed.

Loose but complete, these figures can be worth around $10-15.

c1977   Box 12.25in (31cm) wide

$160-240   **MTB**

A Charlie's Angels 'The Slalom Caper' outfit set, by Hasbro, comprizing of two complete outfits.

c1977   Box 12in (30.48cm) high

$80-100   **MTB**

A Charlie's Angels 'Black Magic' outfit set, by Hasbro.

c1977   11in (27.94cm)

$70-90   **MTB**

A C.H.i.P.S. 'Ponch' action figure and motorbike, by Mego Corp., mint and carded.

Despite the popularity of the series, these figures were deemed unexciting by children at the time and were only available for a short period, making them rare today.

c1981   Card 8.5in (21.5cm) high

$60-80   **MTB**

A Chitty Chitty Bang Bang 'Truly Scrumptious' soft vinyl doll, by Mattel, mint and boxed.

Box 14.75in (37.5cm) high

$600-800   **MTB**

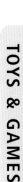

A Chitty Chitty Bang Bang plastic car, by Mattel and Gildrose Productions Ltd, complete with inflatable raft, characters and parts, in unopened packaging, mint and boxed.

This model inspired Corgi to release their diecast version of Chitty Chitty Bang Bang, however they chose not to include the inflatable raft. Examples in this condition with the box are extremely rare. The small parts were often lost or broken, particularly the windscreen.

1968   *Box 7in (18cm) wide*

$200-300   **MTB**

A Chitty Chitty Bang Bang 'Truly Scrumptious' soft vinyl talking doll, by Mattel, mint and boxed.

This talking version is more valuable than the non-talking version on the previous page. The boxes must be in mint condition to be worth this amount of money.

Box 14.75in (37.5cm) high

$800-1,000   **MTB**

A Dempsey and Makepeace action figure set, by Rainbow Toys, licensed by LWT, comprizing Lt. James Dempsey, Chief Supt. Gordon Spikings and a uniformed policeman, complete with accessories and in mint, carded condition.

c1984   *Card 11in (28cm) high*

$35-45   **MTB**

A Dukes of Hazzard 'Luke' action figure, by Mego Corp., mint and carded.

c1980   *11in (28cm) high*

$80-120   **MTB**

A Dune 'Fremen Tarpel Gun', by LJN, battery operated, mint and boxed.

Produced to coincide with the release of David Lynch's 1984 film version, the 'Tarpel Gun' does not appear in the original Frank Herbert novel.

c1984   *Box 11in (28cm) wide*

$60-80   **MTB**

A Dune 'Sand Scout' battery operated vehicle, by LJN, mint and carded.

The rarest toy from this scarce range is the 'Sandworm', and is hidden under the 'Top Secret' banner above. It seems few were ever sold and today they can be worth over $300.

c1984   *10in (25cm) wide*

$40-60   **MTB**

A Happy Days boardgame, by Parker Bros., complete and boxed.

c1976   *Box 18.25in (46.5cm) wide*

$12-18   **BH**

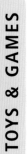

An International Velvet 'Sarah Velvet Brown' action figure, by Kenner, complete with clothing, mint and boxed.

1978   13.25in (33.5cm) high

$70-90   MTB

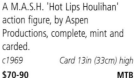

A M.A.S.H. 'Hot Lips Houlihan' action figure, by Aspen Productions, complete, mint and carded.

c1969   Card 13in (33cm) high

$70-90   MTB

A Mork & Mindy 'Mindy' doll, by Mattel, mint and boxed.

c1979   9.75in (25cm) high

$80-100   MTB

A Mork & Mindy 'Mork' talking doll, by Mattel, mint and boxed.

As with most Mattel talking dolls, Mork is made to speak by pulling a cord in his back, which operates a small spinning record. This mechanism was notorious for breaking easily. Examples with broken mechanisms are worth about a third less than this example.

1979

$110-130   Box 14.25in (36cm) high   MTB

A Muppet Show 'Rowlf' figure, by Bendy Toy, mint and boxed.

1980   Box 8.75in (22cm) high

$30-50   MTB

A Police Woman 'Sgt. Leanne "Pepper" Anderson' action figure, by Horseman Dolls, USA, in original box.

Box 12in (30.48cm) high

$50-80   MTB

A Robotech 'Miriya' action figure, by Harmony Gold, mint and carded.

Robotech was adapted from three Japanese mecha anime series, which were re-written and dubbed into English. This combination resulted in three 'generations', with story arcs taken from each of the original series. A number of follow-up films and series were planned but only some were released. This character is based on 'Milia Fallyna Jenius' from The Super Dimension Fortress Macross, which formed the first generation of Robotech.

c1992   9in (22.5cm) high

$15-20   MTB

A Robotech 'Rook Bartley' action figure, by Harmony Gold, mint and carded.

Rook is based on the character Houquet et Rose from 'Genesis Climber MOSPEADA', which formed the third generation of the Robotech storyline.

c1992   9in (22.5cm) high

$15-20   MTB

A Robotech 'Micronized Zentraedi Warrior' action figure, by Harmony Gold, mint and carded.

The evil Zentraedi appeared as giants in the animated show and the original Zentraedi figures made by Matchbox were much larger than the Robotech figures, although not to scale. This is a 'Micronized' figure, so it the same size as the human characters.

c1992   9in (22.5cm) high
$15-20   MTB

A Six Million Dollar Man 'Steve Austin' action figure, by Denys Fisher, in mint condition, complete with carrying case.

Mint and boxed, the value can rise to $150-250. The case on its own can be worth $15.

12.75in (32.5cm) high
$25-35   MTB

A Space 1999 'Commander Koenig' action figure, by Mattel, mint and carded.

These figures are rare, particularly in unopened, mint condition.

1975   12in (30.5cm) high
$100-150   MTB

A Space 1999 'Doctor Russell' action figure, no. 9544, by Mattel, mint and carded.

The rarest 9in figure is the alien 'Zython'. Planned for release in 1976, the figure was dropped from production and only a few examples, possibly samples or prototypes, were released. The second, and final, season of the series was not as successful as the first and this may account for further toys not being released.

1975   12in (30.5cm) high
$100-150   MTB

A Star Trek – The Motion Picture 'Klingon' action figure, by Mego Corp., with signs of discoloration to his face, mint and boxed.

The modelling of the Klingon's head differs greatly from the action figure produced for the original Star Trek series. In the original series the Klingons generally appear human. For the first motion picture, an increased budget for make-up and better techniques meant the race was redesigned with the now typical ridged forehead, and the new figure reflects this. This change was given an official explanation in the Star Trek: Enterprise episodes "Affliction" and "Divergence".

1979   Box 12.5in (32cm) high
$100-150   MTB

A Starsky & Hutch 'Starsky' action figure, by Mego Corp., mint and carded.

1975   9.25in (23cm) high
$60-100   MTB

A Meccano no. 01 Constructor Car, expertly repainted in cream and red with a number of spare components including seat, hood and others.

$400-600   VEC

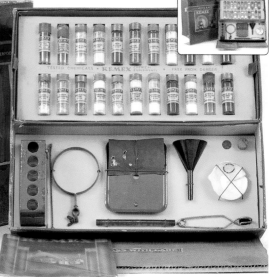

A Hornby Meccano Racer 3 speedboat, finished in two-tone blue and white, contained in original box with key and instruction booklet dated "12/37", in very good condition.

$500-700   VEC

A rare Meccano 'Kemmex 2B' outfit, including glassware, chemical bottles, stand, funnel and other items, together with the instruction booklet for outfits no. 2 and no. 3, contents in good to excellent condition, box in fair condition.

c1933-34

$700-900   VEC

An American Hubley cast iron Racing Car, in light brown with black driver, plated wheels, operating engine cylinders, some wear to edges, otherwise in good condition.

31.75in (27cm) long

$80-120   VEC

An American Kingsbury pressed steel clockwork two-door coupé, yellow with black chassis, opening rear Dickey seat, wired for electric lights, some cracking to the rubber tires and light wear, with key.

12.5in (32cm) long

$360-440   VEC

An American Wyandotte pressed steel WWII Navy Airplane model, with blue wings, silver fuselage, 'US Navy' stencil, four engines and some scratching to paintwork.

c1944   14.5in (37cm) wide

$600-800   BER

An early 1960s Louis Marx plastic friction-powered 'Vanwall Racing Car', made in Hong Kong, in mint condition with original box.

Box 6.25in (16cm) long

$30-50   MTB

A rare French Marx Toys plastic La France Pumper Fire Truck, with silver-colored upper, yellow removable plastic ladder, friction drive with siren, in excellent condition, with good condition illustrated card box with French printing.

9.5in (24cm) long

$140-200   VEC

ESSENTIAL REFERENCE

- Chess, in its closest format to the game known today, is thought to have originated in 6thC India, where it was known as 'Chaturanga'. However, a similar game was developed in China during the 2ndCBC. Today's rules were set down in Italy during the 15thC, but it wasn't until the 18thC and 19thC that the game mushroomed in popularity.
- Although older sets are known, collectors are most likely to come across those dated no earlier than the late 18thC, but most will date from the 19thC and 20thC. The game of chess crosses language barriers and is internationally played, so sets were produced in many countries, with the Eastern export markets of China and India being particularly strong. Sets were also made in the UK and the rest of Europe.
- The form and style of figures differ from country to country, as does the material used. Ivory was commonly used in India and China, with hardwoods the favored material in Europe, although bone and ceramic were also used. Styles

also changed over time, particularly during the late 18thC and early 19thC, with some named after famous chess players or locations.
- The quality of the carving affects value. Eastern sets are usually intricately carved. Most central European sets, and those by the best London makers, although well-carved, are simpler. Sets should be complete and undamaged to be of interest to most collectors, unless very early or very well-carved. Boxes can add value, particularly if they were made for the set, or are similarly well-made.
- The market continues to be strong, with interest across the globe. Although the Internet sees a lively trade, the traditional auction world offers some of the highest quality sets available. Older, good quality sets are becoming harder to find and more valuable, meaning previously less expensive versions are rising in value. Before buying or selling, learn about any national limitations on the trade and transport of ivory and certain woods and bones.

An English ivory chess set by John Calvert, one side stained red, the other natural, kings with double 'fountains', queens with single 'fountains', bishops with miters, knights as horses' heads, rooks as turrets, white king signed "Calvert Maker 189 Fleet Strt London".
c1810   *King 3.5in (9cm) high*

$2,400-3,600   **BLO**

An English ivory chess set by John Calvert, with one side stained red, the other natural, kings with Maltese crosses and punched decoration, queens with fleur-de-lys , bishops with open miters, knights as horses' heads, rooks as turrets, white king signed, "Calvert Maker 189 Fleet Strt London".

John Calvert, a member of the Worshipful Company of Turners, was located at Fleet Street, London, from c1790 to 1840. He specialized in finely detailed chess sets for the English aristocracy and London coffee shops, where chess was a popular pastime. This type, typified by the other examples on this page, was reproduced later in the mid-19thC by John Jaques and Lund. Many 'Old English' pieces are 'monobloc', ie; made from a single piece of wood.
c1810

$3,000-4,000   **BLO**

An English ivory chess set by John Calvert, one side stained red, the other natural, kings with double pierced 'fountains', queens with single 'fountains', bishops with miters, knights as horses' heads, rooks as turrets, the white king signed "Calvert Maker 189 Fleet Strt London".
c1810   *King 3.5in (9cm) high*

$2,400-3,600   **BLO**

A 19thC English small-size 'Lund' pattern ivory chess set, one side natural, the other stained red, kings with Maltese crosses, queens with reeded ball finials, bishops with miters, knights as horses' heads, rooks as turrets, pawns with reeded ball finials, in mahogany box.
                           King 2.75in (7cm) high

$500-700   **BLO**

A weighted machined-brass chess set, by Carlton of England, one side with black patination, the other in unfinished brass, knights with horses' heads, lead heads on brass side, stamped "Carlton England", in wooden box with sliding lid.
c1930   *King 3.25in (8cm) high*

$340-400   **BLO**

A 19thC English 'Old English' pattern chess set, one side in rosewood, the other in boxwood, kings surmounted with Maltese crosses, queens with ball finials topped with spikes, bishops as miters, knights as horses' heads, rooks as turrets, pawns with ball finials.

King 4.75in (12cm) high

$400-600 **BLO**

A 19thC 'Old English' pattern boxwood and ebonized chess set, the king and queens with ball finials, knights as horses' heads and bishops as miters.

King 4.75in (12cm) high

$200-300 **BLO**

EXPERT EYE – AN 'OLD ENGLISH' CHESS SET

The turned single-piece forms identify this as being in the 'Old English' style, particularly the handling of the rook and the rounded disks on the other pieces.

This set may be by Jaques considering the precise design. It is also a large, weighted set.

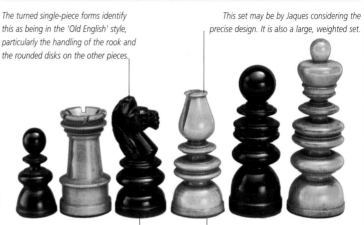

Always examine knights carefully, as they had to be carved rather than turned – the better and more finely detailed the carving, the greater the set is likely to be worth.

The bases have been re-covered with felt over the original pads, and the set has possibly been revarnished at some point, but the 'toffee' patination is attractive and desirable.

A 19thC English 'Old English' pattern boxwood and ebony large-size weighted chess set, probably re-varnished and with new felt bases.

King 4.75in (12cm) high

$1,000-1,200 **BLO**

An English silver and silver-gilt chess set, the kings surmounted with crosses, queens with petal-shaped tops, and bishops with miters and chased crucifix decoration, with hallmarks for Birmingham, 1974, in a leather covered and gilt-tooled casket.

1974 *King 4in (10cm) high*

$4,400-5,200 **BLO**

An unusual 19thC Scottish boxwood and ebony chess set, in a late 19thC brass-mounted oak box with steel carrying handle.

This unusual set is similar in style to both the 'Staunton' and 'Edinburgh Upright' forms and, partly due to the latter, is most probably Scottish in origin.

King 4in (10cm) high

$900-1,100 **BLO**

A 'Silette' Catalin chess set, by Grays of Cambridge, with one side black, the other side yellow, in mahogany box with sliding lid.

c1925 *King 2.75in (7cm) high*

$180-240 **BLO**

An English 'Rose Chess' set, one side black, the other side red, in original card box.

King 2.25in (6cm) high

$300-400 **BLO**

A 19thC Jaques 'In Status Quo' traveling chess set, with bone pieces stained red and natural, in mahogany board, signed, "J. Jaques & Son, Makers, London".

Board 9in (23cm) wide

$760-840 **BLO**

ESSENTIAL REFERENCE – STAUNTON SETS

As chess became ever more popular during the late 18thC and early 19thC, demand grew for a standardized set. The vast array of styles available were typically tall and cumbersome in play. Also, a different style may put certain players off their game, being unfamiliar. In 1849, legendary sports and games equipment maker, John Jaques of London, England, devised a set that would become the standard across the world. Attributed to his brother-in-law, Nathaniel Cook, the design was registered in March 1849. The set is characterized by simple curving necks on a standard base, each topped with a different 'head' representing the piece. As well as being elegant and well-proportioned, it was also easy and economical to carve and produce. It was given the name 'Staunton' in honor of the then chess world champion, Howard Staunton (1810-74), who endorsed and promoted it heavily. Weighted sets, like this one, and those carved from ivory are highly desirable. Green is a rare color. 'Staunton pattern' sets that were not made by Jaques tend to be less desirable.

A 19thC Jaques 'Staunton' weighted boxwood and ebony chess set, the white king stamped, "Jaques London", in mahogany box.

$3,000-4,000   BLO

A 19thC Jaques 'Staunton' weighted boxwood and ebony chess set, both kings stamped, "Jaques London", in mahogany box.

King 4in (10cm) high

$2,000-3,000   BLO

A 19thC Jaques 'Staunton' boxwood and ebony chess set, the white king stamped "Jaques London", in mahogany box with sliding lid.

King 3.5in (9cm) high

$1,100-1,300   BLO

A mid-19thC Jaques 'Staunton' boxwood and ebony chess set, the white king stamped "Jaques London", including a number of pieces with chipped collars and other areas, and loss to varnish.

King 3.25in (8.5cm) high

$200-300   BLO

A Jaques 'Staunton' ivory chess set, one side stained red, the other natural, in red leather mounted casket of sarcophagus shape with "The Staunton Chessmen" on lid.

Ivory Staunton sets are scarcer than wood, particularly when well-carved, as this set is. The box is both appealing and rare, and adds to the desirability and value.

Casket 7in (18cm) wide

$8,000-10,000   BLO

A 20thC Staunton-style boxwood and ebony weighted chess set, one side in boxwood, the other side black.

King 4.25in (11cm) high

$360-440   BLO

TOYS & GAMES

A Chinese export Cantonese ivory figural 'King George' chess set, one side stained red, the other side natural, the Chinese versus the Europeans, white king and queen as King George III and Queen Charlotte of the UK.

c1810   *King 5.5in (14cm) high*

$3,600-4,400   **BLO**

An early 19thC Chinese export ivory 'Bust' chess set, one side stained red, the other side natural, the king and queen as monarchs' heads, bishops as mandarins or counselors, knights as horses' heads, rooks as turrets with flags, pawns as foot soldiers.

King 3.5in (9cm) high

$2,400-3,600   **BLO**

EXPERT EYE – A CHINESE EXPORT CHESS SET

The style of carving on both sides is identical, so we can be sure that this is a complete set from one workshop.

Chinese export sets are usually stained in red, with green being a very unusual and rare color.

As with other Cantonese sets, the carving is typically complex, with many fine details.

Each side has an identical European king and consort queen, which is another rare feature. European monarchs are usually limited to one side, or do not appear at all.

A Chinese export Cantonese ivory 'King George' chess set, one side stained green, the other side left natural, kings as King George III of Great Britain, queens as Charlotte, his consort, bishops as clergy, knights as rearing horses, rooks as elephants bearing towers, pawns as foot soldiers with shields and raised spears.

c1800   *King 5in (12.5cm) high*

$5,000-6,000   **BLO**

An early 19thC Cantonese 'Burmese' pattern ivory chess set, one side stained red, the other natural, the chessmen with intricate carved foliate decoration, knights as horses' heads, rooks as turrets with flags, the white rook with the United Kingdom Union flag.

King 3.25in (8cm) high

$900-1,100   **BLO**

A 20thC Chinese hardwood 'puzzleball' chess set, made in Hong Kong, one side in boxwood, the other side in coromandel, kings surmounted with crosses, queens with crowns, bishops with split miters, knights as horses, rooks as turrets, pawns with spire finials, contained in a wooden box.

King 6in (15.5cm) high

$140-180   **BLO**

An early 19thC Chinese export Cantonese ivory king chess piece, the figure depicting an Emperor or Chinese Worthy, holding a fan in his right hand, with pearls around his neck and a pigtail under his cap, seated on a Chinese-style chair or throne.

Early or finely carved single pieces can hold a value of their own. This sculptural and realistic piece is one such example.

3.5in (9cm) high

$560-640   **BLO**

A 19thC Indian export ivory chess set, one side stained green, the other side left natural, kings with pierced tops and spray finials, over nautical crown collars, queens with bud finials, bishops with feathered miters, knights as horses' heads, rooks as rusticated turrets with spire finials, pawns with baluster knops, in a mahogany and boxwood inlaid box/board.

King 3in (7.5cm) high

$600-800   **BLO**

An early 19thC Indian ivory chess set, probably from Vizagapatam, one side stained red, the other side natural, kings with large reeded ball finials over castelated galleries, queens similar in smaller size, bishops with unusually shaped miters, knights as horses' heads, rooks with spiked or petal-shaped finials, pawns with baluster knops.

King 3.25in (8cm) high

$2,000-3,000   **BLO**

A 19thC Anglo-Indian 'Staunton' pattern ivory chess set, one side stained red, the other side left natural, in a mahogany box with a sliding lid.

King 2.75in (7cm) high

$800-1,200   **BLO**

A 20thC Indian carved stone chess set, one side black, the other side a light green color, kings with pierced crowns, queens similar, bishops with further pierced decoration and elongated finials, knights as horses' heads, rooks as turrets, pawns with domes, all raised on circular bases, together with a wooden box carved with intricate floral patterns.

King 2.75in (7cm) high

$100-140   **BLO**

An East India (John Company) ivory sepoy (Indian soldier) pawn, wearing a shako, pearls around neck, holding a musket.

c1850   *3.125in (8cm) high*

$360-440   **BLO**

An 18thC collection of Indian ivory chessmen, from Rajasthan, including two elephant kings, two elephant queens, four temple bishops or rooks, three horsemen knights and 12 foot soldier pawns, with polychrome decoration, some restoration.

King 3.25in (8cm) high

$6,500-7,500   **BLO**

A 19thC French 'Régence' pattern boxwood and ebony chess set, with rosewood, boxwood and mahogany edged chess board.

This set is so-named due to its association with the Café de la Régence in Paris, France, during the mid-19thC. A haunt of Voltaire, Diderot and Benjamin Franklin, it was a popular place for thinkers and 'celebrities' to play chess.

King 3.5in (9cm) high

$440-560   **BLO**

TOYS & GAMES

An early German tennis-themed printed card and tinplate dexterity game, marked "Germany".

1.5in (3.5cm) diam

$60-90   **BH**

A 1920s-30s English 'Performing Seal' printed tinplate, card and glass dexterity game, printed "Made in England".

Note how different makers in different countries copied each other when a scene proved popular.

2.25in (5.5cm) diam

$40-60   **BH**

A 1920s-30s German 'Performing Seals' dexterity game, with mirror back, printed "Made in Germany".

2.25in (5.5cm) diam

$30-50   **BH**

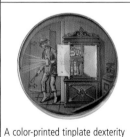

A 1920s-30s German 'Wer Gewinnt – Rot Oder Blau' printed card and tinplate hockey dexterity game, with mirror back and star-printed paper insert inside.

The text translates as 'Who will win? Red or blue?'.

2.25in (5.5cm) diam

$35-45   **BH**

A 1920s 'Drivers' printed card and tinplate dexterity game, with mirror back.

Sporting or automotive themes are very popular and are usually more valuable. This is due to added demand from sporting or automobilia collectors. Examples such as the three on this page are also interesting as they show early forms of dress. This example also shows an early car.

2.25in (3.5cm) diam

$60-90   **BH**

A color-printed tinplate dexterity game, probably German.

Here the old man has come down from his bedroom, having been disturbed by a burglar. The aim of the game is to get both of the hinged, reflective cupboard doors closed.

2.5in (6cm) diam

$50-70   **BH**

An early German printed card and metal dexterity game.

The aim of the game is to place the balls on the girl's earlobes, to give her earrings.

1.75in (4.5cm) diam

$45-55   **BH**

A printed tinplate and card dexterity game, possibly French, showing a lady in a hat.

1.5in (4cm) diam

$30-40   **BH**

A 1920s-30s German double-sided red and green star dexterity game, marked '"D.R.G.M."

2in (5cm) diam

$45-55   **BH**

An early R. Journet 'The Dovecote Puzzle' paper-covered wood and glass dexterity game.

5.5in (14cm) high

$30-50　　　　BH

An R. Journet 'The Stork Puzzle' paper-covered wood and glass dexterity game.

Typical of Journet, the game is more complex than just trying to get the plastic pods into the 'bed' slots. Boys are black pods and girls are pink pods – each has to be matched against the respective male or female names.

5in (12.5cm) wide

$80-130　　　　BH

An R. Journet 'Pootles The Pup' paper-covered wood and glass dexterity game.

4.5in (12cm) high

$80-120　　　　BH

An R. Journet 'The Salmon Tin Puzzle' dexterity game, with red tinplate salmon.

Even the tin has an unseen printed paper 'label' around it.

3.5in (8.5cm) high

$100-150　　　　BH

ESSENTIAL REFERENCE – ROBERT JOURNET

Robert Journet started a toy shop in 1878, in Paddington, London, England. Puzzles were initially made by his father during the 1890s, but this expanded to an increasingly large team when sales mushroomed after the company attended trade fairs. Quality remained high, with paper-covered wood frames, vibrantly colored and detailed images and innovative themes. Exports grew rapidly, and the US became a major market. From the 1920s onwards, the company grew to become the most popular producers of 'Popular Perplexing Puzzles' in the world. In 1965, it was sold to Abbey Corinthian Games who continued to produce the puzzles into the 1970s. The growing popularity of the board game and the arrival of the home computer and electronic games led to a decline in sales, and the range was discontinued. The back of each puzzle advertised the other games available (starting at no. 50) and acts as a handy checklist for collectors, although variations of popular games do exist, widening the variety available.

An R. Journet 'The Brooch Puzzle' printed card and paper-covered wood dexterity game.

Note the nicely decorated embossed paper frame. Like many Journet games, the reverse bears a label showing the many games the company produced.

4.5in (11cm) high

$70-100　　　　BH

An R. Journet 'The Whirlpool Puzzle' paper-covered card and glass dexterity game.

5.25in (13cm) high

$15-25　　　　BH

An R. Journet 'Motorist Puzzle' paper-covered wood and glass dexterity game, signed "R.J. London".

5.25in (13cm) wide

$25-35　　　　BH

An R. Journet 'Four Leaf Clover' printed tinplate and glass dexterity game.

4.25in (10.5cm) high

$28-32　　　　BH

An R. Journet 'The Television Puzzle' paper-covered wood and glass dexterity game.

This can be dated to the early 1950s from the style of the TV set. Television, at that time, was just beginning to proliferate in homes across the Western world. When the coronation of Queen Elizabeth II took place in 1953, 2.5million TV sets were in use across the UK.

5in (12.5cm) high

$30-50 BH

An R. Journet 'The Hand-Some Puzzle' paper-covered wood and glass dexterity game, made for Woolworths.

3.25in (8.5cm) high

$40-60 BH

An R.Journet 'The Green Eyed Kitty Puzzle' paper-covered wood and glass dexterity game, and made for Woolworths, printed "Made in England".

The use of the yellow card and red box is typical of R. Journet. Journet made a series of 12 dexterity games for Woolworths.

2.5in (9cm) high

$80-120 BH

An early 1940s 'V For Victory' printed card, metal and glass dexterity game, printed "Made in U.S.A."

The aim of the game is to fill up the 'V' with the colored rods and fill the holes with silver balls.

5.25in (13cm) high

$25-35 BH

EXPERT EYE – A DEXTERITY GAME

This game is by a named US maker, and is thus desirable. It is a more difficult version of the 'put the ball in the hole' game and this also makes it sought-after.

Games with individual themes are often more desirable and valuable. As quins are an unusual subject, this is rare.

Although not dated, this is likely to have been made in late 1934. In May that year the Dionne Quintuplets were born, becoming the first identical quins to survive birth.

This is borne out by the style of the wording, and the general style and choice of colors, which are all strongly Art Deco.

A James R. Irvin & Co. Inc. of Chicago printed card and tinplate 'Quintuplets The Five Baby Game' dexterity game.

4.5in (11cm) high

$35-45 BH

A 1930s Japanese printed paper-over-card and glass dexterity game, showing an owl perched on a branch with a town in the background, marked "Made in Japan".

2.5in (6cm) high

$30-50 BH

A 1940s American 'Flight Formation' painted tin, card and glass dexterity game.

5.25in (13cm) wide

$35-45 BH

A 1940s 'Wot! No Eyes?' printed card, paper-over-card and glass dexterity game.

Known as Chad or Kilroy, this popular form of graffito was first seen during WWI, primarily in response to rationing, where any particular item could be added after "Wot no...".

2.5in (6.5cm) high

$40-60 BH

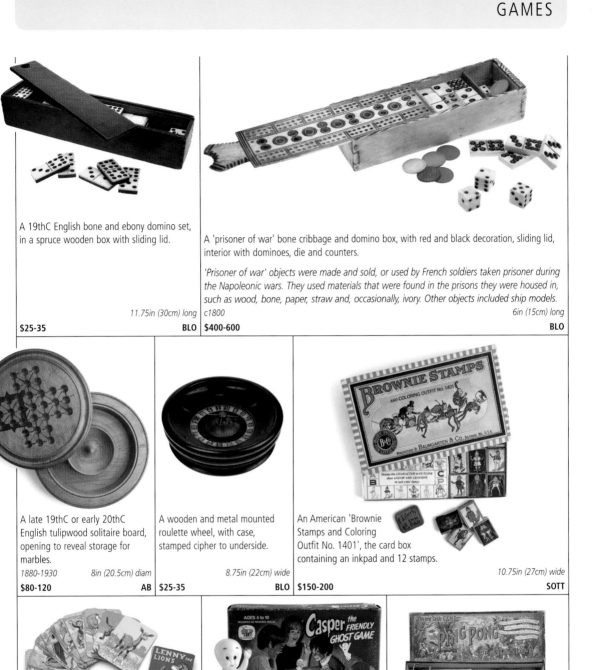

A 19thC English bone and ebony domino set, in a spruce wooden box with sliding lid.

11.75in (30cm) long

$25-35 BLO

A 'prisoner of war' bone cribbage and domino box, with red and black decoration, sliding lid, interior with dominoes, die and counters.

'Prisoner of war' objects were made and sold, or used by French soldiers taken prisoner during the Napoleonic wars. They used materials that were found in the prisons they were housed in, such as wood, bone, paper, straw and, occasionally, ivory. Other objects included ship models.

c1800 6in (15cm) long

$400-600 BLO

A late 19thC or early 20thC English tulipwood solitaire board, opening to reveal storage for marbles.

1880-1930 8in (20.5cm) diam

$80-120 AB

A wooden and metal mounted roulette wheel, with case, stamped cipher to underside.

8.75in (22cm) wide

$25-35 BLO

An American 'Brownie Stamps and Coloring Outfit No. 1401', the card box containing an inkpad and 12 stamps.

10.75in (27cm) wide

$150-200 SOTT

A set of 1950s 'Lenny The Lion's Snap!' playing cards, with original box.

3.75in (9.5cm) high

$20-30 MTB

A Schaper Manufacturing Company 'Casper The Friendly Ghost' board game, licenced by Harvey Friendly Comics Inc.

1974 11.5in (29cm) wide

$25-35 SOTT

A J. Jaques & Son and Hamley Bros. 'Ping Pong or Gossima' set, including two vellum covered bats, with original box, in very good condition.

c1900 Box 18.5in (47cm) long

$100-150 VEC

WATCHES

ESSENTIAL REFERENCE

- Interest in vintage wristwatches, and wristwatches in general, has grown over the past few years. This has been led by attention from men's fashion magazines, and a generally smarter and more luxurious look returning to fashion. Wristwatches are now more widely sought-after not only by collectors, but by those wishing to own an elegant watch different from high street examples. Many also buy as an investment, particularly high quality, complex watches, or those produced in limited editions.

- There are a number of indicators to value, including the maker, the complexity of the movement, the style and the materials used. High-end brands such as Patek Philippe and Rolex will always be sought-after due to their high quality. Within their ranges, iconic models will be the most desirable. The more complex a watch is, the more it is likely to be worth; chronographs and watches with extra features such as moon phases, alarms or perpetual calendars will usually be valuable.

- The style of a watch can also help you to date it, as well as adding value. Small, round pocket watch-like examples generally date from the early 20thC. Rectangular watches are typically 1930s, although examples were produced in the 1950s too. From the late 1940s onwards, watch cases became more stylized and innovative in form, often taking on period jewelry styles. During the 1950s, simple circular styles with pared down faces were also popular. During the late 1960s and '70s, watches became strongly influenced by fashion and often had large, sculptural cases and futuristic styles.

A 1930s Hamilton 'Perry' wristwatch, with white gold-filled oval dial, luminous hands and markers, and Hamilton 987 17-jewel movement.

White gold-filled versions of this watch are always a little more valuable than yellow gold-filled, as they are rarer.

$300-380   ML

A 1930s Hamilton 'Perry' wristwatch, with yellow gold-filled oval dial, luminous hands and markers, and Hamilton 987 17-jewel movement.

$275-325   ML

A 1930s Hamilton 'Sidney' wristwatch, the gold-filled case with 18ct solid gold applied numbers, and 17-jewel movement.

Interestingly, all applied numbers on Hamilton watches from the 1930s are solid gold, regardless of whether the case is solid gold or not.

$175-250   ML

A 1930s Hamilton 'Cushion' wristwatch, with 10ct yellow gold-filled shaped case, silvered dial with luminous 'exploding' Arabic numbers and subsidiary seconds dial at six o'clock, and 17-jewel movement.

$225-275   ML

A 1930s Hamilton 'Greenwich' wristwatch, the yellow gold-filled case with stepped bezel, white dial with luminous hands and numbers, subsidiary seconds dial at six o'clock, and 17-jewel movement.
c1931

$275-325   ML

A 1930s Hamilton wristwatch, with white gold-filled 'cut corner' case, white dial with black Arabic numerals, and Hamilton 17-jewel movement.

$250-300   ML

A 1930s Hamilton 'Square B' wristwatch, with white gold-filled case, white dial with luminous numbers, subsidiary seconds dial at six o'clock, and Hamilton 987 17-jewel movement.

This case is typical of the 1930s and can also be found with engraved decoration.

$275-325　　　　ML

A 1940s Hamilton 'Myron' wristwatch, with curving rectangular 10ct gold-filled case, silvered dial with Arabic numerals, subsidiary seconds dial at six o'clock, and Hamilton 980 17-jewel movement.

This is a very popular watch due to the shaped lugs.

$175-225　　　　ML

EXPERT EYE – A HAMILTON WRISTWATCH

This is an early driver's watch, and was introduced in c1938.

The curved case was made to fit on the side of the wrist so that it could be more easily seen when driving.

A 1930s Hamilton 'Stanley' wristwatch, with yellow gold-filled case, solid gold applied numbers and subsidiary seconds dial at six o'clock, and Hamilton 401 17-jewel movement.

The 401 is the rarest of Hamilton's movements. Only a few of the desirable Stanley models were fitted with this movement, making this example doubly desirable. c1931

$700-800　　　　ML

The overall elongated rectangular shape is typical of 1930s watches.

The streamlined tapered and curved form is reminiscent of automobile design, such as a radiator grille, and is an appealing feature.

A late 1930s Hamilton 'Brooke' wristwatch, with shaped gold-filled case, subsidiary seconds dial at six o'clock, and 17-jewel movement.

$450-500　　　　ML

A 1930s Hamilton 'Sienna' wristwatch, with 14ct solid gold elongated case, and Hamilton 982 19-jewel movement.

Although similar to the Linwood, the case is not as long, nor as curved, as that watch. Fewer of this model were made in solid 14ct gold, so rarity accounts for much of its value.

$600-700　　　　ML

A 1930s Hamilton Art Deco wristwatch, the platinum rectangular case with hooded 'barrel' lugs, diamond markers, and Hamilton 980 17-jewel movement.

The hooded 'barrel' lugs are a typical feature of 1930s watches.

$2,200-2,500　　　　ML

A 1930s Hamilton wristwatch, the 14ct solid white gold case with ribbed bezel at the top and bottom, diamond-set dial, subsidiary seconds dial at six o'clock, and Longines 17-jewel movement.

Many diamond dial watches have curved or cut crystals to accommodate the diamonds which protrude from the dial.

$850-1,050　　　　ML

WATCHES

A 1950s Swiss Movado wristwatch, with gold-filled case, and a Zenith 17-jewel manual wind movement.

$175-250   ML

A 1940s Movado chronograph, with 18ct solid gold case, and 17-jewel movement, signed on the case, dial and movement.

The presence of pulsations at the end of a time period and the additional registers may indicate that this was an aviator's watch.

$2,200-2,500   ML

A 1950s Movado 'Kingmatic' wristwatch, with stainless steel case, the silvered face with day and date apertures, and 28-jewel movement.

This was a high quality and expensive watch during the 1950s. The back is stamped "Sub-Sea" indicating it is waterproof.

$250-300   ML

A limited edition Swiss Franck Muller 'Endurance 24' manual-wind chronograph wristwatch, from an edition of 500, with stainless steel case, true 24-hour orange dial, and original signed Franck Muller strap.

Surprisingly, manuals are worth more than automatics, as fewer were made. Born in 1958, Franck Muller is known as the 'master of complications' due to his highly complex watches. He studied at the famous Geneva School of Watchmaking and launched his first watches in 1983. The car racing theme is also desirable.
1995

$4,000-5,000   ML

EXPERT EYE – A ROLEX 'BUBBLE BACK'

The 'bubble back' was launched in 1934 and was produced until the 1950s – the reference number allows this watch to be dated to around 1942-45.

Look out for the 'hooded' version, filled in between the lugs, which was introduced in 1941. It was not as popular making it rarer today.

The term 'bubble back' refers to the bulging back containing a rotor that moved 360 degrees – its size required a thicker case.

The case is made from solid gold, and is in excellent condition with the original face and intact back milling, hence the high value.

A Rolex 'Bubble Back' wristwatch, with 14ct solid yellow gold case, and 18-jewel automatic movement, reference no. 3131.

$2,700-3,300   ML

A 1960s Omega 'Constellation' wristwatch, the stainless steel case with 'Observatory' back, and Omega Caliber 561 24-jewel movement with five adjustments.

As this contains a 561 movement, it is deemed a true Constellation. In 2007, an Omega Constellation Grand Luxe in platinum from 1958 sold for $351,000 setting the world record price for an Omega watch.

$600-800   ML

A late 1950s Rolex 'Air King' Oyster Perpetual automatic wristwatch, with brushed stainless steel case and band, and signed Rolex 26-jewel full-rotor movement.

Introduced in the late 1950s, the Air King is one of the less valuable Rolex watches, but is still of excellent quality.

$1,100-1,300   ML

A 1930s Swiss Art Deco Semca wristwatch, the yellow and white gold case with engraved bezel, and 15-jewel movement.

This was intended for the Swiss or Canadian market, rather than the US or European market.

$375-450   ML

A 1970s Tressa Lux 'Spaceman' automatic wristwatch, designed by André Le Marquand the brushed stainless steel oval case with black face, and original 'Corfam' plastic strap.

Values drop by more than a third if the strap has been replaced or is in poor condition.

$160-240   RSS

A Tudor military-style 'Ranger' wristwatch, with stainless steel Oyster case, matching articulated strap, black dial, and ETA 25-jewel movement.

Tudor is a sub-brand of Rolex, and was launched in 1945. Other sub-brands include Unicorn and Rolco.

$650-750   ML

A 1990s Swiss Universal 'Compax' manual-wind chronograph wristwatch, the white dial with three registers, sapphire crystal, and signed Universal Geneve 31-jewel movement, signed seven times.

A desirable watch, the manual version is rarer than the automatic. In solid gold this watch could be worth $6,000-7,000.

$1,200-1,500   ML

A 1930s Waltham Ford Merit Club presentation watch, with elongated white gold-filled case, silvered dial with gold Arabic Art Deco style markers, and 17-jewel movement.

Presentation engravings usually devalue a watch, however this example was presented by the Ford Merit Club in 1935, which makes it more interesting and valuable. The length of the case, at 42mm, is rare as it was very large for the time.

$225-275   ML

A 1930s Waltham 'Cushion' wristwatch, with white gold-filled case, the white dial with luminous hands and numbers, subsidiary seconds dial at six o'clock, and with 17-jewel movement.

$150-200   ML

A 1930s Waltham wristwatch, the 14ct white gold 'Solidarity' case with highly engraved bezel, silvered dial with subsidiary seconds dial at six o'clock, and matching Solidarity engraved solid 14ct white gold buckle.

It is hard to find the buckle and watch together. It is also hard to find a watch with this much decoration on the case.

$400-450   ML

A 1970s Zenith 'Respirator' automatic wristwatch, with stainless steel case and matching articulated bracelet, and blue face.

$500-600   RSS

WATCHES

A 1940s Bailey Banks & Biddle wristwatch, with solid platinum case, hooded lugs, diamond-set dial, and Swiss-made 27-jewel movement, the back stamped "Platinum".

High-end jewelry retailer Bailey Banks & Biddle was founded in Philadelphia in 1832 and now has over 70 stores in 24 US states. This watch would have been made and assembled in Switzerland under contract, and the dial marked with their name. A number of retailers sold watches marked and produced in this way.

A 1970s Zenith 'Respirator' automatic watch, with rectangular metal case and matching bracelet, the silvered face with date aperture.

$600-700   **RSS**

A 1960s Swiss Zodiac 'Seawolf' automatic diver's wristwatch, in sealed case, with date and two-tone high fluorescent bezel and dial chapter ring.

$225-275   **ML**

$2,200-2,700   **ML**

A 1940s May's wristwatch, with 14ct solid pink gold square case and Swiss made 17-jewel movement.

Made for May's, the parent company of Macey's, this is another example of a 'contract' watch.

$300-350   **ML**

A Tiffany & Co. 18ct gold demi-hunter wristwatch, with presentation engraving inside back "1871 Sept 7th 1896", signed on the dial and movement, and the case signed "Tiffany & Co. 18K".
c1895

$1,000-1,200   **ML**

A 1960s Pierre Cardin wristwatch, with brushed stainless steel case, silvered dial, and Jaeger 17-jewel movement.

Early Pierre Cardin branded watches like this example were fitted with high quality Jaeger movements. The stainless steel case is unusual.

$225-275   **ML**

A Schochet 'Coin' wristwatch, the solid 18ct gold case made from a $20 coin, and with an unsigned movement, marked "Schochet" on the gold-tone face.

This was probably made by a jeweler, as it is not quite as well-made as the Piaget coin watch on the next page. For example, compare the two catches – the catch on this example is not as well concealed.

$1,500-1,800   **ML**

EXPERT EYE – A LADY'S PENDANT WATCH

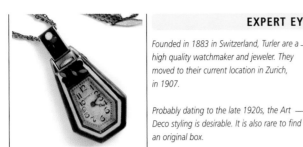

A late 1920s-30s Art Deco Roxy lady's pendant watch, the sterling silver case with enameled design, and Swiss 17-jewel movement, with restored enamel.

$400-500   **ML**

Founded in 1883 in Switzerland, Turler are a high quality watchmaker and jeweler. They moved to their current location in Zurich, in 1907.

Probably dating to the late 1920s, the Art Deco styling is desirable. It is also rare to find an original box.

Twisting the bottom hemisphere makes the top hemisphere open like an iris to reveal the watch face - this is a complex mechanism.

The black enameled exterior with enameled gold dots is in excellent condition with no damage, and it retains its original leather strap and bow.

A 1920s-30s Swiss lady's pendant watch, with hand-engraved Sterling silver hexagonal case, and Swiss 17-jewel movement.

The 12 o'clock is at the bottom of the pendant, allowing it to be 'turned up' and easily read.

$300-350   **ML**

This example has superb iridescence, making it more desirable.

A Swiss Turler lady's pendant watch, within a spherical case decorated with black enamel and gold enamel dots, stamped "Swiss Watch Co.", with an ETA movement, together with leather strap and bow and original box.

$300-350   **ML**

A Swiss Gallet & Co. lady's pendant watch, the conical sterling silver case decorated with alternate bands of black and green enamel and stamped ".935" and "Gallet & Co Geneva Switzerland", with sterling silver rose bud and leaf finial, unsigned face and Gallet 15-jewel movement with two adjustments.

$300-400   **ML**

A Swiss Movado 'Ermeto' traveling watch, solid 9ct gold case sliding open and closed to wind the watch, decorated with Japanese maki-e lacquer scenes of the Nihon Bashi in Kyoto, import marks for Glasgow 1929, and signed Movado 17-jewel movement.

c1929

$3,000-3,500   **DN**

A Piaget 'Coin Watch', the solid 18ct gold case made from a $20 coin, the spring-loaded flap activated by a hidden side release, with Piaget signed 17-jewel movement.

This is a superbly and finely engineered example, with the opening catch being skillfully concealed inside the milled edge of the coin. A number of companies made these, including Corum and Piaget, as well as a number of jewelers, and qualities vary. They were usually carried around in a bag or used on a night stand.

$2,500-3,000   **ML**

A

Acid etching A technique using acid to decorate glass to produce a matt or frosted appearance.

Albumen print Photographic paper is treated with egg white (albumen) to enable it to hold more light-sensitive chemicals. After being exposed to a negative, the resulting image is richer with more tonal variation.

Applied Refers to a separate part that has been attached to an object, such as a handle.

Automatic Used to describe a wristwatch movement that is wound using a revolving weighted disc or half-disc. As the wearer's wrist moves, the disc revolves and winds the watch. Automatic movements became commercially widespread from the 1930s onwards.

B

Baluster A curved form with a bulbous base and a slender neck.

Base metal A term describing common metals such as copper, tin and lead, or metal alloys, that were usually plated in gold or silver to imitate more expensive and luxurious metals. In the US, the term 'pot metal' is more commonly used.

Bisque A type of unglazed porcelain used for making dolls from c1860 to c1925.

Boards The hard covers of a book.

Brassing On plated items, where the plating has worn off to reveal the underlying base metal.

C

Cabochon A large, protruding, polished, but not faceted, stone.

Cameo Hardstone, coral or shell that has been carved in relief to show a design in a contrasting z.

Cameo glass Decorative glass made from two or more layers of differently colored glass, which are then carved or etched to reveal the color beneath.

Cartouche A framed panel, often in the shape of a shield or paper scroll, which can be inscribed.

Cased Where a piece of glass is covered with a further layer of glass, sometimes of a contrasting color, or clear and colorless. In some cases the casing will be further worked with cutting or etching to reveal the layer beneath.

Charger A large plate or platter, often for display, but also for serving.

Chromolithography A later development of 'lithography', where a number of printing stones are used in succession, each with a different color, to build up a multi-colored image.

Composition A mixture including wood pulp, plaster and glue used as a cheap alternative to bisque in the production of dolls' heads and bodies.

Compote A dish, usually on a stem or foot, to hold fruit for the dessert course.

Craze/Crazed/Crazing A network of fine cracks in the glaze caused by uneven shrinking during firing. It also describes plastic that is slowly degrading and has the same surface patterning.

Cuenca A technique used for decorating tiles where molded ridges separate the colored glazes, like the 'cloisonné' enameling technique.

Cultured pearl A pearl formed when an irritant is artificially introduced to the mollusc.

D

Damascened Metal ornamented with inlaid gold or silver, often in wavy lines. Commonly found on weapons or armour.

Dichroic Glass treated with chemicals or metals that cause it to appear differently colored depending on how it is viewed in the light.

Diecast Objects made by pouring molten metal into a closed metal die or mold.

Ding A very small dent in metal.

E

Earthenware A type of porous pottery that requires a glaze to make it waterproof.

Ebonized Wood that has been blackened with dye to resemble ebony.

E.P.N.S. Found on metal objects and standing for 'electroplated nickel silver', meaning the object is made from nickel which is then electroplated with silver.

F

Faience Earthenware that is treated with an impervious tin glaze. Popular in France from the 16th century and reaching its peak during the 18th century.

Faceted A form of decoration where a number of flat surfaces are cut into the surface of an object such as a gem or glass.

Faux A French word for 'false'. The intention is not to deceive fraudulently but to imitate a more costly material.

Finial A decorative knob at the end of a terminal, or on a lid.

Foliate Leaf and vine motifs.

G

Gather The term used to describe the mass of molten glass that the glassmaker forms into an object.

Guilloché An engraved pattern of interlaced lines or other decorative motifs, sometimes enameled over with translucent enamels.

H

Hallmark The series of small stamps found on gold or silver that can identify the maker, the standard of the metal and the city and year of manufacture. Hallmarks differ for each country and can consist only of a maker's or a city mark. Nearly all English silver made after 1544 was required to be fully marked.

Hotworked Descriptive of a technique in glassmaking, where the shape and decoration are created and finished by the glassmaker at the furnace, when the glass is still hot and molten. The mass of glass is often re-inserted into the furnace to keep it molten and at a high enough temperature to ensure it can be 'worked'.

IJKL

Incised Applied to surface decoration or a maker's mark that has been scratched into the surface of an object with a sharp instrument.

Inclusions Used to describe all types of small particles of decorative materials embedded in glass.

Inscribed Usually related to a signature on the base of a piece, or else a design, which has been scratched into the surface using a sharp tool.

Iridescent A lustrous finish that subtly changes color depending on how light hits it. Often used to describe the finish on ceramics and glass.

Lithography A printing technique developed in 1798 and employing the use of a stone upon which a pattern or picture has been drawn with a grease crayon. The ink adheres to the grease and is transferred to the paper when pressed against it.

MNO

Manual Used to describe a wristwatch movement that needs to be wound using a winder on the side of the case.

Millefiori An Italian term meaning 'thousand flowers' and used to describe cut, multi-colored glass canes which are arranged and cased in clear glass. When arranged with the cut side facing the exterior, each circular disc (or short cane) resembles a small flower.

Mint A term used to describe an object in unused condition with no signs of wear and derived from coinage. Truly 'mint' objects will command a premium.

Mold Blown Descriptive of glass which has been blown into a mold to give it form. The inside of the mold is usually decorated with a three dimensional design, giving the surface of the piece a raised pattern.

Mount A metal part applied to an object made of ceramic, glass or another material, with a decorative or functional use.

Murrine Slices of colored transparent, translucent or opaque glass canes, typically with an internal pattern ranging from stylised flowers to abstract patterns. They are usually applied to the exterior of a vase and melted into and bonded to it in the furnace.

Nappy A shallow dish or bowl with a handle used for drinking.

Opalescent An opal-like, milky glass with subtle gradations of color between thinner more translucent areas and thicker, more opaque areas.

P

Paisley A stylized design based on pinecones and foliage, often with added intricate decoration. It originated in India and is most often found on fabrics, such as shawls.

Paste (jewelry) A hard, bright glass cut the same way as a diamond and made and set to resemble them.

Patera An oval or circular decorative motif often with a fluted or floral centre. The plural is 'paterae'.

Piqué A decorative technique where small strips or studs of gold are inlaid onto ivory or tortoiseshell on a pattern and secured in place by heating.

Pontil A metal rod to which a glass vessel is attached when it is being worked. When it is removed it leaves a raised disc-shaped 'pontil mark'.

Pot metal Please see 'Base metal'.

Pounce pot A small pot made of wood (treen), silver or ceramic. Found on inkwells or designed to stand alone, it held a gum dust that was sprinkled over parchment to prevent ink from spreading. Used until the late 18th century.

Pressed (Press molded) Ceramics formed by pressing clay into a mold. Pressed glass is made by pouring molten glass into a mold and pressing it with a plunger.

R

Reeded A type of decoration with thin raised, convex vertical lines. Derived from the decoration of classical columns. Relief A form of molded, pressed or carved decoration that protrudes above the surface of an object. Usually in the form of figures of foliate and foliage designs, it ranges in height from 'low' to 'high'.

Rhinestone Faceted, highly reflective crystal or glass 'stones' cut to resemble gemstones. The original rhinestones were quartz stones (rock crystal) dug out from the Rhine river in Germany. Usually of great clarity, they may be colorless or colored, and may be treated with chemicals to give an iridescent surface effect.

Repoussé A French term for the raised, 'embossed' decoration on metals such as silver. The metal is forced into a form from one side causing it to bulge.

S

Sgraffito An Italian word for 'little scratch' and used to describe a decorative technique where the outer surface of an object, usually in glazed or colored ceramic, is scratched away in a pattern to reveal the contrasting colored underlying surface.

Sommerso Technique developed in Murano in the 1930s. Translates as 'submerged' and involves casing one or more layers of transparent colored glass within a layer of thick, clear, colorless glass.

Stoneware A type of ceramic similar to earthenware and made of high-fired clay mixed with stone, such as feldspar, which makes it non-porous.

T

Tazza A shallow cup with a wide bowl, which is raised up on a single pedestal foot.

Tinplate A thin sheet of steel which has been plated with tin to prevent rusting. It is usually die-cut and bent into shapes and may also be decorated with painted or transfer printed designs.

Tooled Collective description for a number of decorative techniques applied to a surface. Includes engraving, stamping, punching and incising.

V

Vermeil Gold-plated silver. Vesta case A small case or box, usually made from silver, for carrying matches.

W

White metal Precious metal that is possibly silver, but not officially marked as such.

Y

Yellow metal Precious metal that is possibly gold, but not officially marked as such.

Every item illustrated in the Miller's Collectibles Price Guide by Judith Miller and Mark Hill has a letter code that identifies the dealer, auction house or private collector that owns or sold it. In this way the source of the item can be identified. The list below is a key to these codes. In the list, auction houses are shown by the letter A, dealers by the letter D, and private collectors by the letter P. Inclusion in this book in no way constitutes or implies a contract or a binding offer on the part of any of our contributors to supply or sell the goods illustrated, or similar items, at the prices stated.

AAC Ⓐ
ALDERFER AUCTION COMPANY
501 Fairground Road,
Hatfield, PA 19440
Tel: 215 393 3000
info@alderferauction.com
www.alderferauction.com

AB Ⓐ Ⓓ
AUCTION BLOCKS
P.O. Box 241
Shelton, CT 06484
blockship@yahoo.com

AEM Ⓓ
ANTIQUES EMPORIUM
29 Division Street,
Somerville, NJ 08876
Tel: 908 218 1234
bkr63@patmedia.net

AMAC Ⓓ
ANDREW MCAULAY
The Quad, Alfie's Antiques Market,
13 Church Street,
London NW8 8DT, UK
www.alfiesantiques.com

ANT Ⓓ
THE ANTIQUE GALLERY
8523 Germantown Avenue,
Philadelphia, PA 19118
Tel: 215 248 1700
info@antiquegal.com
www.antiquegal.com

ART Ⓓ
ARTIUS GLASS
Street, Somerset BA16 0AN, UK
Tel: +44 (0) 1458 443694
Mob: +44 (0) 7860 822666
wheeler.ron@talktalk.net
www.artiusglass.co.uk

ATK Ⓐ
AUCTION TEAM KÖLN
Otto-Hahn-Str. 10
50997 Köln (Godorf),
Germany
Tel: (0049) 2236 38 4340
auction@breker.com
www.breker.com

BA Ⓓ
BRANKSOME ANTIQUES
370 Poole Road, Branksome,
Poole, Dorset BH1 1AW, UK
Tel: +44 (0)1020 763 324

BAD Ⓓ
BETH ADAMS
Unit GO23-25
Alfies Antique Market,
13 Church Street, Marylebone,
London NW8 8DT, UK
Mob: +44 (0)7776 136 003
www.alfiesantiques.com

BB Ⓓ
BARBARA BLAU
South Street Antiques Market,
615 South 6th Street,
Philadelphia, PA 19147-2128
Tel: 215 592 0256
bbjools@msn.com

BEL Ⓐ
BELHORN AUCTION SERVICES
P.O. Box 20211,
Columbus, OH 43220
Tel: 614 921 9441
auctions@belhorn.com
www.belhorn.com

BER Ⓐ
BERTOIA AUCTIONS
2141 De Marco Drive,
Vineland, NJ 08360
Tel: 856 692 1881
toys@bertoiaauctions.com
www.bertoiaauctions.com

BEV Ⓓ
BEVERLEY ADAMS
Ground Floor,
Alfie's Antiques Market,
13 Church Street,
London NW8 8DT, UK
Mob: +44 (0)7776 136 003
www.alfiesantiques.com

BGL Ⓓ
BLOCK GLASS LTD
blockglss@aol.com
www.blockglass.com

BH Ⓓ
ANTIQUES SHOWCASE AT THE BLACK HORSE
P.O. Box 343, 2180 North Reading
Road, Denver PA, 17517
Tel: 717 335 3300
www.blackhorselodge.com/Antiques
.asp

BIG Ⓐ
BIGWOOD AUCTIONEERS
The Old School, Tiddington
Stratford-upon-Avon,
Warwickshire CV37 7AW, UK
Tel: +44 (0)1789 269 415
www.bigwoodauctioneers.co.uk

BLNY Ⓐ
BLOOMSBURY AUCTIONS NEW YORK
6 West 48th Street, New York
NY 10036-1902
Tel: 212 719 1000
newyork@bloomsburyauctions.com
www.bloomsburyauctions.com

BLO Ⓐ
BLOOMSBURY AUCTIONS
Bloomsbury House, 24 Maddox St,
London W1 S1PP, UK
Tel: +44 (0)20 7495 9494
info@bloomsburyauctions.com
www.bloomsburyauctions.com

BRI Ⓐ
BRIGHTWELLS
Easters Court, Leominster
Herefordshire HR6 0DE, UK
Tel: +44 (0)1568 611 166
www.brightwells.com

C Ⓐ
COTTEES
The Market, East Street, Wareham,
Dorset BH20 4NR, UK
Tel: +44 (0)1929 552 826
auctions@cottees.fsnet.co.uk
www.auctionsatcottees.co.uk

CHT Ⓐ
CHARTERHOUSE
The Long Street Salerooms,
Sherborne,
Dorset DT9 3BS, UK
Tel: +44 (0)1935 812 277
enquiry@charterhouse-
auctions.co.uk
www.charterhouse-auctions.co.uk
www.clevedon-salerooms.com

CN Ⓓ
COLIN NARBETH
Colin Narbeth & Sons Ltd,
20 Cecil Court,
Leicester Square,
London WC2N 4HE, UK
Tel: +44 (0)207 379 6975
colin.narbeth@btinternet.com
www.colin-narbeth.com

CO Ⓓ Ⓐ
COOPER OWEN
Tel: 01753 855 858
enquiry@cooperowen.com
www.cooperowen.com

CRA Ⓐ
CRAFTSMAN AUCTIONS
333 North Main Street,
Lambertville, NJ 08530
Tel: 609 397 9374
info@ragoarts.com
www.ragoarts.com

CW Ⓟ
CHRISTINE WILDMAN
wild123@allstream.net

DN Ⓐ
DREWEATTS
Donnington Priory Salerooms,
Donnington, Newbury,
Berkshire RG14 2JE, UK
Tel: +44 (0)1635 553 553
donnington@dnfa.com
www.dnfa.com/donnington

DRA Ⓐ
DAVID RAGO AUCTIONS
333 North Main Street,
Lambertville, NJ 08530
Tel: 609 397 9374
info@ragoarts.com
www.ragoarts.com
www.fellows.co.uk

FLD Ⓐ
FIELDING'S AUCTIONEERS
Mill Race Lane, Stourbridge,
West Midlands DY8 1JN UK
Tel: +44 (0)1384 444140
info@fieldingsauctioneers.co.uk
www.fieldingsauctioneers.co.uk

FRE Ⓐ
FREEMAN'S
1808 Chestnut Street,
Philadelphia, PA 19103
Tel: 215 563 9275
info@freemansauction.com
www.freemansauction.com

GAZE Ⓐ
THOS. WM. GAZE & SON
Diss Auction Rooms, Roydon Rd,
Diss, Norfolk IP22 4LN, UK
Tel: +44 (0)1379 650 306
sales@dissauctionrooms.co.uk
www.twgaze.com

GBA Ⓐ
GRAHAM BUDD AUCTIONS
P.O. Box 47519, London N14 6XD, UK
Tel: +44 (0)20 8366 2525
gb@grahambuddauctions.co.uk
www.grahambuddauctions.co.uk

GC Ⓟ
GRAHAM COOLEY COLLECTION
Mob: +44 (0)7968 722 269
graham.cooley@universalsensors.co.uk

GCA Ⓟ
GRIFFIN COOPER ANTIQUES
South Street Antiques Market,
615 South 6th Street,
Philadelphia, PA 19147-2128
Tel: 215 592 0256

GCHI Ⓓ
THE GIRL CAN'T HELP IT!
Grand Central Window, Ground
Floor, Alfie's Antiques Market,
13-25 Church Street, London
NW8 8DT, UK
Tel: +44 (0)207 724 8984
Mob: +44 (0)7958 515 614
info@thegirlcanthelpit.com
www.thegirlcanthelpit.com

GGRT Ⓓ
GARY GRANT CHOICE PIECES
18 Arlington Way,
London EC1R 1UY, UK
Tel: +44 (0)20 7713 1122
garyjamesgrant@btinternet.com

GHOU Ⓐ
GARDINER HOULGATE
Bath Auction Rooms, 9 Leafield Way,
Corsham, Nr Bath SN13 9SW, UK
Tel: +44 (0)1225 812 912
auctions@gardinerhoulgate.co.uk
www.gardinerhoulgate.co.uk

GM Ⓓ
GALERIE MAURER
Kurfürstenstrasse 17, D-80799
Munich, Germany
Tel: +49 89 271 13 45
info@galeriemaurer.de
www.galerie-objekte-maurer.de

GORL Ⓐ
GORRINGES, LEWES
15 North Street, Lewes,
East Sussex, BN7 2PD, UK
Tel: +44 (0)1273 472 503
clientservices@gorringes.co.uk
www.gorringes.co.uk

GROB Ⓓ
GEOFFREY ROBINSON
Stands GO77-78 & GO91-92,
Alfies Antiques Market, 13-25
Church Street, London NW8 8DT, UK
Tel: +44 (0)20 7723 0449
www.alfiesantiques.com

HLM Ⓓ
HI & LO MODERN
161 Montclair Avenue,
Montclair, NJ 07042
sales@hiandlomodern.com
www.hiandlomodern.com

JDJ Ⓐ
JAMES D. JULIA INC
P.O. Box 830, Fairfield
Maine 04937
Tel: 207 453 7125
jjulia@juliaauctions.com
www.juliaauctions.com

JN Ⓐ
JOHN NICHOLSON AUCTIONEERS
The Auction Rooms, 'Longfield',
Midhurst Road, Fernhurst,
Haslemere, Surrey GU27 3HA, UK
Tel: +44 (0)1428 653727
sales@johnnicholsons.com
www.johnnicholsons.com

KCS Ⓓ
KCS CERAMICS
Tel: +44 (0)20 8384 8981
karen@kcsceramics.co.uk
www.kcsceramics.co.uk

KNK Ⓓ
KITSCH-N-KABOODLE
South Street Antiques Market,
615 South 6th Street,
Philadelphia, PA 19147-2128
Tel: 215 382 1354
kitschnkaboodle@yahoo.com

KT Ⓐ
KERRY TAYLOR AUCTIONS
Unit C25,
Parkhall Road Trading Estate
40 Martell Road, Dulwich,
London SE21 8EN, UK
Tel: +44 (0)208 676 4600
info@kerrytaylorauctions.com
www.kerrytaylorauctions.com

L&T Ⓐ
LYON AND TURNBULL
33 Broughton Place,
Edinburgh EH1 3RR, UK
Tel: +44 (0)131 557 8844
info@lyonandturnbull.com
www.lyonandturnbull.com

MA Ⓓ
MANIC ATTIC
Alfies Antiques Market,
Stand S48/49,
13-25 Church Street,
London NW8 8DT, UK
Tel: +44 (0)20 7723 6105
ianbroughton@hotmail.com

MAS Ⓐ
MASTRO AUCTIONS
7900 South Madison Street,
Burr Ridge,
Illinois 60527
Tel: 630 472 1200
customerservice@mastroauctions.com
www.mastroauctions.com

MEM Ⓓ
MEMORY LANE
45-40 Bell Blvd, Suite 109
Bayside, NY 11361
Tel: (001) 718 428 8181
memlnny@aol.com

MHC Ⓟ
MARK HILL COLLECTION
Mob: +44 (0)7798 915 474
books@markhillpublishing.com
www.markhillpublishing.com

MHT Ⓓ
MUM HAD THAT
info@mumhadthat.com
www.mumhadthat.com

ML Ⓓ
MARK LAINO
Mark of Time
132 South 8th Street,
Philadelphia,
PA 19107
Tel: 215 922 1551
lecoultre@verizon.net
eBay ID: lecoultre

MTB Ⓓ
THE MAGIC TOYBOX
210 Havant Road,
Drayton, Portsmouth,
Hampshire PO6 2EH, UK
Tel: +44 (0)2392 221 307
magictoybox@btinternet.com
www.magictoybox.co.uk

MTS Ⓓ
THE MULTICOLOURED TIMESLIP
dave_a_cameron@hotmail.com
eBay ID: dave65330

NEA Ⓐ
NEALES OF NOTTINGHAM
192 Mansfield Road,
Nottingham NG1 3HU, UK
Tel: +44 (0)115 962 4141
nottingham@dnfa.com
www.dnfa.com/nottingham

NOR Ⓓ
NEET-O-RAMA
14 Division Street,
Somerville,
NJ 08876
Tel: 908 722 4600
www.neetstuff.com

ON Ⓐ
ONSLOWS
The Coach House,
Manor Road, Stourpaine,
Dorset DT11 8TQ, UK
Tel: +44 (0)1258 488 838
enquiries@onslows.co.uk
www.onslows.co.uk

OUT Ⓓ
OUTERNATIONAL
14 Lübeckerstrasse,
Cologne 50670, Germany
info@outernational.eu
www.outernational.eu

P&I Ⓓ
PAOLA & IAIA
Unit S057-058, Alfie's Antiques
Market, 13-25 Church Street,
London NW8 8DT
Tel: 07751 084 135
paolaeiaialondon@hotmail.com

PAS Ⓓ
PAST CARING
54 Essex Road, London N1 8LR, UK

PC Ⓟ
PRIVATE COLLECTION

PGO Ⓓ
PAMELA GOODWIN
Goodwin Antiques, 11 The Pantiles,
Royal Tunbridge Wells,
Kent TN2 5TD, UK
Tel: 01435 882200
mail@goodwinantiques.co.uk
www.goodwinantiques.co.uk

PWE Ⓐ
**PHILIP WEISS AUCTION
GALLERIES**
1 Neil Court, Oceanside, NY 11572
Tel: 516 594 073
info@philipweissauctions.com
www.philipweissauctions.com

QU Ⓐ
**QUITTENBAUM
KUNSTAUKTIONEN**
Hohenstaufenstrasse 1,
D-80801 Munich, Germany
Tel: +49 89 33 00 756
info@quittenbaum.de
www.quittenbaum.de

RAON Ⓓ
R.A. O'NEILL
No longer trading

ROS Ⓐ
ROSEBERY'S
74-76 Knight's Hill, West Norwood,
London SE27 0JD, UK
Tel: +44 (0)20 8761 2522
auctions@roseberys.co.uk
www.roseberys.co.uk

RSS Ⓐ
ROSSINI SVV
7 Rue Drouot, Paris 75009, France
+33 1 (0)53 34 55 00
contact@rossini.fr
www.rossini.fr

RTC Ⓐ
RITCHIES
380 King Street East, Toronto
Ontario, M5A 1K9 Canada
Tel: 416 364 1864
auction@ritchies.com
www.ritchies.com

SAE Ⓓ
ANTIQUES EMPORIUM
29 Division Street,
Somerville, NJ 08876
Tel: 908 218 1234
bkr63@patmedia.net

SAS Ⓐ
SPECIAL AUCTION SERVICES
Kennetholme, Midgham,
Nr. Reading, Berkshire RG7 5UX, UK
Tel: +44 (0)118 971 2949
mail@specialauctionservices.com
www.specialauctionservices.com

SDR Ⓐ
**SOLLO:RAGO MODERN
AUCTIONS**
333 North Main Street,
Lambertville, NJ 08530
Tel: 609 397 9374
info@ragoarts.com
www.ragoarts.com

SHAND Ⓓ
THE SHAND GALLERY
Toronto Antiques on King
276 King Street West, Toronto,
Ontario M5V 1J2 Canada
Tel: 416 260 9056
kenshand@allstream.net
www.torontoantiquesonking.com

SK Ⓐ
SLOANS & KENYON
7034 Wisconsin Avenue,
Chevy Chase, Maryland 20815
Tel: 301 634 2330
info@sloansandkenyon.com
www.sloansandkenyon.com

SOTT Ⓓ
SIGN OF THE TYMES
Mill Antiques Center,
12 Morris Farm Road,
Lafayette, NJ 07848
Tel: 973 383 6028
jhap@nac.net
www.millantiques.com

SWA Ⓐ
SWANN GALLERIES
Image Library, 104 East 25th Street,
New York, NY 10010
Tel: 212 254 4710
swann@swanngalleries.com
www.swanngalleries.com

SWO Ⓐ
SWORDERS
14 Cambridge Road,
Stansted Mountfitchet,
Essex CM24 8BZ, UK
Tel: +44 (0)1279 817 778
auctions@sworder.co.uk
www.sworder.co.uk

TAC Ⓓ
CYNTHIA FINDLAY
Toronto Antiques on King
276 King Street West, Toronto,
Ontario M5V 1J2 Canada
Tel: 416 260 9057
askcynthia@cynthiafindlay.com
www.cynthiafindlay.com
www.torontoantiquesonking.com

TAM Ⓓ
ANTIQUES & MILITARIA
Toronto Antiques on King
276 King Street West, Toronto,
Ontario M5V 1J2 Canada
Tel: 416 260 9057
sales@antiquesandmilitaria.com

TCF Ⓓ
CYNTHIA FINDLAY
Toronto Antiques on King
276 King Street West, Toronto,
Ontario M5V 1J2 Canada
Tel: 416 260 9057
askcynthia@cynthiafindlay.com
www.cynthiafindlay.com
www.torontoantiquesonking.com

TDG Ⓓ
THE DESIGN GALLERY
5 The Green, Westerham,
Kent TN16 1AS, UK
Tel: +44 (0)1959 561 234
sales@designgallery.co.uk
www.designgallery.co.uk

TGM Ⓓ
THE STUDIO GLASS MERCHANT
Tel: +44 (0)7775 683 961
Tel: +44 (0)208 668 2701
info@thestudioglassmerchant.co.uk
www.thestudioglassmerchant.co.uk

THA Ⓓ
HELEN ASTLEY
Toronto Antiques on King
276 King Street West, Toronto,
Ontario M5V 1J2 Canada
Tel: 416 260 9057
www.torontoantiquesonking.com

THG Ⓓ
HERITAGE
Toronto Antiques on King
276 King Street West, Toronto,
Ontario M5V 1J2 Canada
Tel: 416 260 9057
www.torontoantiquesonking.com

TOA Ⓓ
THE OCCUPIED ATTIC
Tel: 518 899 5030
occattic@aol.com
seguin12@aol.com

TOJ Ⓓ
THESE OLD JUGS
Tel: 410 626 0770
susan@theseoldjugs.com
www.theseoldjugs.com

TPF Ⓓ
PAM FERRAZZUTTI
Toronto Antiques on King
276 King Street West, Toronto,
Ontario M5V 1J2 Canada
Tel: 416 260 9056
pam@pamferrazzuttiantiques.com
www.pamferrazzuttiantiques.com
www.torontoantiquesonking.com

TSG Ⓓ
SHAND GALLERY
Toronto Antiques on King
276 King Street West, Toronto,
Ontario M5V 1J2 Canada
Tel: 416 260 9056
kenshand@allstream.net
www.torontoantiquesonking.com

TSIS Ⓓ
THREE SISTERS
South Street Antiques Market,
615 South 6th Street,
Philadelphia, PA 19147-2128
Tel: 215 592 0256

TWF Ⓓ
TWICE FOUND
608 Markham Street,
Mirvish Village,
Toronto, Ontario
M6G 2L8 Canada
Tel: 416 534 3904
twicefound@bellnet.ca

UCT Ⓓ
UNDERCURRENTS
28 Cowper Street,
London, EC2A 4AS, UK
Tel: +44 (0)207 251 1537
shop@undercurrents.biz
www.undercurrents.biz

VE Ⓓ
**VINTAGE EYEWEAR OF NEW
YORK CITY INC.**
1A The Fantastic Umbrella Factory
4820 Old Post Road,
Charlestown, Rhode Island
Tel: 917 721 6546
vintageyes60@yahoo.com

VEC Ⓐ
VECTIS AUCTIONS LTD
Fleck Way, Thornaby,
Stockton on Tees,
TS17 9JZ, UK
Tel: +44 (0)1642 750 616
admin@vectis.co.uk
www.vectis.co.uk

VSA Ⓐ
VAN SABBEN AUCTIONS
Appelsteeg 1-B, NL-1621 BD,
Hoorn, Netherlands
Tel: +31 (0)229 268 203
uboersma@vansabbenauctions.nl
www.vansabbenauctions.nl

VZ Ⓐ
VON ZEZSCHWITZ
Friedrichstrasse 1a, 80801 Munich,
Germany
Tel: +49 89 38 98 930
www.von-zezschwitz.de

W&L Ⓓ
W&L Antiques
Stand G060, Alfie's Antiques
Market, 13-25 Church Street,
London NW8 8DT, UK
Tel: +44 (0)207 723 6066
Mob: +44 (0)7788 486 297
teddylove@blueyonder.co.uk

WAD Ⓐ
WADDINGTON'S AUCTIONEERS
111 Bathurst Street, Toronto,
Ontario, Canada M5V 2R1
Tel: 416 504 9100
www.waddingtons.ca

W&W Ⓐ
WALLIS & WALLIS
West Steet Auction Galleries, Lewes,
East Sussex BN7 2NJ, UK
Tel: +44 (0)1273 480 208
auctions@wallisandwallis.co.uk
www.wallisandwallis.co.uk

WW Ⓐ
WOOLLEY & WALLIS
51-61 Castle Street, Salisbury,
Wiltshire SP1 3SU, UK
Tel: +44 (0)1722 424 500
enquiries@woolleyandwallis.co.uk
www.woolleyandwallis.co.uk

If you wish to have any item valued, it is advisable to contact the dealer or specialist in advance to check that they will carry out this service and whether there is a charge. While most dealers will be happy to help you with an enquiry, do remember that they are busy people with businesses to run. Telephone valuations are not possible. Please mention the Miller's Collectibles Price Guide 2009 by Judith Miller and Mark Hill when making an enquiry.

ADVERTISING

Senator Phil Arthurhultz
P.O. Box 12336, Lansing,
MI 48901
Tel: 517 334 5000
Mob: 517 930 3000

Phil & Karol Atkinson
May-Oct:
713 Sarsi Tr, Mercer, PA 16137
Tel: 724 475 2490
Nov-Apr:
7188 Drewry's Bluff Road,
Bradenton, FL 34203
Tel: 941 755 1733

Awsum Advertising
P.O. Box 1782, Linden,
NJ 07036
Tel: 732 331 2951
awsumadvertising@aol.com

**Kit Barry Ephemera &
Supplies**
74 Cotton Mill Hill, #A252,
Brattleboro, VT 05301

The Nostalgia Factory
Original Movie Posters &
Related Ephemera,
Charlestown Commerce Center,
50 Terminal St., Bldg. 2,
Boston MA 02129
Tel: 617-241-8300 /
800-479-8754
Fax: 617-241-0710
posters@nostalgia.com
www.nostalgia.com

Toy Road Antiques
200 Highland Street, Canal,
Winchester OH 43110
Tel: 614 834 1786
toyroadantiques@aol.com
www.goantiques.com/
members/toyroadantiques

AMERICANA

**Bucks County Antique
Center**
Route 202,
Lahaksa, PA 18931
Tel: 215 794 9180

Larry and Dianna Elman
PO Box 415, Woodland Hills,
CA 91365

Olde Hope Antiques
P.O. Box 718,
New Hope, PA 18938
Tel: 215 297 0200
info@oldehope.com
www.oldehope.com

Fields of Glory
55 York St, Gettysburg,
PA 17325
Tel: 717 337 2837
foglory@cvn.net
www.fieldsofglory.com

The Splendid Peasant
Route 23 & Sheffield Rd,
P.O. Box 536, South Egremont,
MA 01258
Tel: 413 528 5755
folkart@splendidpeasant.com
www.splendidpeasant.com

Patricia Stauble Antiques
180 Main Street,
P.O. Box 265, Wiscasset,
ME 04578
Tel: 207 882 6341
pstauble@midcoast.com

AUTOGRAPHS

Autographs of America
P.O. Box 461, Provo,
UT 84603-0461
tanders3@autographsof
america.com
www.autographsofamerica.com

Platt Autographs
PO Box 135007,
Clermont,
FL 34711
Tel: 352 241 9164
ctplatt@ctplatt.com
www.ctplatt.com

AUTOMOBILIA

Dunbar's Gallery
54 Haven St. Milford,
MA 01757
Tel: 508 634 8697
Fax: 508 634 8697
dunbarsgallery@comcast.net
http://dunbarsgallery.com

BOOKS

Abebooks
www.abebooks.com

Aleph-Bet Books
85 Old Mill River Rd.,
Pound Ridge, NY 10576
Tel: 914 764-7410
Fax: 914 764-1356
helen@alephbet.com
www.alephbet.com

Bauman Rare Books
535 Madison Ave, between
54th & 55th Streets,
New York, NY 10022
Tel: 212 751 0011
brb@baumanrarebooks.com
www.baumanrarebooks.com

Deer Park Books
Abebooks Inc.,
#4 - 410 Garbally Road,
Victoria,
BC V8T 2K1 Canada
Tel/Fax: 860 350 4140
deerparkbk@aol.com
www.deerparkbooks.com

CANADIANA

Toronto Antiques on King
276 King Street West, Toronto,
Ontario M5V 1J2, Canada
Tel: 416 260 9057
www.torontoantiquesonking
.com

The Blue Pump
178 Davenport Road,
Toronto, Canada M5R 1J2
Tel: 416 944 1673
www.thebluepump.com

CERAMICS

Charles & Barbara Adams
By appointment only
289 Old Main St,
South Yarmouth,
MA 02664
Tel: 508 760 3290
adams_2430@msn.com

Mark & Marjorie Allen
300 Bedford St. Suite 421,
Manchester, NH 03101
Tel: 603 644 8989
mandmallen@adelphia.net
www.antiquedelft.com

British Collectibles
917 Chicago Avenue,
Evanston, Illinois 60202
Tel: 800 634 0431
kevin@britishcollectibles.com
sheila@britishcollectibles.com
britcol@msn.com

Cynthia Findlay
Toronto Antiques on King
276 King Street West,
Toronto, Ontario M5V 1J2,
Canada
Tel: 416 260 9057
www.torontoantiquesonking
.com

Happy Pastime
P.O. Box 1225, Ellicott City,
MD 21041-1225
Tel: 410 203 1101
hpastime@bellatlantic.net
www.happypastime.com

Hi & Lo Modern
161 Montclair Avenue,
Montclair NJ 07042 USA
sales@hiandlomodern.com
www.hiandlomodern.com

Keller & Ross
47 Prospect Street,
Melrose, MA 02176
Tel: 781 662 7257
kellerross@aol.com
http://members.aol.com/
kellerross

Ken Forster
5501 Seminary Road,
Ste 1311, South Falls
Church, VA 22041
Tel: 703 379 1142
(Art Pottery)

Mary's Memories
P.O. Box 2342
Centreville,
VA 20122
mcmonet@hughes.net
www.tias.com/stores/mm

Mellin's Antiques
P.O. Box 1115,
Redding CT 06875
Tel: 203 938 9538
remellin@aol.com

Mary Ann's Collectibles
South Street Antiques Center
615 South 6th Street,
Philadelphia,
PA 19147-2128
Tel: 001 215 592 0256

Pair Antiques
12707 Hillcrest Dr,
Longmont,
CO 80501-1162
Tel: 303 772 2760

Pascoe & Company
253 SW 22nd Avenue,
Miami, Florida 33135
Tel: 800 872 0195/
305 643 2550
www.pascoeandcompany.com

The Perrault-Rago Gallery
333 North Main Street,
Lambertville, NJ 08530
Tel: 609 397 1802
www.ragoarts.com

These Old Jugs
Susan L. Tillipman
Tel: 410 626 0770
susan@theseoldjugs.com
www.theseoldjugs.com

Twice Found
608 Markham Street,
Mirvish Village, Toronto,
Ontario M6G 2L8, Canada
Tel: 416 534 3904
twicefound@bellnet.ca

Greg Walsh
P.O. Box 747,
Potsdam,
NY 13676-0747
Tel: 315 265 9111
gwalsh@northnet.org
www.walshauction.com

CHARACTER COLLECTIBLES

What A Character!
hugh@whatacharacter.com
bazuin32@aol.com
www.whatacharacter.com

COMICS

Carl Bonasera
A1-American Comic Shops,
3514 W. 95th St,
Evergreen Park, IL 60642
Tel: 708 425 7555

The Comic Gallery
4224 Balboa Ave,
San Diego,
CA 92117
Tel: 619 483 4853

Metropolis Collectibles Inc.
873 Broadway, Suite 201,
New York,
NY 10003
Tel: 212 260 4147
Fax: 212 260 4304
orders@metropoliscomics.com
www.metropoliscomics.com

COSTUME & ACCESSORIES

Fayne Landes Antiques
593 Hansell Road,
Wynnewood,
PA 19096
Tel: 610 658 0566
fayne@comcast.net

Andrea Hall Levy
P.O. Box 1243,
Riverdale,
NY 10471
Tel: 646 441 1726
barangrill@aol.com

Lucy's Hats
1118 Pine Street,
Philadelphia, PA

Mod Girl
South Street Antiques Market
615 South 6th Street,
Philadelphia, PA 19147
Tel: 215 592 0256
modgirljill@comcast.net

Yesterday's Threads
206 Meadow St, Branford,
CT 06405-3634
Tel: 203 481 6452

Vintage Eyewear of New York City inc.
1A The Fantastic Umbrella
Factory, 4820 Old Post Road,
Charlestown, Rhode Island
Tel: 917 721 6546
vintageyes60@yahoo.com

Vintage Swank
212 East Main Street,
Front Royal,
VA 22630
Tel: 540 636 0069
www.vintageswank.com

COSTUME JEWELRY

Aurora Bijoux
Tel: 215 872 7808
aurora@aurorabijoux.com
www.aurorabijoux.com

Barbara Blau
South Street Antiques Market,
c/o South Street Antiques
Market 615 South 6th Street,
Philadelphia,
PA 19147-2128
Tel: 215 592 0256
bbjools@msn.com

The Junkyard Jeweler
www.junkyardjeweler.com

Mod-Girl
South Street Antiques Market,
615 South 6th Street,
Philadelphia, PA 19147
Tel: 215 592 0256
modgirljill@comcast.net

Terry Rodgers & Melody LLC
30 & 31 Manhattan Art &
Antique Center,
1050 2nd Avenue,
New York, NY 10022
Tel: 212 758 3164
melodyjewelnyc@aol.com

Roxanne Stuart
Langhorne PA
Tel: 215 750 8868
gemfairy@aol.com

Vintique Vintage Jewelry
Tel: 612 968 4600
www.rubylane.com/shops/
sparkles

Bonny Yankauer
Tel: 201 825 7697
bonnyy@aol.com

DISNEYANA

MuseumWorks
525 East Cooper Avenue,
Aspen CO 81611
Tel: 970-544-6113
Fax: 970-544-6044
www.mwhgalleries.com

Sign of the Tymes
Mill Antiques Center,
12 Morris Farm Road,
Lafayette, NJ 07848
Tel: 973 383 6028
jhap@nac.net
www.millantiques.com

DOLLS

All Dolled Up
Tel: 519 745 2122
jenn@alldolledup.ca
www.alldolledup.ca

Memory Lane
45-40 Bell Blvd, Suite 109,
Bayside, NY 11361
Tel: 718 428 8181
memlnny@aol.com
www.tias.com/stores/memlnny

Treasure & Dolls
518 Indian Rocks Rd,
N. Belleair Bluffs, FL 33770
Tel: 727 584 7277
dolls@treasuresanddolls.com
www.treasuresanddolls.com

FIFTIES & SIXTIES

Deco Etc
122 West 25th Street
(btw 6th & 7th Aves),
New York, NY 10001
Tel: 212 675 3326
deco_etc@msn.com
www.decoetc.net

Kathy's Korner
Tel: 516 624 9494

Lois' Collectibles
Market III, 413 W Main St,
Saint Charles,
IL 60174-1815
Tel: 630 377 5599

Modcats
info@modcats.com
www.modcats.com

Nifty Fifties
Tel: 734 782 3974

Neet-O-Rama
14 Division Street,
Somerville,
NJ 08876
Tel: 908 722 4600
www.neetstuff.com

Steve Colby
Off The Deep End, 712 East St,
Frederick,
MD 21701-5239
Tel:800 248 0645
Fax: 301-766-0215
contact@offthedeepend.com
www.offthedeepend.com

Vintage Swank
212 East Main Street,
Front Royal,
VA 22630
Tel: 540 636 0069
www.vintageswank.com

FILM MEMORABILIA
George Baker
CollectorsMart, P.O. Box
580466, Modesto, CA 95358
Tel; 290 537 5221
Fax: 209 531 0233
georgeb1@thevision.net
www.collectorsmart.com

Norma's Jeans
3511 Turner Lane, Chevy Chase,
MD 20815-2313
Tel: 301 652 4644
Fax: 301 907 0216

STARticles
58 Stewart St, Studio 301,
Toronto,
Ontario, M5V 1H6 Canada
Tel/fax: 416 504 8286
info@starticles.com

Wonderful World of Animation
9517 Culver Blvd,
Culver City,
CA 90232
Tel: 310 836 4992
www.wonderfulworldofanimation
.com

GLASS
Block Glass Ltd
blockglss@aol.com

City Scavenger Vintage Glass & Goods
563N 66th Street,
Wallwatosa, WI 53213
Tel: 414 763 5734
www.justglassmall.com/stores/
ballerinalady

The End of History
548 1/2 Hudson Street,
New York, NY 10014
Tel: 212 647 7598
Fax: 212 647 7634

Cynthia Findlay
Toronto Antiques on King
276 King Street West, Toronto,
Ontario M5V 1J2 Canada
Tel: 416 260 9057
www.torontoantiquesonking
.com

Hi & Lo Modern
161 Montclair Avenue
Montclair NJ 07042 USA
sales@hiandlomodern.com
www.hiandlomodern.com

Mary Ann's Collectibles
South Street Antiques Center
615 South 6th Street,
Philadelphia,
PA 19147-2128 USA
Tel: 001 215 592 0256

Past-Tyme Antiques
Tel: 703 777 8555
pasttymeantiques@aol.com

Jeff F. Purtell
31 Pleasant Point Drive,
Portsmouth, NH 03801
Tel: 800-973-4331
jfpurtell@steubenpurtell.com
www.steubenpurtell.com
(Steuben)

Paul Reichwein
2321 Hershey Ave,
East Petersburg,
PA 17520
Tel: 717 569 7637
paulrdg@aol.com

Retro Art Glass
California
Tel: 951-639-3032
www.retroartglass.com

Paul Stamati Gallery
1050 2nd Avenue, New York,
NY 10022
Tel: 212 754 4533
Fax: 212 754-4552
www.stamati.com

Suzman's Antiques
P.O. Box 301, Rehoboth,
MA 02769
Tel: 508 252 5729

Twice Found
608 Markham Street,
Mirvish Village, Toronto,
Ontario M6G 2L8, Canada
Tel: 001 416 534 3904
twicefound@bellnet.ca

HOLIDAY MEMORABILIA
Chris & Eddie's Collectibles
c/o South Street Antiques
Market, 615 South 6th Street,
Philadelphia, PA 19147
Tel: 215 592 0256

Sign of the Tymes
Mill Antiques Center,
12 Morris Farm Road, Lafayette,
NJ 07848
Tel: 973 383 6028
jhap@nac.net
www.millantiques.com

KITCHENALIA
Dynamite Antiques & Collectibles
eb625@verizon.net

Village Green Antiques
Port Antiques Center,
289 Main Street,
Port Washington,
NY 11050
Tel: 516 625 2946
amysdish@optonline.net

LIGHTING
Chameleon Fine Lighting
223 East 59th Street,
New York, NY 10022
Tel: 212 355 6300
mail@chameleon59.com
www.chameleon59.com

LUNCH BOXES
Seaside Toy Center
Joseph Soucy
179 Main St,
Westerly,
RI 02891
Tel: 401 596 0962

MARBLES
Auction Blocks
P.O. Box 2321, Shelton,
CT 06484
Tel: 203 924 2802
auctionblocks@aol.com
www.auctionblocks.com

MECHANICAL MUSIC
Mechantiques
The Crescent Hotel,
75 Prospect St,
Eureka Springs,
AR 72632
Tel: 479-253-0405
mroenigk@aol.com
www.mechantiques.com

The Music Box Shop
6102 North 16th Street,
Phoenix, AZ 85016
Tel: 602 277-9615
musicboxshop@home.com
www.themusicboxshop.com

MILITARIA
Antiques & Militaria
Toronto Antiques on King
276 King Street West,
Toronto, Ontario M5V 1J2
Canada
Tel: 001 416 260 9057
sales@antiquesandmilitaria
.com

Articles of War
358 Boulevard,
Middletown, RI 02842
Tel: 401 846 8503
dutch5@ids.com

PENS & WRITING EQUIPMENT

Fountain Pen Hospital
10 Warren Street,
New York, NY 10007
Tel: 212 964 0580
info@fountainpenhospital.com
www.fountainpenhospital.com

Gary & Myrna Lehrer
16 Mulberry Rd, Woodbridge,
CT 06525-1717
Tel: 203 389 5295
Fax: 203 389 4515
garylehrer@aol.com
www.gopens.com

David Nishimura
Vintage Pens,
P.O. Box 41452
Providence,
RI 02940-1452
Tel: 401 351 7607
www.vintagepens.com

Pendemonium
619 Avenue G,
Fort Madison, IA 52627
Tel: 319 372 0881
Fax: 319 372 0882
www.pendemonium.com

Sandra & L. 'Buck' van Tine
Lora's Memory Lane,
13133 North Caroline St,
Chillicothe,
IL 61523-9115
Tel: 309 579 3040
Fax: 309 579 2696
lorasink@aol.com

PLASTICS

Dee Battle
9 Orange Blossom Trail,
Yalaha,
FL 34797
Tel: 352 324 3023

Malabar Enterprises
172 Bush Lane,
Ithaca,
NY 14850
Tel: 607 255 2905
Fax: 607 255 4179
asn6@cornell.edu

POSTERS

La Belle Epoque
11661 San Vincente,
3304 Los Angeles,
CA 90049-5110
Tel: 310 442 0054
Fax: 310 826 6934

Chisholm Larsson
145 8th Avenue,
New York, NY 10011
Tel: 212 741 1703
www.chisholm-poster.com

Posteritati
239 Center St, New York,
NY 10013
Tel: 212 226 2207
Fax: 212 226 2102
mail@posteritati.com
www.posteritati.com

Vintage Poster Works
P.O. Box 88, Pittford,
NY 14534
Tel: 585 381 9355
debra@vintageposterworks.com
www.vintageposterworks.com
ktscicon@ix.netcom.com

RADIOS

Catalin Radios
5443 Schultz Drive, Sylvania,
OH 43560
Tel: 419 824 2469
Mob: 419 283 8203
steve@catalinradio.com
www.catalinradio.com

ROCK & POP

Heinz's Rare Collectibles
P.O. Box 179, Little Silver,
NJ 07739-0179
Tel: 732 219 1988
Fax: 732 219 5940
(The Beatles)

Tod Hutchinson
P.O. Box 915, Griffith,
IN 46319-0915
Tel: 219 923 8334
toddtcb@aol.com
(Elvis Presley)

SCENT BOTTLES

Oldies But Goldies
860 NW Sorrento Ln.
Port St. Lucie, FL 34986
Tel. 772 873 0968
email@oldgood.com
www.oldgood.com

Monsen & Baer Inc
P.O. Box 529, Vienna,
VA 22183-0529
Tel: 703 938 2129
monsenbaer@erols.com

SCIENTIFIC & TECHNICAL, INCLUDING OFFICE & OPTICAL

George Glazer Gallery
28 East 2nd Street,
New York, NY 10021
Tel: 212 535 5706
Fax 212 658 9512
worldglobe@georgeglazer.com
www.georgeglazer.com

Jane Hertz
Fax: 941 925 0487
auction01122@aol.com
auction@breker.com
www.breker.com
(Cameras, Office & Technical
Equipment)

KARS Unlimited
P.O. Box 895340,
Leesburg, FL 34789-5340
Tel: 352 365 0229
karsunltd@aol.com
www.kars-unlimited.com

The Olde Office
68-845 Perez Rd, Ste 30,
Cathedral City,
CA 92234
Tel: 760 346 8653
Fax: 760 346 6479
info@thisoldeoffice.com
www.thisoldeoffice.com

Harry Poster
1310 Second Street,
Fair Lawn,
NJ 07410
tvs@harryposter.com
www.harryposter.com

Tesseract
coffeen@aol.com
www.etesseract.com

SMOKING

Mike Cassidy
1070 Bannock #400,
Denver, CO 80204
Tel: 303 446 2726

Chuck Haley
Sherlock's,
13926 Double Girth Ct.,
Matthews,
NC 28105-4068
Tel: 704 847 5480

Ira Pilossof
Vintage Lighters Inc.,
P.O. Box 1325, Fairlawn,
NJ 07410-8325
Tel: 201 797 6595
vintageltr@aol.com

Richard Weinstein
International Vintage Lighter
Exchange, 30 W. 57th St,
New York, NY 10019
Tel: 212 586 0947
info@vintagelighters.com
www.vintagelighters.com

SPORTING MEMORABILIA

Classic Rods & Tackle
P.O. Box 288, Ashley Falls,
MA 01222
Tel: 413 229 7988

Larry Fritsch Cards Inc
735 Old Wassau Rd,
P.O. Box 863, Stevens Point,
WI 54481
Tel: 715 344 8687
Fax: 715 344 1778
larry@fritschcards.com
www.fritschcards.com
(Baseball Cards)

George Lewis
Golfiana, P.O. Box 291,
Mamaroneck, NY 10543
Tel: 914 698 4579
findit@golfiana.com
www.golfiana.com

Golf Collectibles
P.O. Box 165892,
Irving, TX 75016
Tel: 800 882 4825
furjanic@directlink.net
www.golfforallages.com

The Hager Group
P.O. Box 952974, Lake Mary,
FL 32795
Tel: 407 788 3865
(Trading Cards)

Hall's Nostalgia
21-25 Mystic St, P.O. Box 408,
Arlington, MA 02174
Tel: 781 646 7757

Tom & Jill Kaczor
1550 Franklin Rd,
Langhorne, PA 19047
Tel: 215 968 5776
Fax: 215 946 6056

Vintage Sports Collector
3920 Via Solano,
Palos Verdes Estates, CA 90274
Tel: 310 375 1723

TEDDY BEARS & SOFT TOYS

The Calico Teddy
Tel: 410 433 9202,
calicteddy@aol.com
www.calicoteddy.com

Harper General Store
Tel: 717 964 3453
lauver5@comcast.com
www.harpergeneralstore.com

Marion Weis
Division St Antiques, P.O. Box
374, Buffalo, MN 55313-0374
Tel: 612 682 6453

TOYS & GAMES

Atomic Age
318 East Virginia Road,
Fullerton, CA 92831
Tel: 714 446 0736
Fax: 714 446 0436
atomage100@aol.com

Barry Carter
Knightstown Antiques Mall,
136 W. Carey St, Knightstown,
IN 46148-1111
Tel: 765 345 5665
bcarter@spitfire.net

France Antique Toys
Tel: 631 754 1399

Roger & Susan Johnson
6264 Valley Creek,
Pilot Point,
TX 76258
Tel: 940 686 5686
czarmann@aol.com

Kitsch-N-Kaboodle
c/o South Street Antiques
Market,
615 South 6th Street,
Philadelphia,
PA 19147-2128
Tel: 215 382 1354
kitschnkaboodle@yahoo.com

Litwin Antiques
P.O. Box 5865, Trenton,
NJ 08638-0865
Tel/Fax: 609 275 1427
(Chess)

Harry R. McKeon, Jr.
18 Rose Lane, Flourtown,
PA 19031-1910
Tel: 215 233 4094
toyspost@aol.com
(Tin Toys)

The Old Toy Soldier Home
977 S. Santa Fe, Ste 11
Vista, CA 92083
Tel: 760 758 5481
oldtoysoldierhome@earthlink.net
www.oldtoysoldierhome.com

Jessica Pack Antiques
Chapel Hill, NC
Tel: 919 408 0406
jpants1@aol.com

Trains & Things
210 East Front Street, Traverse
City, Michigan 49684
Tel: 231 947 1353
www.tctrains.com

WATCHES

Mark Laino
Mark of Time
132 South 8th Street,
Philadelphia, PA 19107
Tel: 215 922 1551
lecoultre@verizon.net

Texas Time
3076 Waunuta St, Newbury
Park, CA 1320
Tel: 805 498 5644
paul@dock.net

WINE & DRINKING

Donald A. Bull
P.O. Box 596, Wirtz, VA 24184
Tel: 540 721 1128
Fax: 540 721 5468
corkscrew@bullworks.net

**Steve Visakay Cocktail
Shakers**
P.O. Box 1517 West Caldwell,
NJ 07007-1517
svisakay@aol.com

Derek White
The Corkscrew Pages,
769 Sumter Dr, Morrisville,
PA 19067
Tel: 215 493 4143
Fax: 609 860 5380
dswhite@marketsource.com
www.taponline.com

DIRECTORY OF SPECIALISTS

The following list of general antiques and collectibles centres and markets is organised by state. Any proprietor who would like to be listed in the our next edition, space permitting, or to update their contact information, should email info@millersguides.com by 1st February 2009

ALABAMA

Birmingham Antique Mall
2309 2nd Avenue South
Birmingham, AL 35205
Tel: 205 328 7761
Fax: 205 328 0794
bhamantiquemall@bellsouth
.net

ALASKA

Pack Rat Mall
5911 Old Seward Hwy
Anchorage, AK 99518
Tel: 907 522 5272

ARIZONA

American Antique Mall
3130 E Grant Rd
Tucson, AZ 85716
Tel: 520 326 3070

The Antique Centre
2012 North Scottsdale Road,
Scottsdale, AZ
Tel: 480 657 9500
info@the-antique-centre.com
www.the-antique-centre.com

ARKANSAS

**Antique Mall of
Van Buren**
415 Main St.,
Van Buren, AR 72956
Tel: 479 474 7896

CALIFORNIA

**San Francisco Antique
and Design Mall**
701 Bayshore Blvd.,
San Francisco, CA 94124-1902
Tel: 415 656 3530
info@sfantique.com
www.sfantique.com

**Ocean Beach
Antique Mall**
4926 Newport Ave.
San Diego, CA 92107
Tel: 619 223 6170

**Westchester Faire
Antique Mall**
8655 So. Sepulveda Blvd.,
Los Angeles, CA 90045
Tel: 310 670 4000

COLORADO

**Colorado Country
Antique Mall**
2109 Broadway St
Colorado Springs, CO 80904
Tel: 719 520 5680

CONNECTICUT

**Debbie's Stamford
Antiques Center**
735 Canal Street
Stamford, CT 06092
Tel: 203 357 0622

DELAWARE

Antique Village Mall
221 Highway One
Lewes,
DE 19958
Tel: 302 644 0842

FLORIDA

**Inglenook Antiques &
Collectibles**
3607 N. Scenic Hwy,
Lake Wales, FL 33898
Tel: 863 678 1641

Avonlea Antique Mall
8101 Philips Highway,
Jacksonville, FL 32256
Tel: 904 636 8785
Fax: 904 636 8732
Email: info@avonleamall.com
www.avonleamall.com

GEORGIA

Athens Antique Mall
4615 Atlanta Hwy.,
Bogart, GA 30622
Tel: 706 654 0108
www.athensantiquemall.com

HAWAII

Antique Alley
1347 Kapiolani Blvd Ste 101,
Honolulu, HI 96814
Tel: 808 941 8551

IDAHO

Antique Hub
2244 Warm Springs Ave,
Boise, ID 83712-8429
Tel: 208 336 4748

ILLINOIS

**Second Time Around
Antique Market**
151 Will Road,
Braidwood,
IL 60408
Tel: 815 458 2034

INDIANA

**Manor House Antique
Mall**
5454 US 31 South,
Indianapolis, IN 46227
Manorhouse007z@aol.com
www.manorhouseantiques.co

IOWA

**The Brass Armadillo
Des Moines**
701 NE 50th Avenue
Des Moines, Iowa 50313
Tel: 515-282-0082
www.brassarmadillo.com/dsmst
ore.htm

KANSAS

**Flying Moose
Antique Mall**
9223 W Kellogg Dr.,
Wichita, KS 67209
Tel: 316 721 6667
Fax: 316 721 9529
www.flying-moose.com

KENTUCKY

**The Red Door
Antiques Mall**
35 US Hwy 641 North,
Eddyville, KY 42038
Tel: 270 388 1957
Fax: 270 388 1958
red_door@bellsouth.net
www.thereddoorantiques.com

LOUISANA

Magazine Antique Mall
3017 Magazine Street,
New Orleans, LA 70115
Tel: 504 869 9994
www.magazineantiquemall.com

MAINE

Cornish Trading Company
19 Main St.,
Cornish, ME 04020
Tel: 207 625 8387
antiques@cornishtrading.com
www.cornishtrading.com

MARYLAND

**Antique Center I, II, III at
Historic Savage Mill**
8600 Foundry Street,
Savage, MD 20763
Tel: 410 880 0918 or
301 369 4650
www.antique-cntr-savage.com

MASSACHUSETTS

**Showcase Antiques
Centre**
Old Sturbridge Village,
Route 20,
Sturbridge, MA 01566
Tel: 508 347 7190
Fax: 508 347 5420
sales@showcaseantiques.com
www.showcaseantiques.com

MICHIGAN

Michiana Antique Mall
2423 South 11th Street,
Niles, MI 49120
Tel: 269 684 7001
michianaantiquemall@
compuserve.com
www.michianaantiquemall.com

MINNESOTA

Lindström Antique Mall
12740 Lake Blvd.,
P.O. Box 668,
Lindström, MN 55045
Tel: 651 257 3340
kearn@lindstromantiquemall
.com
www.lindstromantiquemall.com

MISSISSIPPI

**Boone's Camp
Antique Mall**
101 E Church St,
Booneville, MS 38829
Tel: 662 728 2227

MISSOURI

**Gingerbread House
Antiques Mall**
Hwy 43 S,
Joplin, MO 64801
Tel: 417 623 6690

MONTANA

**Historic Towey Hotel and
Antiques Mall**
11 South Montana Street,
Butte, MT 59701
Tel: 406 723 0061

NEBRASKA

**Platte Valley Antique
Mall,**
13017 238th St.,
Greenwood, NE 68037
Tel: 402 944 2949
Fax: 402 944 317

NEVADA

Red Rooster Antique Mall
1109 Western Avenue,
Las Vegas, NV 89102
Tel: 702 382 5253

NEW HAMPSHIRE

Antiques at Colony Mill Marketplace
The Colony Mill Marketplace,
222 West St.,
Keene, NH 03431
Tel: 603 358 6343
www.colonymill.com/Antiques_at_Colony_Mill

Fern Eldridge & Friends
800 First NH Turnpike (Rte. 4),
Northwood, NH 03261
Tel: 603 942 5602

NEW JERSEY

The Lafayette Mill Antiques
12 Morris Farm Road (Just off Rte 15),
Lafayette
NJ 07848
Tel: 973 383 0065
millpartners@inpro.net
www.millantiques.com

Somerville Center Antiques
34 W. Main St.,
Somerville, NJ 08876
Tel: 908 595 1887
www.somervilleantiques.net

NEW MEXICO

Monterey Antique Mall
1400 W 2nd St, Suite H,
Roswell, NM 88201
Tel: 505 623 3347

NEW YORK

L.W. Emporium
6355 Knickerbocker Road,
Ontario, NY 14519
Tel: 315 524 8841
www.lwemporium.com

The Manhattan Art and Antiques Center
1050 Second Avenue at 56th Street,
New York, NY 10022
Tel: 212 355 4400
Fax: 212 355 4403
info@the-maac.com
www.the-maac.com

The Showplace Antiques Center
40 W. 25th St., New York City,
NY 10010
Tel: 212 633 6063
www.nyshowplace.com

NORTH CAROLINA

Fifteen Ten Antiques
1510 Central Ave.,
Charlotte, NC 28205
Tel: 704 342 9005
info@1510-antiques.com

NORTH DAKOTA

Fargo Antique Mall
14 Roberts St.,
Fargo, ND 58102
Tel: 701 235 1145

OHIO

Grand Antique Mall
9701 Reading Road,
Reading, OH 45215
Tel: 513 554 1919
www.grandantiquemall.com

Hartville Market Place and Flea Market
1289 Edison Street NW,
Hartville, Ohio 44632
Tel: 330 877 9860
www.hartvillefleamarket.com

OKLAHOMA

Apple Barrell Antiques Mall
4619 NW 10th St.,
Oklahoma City,
OK 73127
Tel: 405 947 7732

OREGON

Old Town Antique Mall
324 SW Sixth St.
Grants Pass, OR 97527
Tel: 541 474 7525
www.southernoregonantiques.com

PENNSYLVANIA

Antiques Showcase at The Black Horse
P.O. Box 343,
2180 North Reading Road,
Denver, PA 17517
Tel: 717 335 3300
www.blackhorselodge.com/Antiques.asp

South Street Antiques Market,
615 South 6th Street,
Philadelphia, PA 19147-2128
Tel: 215 592 0256

RHODE ISLAND

Providence Antique Center,
442 Wickenden St.,
Providence, RI 02903
Tel: 401 274 5820

SOUTH CAROLINA

Charleston Antique Mall
4 Avondale at Savannah Hwy.
Charleston, SC 29407
Tel: 843-769-6119
www.charlestonantiquemall.net

SOUTH DAKOTA

Black Hills Antiques Mall
524 6th St.,
Rapid City, SD 57701
Tel: 605 341 7182

TENNESSEE

Goodlettsville Antique Mall
213 N. Main St,
Goodlettsville, TN 37072
Tel: 615 859 7002
info@goodlettsvilleantiquemall.com
www.goodlettsvilleantiquemall.com

Madison Avenue Antique Mall
1864 Madison Avenue
Memphis, TN 38104
Tel: 901 728 5453
Fax: 901 728 4582
www.madisonavenueantiquemall.com

TEXAS

Antique Pavilion
2311 Westheimer,
Houston, TX 77098
Tel: 713 520 9755

UTAH

Sugarhouse Antique Mall
2120 Highland Dr,
Salt Lake City, UT 84106
Tel: 801 487 5084

VERMONT

Vermont Antique Mall at Quechee Gorge Village
Quechee Gorge Village,
U.S. Route 4, PO Box 730,
Quechee, VT 05059
Tel: 802 295 1550
www.quecheegorge.com/antiques.html

VIRGINIA

Antique Village
10203 Chamberlayne Rd,
Mechanicsville, VA 23116-4001
Tel: 804 746 8914
www.antiquevillageva.com

WASHINGTON

Antique Gallery Mall
117 Glen Ave,
Snohomish, WA 98290
Tel: 360 568 7644

WEST VIRGINIA

Adams Ave Antique Mall
1460 Adams Ave,
Huntington, WV 25704
Tel: 304 523 7231

WISCONSIN

Red Shed Antiques
15258W County Road B,
Hayward, WI 54843
Tel: 715 634 6088
www.redshed.com

WYOMING

Cy Avenue Antique Mall
1905 CY Ave,
Casper, WY 82604
Tel: 307 237 2293

CANADA

Toronto Antiques on King
276 King Street West, Toronto,
Ontario M5V 1J2, Canada
Tel: 416 260 9057
www.torontoantiquesonking.com

Antique Market
4280 Main Street, Vancouver,
BC, Canada, V5V 3P9
Tel: 778 322 5057
info@antiquemarketvancouver.com
www.antiquesdirect.ca

Post Office Antique Mall
Box 419, 340 Esplanade,
Ladysmith, BC, Canada,
V9G 1A3
Tel: 250 245 7984

Vanity Fair Antique & Collectables Mall
1044 Fort Street, Victoria BC,
Canada, V8V 3K4
Tel: 250 380 7274

Green Spot Antiques
175 Beverly Street #15,
Cambridge, Ontario, N1R 7Y9,
Canada
Tel: 519 623 1049
info@greenspotantiques.com
www.twojjs.com/greenspot

Ucanbuy Vintage Modern
Antiques and Art
50 John Street,
Port Hope, Ontario
Canada L1A 2Z2
Tel: 1 877 775 7979
www.ucanbuy.ca

The following list of auctioneers who conduct regular sales by auction is organised by state. Any auctioneer who would like to be listed in our next edition, space permitting, or to update their contact information, should email info@millersguides.com by 1st February 2009.

ALABAMA

Flomaton Antique Auctions
P.O. Box 1017,
320 Palafox Street,
Flomaton, AL 36441
Tel: 251 296 3059
Fax: 251 296 1974
www.flomatonantiqueauction
.com

Grand View Antiques & Auction
2641 Highway 431
Roanoke, AL 36274
Tel: 334 863 6040
info@grandviewauction.com

ARIZONA

Dan May & Associates
4110 N. Scottsdale Road,
Scottsdale, AZ 85251
Tel: 602 941 4200

ARKANSAS

Ponders Auctions
1504 South Leslie,
Stuttgart, AR 72160
Tel: 501 673 6551

CALIFORNIA

Aurora Galleries International
30 Hackamore Lane, Ste 2,
Bell Canyon, CA 91307
Tel: 818 884 6468
Fax: 818 227 2941
vcampbell@auroraauctions.com
www.auroragalleriesonline.com

Butterfield & Butterfield
7601 Sunset Blvd,
Los Angeles,
CA 90046
Tel: 323 850 7500
Fax: 323 850 5843
info@butterfields.com
www.butterfields.com

Butterfield & Butterfield
220 San Bruno Ave,
San Francisco,
CA 94103
Tel: 415 861 7500
Fax: 415 861 8951
info@butterfields.com
www.butterfields.com

Clark Cierlak Fine Arts
14452 Ventura Blvd,
Sherman Oaks,
CA 91423
Tel: 818 783 3052
Fax: 818 783 3162
gallery@pacbell.net
www.estateauctionservice.com

I.M. Chait Gallery
9330 Civic Center Dr,
Beverly Hills, CA 90210
Tel: 310 285 0182
Fax: 310 285 9740
chait@chait.com
www.chait.com

Cuschieri's Auctioneers & Appraisers
863 Main Street,
Redwood City,
CA 94063
Tel: 650 556 1793
Fax: 650 556 9805
www.cuschieris.com

eBay, Inc
2005 Hamilton Ave, Ste 350,
San Jose, CA 95125
Tel: 408 369 4839
www.ebay.com

L.H. Selman
123 Locust St,
Santa Cruz, CA 95060
Tel: 800 538 0766
Fax: 408 427 0111
leselman@got.net

Malter Galleries
17003 Ventura Blvd,
Encino, CA 91316
Tel: 818 784 7772
Fax: 818 784 4726
www.maltergalleries.com

PBA Galleries
133 Kearny Street, 4th Floor,
San Francisco, CA 94108
Tel: 415 989 2665
www.pbagalleries.com

Poster Connection Inc
43 Regency Dr,
Clayton, CA 94517
Tel: 925 673 3343
Fax: 925 673 3355
sales@posterconnection.com
www.posterconnection.com

Profiles in History
110 North Doheny Dr,
Beverly Hills, CA 90211
Tel: 310 859 7701
Fax: 310 859 3842
www.profilesinhistory.com

San Rafael Auction Gallery
634 Fifth Avenue,
San Rafael, CA 9490
Tel: 415 457 4488
Fax: 415 457 4899
www.sanrafael-auction.com

Slawinski Auction Co.
The Scotts Valley Sports Center,
251 Kings Village Road,
Scotts Valley, CA 95066
Tel: 831 335 9000
www.slawinski.com

COLORADO

Aristocrat
1152 S. Lipan Street
Denver, CO 80223
Tel: 720 298 5101
AristocratEstate@aol.com

CONNECTICUT

Alexander Autographs
100 Melrose Ave,
Greenwich,
CT 06830
Tel: 203 622 8444
Fax: 203 622 8765
info@alexautographs.com
www.alexautographs.com

Norman C. Heckler & Co.
79 Bradford Corner Road,
Woodstock Valley,
CT 0682
Tel: 860 974 1634
Fax: 860 974 2003
www.hecklerauction.com

Lloyd Ralston Gallery
350 Long Beach Blvd,
Stratford, CT 016615
Tel: 203 386 9399
Fax: 203 386 9519
lrgallery@sbcglobal.net
www.lloydralstontoys.com

DELAWARE

Remember When Auctions Inc.
Tel: 302 436 4979
Fax: 302 436 4626
sales@history-attic.com
www.history-attic.com

FLORIDA

Auctions Neapolitan
995 Central Avenue,
Naples, FL 34102
Tel: 941 262 7333
kathleen@auctionsneapolitan
.com
www.auctionsneapolitan.com

Burchard Galleries
2528 30th Ave N,
St Petersburg, FL 33713
Tel: 727 821 1167
www.burchardgalleries.com

Dawson's, now trading as Dawson's & Nye
P.O. Box 646,
Palm Beach, FL 33480
Tel: 561 835 6930
Fax: 561 835 8464
info@dawsons.org
www.dawsons.org

Arthur James Galleries
615 E. Atlantic Ave,
Delray Beach, FL 33483
Tel: 561 278 2373
Fax: 561 278 7633
www.arthurjames.com

Kincaid Auction Company
3809 East CR 542,
Lakeland, FL 33801
Tel: 800 970 1977
www.kincaid.com

Sloan's Auction Galleries
8861 NW 19th Terace,
Ste 100,
Miami, FL 33172
Tel: 305 751 4770
sloans@sloansauction.com
www.sloansandkenyon.com

GEORGIA

Great Gatsby's
5070 Peachtree Industrial Blvd,
Atlanta, GA 30341
Tel: 770 457 1903
Fax: 770-457-7250
www.gatsbys.com

My Hart Auctions Inc
P.O. Box 2511,
Cumming, GA 30028
Tel: 770 888 9006
www.myhart.net

Red Baron's Antiques
6450 Roswell Road
Atlanta, GA 30328
Tel: 404 252 3770
Fax: 404 257 0268
www.redbaronsantiques.com

IDAHO

**The Coeur D'Alene
Art Auction**
P.O. Box 310,
Hayden, ID 83835
Tel: 208 772 9009
Fax: 208 772 8294
cdaartauction@cdaartauction
.com
www.cdaartauction.com

ILLINOIS

Leslie Hindman Inc.
122 North Aberdeen Street,
Chicago, IL 60607
Tel: 312 280 1212
Fax: 312 280 1211
www.lesliehindman.com

Joy Luke
300 East Grove Street,
Bloomington, IL 61701
Tel: 309 828 5533
Fax: 309 829 2266
robert@joyluke.com
www.joyluke.com

Mastro Auctions
7900 South Madison Street,
Burr Ridge, IL 60527, USA
Tel: 630 472 1200
customerservice@
mastroauctions.com
www.mastroauctions.com

INDIANA

**Curran Miller Auction &
Realty Inc**
4424 Vogel Rd, Ste 400,
Evansville, IN 47715
Tel: 812 474 6100
Fax: (812) 474-6110
cmar@curranmiller.com
www.curranmiller.com

Kruse International
5540 County Rd 11A,
Auburn, IN 46706
Tel: 800 968 4444
info@kruseinternational.com
www.kruseinternational.com

Lawson Auction Service
P.O. Box 885,
North Vernon, IN 47265
Tel: 812 372 2571
www.lawsonauction.com

Stout Auctions
529 State Road 28 East,
Willamsport, IN 47993
Tel: 765 764 6901
Fax: 765-764-1516
info@stoutauctions.com
www.stoutauctions.com

Strawser Auction Group
PO Box 332,
200 North Main Street
Wolcottville, IN 46795-0332
Tel: 260 854 2859
Fax: 260 854 3979
info@strawserauctions.com
www.strawserauctions.com

IOWA

**Jackson's Auctioneers &
Appraisers**
2229 Lincoln St,
Cedar Falls, IA 50613
Tel: 319 277 2256
Fax: 319-2771252
www.jacksonsauction.com

Tom Harris auctions
2035 18th Ave,
Marshalltown, IA 50158
Tel: 641 754 4890
Fax: 641 753 0226
tomharris@tomharrisauctions
.com
www.tomharrisauctions.com

Tubaugh Auctions
1702 8th Ave,
Belle Plaine, IA 52208
Tel: 319 444 2413 /
319.444.0169
www.tubaughauctions.com

KANSAS

CC Auctions
416 Court St,
Clay Center, KS 67432
Tel: 785 632 6021
dhamilton@cc-auctions.com
www.cc-auctions.com

**Manion's International
Auction House**
4411 North 67th Street
Kansas City,
KS 66104
Tel: 913 299 6692
Fax: 913 299 6792
collecting@manions.com
www.manions.com

Brian Spielman Auctions
PO Box 884,
Emporia, KS 66801
Tel: 620 341 0637 or
620 437 2424
spielman@madtel.net

Woody Auction
P.O. Box 618
317 S. Forrest
Douglass, KS 67039
Tel: 316 747 2694
Fax: 316 747 2145
www.woodyauction.com
info@woodyauction.com

KENTUCKY

Hays & Associates Inc
120 South Spring Street,
Louisville,
KY 40206
Tel: 502 584 4297
kenhays@haysauction.com
www.haysauction.com

**Steffens Historical
Militaria**
P.O. Box 280,
Newport,
KY 41072
Tel: 859 431 4499
Fax: 859 431 3113
www.steffensmilitaria.com

LOUISIANA

Neal Auction Company
4038 Magazine Street
New Orleans,
Louisiana 70115
Tel: 504 899 5329
Fax: 504 897 3808
www.nealauction.com

**New Orleans Auction
Galleries**
801 Magazine Street,
New Orleans, LA 70130
Tel: 504 566 1849
Fax: 504 566 1851
info@neworleansauction.com
www.neworleansauction.com

MAINE

**James D. Julia
Auctioneers Inc.**
P.O. Box 830,
Fairfield, ME 04937
Tel: 207 453 7125
jjulia@juliaauctions.com
www.juliaauctions.com

Thomaston Place
Auction Galleries
P.O. Box 300,
Thomaston, ME 04861
Tel: 207 354 8141
Fax: 207 354 9523
barbara@kajav.com
www.thomastonauction.com

MARYLAND

Guyette & Schmidt
PO Box 1170,
St. Michaels,
MD 21663.
Tel: 410 745 0485
Fax: 410 745 0457
decoys@guyetteandschmidt
.com
www.guyetteandschmidt.com

**Hantman's Auctioneers
& Appraisers**
P.O. Box 59366,
Potomac,
MD 20859
Tel: 301 770 3720
Fax: 301 770 4135
hantman@hantmans.com
www.hantmans.com

Isennock Auctions & Appraisals
4106B Norrisville Road,
White Hall, MD 21161
Tel: 410 557 8052
Fax 410 692 6449
isennock@isennockauction.com
www.isennockauction.com

Sloans & Kenyon
7034 Wisconsin Avenue,
Chevy Chase, MD 20815
Tel: 301 634-2330
Fax: 301 656-7074
info@sloansandkenyon.com
www.sloansandkenyon.com

Theriault's
P.O. Box 151
Annapolis, MD 21404
Tel: 410 224 3655
Fax: 410 224 2515
info@theriaults.com
www.theriaults.com

MASSACHUSETTS

Eldred's
P.O. Box 796, 1483 Route 6A
East Dennis, MA 02641
Tel: 508 385 3116
Fax: 508 385 7201
info@eldreds.com
www.eldreds.com

Grogan & Company
22 Harris St,
Dedham, MA 02026
Tel: 800-823 1020
Fax: 781 461 9625
grogans@groganco.com
www.groganco.com

Simon D. Hill & Associates
420 Boston Turnpike,
Shrewsbury, MA 01545
Tel: 508 845 2400
Fax: 978 928 4129
www.simondhillauctions.com

Skinner Inc
The Heritage on the Garden,
63 Park Plaza,
Boston, MA 02116
Tel: 617-350-5400
Fax: 617-350-5429
info@skinnerinc.com
www.skinnerinc.com

Willis Henry Auctions
22 Main St,
Marshfield,
MA 02050
Tel: 781 834 7774
Fax: 781 826 3520
wha@willishenry.com
www.willishenry.com

MICHIGAN

DuMouchelles
409 East Jefferson Ave,
Detroit, MI 48226
Tel: 313 963 6255
Fax: 313 963 8199
info@dumouchelles.com
www.dumouchelles.com

MINNESOTA

Rose Auction Galleries
3180 Country Drive,
Little Canada, MN 55117
Tel: 651 484 1415 /
888-484-1415
Fax: 651 636 3431
auctions@rosegalleries.com
www.rosegalleries.com

MISSISSIPPI

Edens
3720 Flowood Drive,
Flowood, MS 39232
Tel: 601 946 1501
www.edensauctions.com

MISSOURI

Ivey-Selkirk
7447 Forsyth Blvd,
Saint Louis, MO 63105
Tel: 314 726 5515
Fax: 314 726 9908
www.iveyselkirk.com

MONTANA

Allard Auctions Inc
P.O. Box 1030,
St Ignatius,
MT 59865
Tel: 406 745 0500
Fax: 406 745 0502
www.allardauctions.com

NEBRASKA

Helberg & Nuss
1145 M Street
Gering, NE 69341
Tel: 308 436 4056
www.helbergnussauction.com

NEVADA

Lightning Auctions, Inc.
870 South Rock Blvd.
Sparks, Nevada 89431
Tel: 775 331 4222
Fax: 775 331 4281
www.lightningauctions.com

NEW HAMPSHIRE

Northeast Auctions
93 Pleasant St,
Portsmouth, NH 03801-4504
Tel: 603 433 8400
Fax: 603 433 0415
contact@northeastauctions.com
www.northeastauctions.com

NEW JERSEY

Bertoia Auctions
2141 Demarco Dr,
Vineland, NJ 08360
Tel: 856 692 1881
Fax: 856 692 8697
www.bertoiaauctions.com

David Rago Auctions
333 North Main St,
Lambertville, NJ 08530
Tel: 609 397 9374
Fax: 609 397 9377
info@ragoarts.com
www.ragoarts.com

David Rago: Nicholas Dawes Lalique Auctions
333 North Main St,
Lambertville, NJ 08530
Tel: 609 397 9374
Fax: 609 397 9377
info@ragoarts.com
www.ragoarts.com

Dawson & Nye
128 American Road,
Morris Plains, NJ 07950
Tel: 973 984 6900
Fax: 973 984 6956
info@dawsonandnye.com
www.dawsonandnye.com

Sollo: Rago Modern Auctions
333 North Main St,
Lambertville, NJ 08530
Tel: 609 397 9374
Fax: 609 397 9377
info@ragoarts.com
www.ragoarts.com

NEW MEXICO

Manitou Gallery
123 West Palace Avenue,
Santa Fe, NM 87501
Tel: 800 986 0440
info@manitougalleries.com
www.manitougalleries.com

Parker-Braden Auctions
P.O. Box 1897,
4303 National Parks Highway,
Carlsbad, NM 88220
Tel: 505 885 4874
Fax: 505 885 4622
www.parkerbraden.com

NEW YORK

Bloomsbury Auctions
6 West 48th Street
New York, NY 10036-190
Tel: 212 719 1000
Fax: 212 719 1400
http://ny.bloomsburyauctions
.com

Christie's
20 Rockefeller Plaza,
New York,
NY 10020
Tel: 212 636 2000
Fax: 212 636 2399
info@christies.com
www.christies.com

TW Conroy
36 Oswego Street,
Baldwinsville,
NY 13027
Tel: 315 638 6434
Fax: 315 638 7039
info@twconroy.com
www.twconroy.com

Samuel Cottone Auctions
15 Genesee Street,
Mount Morris,
NY 14510
Tel: 585 658 3119
Fax: 585 658 3152
scottone@rochester.rr.com
www.cottoneauctions.com

William Doyle Galleries
175 E. 87th Street,
New York, NY 10128
Tel: 212 427 2730
Fax: 212 369 0892
info@doylenewyork.com
www.doylenewyork.com

Guernsey's Auctions
108 East 73rd St,
New York, NY 10021
Tel: 212 794 2280
Fax: 212 744 3638
auctions@guernseys.com
www.guernseys.com

Phillips, De Pury & Luxembourg
450 West 15 Street,
New York, NY 10011
Tel: 212 940 1200
Fax: 212 924 3306
info@phillipsdepury.com
www.phillips-dpl.com

Sotheby's
1334 York Ave at 72nd St,
New York, NY 10021
Tel: 212 606 7000
Fax: 212 606 7107
info@sothebys.com
www.sothebys.com

Swann Galleries Inc
104 E. 25th St,
New York, NY 10010
Tel: 212 254 4710
Fax: 212 979 1017
swann@swanngalleries.com
www.swanngalleries.com

Philip Weiss Auctions
1 Neil Court,
Oceanside, NY 11572
Tel: 516 594 073
info@prwauctions.com
www.philipweissauctions.com

NORTH CAROLINA

Raynor's Historical Collectible Auctions
1687 West Buck Hill Road
Burlington, NC 27215
Tel: 336 584 3330
Fax: 336 570 2748
auctions@hcaauctions.com
www.hcaauctions.com

Robert S. Brunk
P.O. Box 2135,
Asheville, NC 28802
Tel: 828 254 6846
Fax: 828 254 6545
auction@brunkauctions.com
www.brunkauctions.com

NORTH DAKOTA

Curt D Johnson Auction Co.
4216 Gateway Dr.,
Grand Forks, ND 58203
Tel: 701 746 1378
figleo@hotmail.com
www.curtdjohnson.com

OHIO

Belhorn Auction Services
PO Box 20211,
Columbus, OH 43220 USA
Tel: 614 921 9441
auctions@belhorn.com
www.belhorn.com

Cincinnati Art Galleries
225 East Sixth Street
Cincinnati, Ohio 45202
Tel: 513 381 2128
Fax: 513 381 7527
www.cincinnatiartgalleries.com

Cowans Historic Americana
673 Wilmer Avenue,
Cincinnati, OH 45226
Tel: 513 871 1670
Fax: 513 871 8670
www.historicamericana.com

DeFina Auctions
1591 State Route 45 Sth,
Austinburg, OH 44010
Tel: 440 275 6674
Fax: 440.275.2028
info@definaauctions.com
www.definaauctions.com

Garth's Auctions
2690 Stratford Rd,
Box 369,
Delaware, OH 43015
Tel: 740 362 4771
Fax: 740 363 0164
info@garths.com
www.garths.com

Metropolitan Galleries
3910 Lorain Ave,
Cleveland, OH 44113
Tel: 216 631 2222
Fax: 216 529 9021
www.metropolitangalleries.com

OKLAHOMA

Buffalo Bay Auction Co
825 Fox Run Trail,
Edmond, OK 73034
Tel: 405 285 8990
buffalobayauction@hotmail
.com
www.buffalobayauction.com

OREGON

Dale Johnson Auction Service
P.O. Box 933,
Prineville, OR 97754-0933
Tel: 541 416 8315
d2john@earthlink.net
www.dalejohnauctionsvc.com

PENNSYLVANIA

Alderfer Auction Gallery
501 Fairgrounds Rd,
Hatfield PA 19440
Tel: 215 393 3000
Fax: 215 368-9055
info@alderferauction.com
www.alderferauction.com

Noel Barrett
P.O. Box 300,
Carversville, PA 18913
Tel: 215 297 5109
www.noelbarrett.com

Dargate Auction Galleries
214 North Lexington,
Pittsburgh, PA 15208
Tel: 412 362 3558
info@dargate.com
www.dargate.com

Freeman's
1808 Chestnut Ave,
Philadelphia, PA 19103
Tel: 610 563 9275
info@freemansauction.com
www.freemansauction.com

Hunt Auctions
256 Welsh Pool Rd.
Exton, PA 19341
Tel: 610 524 0822
Fax: 610 524 0826
info@huntauctions.com
www.huntauctions.com

Pook & Pook Inc
463 East Lancaster Ave,
Downington, PA 19335
Tel: 610 269 4040
Fax: 610 269 9274
info@pookandpook.com
www.pookandpook.com

Skinner's Auction Co.
170 Northampton St,
Easton, PA 18042
Tel: 610 330 6933
skinnauct@aol.com
www.skinnersauction.com

Stephenson's Auctions
1005 Industrial Blvd,
Southampton, PA 18966
Tel: 215 322 618
info@stephensonsauction.com
www.stephensonsauction.com

RHODE ISLAND

Web Wilson
P.O. Box 506,
Portsmouth, RI 02871
Tel: 800 508 0022
hww@webwilson.com
www.webwilson.com

SOUTH CAROLINA

Charlton Hall Galleries Inc.
912 Gervais St
Columbia, SC 29201
Tel: 803 799 5678
Fax: 803 733 1701
www.charltonhallauctions.com

SOUTH DAKOTA

Girard Auction & Land Brokers, Inc.
P.O. Box 358
Wakonda, SD 57073
Tel: 605 267 2421
Fax: 605 267 2421
www.girardauction.com

TENNESSEE

Berenice Denton Estate Sales and Appraisals
2209 Bandywood Drive,
Suite C
Nashville, TN 37215
Tel: 615 292 5765
info@berenicedenton.com
www.berenicedenton.com

Kimball M. Sterling Inc
125 W. Market St, Johnson City,
TN 37604
Tel: 423 928 1471
www.sterlingsold.com

TEXAS

Austin Auctions
8414 Anderson Mill Rd,
Austin, TX 78729-4702
Tel: 512 258 5479
Fax: 512 219 7372
www.austinauction.com

Dallas Auction Gallery
1518 Socum St,
Dallas, TX 75207
Tel: 213 653 3900
Fax: 213 653 3912
info@dallasauctiongallery.com
www.dallasauctiongallery.com

Heritage-Slater Americana
3500 Maple Avenue
Dallas, TX 75219
Tel: 214 528 3500
www.heritagegalleries.com

Heritage Galleries
3500 Maple Avenue
Dallas, TX 75219
Tel: 214 528 3500
www.heritagegalleries.com

UTAH

America West Archives
P.O. Box 100,
Cedar City, UT 84721
Tel: 435 586 9497
Fax: 435 586 9497
info@americawestarchives.com
www.americawestarchives.com

VERMONT

Eaton Auction Service
Chuck Eaton, 3428
Middlebrook Road,
Fairlee, VT 05045
Tel: 802 333 9717
eas@sover.net
www.eatonauctionservice.com

VIRGINIA

Green Valley Auctions, Inc.
2259 Green Valley Lane
Mt. Crawford, VA 22841
Tel: 540 4344260
Fax: 540 434 4532
info@greenvalleyauctions.com
www.greenvalleyauctions.com

Ken Farmer Auctions & Estates
105A Harrison St,
Radford, VA 24141
Tel: 540 639 0939
Fax: 540 639 1759
info@kfauctions.com
www.kfauctions.com

Phoebus Auction Gallery
14-16 E. Mellen St,
Hampton, VA 23663
Tel: 757 722 9210
Fax: 757 723 2280
bwelch@phoebusauction.com
www.phoebusauction.com

Quinn's Auction Galleries
431 N. Maple Avenue
Falls Church,
VA 22046-4203
Tel: 703 532 5632
Fax: 703 532 4910
info@quinnsauction.com
www.quinnsauction.com

Signature House
407 Liberty Ave,
Bridgeport, WV 25330
Tel: 304 842 3386
Fax: 304 842 3001
editor@signaturehouse.net
www.signaturehouse.net

WASHINGTON

Ingrid O'Neil
Sports & Olympic Memorabilia
PO Box 872048
Vancouver WA 98687
Tel: 360 834 5202
Fax: 360 834 2853
ingrid@ioneil.com
www.ioneil.com

WASHINGTON DC

Weschlers
909 E Street, NW Washington,
DC 20004
Tel: 202 628 1281
Fax: 202 628 2366
fineart@weschlers.com
www.weschlers.com

WEST VIRGINIA

Cozart Auction & Appraisal Services
P.O. Box 11
New Martinsville,
WV 26155
Tel: 304 771 3722
tcozart@suddenlink.net
www.cozartauction.com

WISCONSIN

Krueger Auctions
P.O. Box 275,
Iola, WI 54945-0275
Tel: 715 445 3845

Schrager Auction Galleries
2915 North Sherman Blvd,
P.O. Box 100043,
Milwaukee, WI 53210
Tel: 414 873 3738
Fax: 414 873 5229
askus@schragerauction.com
www.schragerauction.com

WYOMING

Cody Old West Show & Auction
P.O. Box 2038,
37555 Hum Rd, Ste 101,
Carefree, AZ 85377
Tel: 307-587-9014
brian@codyoldwest.com
www.codyoldwest.com

CANADA

Ritchies
380 King Street East,
Toronto, Ontario,
Canada M5A 1K4
Tel: 416 364 1864
www.ritchies.com

Waddington's
Auctioneers & Appraisers
111 Bathurst St., Toronto,
Ontario, Canada M5V 2R1
Tel: 416 504 9100
www.waddingtons.ca

Walkers
81 Auriga Drive, Suite 18,
Ottawa, Ontario,
Canada K2E 7Y5
Tel: 613 224 5814
www.walkersauctions.com

ADVERTISING

Antique Advertising Association of America
P.O. Box 1121,
Morton Grove, IL 60053
Tel: 708 446 0904
www.pastimes.org

Coca Cola Collectors' Club International
P.O. Box 49166,
Atlanta, GA 30359-1166

The Coca-Cola Collectors Club
www.cocacolaclub.org

Tin Container Collectors' Association
P.O. Box 440101 Aurora,
CO 80044

AMERICANA

Folk Art Society of America
P.O. Box 17041,
Richmond, VA 23226-70

American Political Items Collectors
P.O. Box 340339,
San Antonio,
TX 8234-0339
http://apic.us

AUTOGRAPHS

International Autograph Collectors' Club & Dealers' Alliance
4575 Sheridan St, Ste 111,
Hollywood, FL 33021-3515
Tel: 561 736 8409
www.iada-cc.com

Universal Autograph Collectors Club
PO Box 1205, Welaka,
FL 32193
Tel: 352 383 1958
www.uacc.org

AUTOMOBILIA

Automobile Objets d'Art Club
252 N. 7th St. Allentown,
PA 18102-4204
Tel: 610 432 3355
oldtoy@aol.com

BOOKS

Antiquarian Bookseller's Association of America
20 West 44th St, 4th Floor,
New York, NY 10036
Tel: 212 944 8291

The Alice in Wonderland
Collectors Network
Joel Birenbaum, 2765
Shellingham Drive,
Lisle, IL 60532-4245

CERAMICS

American Art Pottery Association
2 Julian Woods Place
The Woodlands,
TX 77382
www.aapa.info

American Ceramic Circle
P.O. Box 224
Williamsburg,
VA 23187-0224
Tel: 804 693 7649
www.amercercir.org

American Cookie Jar Association
1600 Navajo Rd, Norman,
OK 73026
davismj@ionet.net

U.S. Chintz Collectors' Club
P.O. Box 50888,
Pasadena, CA 91115
Tel: 626 441-4708
Fax: 626 441-4122
www.chintz.net

Goebel Networkers
P.O. Box 396,
Lemoyne, PA 17043

Homer Laughlin China Collectors' Association
P.O. Box 1093
Corbin KY 40702-1093
www.hlcca.org
(Fiesta ware)

Hummel Collectors Club
1261 University Dr, Yardley,
PA 19067-2857
Tel: 888 548 6635
Fax: 215 321 7367
www.hummels.com

Roseville of The Past Pottery Club
P.O. Box 656 Clarcona,
FL 32710-0656
Tel: 407 294 3980
Fax: 407 294 7836
rosepast@bellsouth.net

Royal Doulton International Collectors' Club
700 Cottontail Lane,
Somerset, NJ 08873
Tel: 800 682-4462
Fax: 732 764-4974

National Shelley China Club
591 W. 67th Ave.
Anchorage,
AK 99518-1555
www.nationalshelleychinaclub
.com

Stangl & Fulper Club
P.O. Box 538,
Flemington,
NJ 08822
Tel: 908 995 2696
kenlove508@aol.com

American Stoneware Collectors' Society
P.O Box 281, Bay Head,
NJ 08742
Tel: 732 899 8707

COINS, BANKNOTES & PAPER MONEY

International Bank Note Society
www.theibns.org

International Bond and Share Society
www.scripophily.org

COSTUME JEWELRY

Leaping Frog Antique Jewelry & Collectible Club
4841 Martin Luther King Blvd,
Sacramento, CA 95820-4932
Tel: 916 452 6728
pandora@cwia.com

Vintage Fashion & Costume Jewelry Club
P.O. Box 265, Glen Oaks,
NY 11004-0265
Tel: 718 939 3095
vfcj@aol.com
www.lizjewel.com/vf

DISNEYANA

National Fantasy Club For Disneyana Collectors
P.O. Box 106, Irvine,
CA 92713-9212
Tel: 714 731 4705
info@nffc.org
www.nffc.org

Walt Disney Collectors' Society
500 South Buena Vista St,
Burbank, CA 91521-8028
Tel: 800 932 5749

EPHEMERA

American Business Card Club US
5503 215th St. SW,
Mountlake Terrace,
WA 98043-3044

American Matchcover
Collecting Club
P.O. Box 18481,
Asheville, NC 28814-0481
www.matchcovers.com
bill@matchcovers.com

FIFTIES & SIXTIES

Head Hunters Newsletters
P.O. Box 83H,
Scarsdale, NY 10583
Tel: 914 472 0200

FILM & TV MEMORABILIA

The Animation Art Guild
330 W. 45th St, Ste 9D,
New York, NY 10036-3864
Tel: 212 765 3030
theaagltd@aol.com

Lone Ranger Fan Club
P.O. Box 9561
Amarillo, TX 79105
www.lonerangerfanclub.com

GLASS

American Carnival Glass Association
9621 Springwater Lane,
Miamisburg, OH 45342

Land of Sunshine Depression Glass Club
P.O. Box 560275,
Orlando, FL 32856-0275
Tel: 407 298 3355

HATPINS

American Hatpin Society
20 Montecillo Dr,
Rolling Hills Estates,
CA 90274-4249
Tel: 310 326 2196
info@americanhatpinsociety.com
www.americanhatpinsociety.com

HOUSEHOLD

American Lock Collectors Association
8576 Barbara Drive,
Mentor, Ohio 44060
admin@alca.us
www.alca.name

Antique Fan Collectors' Association
P.O. Box 5473,
Sarasota, FL 34277-5473
president@fancollectors.org
www.fancollectors.org

KITCHENALIA

Kitchen Antiques & Collectibles News
4645 Laurel Ridge Dr,
Harrisburg, PA 17119

MARBLES

Marble Collectors Unlimited
P.O. Box 206,
Northborough,
MA 01532-0206
marblesbev@aol.com

MECHANICAL MUSIC

Musical Box Society International
700 Walnut Hill Rd,
Hockessin, DE 19707
Tel: 302 239 5658
www.mbsi.org

MILITARIA

Association of American Military Uniform Collectors
AAMUC FOOTLOCKER
P. O. Box 1876
Elyria, OH 44036
AAMUCFL@comcast.net
www.naples.net/clubs/aamuc/

OPTICAL, MEDICAL, SCIENTIFIC & TECHNICAL

Antique Wireless Association (AWA)
P.O. Box 478,
2 Walnut Place,
Apalachin, NY 137232
www.antiquewireless.org

International Association of Calculator Collectors
P.O. Box 345,
Tustin, CA 92781-0345
Tel: 714 730 6140
Fax: 714 730 6140
mrcalc@usa.net

PENS & WRITING

The Society of Inkwell Collectors
P.O. Box 324,
Mossville, IL 61552
Tel: 309 579 3040
director@soic.com
www.soic.com

Pen Collectors of America
P.O. Box 447
Fort Madison, IA 52627-0447
librarian@pencollectors.com
www.pencollectors.com

PEZ

Pez Collectors News
P.O. Box 14956, Surfside Beach,
SC 29587
info@pezcollectorsnews.com
www.pezcollectorsnews.com

ROCK N ROLL

Elvis Forever TCB Fan Club
P.O. Box 1066,
Miami, FL 33780-1066

Working Class Hero Beatles Club
3311 Niagara St, Pittsburgh,
PA 1213-4223

SCENT BOTTLES

National Association of Avon Collectors
P.O. Box 7006
Kansas City, MO 64113

International Perfume Bottle Association
396 Croton Rd,
Wayne, PA 19087
Tel: 610-995-9051
jcabbott@bellatlantic.net
www.perfumebottles.org

SMOKING

On The Lighter Side
flames@otls.com
www.otls.com

Pocket Lighter Preservation Guild & Historical Society, Inc.
P.O. Box 1054, Addison,
IL 60101-8054
Tel: 708 543 9120

Snowdomes
Snowdome Collectors' Club
P.O. Box 53262,
Washington, DC 20009-9262

SPORTING MEMORABILIA

American Fish Decoy Collectors Association
P.O. Box 252,
Boulder Junction,
WI 54512

Boxing & Pugilistica Collectors International
P.O. Box 83135,
Portland, OR 97283-0135
Tel: 502 286 3597

Golf Collectors' Society
Attn. Karen Bednarski
P.O. Box 2386
Florence, OR 97439
Tel: 216 861 1615
www.golfcollectors.com

National Fishing Lure Collectors' Club

H.C. 33, Box 4012,
Reeds Spring, MO 65737
spurr@kingfisher.com

Society for American Baseball Research
812 Huron Rd, E. 719,
Cleveland, OH 441155
info@sabr.org
www.sabr.org

TEDDY BEARS & SOFT TOYS

Bearly Ours Teddy Club
54 Berkinshaw Cres.,
Don Mills, Ontario M3B 2T2,
Canada

Steiff Club – North America
425 Paramount Drive
Raynham, MA 02767
Tel: 508 828 2377
Fax: 508 821 4477
www.steiffusa.com

TEXTILES & COSTUME

The Costume Society of America
203 Towne Centre Drive
Hillsborough, NJ 08844
Tel: 410 275 1619
www.costumesocietyamerica.com

American Fan Collectors' Association
P.O. Box 5473,
Sarasota, FL 34277-5473
Tel: 817 267 9851
Fax: 817 267 0387

International Old Lacers
P.O. Box 554, Flanders,
NJ 07836
iolinc@aol.com

TOYS & GAMES

American Toy Emergency Vehicle (ATEV) Club,
Jeff Hawkins,
11415 Colfax Road,
Glen Allen, VA 23060

Annalee Doll Society
P.O.Box 1137,
Meredith, NH 03253
Tel: 800 433-6557
Fax: 603 279-6659

The Antique Toy Collectors of America, Inc
C/o Carter, Ledyard & Milburn,
Two Wall St (13th Floor),
New York, NY 10005

Chess Collectors' International

P.O. Box 166, Commack,
NY 11725-0166
Tel: 516 543 1330
lichness@aol.com

National Model Railroad Association
4121 Cromwell Rd,
Chattanooga, TN 37421
Tel: 423 892 2846
nmra@tttrains.com

Toy Soldier Collectors of America
5340 40th Ave N,
Saint Petersburg,
FL 33709
Tel: 727 527 1430

United Federation of Doll Clubs
10920 N. Ambassador Dr,
Kansas City, MO 64153
Tel: 816-891-7040
ufdc@aol.com

WATCHES

Early American Watch Club
P.O. Box 81555,
Wellesley Hills,
MA 02481-1333

National Association of Watch & Clock Collectors
514 Poplar St,
Columbia, PA 17512
Tel: 717 684 8261
www.nawcc.org

WINE & DRINKING

International Correspondence of Corkscrew Addicts
670 Meadow Wood Road
Mississauga Ontario,
L5J 2S6 Canada
dugohuzo@aol.com
www.icca-corkscrew.com

Collectibles are particularly suited to online trading. When compared with many antiques, most collectibles are easily defined, described and photographed, whilst shipping is relatively easy, due to average sizes and weights. Collectibles are also generally more affordable and accessible, and the internet has provided a cost effective way of buying and selling without the overheads of shops and auction rooms. A huge number of collectibles are offered for sale and traded daily over the internet, with websites varying from global online marketplaces, such as eBay, to specialist dealers' sites.

• There are a number of things to be aware of when searching for collectibles online. Some items being sold may not be described accurately, meaning that general category searches, and even purposefully misspelling a name, can yield results. If something looks, or sounds, too good to be true, it probably is. Using this book should give you a head start in getting to know your market, and also enable you to tell the difference between a real bargain, and something that sounds like one. Good color photography is absolutely vital – try to find online listings that include as many images as possible, including detail shots, and check them carefully. Be aware that colors can appear differently between websites, and even between computer screens.

• Always ask the vendor questions about the object, particularly regarding condition. If no image is supplied, or you want to see another aspect of the object, ask for more information. A good seller should be happy to cooperate if approached politely and sensibly.

• As well as the 'e-hammer' price, you will very likely have to pay additional transactional fees such as packing, shipping and possibly state or national taxes. Ask the seller for an estimate of these additional costs before leaving a bid, as this will give you a better idea of the overall amount you will end-up paying.

• In addition to large online auction sites, such as eBay, there are a host of other online resources for buying and selling. The internet can also be an invaluable research tool for collectors, with many sites devoted to providing detailed information on a number of different collectibles – however, it is always best to use trusted names or compare information between sites.

INTERNET RESOURCES

Live Auctioneers
www.liveauctioneers.com
info@liveauctioneers.com
A free online service that allows users to search catalogs from selected auction houses in Europe, the USA and the United Kingdom. Visitors to the site can bid live via the internet into salerooms as auctions happen. Registered users can also search through an archive of past catalogues and receive a free e-mail newsletter.

The Saleroom.com
www.the-saleroom.com
A free online service that allows users to search catalogs from selected auction houses in Europe, the USA and the United Kingdom. Visitors to the site can bid live via the internet into salerooms as auctions happen. Registered users can also search through an archive of past catalogues and receive a free e-mail newsletter.

ArtFact
info@artfact.com
www.artfact.com
Provides a comprehensive database of worldwide auction listings from over 2,000 art, antiques and collectibles auction houses. User can search details of both upcoming and past sales and also find information on a number of collectors' fields. Basic information is available for free, access to more in depth information requires a subscription. Online bidding live into auctions as they happen is also offered.

Invaluable.com
www.invaluable.com
sales@invaluable.com
A subscription service allowing users to search selected auction house catalogs from the United Kingdom and Europe. Also offers an extensive archive for appraisal uses.

The Antiques Trade Gazette
www.atg-online.com
The online edition of the UK antiques and collectibles trade newspaper, including British auction and fair listings, news and events.

Maine Antique Digest
www.maineantiquedigest.com
Online version of the US antiques and collectibles trade newspaper including news, articles, fair and auction listings and more.

La Gazette du Drouot
www.drouot.com
The online home of the magazine listing all auctions to be held in France at the Hotel de Drouot in Paris. An online subscription enables you to download the magazine online.

AuctionBytes
www.auctionbytes.com
Auction resource with community forum, news, events, tips and a weekly newsletter.

Auction.fr
www.auction.fr
An online database of auctions at French auction houses. A subscription allows users to search past catalogs and prices realised.

Auctiontalk
www.internetauctionlist.com
Auction news, online and offline auction search engines and chat forums.

Go Antiques/Antiqnet
www.goantiques.com
www.antiqnet.com
An online global aggregator for art, antiques and collectibles dealers. Dealers' stock is showcased online, with users able to browse and buy.

eBay
www.ebay.com
Undoubtedly the largest and most diverse of the online auction sites, allowing users to buy and sell in an online marketplace with over 78 million registered users from across the world.